RICHARD EBERHART
A Descriptive Bibliography
1921-1987

MECKLER'S LITERARY BIBLIOGRAPHIES

Walker Percy: A Bibliography: 1930-1984
by Stuart Wright
ISBN 0-88736-046-7 CIP 1986

The Bibliography of Contemporary American
Poetry, 1945-1985: An Annotated Checklist
by William McPheron
ISBN 0-88736-054-8 CIP 1986

Harry Crews: A Bibliography
by Michael Hargraves
ISBN 0-88736-060-2 CIP 1986

William Goyen: A Descriptive Bibliography,
1938-1985
by Stuart Wright
ISBN 0-88736-057-2 CIP 1986

Stevie Smith: A Bibliography
by Jack Barbera, William McBrien
& Helen Bajan
ISBN 0-88736-101-3 CIP 1987

Sylvia Plath: An Analytical Bibliography
by Stephen Tabor
ISBN 0-88736-100-5 CIP 1987

H. Rider Haggard: A Bibliography
by D.E. Whatmore
ISBN 0-88736-102-1 CIP 1987

Robert Gover: A Descriptive Bibliography
by Michael Hargraves
ISBN 0-88736-165-X CIP 1988

Confederate Broadside Poems:
An Annotated Descriptive Bibliography
by William Moss
ISBN 0-88736-163-3 CIP 1988

Alice Malsenior Walker:
An Annotated Bibliography: 1968-1986
by Louis H. Pratt and Darnell D. Pratt
ISBN 0-88736-156-0 CIP 1988

Supplement to A Bibliography of
George Moore
by Edwin Gilcher
ISBN 0-88736-199-4 CIP 1988

Alan Sillitoe: A Bibliography
by David Gerard
ISBN 0-88736-104-8 CIP 1988

John Wain: A Bibliography
by David Gerard
ISBN 0-88736-103-X CIP 1988

The Making of the Shelley Myth:
An Annotated Bibliography of Criticism of
P.B. Shelley, 1822-1860
by Karsten Klejs Engelberg
ISBN 0-88736-298-2 CIP 1988

PKD: A Philip K. Dick Bibliography,
Revised Edition
by Daniel J. H. Levack and Steven Owen
Godersky
ISBN 0-88736-096-3 CIP 1988

Dune Master: A Frank Herbert
Bibliography
by Daniel J. H. Levack and Mark Willard
ISBN 0-88736-099-8 CIP 1988

Gothic Fiction: A Master List of
Twentieth Century Criticism
and Research
by Frederick S. Frank
ISBN 0-88736-218-4 CIP 1988

The Bibliography of Contemporary
American Fiction, 1945-1988:
An Annotated Checklist
by William McPheron and
Jocelyn Sheppard
ISBN 0-88736-167-6 CIP 1989

Robinson Crusoe: An Annotated
Checklist of English Language Editions,
1719-1985
by Robert Lovett
ISBN 0-88736-058-0 CIP forthcoming

Donald Davie: A Descriptive Bibliography
by Stuart Wright
ISBN 0-88736-059-9 CIP forthcoming

John Ciardi: A Descriptive Bibliography
by Charles C. Lovett and
Stephanie B. Lovett
ISBN 0-88736-056-4 CIP forthcoming

Lewis Carroll's Alice: An Annotated
Checklist of Editions in English
by Charles C. Lovett and
Stephanie B. Lovett
ISBN 0-88736-166-8 CIP forthcoming

Robert Lowell: A Descriptive
Bibliography
by Stephen Gould Axelrod
ISBN 0-88736-227-3 CIP forthcoming

James Tate: A Descriptive Bibliography
by Gene DeGruson
ISBN 0-88736-229-X CIP forthcoming

Richard Eberhart: A Descriptive
Bibliography, 1921-1987
by Stuart Wright
ISBN 0-88736-346-6 CIP 1989

Clifford Odets: An Annotated
Bibliography of Criticism
by Robert Cooperman
ISBN 0-88736-326-1 CIP forthcoming

RICHARD EBERHART

A Descriptive Bibliography

1921-1987

STUART WRIGHT
Assisted by Charles and Stephanie Lovett

Meckler
Westport • London

Library of Congress Cataloging-in-Publication Data

Wright, Stuart T.
    Richard Eberhart : a descriptive bibliography, 1921-1987 / Stuart
  Wright.
      p. cm.
    ISBN 0-88736-346-6 (alk. paper) : $
    1. Eberhart, Richard, 1904 -   --Bibliography. I. Title.
  Z8253.87. W75   1989
  [PS3509.B456]
  016.811 ' 52--dc20   89-12948
                                                              CIP

British Library Cataloguing in Publication Data

Wright, Stuart
    Richard Eberhart: a descriptive bibliography, 1921 -
    1987.
    1. Poetry in English. American writers. Eberhart,
    Richard, 1904 - - Bibliographies
    I. Title
    016 ' . 811 ' 52

    ISBN 0-88736-346-6

Meckler Corporation, 11 Ferry Lane West, Westport, CT 06880.
Meckler Ltd., Grosvenor Gardens House, Grosvenor Gardens,
  London SW1W 0BS, U.K.

Printed on acid free paper.
Printed in the United States of America.

for Dick and Betty

Great praises are in the air!

Contents

Acknowledgments ix

Bibliographical Method xi

Abbreviations xv

A. Separate Publications 1

B. Contributions to Books and Pamphlets 185

C. Contributions to Periodicals 273

D. Blurbs 341

E. Interviews and Published Comments 347

F. Material Duplicated from Typescript 355

G. Recordings 365

H. Musical Settings 373

I. Translations 375

J. Odds and Ends 377

Index 379

Acknowledgments

My greatest debt in the preparation of this bibliography is to Richard Eberhart. Without his encouragement, invaluable assistance, and friendship, my task would have been much more difficult. Betty Eberhart, the poet's wife, proved a warm and generous hostess on a number of visits to Hanover, New Hampshire.

I owe a very special debt of gratitude to the staff of the Baker Library, Dartmouth College, especially to Stanley W. Brown (Curator of Rare Books) and Philip N. Cronenwett (Curator of Manuscripts and Chief of Special Collections). These gentlemen generously tolerated my many queries with gracious equanimity: their assistance was invaluable.

The staffs of Richard Eberhart's publishers were most helpful in providing information about his books. I would like to acknowledge the following individuals for their assistance: Gillian Auld (Secker & Warburg); Barbara Bartolotta (Scott, Foresman); Jamie Berger (New Directions); Gerald Costanzo (Carnegie-Mellon University Press); Arthur B. Evans (University of Pennsylvania Press); Morris A. Gelfand (Stone House Press); Brenda Kolb (University Presses of Florida); Frances B. Krouse (Vermont Academy of Arts and Sciences); Sarah Lindsay (Unicorn Press); Helga Low (University Press of New England); Richard Matthews (Konglomerati Press); Mimi Melek (Oxford University Press); William Plumley (Mountain State Press); Kristine Rumery (St. Martin's Press); June Sirc (*The Observer*, London); Carol Sturm (Nadja); Mary Wheatley (University Press of Virginia); John Wilson (Ohio University Press).

It is impossible for me to acknowledge everyone else who has offered assistance and encouragement, so I must accept responsibility for any omissions here. But those I would now acknowledge include: special thanks to Michael Bott, Keeper of Archives and Manuscripts, University of Reading, England, depository of the Chatto & Windus archive; Bertie Babcock; Anne Bailey (Fondren Library, SMU); Robert J. Bertholf (SUNY-Buffalo); Professor Fred Chappell; Edna Cherry; Michelle Cromwell; Susan Edmonds (Special Collections, Western Washington University Library); Christine Erdham (Morse Library, Beloit College); Laney Evans (Old Town Club Library); Renate Evans (Reynolds Library, Wake Forest University); William Ferguson; Professor George P. Garrett; Professor Robert W. Lovett; Professor Joseph O. Milner; Professor William Moss; K. Rainford (*Yorkshire Post*); Helen D. Rifas (Reynolds Library, Wake Forest University); Pauline Thomson (National Library of Scotland); Henry E. Turlington; John Updike; Robert Penn Warren; Richard Wilbur; Charles Wilt (Chalmers Library, Kenyon College). Mention is made of those who were not acknowledged in *The Miracle on*

Hawthorne Hill: Bert Bennett; Feathers Cuningham; John Gallaher; Jim Holmes; Gene Hooks; Berk Ingram; Matt Long; Gene Lucas; Manson Meads; Dick Port; Garnett Saunders; Bill Smith; Flake Steele; Luther Upton; Skip Wanders; Bob Warhover; Ernie Yount.

My final acknowledgment is to Gerald W. Esch, Dean of the Graduate School, Wake Forest University, for making available grants from the Research and Publications Fund for preparation and publication of this manuscript.

Bibliographical Method

This bibliography lists and describes the known publications of American poet Richard Eberhart, winner of both Pulitzer and Bollingen prizes. It derives in part from the "Selected Bibliography" in Joel Roache, *Richard Eberhart: The Progress of an American Poet*(New York: Oxford University Press, 1971), pp. 263-88. I am deeply indebted to the pioneering work of Professor Roache.

Section A, which contains separate publications (books, pamphlets, and broadsides) by Richard Eberhart lists titles chronologically by edition and by country. For each of Eberhart's books there is a detailed description of the first American and first English edition. Subsequent printings are described in such detail as distinguishes them from earlier printings. A simple numbering system has been employed for entries in this section. **A3b**, for example, signifies the first edition, American issue (from English sheets) of *Song and Idea*. **A** refers to the section, **3** indicates that this is Eberhart's third separate publication, and **b** designates the proper chronological position within the sequence of published issues of this title. Advance proof copies issued for review purposes are described in the *Notes* paragraph (see below).

The descriptive formularies are taken from Fredson Bowers, *Principles of Bibliographical Description* (Princeton, NJ: Princeton University Press, 1949), with modifications from G. Thomas Tanselle, and further modifications from James L.W. West III. Descriptions for each book contain a paragraph for collation, contents, publication information, locations, and first appearance of new material (republication information relative to first appearance material is regularly noted in this paragraph as well). Leaf, board, and dust jacket measurements in descriptions of first printings are given in inches and millimeters; all other measurements are given in millimeters only.

Title Page: Title pages of first editions have been photographically reproduced from the originals; all printing is in black ink unless indicated otherwise.

Copyright Page: This page is also reproduced from the original, occasionally in compressed format.

Collation: The standard Bowers formulary is used with two changes: there is no indication of format ($8°$, $16°$), and dimensions of leaves are given in the description of the paper below.

Running Titles: The location of the running title (at head or foot) is first given. Then the printing is quasi-facsimiled from the left margin of the verso page across the gutter (indicated by a vertical rule) to the right margin of the recto page.

Typography: Here the method is adapted from Tanselle's "The Identification of Type Faces in Bibliographical Description," PBSA, 60, (1966), 185–202.

Paper and Binding: Tanselle's "The Bibliographical Description of Paper," SB, 24 (1971), 26-67, serves as the guide here. Sheet size and bulking measurements are not given. Binding descriptions are based on Tanselle's "Book-Jackets, Blurbs, and Bibliographers," *The Library*, 5th ser., 26 (June 1971), 81-134.

Text Contents: This paragraph lists the items included.

Publication: The date of publication and price are given first, followed by the number of copies printed (if known). The dates and size of subsequent printings complete this paragraph.

Locations: Although no fewer than ten copies of each book were examined, only the following collections or institutional libraries have been noted.

DLC   Library of Congress
NcGU University of North Carolina at Greensboro
NcU   University of North Carolina at Chapel Hill
NhD   Special Collections, Baker Library, Dartmouth College
RE   Richard Eberhart Collection, Hanover, New Hampshire
SW   Stuart Wright Collection, Winston-Salem, NC
ViU   University of Virginia, Charlottesville

First Appearance: This paragraph identifies poetry and prose by Eberhart that appears in print for the first time; reprinted appearances of this material are regularly noted within this paragraph as well. Variants in subsequent printings of poems are also listed here.

Notes: These paragraphs contain descriptions of advance proof copies, oddities of manufacture, and miscellaneous supplemental material pertaining to the book or title described.

Section B lists chronologically books and pamphlets edited by Eberhart and books containing first appearances or first book appearances of material by him. Subsequent textual variants are listed for those items that are appearing in print for the first time.

Section C lists chronologically first periodical appearances by Eberhart, including juvenilia, poems, criticism, and written prose statements (as opposed to quoted comments and statements from interviews). Reprinted appearances of this material in books and periodicals, along with any textual variants in poems, are also listed.

Section D contains dust jacket blurbs and statements promoting the work of other writers.

Section E contains an annotated chronological listing of interviews with Richard Eberhart as well as published comments by him.

Section F contains an alphabetical listing of items principally reproduced from Eberhart's typescript originals, generally by spirit duplication process. Exceptions include press releases and material got up and repro-duced by some other mechanical process (but including spirit duplication) not from Eberhart's original. It should be noted that for a period of some thirty years Eberhart made copies of early versions of his poems by spirit duplica-tion process for his own use in revision and for distribution to friends. For ex-ample, in the compiler's collection are examples Eberhart sent to his friends Louis Untermeyer and John Ciardi. In general, he ran off no more than ten such copies of each poem, as they were intended for limited circulation or simply for personal use. Textually, they are of great interest in the study of Eberhart's method of composition. At the beginning of this section there is a description of the paper upon which each of Eberhart's poems or prose works is reproduced. Because the section is arranged alphabetically, published items are cross-referenced to the published appearance (the date of composition may in fact have been a good deal earlier than first publication).

Section G contains a chronological listing of sound recordings, disc and tape, of Eberhart reading from his work (discs precede tapes). Copies of the tape recordings prepared at the Recording Laboratory of the Library of Congress are identified by the numbering system used in *Literary Recordings: A Checklist of the Archive of Recorded Poetry and Literature in the Library of Congress*, comp. Jennifer Whittington, rev. and enl. ed. (Washington, DC: Poetry Office, Manu-script Division, Research Services, Library of Congress, 1981).

Section H lists chronologically musical settings of poems by Richard Eberhart; all are unpublished.

Section I contains a chronological listing of translations of Eberhart's poems, alphabetically arranged by language.

Section J consists of five odds and ends that do not fit logically into any of the other sections: a recording of Eberhart reading from the work of anoth-er poet; a hectographed program containing an original poem; notes for a phonograph recording sleeve; a published self-portrait; and printed quoted comments on the front of a brochure.

Abbreviations

BE	*A Bravery of the Earth* (1930)
BO	*Burr Oaks* (1947)
CP60	*Collected Poems 1930–1960* (1960)
CP76	*Collected Poems 1930–1976* (1976)
CP88	*Collected Poems 1930–1986* (1988)
CVP	*Collected Verse Plays* (1962)
FG	*Fields of Grace* (1972)
FP	*Florida Poems* (1981)
4P	*Four Poems* (1980)
GP	*Great Praises* (1957)
LR	*The Long Reach: New and Uncollected Poems 1948–1984* (1984)
NH	*New Hampshire: Nine Poems* (1980)
OPP	*Of Poetry and Poets* (1979)
PNS	*Poems New and Selected* (1945)
PP	*Poems to Poets* (1975)
Qu	*The Quarry* (1964)
RS	*Reading the Spirit* (1936)
SB	*Shifts of Being* (1968)
SI	*Song and Idea* (1940)
SP51	*Selected Poems* (1951)
SP65	*Selected Poems 1930–1965* (1965)
Su	*Survivors* (1979)
31S	*Thirty-One Sonnets* (1967)
Un	*Undercliff: Poems 1946–1953* (1953)
WL	*Ways of Light* (1980)

A

Separate Publications

A1 *A BRAVERY OF EARTH*

A1a. First edition, English issue (1930)

A BRAVERY OF EARTH

BY

RICHARD EBERHART

JONATHAN CAPE
THIRTY BEDFORD SQUARE
LONDON

Title Page: 7 5/8 x 4 7/8 in. (193 x 123 mm.)

FIRST PUBLISHED IN MCMXXX

MOTHER
I PRAISE YOU

PRINTED IN GREAT BRITAIN BY
BUTLER & TANNER LTD
FROME

Collation: [unsigned A⁸] B-H⁸; 64 leaves; [1-6] 7-128.

Contents: p. 1: half title; p. 2: blank; p. 3: title page;
p. 4: copyright page and dedication, 'MOTHER I I PRAISE YOU';
p. 5: second half title; p.6: blank; pp. 7-128: text.

Typography: 28 lines per normal page; 118 (122) x 68 mm.;
20 lines = 89 mm

Paper and Binding: leaf measures 7 5/8 x 4 7/8 in. (193 x 123 mm.); yWhite
(92) wove, unwatermarked paper; uncoated smooth; coarse linen-cloth (304c)
boards, 7 13/16 x 5 1/4 in. (198 x 133 mm.), contain threads primarily in s.
Blue (178), brill. G (140), and white; spine: stamped in d. p B (201), '[vert.,

from bottom to top] A BRAVERY OF EARTH [ornament] RICHARD EBERHART'; top and fore-edges rough trimmed; yWhite (92) wove, unwatermarked endpapers.

Dust Jacket: total measurement, 7 13/16 x 18 1/16 in. (198 x 459 mm.); wove, unwatermarked tan paper (no Centroid equiv.); both sides uncoated, rough; lettered in black and brill. G (140); front: '[all within brilliant green ornamental rules frame; in black] *A Bravery of Earth* | by | RICHARD EBERHART | [publisher's device in brilliant green]'; spine: '[in brilliant green, row of type ornaments] | [in black] A | Bravery | of | Earth | by | RICHARD | EBERHART | [publisher's device in brilliant green at base] | [in black] JONATHAN | CAPE | [in brilliant green, row of type ornaments]'; back: unprinted; front flap: '[in black] A BRAVERY OF EARTH | [16 lines prin. in roman, about the book] | [in lower right corner, broken diagonal rule, 64 mm.] | 5 s. net'; back flap: unprinted.

Text Contents: "A Bravery of Earth."

Publication: Published 10 March 1930 at 5s; number of copies printed unknown.

Locations: DLC, NcU, NhD, RE (2), SW (5), ViU.

First Publication: all. The following poems have been collected or reprinted subsequent to original publication:

"This Fevers Me": untitled in BE, 7.1-8.3; in *SP51, CP60; SP65; CP76; CP88*; rept. in *Fifteen Modern American Poets*, ed. George P. Elliott, Rinehart Edition 79 (New York: Rinehart, 1956), p. 21; *The Pattern of Poetry*, ed. William Kean Seymour and John Smith (London: Burke, 1963), p. 32; *Modern Religious Poems*, ed. Jacob Trapp (New York: Harper & Row, 1964), p. 38; *The Distinctive Voice*, ed. William J. Martz (Glenview, Ill.: Scott, Foresman, 1966), p. 146; *The Lyric Potential*, ed. James E. Miller, Jr. (Glenview, Ill.: Scott, Foresman, 1974), p. 192, with RE's previously unpublished note on the poem on p. 193 (see **B116**).
"O Wild Chaos!": untitled in BE, 33.13-22; in *CP60, CP76, CP88*.
"The Bells of a Chinese Temple": untitled in BE: 119.12- 121.12; in *CP60; SP65; CP76; CP88*.

Note: An errata slip, 3 7/8 x 4 5/8 in. (74 x 119 mm.) is tipped in between pp. 6-7 in all copies examined: 'ERRATA | Page 61, line 15. There should be a space separat- | ing line 14, '...out of the pigment' from | 15, 'That night-sent man...' | Page 76, line 18. There should be a space separat- | ing line 17, '...the unhaving' from 18, 'He | girded himself ...' | Page 76, line 28 (last), should read, 'Dull motions | were springe.' | Page 110, line 4 from bottom, should read, 'The | intaking of life like breath.'

A1b. First edition, American issue (English sheets)
All ident. to **A1a** except for:

A BRAVERY OF EARTH

BY

RICHARD EBERHART

NEW YORK
JONATHAN CAPE & HARRISON SMITH
LONDON: JONATHAN CAPE

Title Page: 7 1/2 x 4 7/8 in. (191 x 125 mm.).

Copyright Page: FIRST PUBLISHED IN MCMXXX | PRINTED IN GREAT BRITAIN BY | BUTLER & TANNER LTD | FROME'.

Collation: [A⁸ + ¹] B-H⁸; 65 leaves; one blank leaf, [1-6] 7-128; [A⁸ + ¹] contains a cancel leaf tipped onto the stub of A².

Contents: p. 1: title page; p. 2: copyright page; p.3: dedication (from p. 4 of **A1a**): 'MOTHER | I PRAISE YOU'; p. 4: blank.

Binding: deep Red (13) fine bead-cloth (202b) boards measure 7 3/4 x 5 1/8 in. (196 x 131 mm.); front and back are unstamped; spine: in gold, '[vert. from top to bottom] A BRAVERY OF EARTH [rule] *EBERHART* [horiz. at base, publisher's device]'; all edges trimmed; top edges stained black.

Dust Jacket: total measurement, 7 3/4 x 19 in. (197 x 484 mm.); dull white (no Centroid equiv.) wove, unwatermarked decorated paper, with flecks of grayish blue, pink and orange; both sides uncoated, rough; printed in grayish blue (no Centroid equiv.); front: contains four rectangular panels, the corners of the three top of which touch to frame the title, the fourth of which crosses the bottom edge, '[on right side] A | BRAVERY | OF | EARTH [above panel at bottom] RICHARD EBERHART'; spine: '[rectangular panel at top; vert. from top to bottom] A BRAVERY OF EARTH [horiz. at base, publisher's device]'; back: '[all within a frame of double-rules, the outer of which is thick] *THE TRAVELLER'S LIBRARY* | [3 lines in roman describing the series] | *Already Published* | [list in two columns, the left of which contains 16 authors and titles in roman and ital; and the right, 15 authors in roman and ital] | [3 lines prin. in ital, advertisement for Jonathan Cape & Harrison Smith]'; front flap: '*A Bravery of Earth* | [13 lines prin. in roman, about the book (ident. to front flap of **A1a**)] | $2.00'; back flap: '[27 lines prin. in roman, advertisement for Malachi Whitaker, *Frost in April*, including a Humbet Wolfe blurb from the *The Observer*, and price]'.

Publication: Published in late April or early May 1930 at $2.00; copies were bound in the U.S. from English sheets.

Locations: DLC, NhD, RE, SW (4)

Note: A new errata sheet, 3 x 5-inch (77 x 126 mm.) was printed for the American issue, and tipped on p. 5; the corrections are ident. to those noted in **A1a**.

A2 *READING THE SPIRIT*

A2a. *First edition, English issue* (1936)

READING
THE SPIRIT

By

Richard   Eberhart

1936

CHATTO & WINDUS

LONDON

Title Page: 8 1/2 x 5 5/8 in. (215x 143 mm.).

PUBLISHED BY

Chatto & Windus

LONDON

*

The Macmillan Company
of Canada, Limited

TORONTO

Collation: [unsigned a⁴] A-E⁸; 44 leaves; [i-vi] vii-viii, [1] 2-7 [8-10] 11-29 [30-32] 33-53 [54-56] 57-79 [80].

Contents: p. i: half title; p.ii: *'By the same Author* | A BRAVERY OF EARTH'; p. iii: title page; p. iv: copyright page; p.v: dedication, *'To* | MY FATHER'; p.vi: 'NOTE | [8 lines of acknowledgment in roman and ital]'; pp. vi-viii: table of contents; pp. 1-7: introduction by Michael Roberts; p. 8: blank; pp. 9-79: text, in three sections, numbered I-III; p. 80: colophon, 'Printed in Great Britain | by T. and A. CONSTABLE LTD. | at the University Press | Edinburgh'.

Typography: 37 lines per normal page; 157 (162) x 96.5 mm. (p. 6); 20 lines = 85 mm.

Paper and Binding: leaf measures 8 1/2 x 5 5/8 in. (214 x 145 mm.); yWhite (92) laid paper, vert. chainlines 25 mm. apart, watermarked '[crown device] | [in open-face semi-Gothic] Abbey Mills | Greenfield'; both sides uncoated, smooth; boards; quarter-bound in deep B (approx. 179) bead-cloth (202b) and m. Blue and grayish tan (no Centroid equiv.) decorated paper (ovals and dots broken by diagonals running left to right) boards, 5 5/8 x 5 7/8/ in. (219 x 149 mm.); spine: stamped in gold, '[vert. from bottom to top] Eberhart [wavy rule] READING THE SPIRIT'; top edges trimmed, fore- and bottom edges rough trimmed; yWhite (92) laid endpapers, horiz. chainlines 28 mm. apart; uncoated smooth.

Dust Jacket: total measurement, 8 5/8 x 21 7/16 in. (220 x 545 mm.); tan (no Centroid equiv.) laid paper, vert. chainlines 24 mm. apart; both sides uncoated, smooth; printed in d. Blue (183) and deep Red (13); front: '[in dark blue open-face type] R E A D I N G | T H E | S P I R I T | [in deep red, row of three solid star ornaments, the middle of which is raised] | [in dark blue, roman] RICHARD | EBERHART'; spine: '[in dark blue, vert. from top to bottom; row of three solid star ornaments] [in deep red] Richard Eberhart [in dark blue, thick rule] [in deep red] READING THE SPIRIT [in dark blue, row of three solid star ornaments, like first]'; back: '[in dark blue] POETRY | [in deep red, row of three solid star ornaments, the center of which is raised] | [in dark blue; prin. in roman, list of 12 authors and 14 titles, with prices] | [in deep red, solid star ornament] | [in dark blue] CHATTO & WINDUS | 40-42 CHANDOS STREET, LONDON W.C.2'; front flap: '[in dark blue; 21 lines in roman, about the book] | 6s. [but with '5s.' printed over in dark blue in all copies examined] *NET*'; back flap: unprinted.

Text Contents: Introduction, by Michael Roberts; text divided into three numbered sections; I: "Maze," "Request for Offering," "World's Mere Environment," "In the Evening Stark and Bare," "Fragments," "For a Lamb," "Maya and the Hunter," "Cynic Song," "Necessity," "Caravan of Silence,""Beyond San Rapiña," "If This Be Love," "You, Too, Are Coming Up," "New Year's Eve;" II: "Four Lakes' Days," "Ode to Silence," "Dissertation by Wax Light," "Meditation on the Sun," "The Return of Odysseus," " Where Are Those High and Haunting Skies;" III: "On First Hearing Beethoven's Opus 127, at 23 Fitzroy Square," "Suite in Prison," "The Groundhog," The Rape of the Cataract," "Death is Indescribably Much on Me," "1934," "Job," "In a Hard Intellectual Light," "My Bones Flew Apart," "Song of the Soul," "The Transfer."

Publication: Published 1 Oct. 1936 at 6s (later 5s); 756 copies printed, of which 496 were for distribution in Great Britain. It is likely that fewer than 350 copies were actually bound, as "140 quires [were] destroyed by enemy action on October 18 1940." (Ltr., Michael Bott, Keeper of Archives and Manuscripts, Univ. of Reading, England, to SW, 15 Jan. 1987.) Publisher's records further report that of the copies that were bound, only 200 were sold by March 1940. See **A2b.**

Locations: DLC, NcGU, NcU, NhD, RE (2), SW (4), ViU.

First Appearances: The following poems are here first published; collected and reprinted appearances are regularly noted below and following.

"World's Mere Environment"
"In the Evening Stark and Bare"
"Beyond San Rapiña"
"If This Be Love': rept. in *A Little Treasury of Love Poems from Chaucer to Dylan Thomas*, ed. John Holmes (New York: Scribner's, 1950), pp. 36-37.
"You, Too, Are Coming Up"
"New Year's Eve"
"Four Lakes' Days": in *SP51, CP60, CP76, CP88*; rept. in *Mid-Century American Poets*, ed. John Ciardi (New York: Twayne, 1950), pp.236-37; excpt. rept. in *New York Times Book Review*, 23 Aug. 1953, p. 2.
"Ode to Silence": in *CP60, CP76, CP88*
"Meditation on the Sun"
"Where Are Those High and Haunting Skies": in *SP51, CP60, CP76, CP88*; rept. in *Three Dimensions of Poetry*, ed. Vincent Stewart (New York: Scribner's, 1969), pp. 226-27; *American Literature: The Makers and the*

Making, ed. Cleanth Brooks et al. (New York: St. Martin's, 1973), v. 2, p. 2919.

"On First Hearing Beethoven's Opus 127, at 23 Fitzroy Square"

"Suite in Prison": in *SP51, CP60, CP76, CP88*; part IV first publ. as "From 'Suite from Prison'" (**C87**).

"The Rape of the Cataract": in *CP60, CP76, CP88*; rept. in *The Achievement of Richard Eberhart*, ed. Bernard Engel (Glenview, Ill.: Scott, Foresman, 1968), pp. 56-57.

"Death is Indescribably Much on Me"

"Job"

"In a Hard Intellectual Light": in *SP51, CP60, SP65, CP76, CP88*; rept. in *A Little Treasury of Modern Poetry, English and American*, ed. Oscar Williams, rev. ed. (New York: Scribner's 1952), pp. 433-34, and in "Third College Edition" (1970), pp. 432-33; *Perspectives U.S.A.*, no. 10 (Winter 1955), 28-29; *Fifteen Modern American Poets*, ed. Elliott (1956), pp. 22-23; *Chief Modern Poets of England and America*, ed. Gerald D. Sanders et al., 4th ed. (New York: Macmillan, 1962), v. 2, pp. 403-404, and in 5th ed. (1970), v. 2. pp. 360-61; *The Norton Anthology of Poetry*, ed. Arthur B. Eastman et al. (New York: Norton, 1970), pp. 1067-68.

"My Bones Flew Apart": in *SP51, CP60, CP76, CP88*

"Song of the Soul"

"The Transfer": in *SP51, CP60, CP76, CP88*

A2b. *First edition, American issue* (English sheets), 1937
All ident to **A2a** except for:

READING
THE SPIRIT

By

Richard   Eberhart

NEW YORK

OXFORD UNIVERSITY PRESS

1937

Copyright Page: 'MADE IN GREAT BRITAIN | [at base] ALL RIGHTS RESERVED'.

Binding: quarter-bound in m. Blue (approx. 182) bead cloth (202b) cloth and medium grayish blue (no Centroid equiv.) paper boards, 8 3/4 x 5 13/16 in. (223 x 151 mm.); spine: stamped in gold, '[three rows of type ornaments] [vert. from bottom to top] *EBERHART* [rule, 9 mm..] READING THE SPIRIT [horiz., three rows of type ornaments like first]'.

Dust Jacket: total measurement, 8 13/16 x 21 7/16 in. (222 x 545 mm.); p. Blue (approx. 185) wove paper, watermarked '*T & H Tru-Color Text*'; both sides uncoated, smooth; printed in black; front: READING | THE | SPIRIT | *Poems* | *Richard Eberhart*'; spine: printed in black; ident. to spine of binding; back: 'OXFORD BOOKS | [33 lines in roman and ital, consisting of descriptions and prices of books by Federico Garciá Lorca, Stephané Mallarmé, Helen Cornelius, Gerard Manley Hopkins, and Walter de la Mare] | OXFORD UNIVERSITY PRESS | 114 Fifth Avenue, New York'; front flap: '[16 lines prin. in roman, about the book and author]'; back flap: '[17 lines in roman and ital, about the author]'.

Publication: Published 2 December 1937 at $2.50; 250 copies from English sheets, with Oxford title page, for distribution in the United States.

Locations: DLC, NhD, RE, SW (3)

A3a. *First Edition, English issue (1940)*

Song and Idea

By

RICHARD EBERHART

1940

CHATTO & WINDUS

LONDON

Title Page: 8 1/2 x 5 9/16 in. (215 x 142 mm.).

PUBLISHED BY

Chatto & Windus

LONDON

*

The Macmillan Company
of Canada, Limited

TORONTO

Collation: [a⁴] A-C⁸ D⁴; 32 leaves; [i-iv] v-vii [viii], [1-2] 3-26 [27-28] 29-55 [56].

p. i: half title; p. ii: list of books by RE; p. iii: title page; p. iv: copyright page; pp. v-vii: table of contents; p. viii 'NOTE I [7 lines of acknowledgement in roman and ital]'; pp. 1-55: text, in two numbered sections; p. 56: colophon, 'Printed in Great Britain I by T. and A. CONSTABLE LTD. I at the University Press I Edinburgh'. N.B.: p. 1 contains dedication of section I, '*To I MAIA*', and p. 27 contains dedication of section II, '*To My Sister I ELIZABETH I on her perfect recovery from I a broken neck*'.

Typography: 34 lines per normal page; 155 (160) x 76 mm.; 20 lines = 92 mm.

Paper and Binding: leaf measures 8 9/16 x 5 3/4 in. (218 x 146 mm.); yWhite (92) laid paper, vert. chainlines 24 mm. apart, watermarked '[crown device] I [in open-face semi-Gothic] Abbey Mills I Greenfield'; binding: quarter-bound in m. O (approx. 43) bead-cloth (202b) and decorated laid paper, m. O design of what appears to be a wheat plant on yWhite (92), boards measure 8 3/4 x 5 13/16 in. (223 x 149 mm.); spine: stamped in m. Br (58), '[vert. from top to bottom] SONG AND IDEA [wavy rule] *RICHARD EBERHART*'; top edges trimmed, fore- and bottom edges rough trimmed; yWhite (92) wove, unwatermarked endpapers, uncoated smooth.

Dust Jacket: total measurement, 8 13/16 x 20 in. (223 x 507 mm.); 1. y Br (86) wove paper, watermarked '[rule] BASINGWERK PARCHMENT [rule]'; inner side uncoated, outer side coated smooth; printed in d. Br (approx. 59); front: 'P O E M S [row of 13 circles that decrease in size from left to right] I [running upward from left to right] Song and Idea I [illus. of flower, ident. to title page] I RICHARD I EBERHART'; spine: '[vert. from top to bottom] SONG AND IDEA *by RICHARD EBERHART*'; Back: 'Poetry I [15 lines in roman and ital., including list of 12 authors and 18 titles, the first of which is RE's *Reading the Spirit*] I *Chatto & Windus*'; front flap: '[21 lines prin. in roman, about the book and author] I 6s. NET'; back flap: unprinted.

Text Contents: in two numbered sections; I: "The Scarf of June," "Experience Evoked," "Two Loves," "Burden," "In Prisons of Established Craze," "The Largess," "Let the Tight Lizard on the Wall," "Earth Sanctions Old Men," "The Needle of the Eye," "When Doris Danced," "The Critic With His Pained Eye," "My Desire to Write Poetry Without Money," "Anglo-Saxon Song," "The Young Hunter," "When Golden Flies Upon My Carcase Come," "Now Is the Air Made of Chiming Balls," "The Child," "Opportunity, Tired Cup of Tin," "For Blake," "Realm (To W.H. Auden)," "Christmas Night," "I Went to See

Irving Babbitt"; II: "Grave Piece," "Recollection of Childhood," "When I Think of Her, the Power of Poetry Arises," "Orchard," "Rumination," "The Soul Longs to Return Whence It Came," "Song," "In the Night When Destruction Shall Shake the World," "Song for the Death of My Uncle in Illinois," The Humanist," "The Virgin," "Man's Greed and Envy Are So Great," "The Goal of Intellectual Man," "If I Could Only Live at the Pitch That Is Near Madness,""Wading Through the Thick Mud of Society," "I Walked Out to the Graveyard to See the Dead," "Those Who Love Struggle," "A Meditation," " The Full of Joy Do Not Know; They Need Not."

Publication: Published 21 Nov. 1940 at 6s; 759 copies printed, of which 261 copies were bound for distribution in Great Britain. Bound copies were available to selected reviewers in late October or early November 1940 and contain a review slip listing publication as 7 November 1940.

Locations: DLC, NcGU, NcU, RE, SW(5), ViU.

First Appearances: The following poems are here first published; collected and reprinted appearances are regularly noted.

"Experience Evoked": in *SP51, CP60, SP65, CP76, CP88*; rept. in *Twentieth Century American Poetry*, ed. Conrad Aiken (New York: Modern Library, 1944), pp. 367-68; *The American Experience in Literature*, ed. Sculley Bradley et al., rev. ed. (New York: Norton, 1961), v. 2, p. 1543, and in 3d ed. (1967), p. 1624; *Explicator*, 32 (May 1974), 16, with RE's own explication of this poem in p. 17.

"Burden": in *SP51, CP60, SP65, CP76, CP88*; rept. in *New Republic*, 104 (13 Jan. 1941), 46; *New York Times Book Review*, 29 July 1951, p. 2; *Dartmouth Alumni Magazine*, 44 (June 1952), 25; *This Powerful Rhyme: A Book of Sonnets*, ed. Helen Plotz (New York: Greenwillow, 1979), p. 45.

"In Prisons of Established Craze": in *CP60, SP65, CP76, CP88*; rept. in *American Literature*, ed. Brooks et al. (1973), v. 2, p. 2919.

"Let the Tight Lizard on the Wall": in *CP60, CP76, CP88*

"Earth Sanctions Old Men"

"When Doris Danced": in *SP51, CP60, SP65, CP76, CP88*; rept. in *Erotic Poetry: The Lyrics, Ballads, Idylls, and Epics of Love*, ed. William Cole (New York: Raandom House, 1963); *The Case for Poetry*, ed. Frederick L. Gwynn et al., 2d ed. (New York: Prentice-Hall, 1965); *Chief Modern Poets of England and America*, ed. (1970), pp. 363-64; *The Norton Anthology of Poetry*, ed. Eastman et al. (1970), p. 1068; *Music and Fire: Approaches to Poetry*, ed. H. Edward Richardson and Frederick B. Shroyer (New York; Knopf, 1971), p. 130.

"The Critic With His Pained Eye": in *CP60, SP65, CP76, CP88*.

"The Young Hunter": in *SP51, CP60, CP76, CP88*; rept. in *Explicator*, 6 (Feb. 1948), 24.

"When Golden Flies Upon My Carcase Come": in *SP51, CP60, SP65, CP76, CP88*; rept. in *Fifteen Modern American Poets*, ed. Elliott (1956), pp. 23-24; *The Achievement of Richard Eberhart*, ed. Engel (1968), p. 24.

"The Child": in *SP51, CP60, CP76, CP88*; rept. in *A Century of Winter (1855-1955)*, ed. D.M. Low et al. (London: Chatto & Windus, 1956), p. 571.

"Opportunity, Tired Cup of Tin"

"For Blake"

"Christmas Night"

"Orchard": in *CP60, SP65, CP88*; rept. in *The Achievement of Richard Eberhart*, ed. Engel (1968), pp. 25-26.

"The Soul Longs to Return Whence It Came": in *SP51, CP60, SP65, CP76, CP88*; rept. in *New Poems* 1940, ed. Oscar Williams (New York: Yardstick Press, 1941), pp. 93-95; *The Triumph of Life: Poems of Consolation for the English Speaking Language*, ed. Horace Gregory (New York; Viking, 1943), pp. 87-89; *The Zephyr Book of American Verse*, ed. Ebba Dablin (Stockholm: Continental Book Co., 1945), pp. 264-66; *A Little Treasury of Modern Poetry, English and American*, ed. Oscar Williams (New York: Scribner's, 1946), pp. 133-35, and in rev. ed. (1952), pp. 437-38; *The Pocket Anthology of Modern Verse*, ed. Oscar Williams (New York: Pocket Books, 1954), pp. 462-63; *Exploring Poetry*, ed. M.L. Rosenthal and A.J.M. Smith (New York: Macmillan, 1955), pp. 471-73; *American Poetry*, ed. Karl Shapiro (New York: Crowell, 1960), pp. 208-9; *Chief Modern Poets of England and America*, ed. Sanders et al., 4th ed. (1962), v. 2, pp. 404-6, and in 5th ed. (1970), v. 2, pp. 361-63; *Today's Poets: American and British Poetry Since the 1930's*, ed. Chad Walsh (New York: Scribner's, 1964), pp. 37-39; *The Distinctive Voice*, ed. William J. Martz (Glenview, Ill.: Scott, Foresman, 1966), pp. 147-48; *The Achievement of Richard Eberhart*, ed. Engel (1968), pp. 27-28; *Muse of Fire: Approaches to Poetry*, ed. Richardson and Shroyer (1971), pp. 85-86.

"In the Night When Destruction Shall Take the World": rept. in *Southern Review*, 7 (Spring 1942), 861-62.

"Man's Greed and Envy Are So Great": in *CP60, CP76, CP88*.

"The Goal of Intellectual Man": in *SP51, CP60, SP65, CP76, CP88*; rept. in *Modern Poetry American and British*, ed. Kimon Friar and John Malcolm Brinnin (New York: Appleton-Century-Crofts, 1951) p. 281; *Brandeis University Bulletin*, 18 (Nov. 1968), 18; *American Literature*, ed. Brooks et al. (1973), v. 2, p. 2919.

"Wading Through the Thick Mud of Society"

"The Full of Joy Do Not Know; They Need Not": in *SP51, CP60,*

CP76, CP88; rept. in *The Norton Anthology of Poetry*, ed. Eastman (1970), p. 1068.

Notes: RE submitted the mansucript of Song and Idea to Chatto & Windus in January 1940. It contained 54 titled poems as well as 31 numbered sonnets (later published as **A26**). W. H. Auden, whom Eberhart had brought to St. Mark's School, Southborough, Mass., in 1939 to teach for four months, was instrumental in the selection process. "I am indebted to Auden for reading a Mss. of some 200 poems," Eberhart wrote Michael Roberts at Chatto & Windus, and "from which these have been taken." Auden's selections are marked on the typescript, as follow: "Experience Evoked," "Two Loves," "Burden," "In Prisons of Established Craze," The Largess," "Earth Sanctions Old Men," "The Young Hunter," "Song of Freedom," " ['Auden wants to get his friend Benjamin Britten to set it to music'], "When Golden Flies Upon My Carcass Come," "The Child," "Opportunity," ['Auden has sense enough to see the merit of this (poem); I always liked it but never got it printed.'], "Recollection of Childhood," "The Soul Longs to Return Whence It Came," "The Blindness of Poets," "I Walked Out to the Graveyard to See the Dead," "The Human Being Is a Lonely Creature," "A Meditation," and "The Full of Joy." Apparently Harold Raymond, another Chatto & Windus editor, had already made his own selection, and type had been set by Constable in Edinburgh. Proof copies in a brown wrapper were issued in March or April 1940, listing the publication date as 20 June 1940. RE seemed reasonably pleased with the selection but wanted Raymond to insert "Go to the Shine That's On a Tree" between "Burden" and "In Prisons of Established Craze," and "But to Reach the Archimedean Point" and "The Psychic Life" after "I Went to See Irving Babbitt," to conclude section I. Raymond did not allow these additions, however, but RE did receive editorial permission to make the following changes and corrections, even though the proof copies had already been foliated and sent to reviewers. RE's changes and corrections are noted below; the earlier reading (proof copy) precedes the bracket and corresponds to the published text.

4.5 Sowing] Sewing
12.4 has] knows
14 [title] PAINÈD] PAINED
14.1 painèd] pained
39.6 thy] this
41.8 instead]~)ᴧ
32.12 tomb] womb
46.16 harmony.]~ ,
46.4 What the sun and the moon and the stars broke] That the sun and the moon broke

51.5 (The wind is blowing.) (The wind is blowing.)] (Blowing, the ineffable structure of the wind)

52.11 Beating, beating immemorial mystery.] Contending in immaterial mastery.

52.16 here]~ ,

52.29 machine;] ~:

52.33 builds,]~_∧

53.9 barbed wire, barbed wire.] barbs of fiery wire

53.13 gemut of all] weirs of

53.21 very cold brink] cold, very brink

53.14 beautiful dynamic] captive, cyclic

53.15 as we say in our American slang.] meaning and moral dimension.

54.5 That you] You

54.6 That you] You

54.7 say]~ ,

54.10 For ... about,] (For ... about),

Maia, to whom the first section of *Song and Idea* is dedicated, is Louise Hawkes Padelford, and with whom RE conducted a deeply personal realtion-ship and correspondence from 1926-28. He referred to her as "Maia" or "Maya," and he was Ricco. In addition to specific poems that bear her name, *Thirty One Sonnets* (A26) were written for her between 11 May and 11 June 1932. Mrs. Padelson provided a £30 subsidy that allowed Chatto & Windus to proceed with the publication of *Song and Idea*. See Joel Roache, *Richard Eberhart: The Progress of an American Poet* (New York: Oxford Univ. Press, 1971), pp. 160-61.

A3b. *First edition, American issue* (English sheets, 1942)
All ident to **A3a** except for:

Song and Idea

By

RICHARD EBERHART

NEW YORK

OXFORD UNIVERSITY PRESS

1942

Title Page: 8 7/16 x 5 3/8 in. (214 x 135 mm.)

Copyright Page: 'MADE IN GREAT BRITAIN | ALL RIGHTS RESERVED'.

Collation: [a²] is cancelled leaf containing title and copyright pages.

Paper and Binding: leaf measures 8 7/16 x 5 9/16 in. (214 x 141 mm.); m. Blue (approx. 182 but darker) fine bead-cloth (202b) boards measure 8 11/16 x 5 3/4 in. (222 x 145 mm.); spine: stamped in gold, '[vert. from bottom to top] [type ornament] *EBERHART* [solid star ornament] SONG AND IDEA [type ornament like first]'; top and bottom edges cut, fore-edges rough trimmed; tan (no Centroid equiv.) wove endpapers, unwatermarked; uncoated, smooth.

Dust Jacket: total measurement, 8 11/16 x 21 3/8 in. (221 x 544 mm.); p. Blue (approx. 185) wove paper, watermarked '*T & H Tru-Colour Text*'; both sides uncoated, smooth; printed in v. deep Red (14); front: '*Poems* | [rev. out in open-face fancy type, against a very deep red panel, 69 x 69 mm.] SONG | AND | IDEA | [below panel] *RICHARD EBERHART*'; spine: like spine of binding; back: 'OXFORD BOOKS | [rule, 97 mm.] | READING THE SPIRIT | By Richard Eberhart, 87 Pages $2.50 | [15 lines in roman and ital, including excerpts from reviews by Muriel Rukeyser (*New York Herald Tribune*), *New York Times*, and R.P. Blackmur (*Partisan Review*)] | [rule, 97 mm.] | OXFORD UNIVERSITY PRESS | 114 Fifth Avenue • New York, N.Y.'; front flap: SONG AND IDEA | by | RICHARD EBERHART | [20 lines prin. in roman, about RE, including excerpts from reviews by Harry Brown (*Vice Versa*), John Crowe Ransom (*Furioso*), Nicholas Moore (*Poetry*, London), and Audrey Beecham (*Life and Letters Today*)]'.

Publication: Published 20 Aug. 1942 at $1.50; approx. 188 copies bound from sheets of **A3a** (with cancelled title page) for sale in the United States. RE received his author's copies on 10 August. The 300 quires (312 prepared in July 1941) were destroyed when the ship carrying them was torpedoed by a German U-boat in October 1941. A second set of quires (approx. 188) were successfully shipped to New York in December 1941.

A4 *A WORLD-VIEW*

First edition (1941)

Title Page: 9 x 4 in. (228 x 101 mm.).

Copyright Page: unprinted

Collation: [unsigned 1⁴]; [1-8]

Contents: p. 1: title page; p. 2: blank; pp.3-6: text; p.7: blank; p. 8: statement of limitation.

Typography: 40 lines per page; 180 x 77 mm.; 20 liness = 84 mm.

Paper and Binding: yWhite (92) wove, unwatermarked paper; uncoated, smooth; wire-stitched in thin, light grayish blue (no Centroid equiv.) card cover, 9 x 8 in. (228 x 202 mm.) folded once vertically to 9 x 4 in. (228 x 101 mm.); printed in d. Blue (183); front: 'A World-View l BY RICHARD EBERHART l *Tufts College Phi Beta Kappa Poem, 1941*'.

Text Contents: First separate publication of "A World-View" (**C131**).

Publication: 200 copies privately printed in June 1941 at the Tufts College Press, Medford, Mass.; not for sale.

Locations: DLC, NhD, RE, SW (7)

Statement of Limitation: p. 8: '200 copies of A WORLD-VIEW l were printed in June, 1941 at the l Tufts College Press l (*Reprinted from the Tuftonian*)'.

A5 *FREE GUNNERS HAND BOOK*

A5a. *First edition* [1943]

[Cover title: rev. out in white against pictorial cover, in tones of gray and black, depicting a single truck and ball turret] FREE GUNNERS | HAND BOOK | Aviation Free Gunnery Unit | *RESTRICTED* | [at base, below truck and ball turret] N.A.S. NORFOLK | DAM NECK | VA.

Collation: [unsigned 1¹⁴]; 14 leaves; [i-ii], 1-4 [5] 6-8 [9] 10-19 [20] 21-25 [26].

Contents: p. i: table of contents; p. ii: frontispiece; pp. 1-23: text, diagrams, and tables; pp. 24-25: glossary; p. 26: blank. N.B.: No copyright page present.

Typography: reproduced from typescript original.

Paper and Binding: leaf measures 7 x 5 in. (179 x 128 mm.); yWhite (92) wove, unwatermarked paper; uncoated, smooth; wire-stitched in yWhite (92) self-wrapper (paper ident. to text stock), 7 x 10 in. (179 x 256 mm.), folded once vertically to 7 x 5 in. (179 x 128 mm.); front: see above, description of cover-title; back: printed in black, '[slanted thick rule, 69 mm.] | [printed obliquely, from left to right, bottom to top] | DO NOT TAKE | INTO THE AIR | [slanted rule like first]'; on recto of rear wrapper: in black, 'Graphic Arts Department | Photo-Science lab. | N.A.S. Norfolk'.

Text Contents: "Free Gunners Hand Book"; see *Note.*

Publication: Published 6 Aug. 1943 by the U.S. Navy for use in training aviation free gunners; not for sale.

Locations: NhD, RE, SW (6)

Note: In the compiler's collection is RE's personal copy of *Free Gunners Hand Book*, containing RE's contemporary inscription on the verso of the cover title, in blue ink: "This book was instigated, | compiled, and executed | by | Richard G. Eberhart | Lieut. USNR | at AFGU, Dam Neck, Va. | published Aug. 6, 1943 | a copy to be given each gunnery student."

A5b. *Second edition, first printing* [1944]

[Cover title: in black] Free Gunner's I Hand Book I AVIATION FREE GUNNERY UNIT I RESTRICTED I [photograph of a line of trucks containing ball turrets] I [below photograph] NAS • NORFOLK • DAM NECK, VA.

Collation: [1^{20}]; 20 leaves; 1-40.

Contents: p. 1: spaces for gunnery student's name, rate, squadron, and class or section, with photograph at base; p. 2: prefatory remark by Lieut. W. Berry Grove, dated April 1944; p. 3: table of contents; pp. 4-38: text and tables; pp. 39-40: glossary.

Typography: reprod. from typescript original except for titles.

Paper and Binding: leaf measures 6 15/16 x 4 15/16 in. (177 x 127 mm.); yWhite (92) wove, unwatermarked paper; uncoated, smooth; wire-stitched in light blue (no Centroid equiv.) card cover, 6 15/16 x 9 7/8 in. (177 x 254 mm.), folded once vertically to 6 15/16 x 4 15/16 in. (177 x 127 mm.); cover title: see above; back: '[within a rules frame] DO NOT TAKE I THIS BOOKLET I INTO THE AIR I [at base] PHOTOGRAPHIC DEPARTMENT, N.A.S., NORFOLK, VA.'; inner side unprinted.

Text Contents: RE's substantially revised text for "Free Gunner's Hand Book."

Publication: Published in April 1944; not for sale. A second printing of the second edition was issued in May 1944; not seen.

Locations: DLC, RE (2), SW (2)

A5c. *Third edition, first printing* [1944]
All ident. to **A5b** except for:

Collation: [unsigned 1^{22}]; 22 leaves; 1-43 [44].

Contents: p. 2: introduction for this edition by Lieut. Cmdr. W. Berry Grove, with publication history printed below, as follows: 'First Edition, April 1944 I Revised Edition, May 1944 I Revised Edition, October 1944'; pp. 4-41: diagrams and text; pp. 42-43: glossary; p. 44: blank.

Binding: light blue (no Centroid equiv.) card cover, total measurement 7 x 10 in. (179 x 256 mm.), folded once to 7 x 5 in. (179 x 128 mm.).

Text Contents: RE's second revised text for "Free Gunners Hand Book."

Note: The publication history of *Free Gunner's Hand Book* as described above in the Contents paragraph is somewhat misleading, and does not account for the true first edition (**A5a**), but rather only for the second edition (**A5b**), a second printing, and the third edition, further revised by RE. That is to say, **A5b** is a re-typed, heavily revised version of the first edition; the additional printing and the third edition were prepared from **A5b**, and contain textual changes in the form of several deletions of material or additions to the text and diagrams.

A6 *POEMS NEW AND SELECTED* (1944 [i.e., 1945])

First edition, hardcover issue

R I C H A R D   E B E R H A R T

Poems

N E W   A N D   S E L E C T E D

The Poets of the Year

N E W   D I R E C T I O N S ,   N O R F O L K ,   C O N N E C T I C U T

1944

Title Page: 8 9/16 x 5 3/4 in. (218 x 147 mm.).

ACKNOWLEDGMENTS

Some of the poems in this book have appeared in the following publications, to whom acknowledgment is made for permission to reprint: The Nation, Kenyon Review, The Chimera, Furioso, Partisan Review, Poetry, Diogenes.

"Maze" and "The Groundhog" are from READING THE SPIRIT and "If I Could Only Live at the Pitch that is Near Madness" and "I Walked Out to the Graveyard to See the Dead" are from SONG AND IDEA, both published by the Oxford University Press, New York.

Collation: [unsigned 1¹⁶]; 16 leaves; [1-4] 5-30 [31-32].

Contents: p. 1: half title; p. 2: blank; p. 3: title page; p. 4: copyright page, with acknowledgements; pp. 5-30: text; p. 31: colophon; p. 32: advertisement for "The Poets of the Year" series.

Typography: 35 lines per normal page; 174 x 95 mm.; 20 lines = 99 mm.

Paper and Binding: leaf measures 8 9/16 x 5 3/4 in. (218 x 147 mm.); yWhite (92) wove, unwatermarked; uncoated, smooth; very pale green (no Centroid equiv.) paper-covered boards measure 8 7/8 x 6 1/16 in. (225 x 152 mm.); printed in black and v. 1. G. (approx. 143); front: '[v. 1. G (143) rule] [in black] *RICHARD EBERHART* | [thick, very light green panel, 19 x 59 mm.] | [in black] Poems | [very light green panel, 21 x 59 mm.] | [in black] *NEW AND SELECTED* | [very light green panel, 30 x 59 mm.] | [in black] The Poets of the Year | [very light green thick rule]'; remainder unprinted; all edges cut; tan (no Centroid equiv.) wove, unwatermarked endpapers; uncoated smooth.

Dust Jacket: total measurement, 8 13/16 x 19 5/16 in. (223 x 507 mm.); very pale green unwatermarked paper (ident. to paper-covered boards); uncoated rough; printed in black; front: ident. to front paper-covered board; spine and back: unprinted; front flap: '$1.00 | The Poets of the Year | [8 lines in roman, about the series] | *for 1944* | [12 lines in roman and ital, including 6 titles and 5 authors] the first of which is RE's *Poems New and Selected*] | New Directions | 67 WEST 44TH STREET, NEW YORK 18, N.Y.'; back flap: 'Poems, New and Selected | By Richard Eberhart | [20 lines prin. in roman, about the book and author]'.

Paper Issue
All ident. to hardcover issue except for:

Title Page: 8 15/16 x 5 9/16 in. (224 x 148 mm.)

Binding: wire-stitched in thick, yWhite (92) card cover; total measurement, 8 15/16 x 11 13/16 in. (224 x 299 mm.), folded once vertically to 8 15/16 x 5 7/8 in. (224 x 149 mm.).

Dust Jacket: like **A6** hardcover issue except $1.00 price on front flap of dust jacket has been clipped, and '50c' has been printed in lower right corner.

Text Contents: text divided into five sections; section 1, "Four War Poems": "World War," "The Preacher Sought to Find Out Acceptable Words," "Dam Neck, Virginia," "The Fury of Aerial Bombardment"; section 2: "Triptych"; section 3: "Song ['There is a place stoical autumn, a glass']," "Mysticism Has Not the Patience to Wait for God's Revelation," "The Dream," "The Moment of Vision," "Retrospective Forelook," "The Lyric Absolute," "There Is an Evil in the Air"; section 4, "Poems Selected from Earlier Volumes": "Maze," "The Groundhog," "If I Could Only Live at the Pitch That Is Near Madness," "I Walked Out to the Graveyard to See the Dead."

Publication: Published 28 January 1945; 2,000 copies printed, of which 500 were issued in paper-covered boards at $1.00, and 1,500 in card-cover at 50 cents.

Locations: DLC (hardcover), NhD (both issues), RE (both issues), SW (4 in hardcover, 3 in paper)

First Appearances: The following are here first printed; collected and reprinted appearances are regularly noted.

"World War"; in *SP65, SP76, CP88*; rept. in *The War Poets: An Anthology of the War Poetry of the 20th Century*, ed. Oscar Williams (New York: John Day, 1945), pp. 124-25; *Where Is Vietnam: American Poets Respond*, ed. Walter Lowenfels (Garden City, N.Y.: Doubleday, 1967), p. 31.
"The Moment of Vision": in *BO, SP51, CP60, CP76, CP88*; rept. in *Modern Religious Poems: A Contemporary Anthology* ed. Jacob Trapp (New York: Harper & Row, 1964), pp. 243-44.
"Retrospective Forelook": in *BO, SP51, CP60, SP65, CP76, CP88.*
"The Lyric Absolute": in *BO, CP60, CP76, CP88.*
"There Is an Evil in the Air": in *LR, CP88.*

Colophon: p. 31, 'DESIGNED BY EDMUND B. THOMPSON I AT HAWTHORN HOUSE, WINDHAM, CONNECTICUT, I AND PRINTED IN I BULMER AND LINOTYPE BASKERVILLE I TYPES AT THE WALPOLE PRINTING I OFFICE, MOUNT VERNON, N.Y.'.

A7 *BURR OAKS*

A7a. *First edition, English issue* (1947)

BURR OAKS

By

Richard Eberhart

1947

CHATTO & WINDUS

LONDON

Title Page: 8 9/16 x 5 3/8 in. (218 x 137 mm.).

PUBLISHED BY

Chatto & Windus

LONDON

*

Oxford University Press

TORONTO

PRINTED IN GREAT BRITAIN
BY BUTLER & TANNER LTD.
FROME AND LONDON

Collation: [unsigned A^6 B^8] C-E^8 F^4; 42 leaves, the first and last of which are used as the front and rear pastedowns; [i-iv] vii-viii [1-2] 3-28 [29-30] 31-55 [56-58] 59-68.

Contents: p. i: half title; p. ii: list of books by RE; p. iii: title page; p. iv: copyright page; p. v: dedication, 'To I MY WIFE'; p. vi: acknowledgement; pp. vii-viii: table of contents; pp. 1-68: text.

Typography: 37 lines per normal page; 154 (162) x 90 mm.; 20 lines = 85 mm.

Paper and Binding: leaf measures 8 5/8 x 5 3/8 in. (219 x 137 mm.); yWhite (92) wove, unwatermarked paper; uncoated smooth; v. OY (66) fine linen-cloth (304) boards measure 8 13/16 x 5 5/8 in. (224 x 143 mm.); spine: stamped in gold, '[vert. from top to bottom] *BURR OAKS* [wavy rule] *Richard Eberhart* [horiz., at base; publisher's device]'; all edges trimmed; second and penultimate leaves used as endpapers.

Dust Jacket: total measurement, 8 13/16 x 9 13/16 in. (223 x 503 mm.); light gray (no Centroid equiv.), wove, unwatermarked paper; both sides uncoated, smooth; printed in br. O (54) and d. y G (137); front: '[in brownish orange open-face] B U R R O A K S I [in dark yellowish green, illus. of acorn and oak leaves] I [in brownish orange script] Poems by I [in roman] Richard Eberhart'; spine: '[vert. from top to bottom; in dark yellowish green open-face] BURR OAKS [star ornament] [in brownish orange; roman] Eberhart [in dark yellowish green] CHATTO'; back: '[in brownish orange open-face] POETRY I [in dark yellowish green, roman; list of 16 authors and 25 titles, the first of which is RE with *Reading the Spirit* and *Song and Idea*] I [in brownish orange open-face] CHATTO & WINDUS'; front flap: '[in dark yellowish green, 6 lines prin. in roman, about the book] I 6s. net'; back flap: unprinted.

Text Contents: text in three numbered sections; I: "Rumination," "Cover Me Over," "The Recapitulation," "The Peer," "The Game," "Imagining How It Would Be to Be Dead," "I Walked Over the Grave of Henry James," "My Temples Quake While Fires Exhale," "The Ineffable," "The Magical," "The Full Weakness of Man," "Of Truth," "Song," "Mysticism Has Not the Patience to Wait for God's Revelation," "The Dream," "The Moment of Vision," "Retrospective Forelook," "The Lyric Absolute," "I Will Not Dare to Ask One Question," "New Hampshire, February"; II: "Triptych," "Speech of a Protagonist," Ode to a Chinese Paper Snake," "Burr Oaks"; III: "The Preacher Sought to Find Out Acceptable Words," "Dam Neck, Virginia," "The Fury of Aerial Bombardment," "An Airman Considers His Power," "At the End of War," "A Ceremony by the Sea."

Publication: Published 16 Oct. 1947 at 6s; 1,462 copies printed, of which 1,102 were bound for distribution in Great Britain.

Locations: DLC, NcU, NhD (2), RE (2), SW (6), ViU

First Appearances: The following poems are here first published; collected and reprinted appearances are regularly noted.

"The Peer"

"Imagining How It Would Be to Be Dead": in *SP51, CP60, SP65, CP76, CP88*; rept. in *A Little Treasury of American Poetry*, ed. Oscar Williams (New York: Scribner's, 1948), pp. 688-89; *Perspectives U.S.A.*, no. 10 (Winter 1955), 29-30.

"I Walked Over the Grave of Henry James": in *SP51, CP60, SP65, CP76, CP88*.

"My Temples Quake While Fires Exhale"

"The Ineffable": in *SP51, CP60, CP76, CP88*.

"The Full Weakness of Man"

"I Will Not Dare to Ask One Question": in *CP60, CP76, CP88*.

"Speech of a Protagonist"

"Burr Oaks": in *SP51, CP60, CP76, CP88*; rept. in *The Achievement of Richard Eberhart*, ed. Engel (1968), p. 63; "The Attic," an excpt. from "Burr Oaks," rept. in *Modern American and Modern British Poetry*, ed. Louis Untermeyer, shorter ed. (New York: Harcourt, Brace, 1955), p. 339.

A7b. *First edition, American issue* (British sheets) (1947)
All ident. to **A7a** except for:

BURR OAKS

Bγ

Richard Eberhart

NEW YORK

OXFORD UNIVERSITY PRESS

1947

MADE IN GREAT BRITAIN

PRINTED IN GREAT BRITAIN
BY BUTLER & TANNER LTD.
FROME AND LONDON

Binding: '*OXFORD*' stamped in gold at base of spine.

Dust Jacket: English price clipped from front flap of jacket; back: '[in dark yellowish green] OXFORD BOOKS | [in brownish orange, spiral-like rule, 102 mm.] | [13 lines in roman, including list of books by RE, C. Day Lewis, H.D., and Grierson-Smith] | [in brownish orange, rule like first] | [in dark yellowish green] OXFORD UNIVERSITY PRESS | 114 FIFTH AVENUE • NEW YORK 11, N.Y.'; spine: '[at base, in dark yellowish green] OXFORD'.

Publication: Published 28 Nov. 1947 at $3.00; 360 copies issued from British sheets with Oxford University Press imprint.

Locations: DLC, NcU, NhD, RE (2), SW (4)

A8 *RUMINATION*

First separate edition (1947)

RUMINATION

Collation: broadside, 7 1/2 x 5 1/8 in. (190 x 130 mm.).

Contents: recto: 'RUMINATION | BY | *Richard Eberhart* | [pair of type ornaments] | [8 lines of text, in roman] | Printed at *THE WAYZGOOSE PRESS*, April 29, 1947'; verso: blank.

Typography: 7 lines of text; 36 (79) x 85 mm.; 7 lines = 36 mm.

Paper: pale, yellowish tan (no Centroid equiv.) wove, unwatermarked paper; uncoated, smooth.

Text Contents: "Rumination" (from **A7**).

Publication: Approx. 50 copies printed by RE's brother-in-law, Charles Butcher II, at the Wayzgoose Press, Hanover, N.H., on 29 April 1947; not for sale.

Locations: NhD, RE, SW (3)

A9 *BROTHERHOOD OF MEN*

First limited and signed edition [1949]

RICHARD EBERHART

BROTHERHOOD

OF MEN

THE BANYAN PRESS

Title Page: 8 1/4 x 5 in. (210 x 126 mm.); title in deep red (approx. 13), with ornament in 1. Br (57).

COPYRIGHT 1949 THE BANYAN PRESS

Collation: [unsigned 1⁸]; 16 leaves; [i-ii], 1-11 [12-14].

Contents: p. i: title page; p. ii: copyright page; pp. 1-11: text; p. 12: blank; p. 13: colophon; p. 14: blank.

Typography: 30 lines per normal page; 147 x 88 mm.; 20 lines = 98 mm.

Paper and Binding: leaf measures 8 1/4 x 5 in. (210 x 126 mm.); yWhite (92) laid paper, vert. chainlines 28 mm. apart, watermarked 'E T R U R I A I I T A L Y I [ornamental device]'; uncoated, rough; top edges rough trimmed, fore- and bottom edges deckled; handsewn with brown cord onto thick gy. Y G (122) card cover and printed jacket 8 3/8 x 5 1/16 in. (209 x 128 mm.); uncoated, rough; unprinted.

Printed Jacket: total measurement, 8 1/4 x 10 1/8 in. (209 x 257 mm.), folded once vertically to 8 1/4 x 5 1/16 in. (209 x 128 mm.); pale brown (no Centroid equiv.) laid paper, vert. chainlines 16 or 6 mm. apart; front: printed in black and m. Br. (approx. 58), '[in black; at top, left side] RICHARD EBERHART I [in moderate brown; at bottom, left side] BROTHERHOOD OF MEN'.

Text Contents: First publication of RE's poem, "Brotherhood of Men"; in *SP51, CP60, CP76, CP88*; rept. in *100 Modern Poems*, ed. Selden Rodman (New York: Pelligrini & Cudahy, 1949), pp. 189-91.

Publication: Published 8 Feb. 1949 at $2.00; approx. 226 copies printed.

Colophon: p. 13, '[RE's autograph in blue ink] I [in black] THIS POEM HAS BEEN SET BY HAND AND PRINTED ON ETRURIA I BY MATTHEW FREDERICKS AND MILTON SAUL AT THE BANYAN I PRESS IN PAWLET VERMONT DURING JANUARY 1949. THERE I ARE 200 NUMBERED COPIES FOR SALE, 26 LETTERED COPIES I NOT FOR SALE. THIS IS [arabic number or letter, A-Z, supplied in red ink against a column of five short horiz. rules]'.

Locations: DLC, NhD, RE, SW (7, lettered and numbered)

Note: The 26 copies prepared for review contain a review slip printed in black on yWhite (92) wove paper, 70 x 108 mm., watermarked '[in fancy type] Neenjh | [in open-face} TUDOR LEDGER | [in roman] 100% RAG CONTENT': *'Review copy* | This book, set & bound by hand & issued in a | a [sic] limited, numbered edition, will be published | on [supplied in red ink] 8 February 1949 [printed in black] & will sell for [supplied in red ink] $2.00 [remainder printed in black]. | Copies of any notice that you choose to print | will be appreciated. | *THE BANYAN PRESS* | *Pawlet Vermont'*.

A10 *AN HERB BASKET*

First limited edition (1950)

A N H E R B B A S K E T by
Richard Eberhart. Copyright 1950.
The Cummington Press.

We are fighting still to know
What we are doing in writing.
Are we making an engine, making
It go? Are we playing with a balloon?
Are we inviting Heraclitus?
We are fighting: but do we know?

Title Page: 8 1/16 x 5 13/16 in. (204 x 148 mm.); title in d. y Pink (30), remainder in black.

Collation: [unsigned 1^8]; 16 leaves; [1-16].

Contents: pp. 1-4: blank; p. 5: title page and first six lines of text; pp. 6-11: text; p. 12: conclusion of text and colophon; pp. 13-16: blank.

Typography: 3 numbered 6-line stanzas per normal page; 122 (128) x 86 mm.; 6 lines = 32 mm.

Paper and Decorated Paper Jacket: leaf measures 8 1/16 x 5 13/16 in. (206 x 145 mm.); white wove paper, watermarked, '[in open-face] RIVES'; uncoated, rough; handsewn with white cord; very pale pink (no Centroid equiv.) decorative jacket with regular horiz. design in m. Pink (5), p. r P (244), and black; tipped on spine, first and last leaves; unlettered and issued without label; white protective outer jacket, total measurement 8 1/4 x 15 3/8 in. (210 x 391 mm.).

Text Contents: First publication of RE's poem, "An Herb Basket." In Un.

Publication: Published in June 1950 at $1.00; 155 copies printed.

Colophon: p. 14, '[ornament in d. y Pink (30); remainder in black] One-hundred-fifty-five copies | printed by W W, who etched the cop- | perplate, and H D, who set the type. | Cummington, Masstts. Cummington | School of the Arts. May 1950.'

Locations: DLC, NhD, RE (2), SW (5)

Notes: An unknown number of review copies were issued prior to publication; all ident. to A10 except for: issued in plain, unprinted brownish gray (no Centroid equiv.) paper jacket, horiz. chainlines 20 mm. apart, and watermarked 'FABRIANO (ITALY)'. In the compiler's collection is a review copy in which the title (p. 5) is printed in l. P (222), with the ornament on p. 14 deleted. It is likely that this is a printer's trial copy, preceding the review copy, and does not constitute a separate issue.

A11 *SELECTED POEMS*

A11a. *First edition, English issue* (1951)

SELECTED
POEMS

By

Richard Eberhart

1951

CHATTO & WINDUS

LONDON

Title Page: 8 1/2 x 5 1/4 in. (216 x 136 mm.).

PUBLISHED BY

Chatto & Windus

LONDON

✿

Clarke, Irwin & Co. Ltd.

TORONTO

Collation: [unsigned A^8] B-F^8; 48 leaves; [i-viii] 1-88.

Contents: p. i: half title; p. ii: list of books by RE; p. iii: title page; p. iv: copyright page; p. v: dedication, 'To | BETTY | & | DIKKON'; p. vi: blank; pp. vii-viii : table of contents; pp. 1-86: text; p. 87: blank; p. 88: at base, 'PRINTED IN GREAT BRITAIN | BY SPOTTISWOODE, BALLANTYNE & CO., LTD. | LONDON AND COLCHESTER'.

Typography: 37 lines per normal page; 157 (162) x 86 mm.; 20 lines = 85 mm.

Paper and Binding: leaf measures 8 5/8 x 5 5/16 in. (220 x 135 mm.); yWhite (92) laid paper, vert. chainlines 25 mm. apart; watermarked '[crown ornament] | ANTIQUE DE LUXE | BCM / SH'; uncoated smooth; m. Red (15) fine bead-cloth (202b) boards measure 8 7/8 x 5 5/8 in. (225 x 141 mm.); spine: stamped in gold, '[vert., from top to bottom] EBERHART *Selected Poems* [wavy rule] *Chatto & Windus*'; all edges trimmed; yWhite (92) wove, unwatermarked endpapers.

Dust Jacket: total measurement, 8 7/8 x 19 1/16 in. (225 x 384 mm.); very light greenish gray (approx. 154, but lighter) wove, unwatermarked paper; both sides uncoated, smooth; printed in black and d. Red (16); front: '[all within a dark red double-rules frame; in black] SELECTED | POEMS | BY | Richard Eberhart | [in dark red, reprod. of drawing of groundhog by Trekkie Parsons] | [in black] CHATTO & WINDUS'; spine: '[vert., from top to bottom; in black] Richard Eberhart [in dark red] SELECTED POEMS [in black] CHATTO & WINDUS'; back: '[in dark red, double rule, 93 mm.] | *Some appreciations of the Poetry of* | RICHARD EBERHART | [in black, 35 lines in roman, including blurbs by Dame Edith Sitwell, Conrad Aiken, Robert Penn Warren, and Richard Wilbur] | [in dark red] CHATTO & WINDUS | [double rules, 93 mm.]'; front flap: '[in black] RICHARD EBERHART | [in dark red, fancy rule] | [in black] *Selected Poems* | [10 lines prin. in roman, about the book] | [lower right corner] 6s. | NET'; back flap: unprinted.

Text Contents: "This Fevers Me," "Maze," "Request for Offering," "For a Lamb," "Necessity," "Caravan of Silence," "Four Lakes' Days," "Dissertation by Wax Light," "The Return of Odysseus," "Where Are Those High and Haunting Skies," "Suite in Prison," "The Groundhog," "1934," "In a Hard Intellectual Light," "My Bones Flew Apart," "The Transfer," "The Scarf of June," "Experience Evoked," "Two Loves," "Burden," "In Prisons of Established Craze," "The Largess," "When Doris Danced," "The Young Hunter," "When Golden Flies Upon My Carcass Come," "Now Is the Air Made of Chiming Balls," "The Child," "Recollection of Childhood," "The Soul Longs to Return Whence It Came," "The Humanist," "The Goal of

Intellectual Man," "If I Could Only Live at the Pitch That Is Near Madness,"
"I Walked Out to the Graveyard to See the Dead," "A Meditation," "The Full
of Joy Do Not Know; They Need Not," "Rumination," "Cover Me Over,"
"Imagining How It Would Be to Be Dead," "I Walked Over the Grave of
Henry James," "The Ineffable," "Mysticism Has Not the Patience to Wait for
God's Revelation," "The Dream," "The Moment of Vision," "Retrospective
Forelook," "I Will Not Dare to Ask One Question," "New Hampshire,
February," "Ode to the Chinese Paper Snake," "Burr Oaks," "Dam Neck,
Virginia," "The Fury of Aerial Bombardment," "An Airman Considers His
Power," "At Lake Geneva," "Brotherhood of Men."

Publication: Published 19 March 1951 at 6s; 1250 copies printed, of which
730 were issued in Great Britain. In June 1952, 250 copies of the English issue (with Chatto & Windus imprint) were shipped to Oxford University Press
in New York.

Locations: NhD, RE (3), SW (6)

A11b. *First edition, American issue* (from English sheets) (1951)
All ident. to **A11a** except for:

SELECTED POEMS

By

Richard Eberhart

NEW YORK

OXFORD UNIVERSITY PRESS

1951

Title Page: 8 5/8 x 5 5/16 in. (220 x 136 mm.).

Copyright Page: 'PRINTED IN GREAT BRITAIN I COPYRIGHT 1951 BY RICHARD EBERHART'.

Binding: at base of spine, '[vert. from top to bottom] *Oxford*'.

Dust Jacket: front: contains drawing of groundhog, in black; '[in black] OXFORD I UNIVERSITY PRESS I NEW YORK'; spine: at base, '[vert., from top to bottom] OXFORD UNIVERSITY PRESS'; front flap: in black, at lower right corner, '$2.50 I NET'; back flap: '[in dark red] RECENT OXFORD I BOOKS ON I POETRY I [in black; ornament] I [22 lines prin. in roman, including a list of books by Conrad Aiken, E.E. Cummings, William Gibson, G.M. Hopkins, C. Day Lewis, and W.B. Yeats (ed.)] I [in dark red] *Printed in Great Britain*'.

Publication: Published 29 June 1951 at $2.50; 520 copies issued from English sheets with Oxford Univ. Press imprint on title page. A further 250 copies (with Chatto & Windus imprint) were purchased by Oxford University Press for distribution in the U.S.

Locations: NhD (2), RE (2), SW (4)

A12 *POETRY AS A CREATIVE PRINCIPLE*

First edition (1952)

Cover Title: '[in deep B (179)] Poetry as a Creative Principle I A FOUNDER'S DAY ADDRESS I *by* I RICHARD EBERHART I [seal of Wheaton College] I WHEATON COLLEGE I NORTON, MASSACHUSETTS I APRIL, 1952'.

Copyright Page: 'Copyright by Richard Eberhart, 1952'.

Collation: [unsigned 1^8]; 16 leaves; 1-13 [14-16].

Contents: pp. 1-13: text; p. 14: blank; p. 15: copyright; p. 16: blank.

Typography: 38 lines per normal page; 162 (170) x 101 mm.; 20 lines = 85 mm.

Paper and Card Cover: leaf measures 9 x 5 15/16 in. (228 x 150 mm.); yWhite (92) wove paper, watermarked 'STRATHMORE PASTEL I U.S.A.'; uncoated, rough; wire-stitched in thick yWhite (92) wove, card cover (heavier Strathmore stock than text), 9 x 5 15/16 in. (228 x 150 mm.); title printed on front in deep B (179).

Text Contents: "Poetry As a Creative Principle"; in *OPP*.

Publication: Approx. 300 copies printed for distribution in May 1952; not for sale.

Locations: NhD, RE, SW

First Publication: RE's essay, "Poetry As a Creative Principle."

A13 *UNDERCLIFF: POEMS 1946-1953*

A13a. *First edition, English issue* (1953)

UNDERCLIFF

POEMS
1946–1953

Richard Eberhart

1953
CHATTO & WINDUS
LONDON

Title Page: 8 5/8 x 5 5/16 in. (218 x 136 mm.)

PUBLISHED BY

Chatto & Windus

LONDON

★

Clarke, Irwin & Co. Ltd

TORONTO

COPYRIGHT 1953

BY RICHARD EBERHART

PRINTED IN GREAT BRITAIN

Collation: [unsigned A^8] B-H^8; 64 leaves; [i-vi] vii-ix [x-xii], 13-43 [44-46] 47-94 [95-96] 97-127 [128].

Contents: p. i: half title; p. ii: list of books by RE; p. iii: title page; p. iv: copyright page; p. v: dedication, 'With I Old and New I Affection I for I My I Two I Gretchens'; p. vi: blank; pp. vii-ix: table of contents; p. x: acknowledgments'; pp. 1-127: text, in two numbered parts; p. 128: colophon: 'Printed in Great Britain I at Hopetoun Street, Edinburgh, I by T. and A. CONSTABLE LTD. I Printers to the University of Edinburgh'.

Typography: 36 lines per normal page; 154 (165) x 90 mm.; 20 lines = 88 mm.

Paper and Binding: leaf measures 8 5/8 x 5 5/16 in. (218 x 136 mm.); yellowish white (Centroid 92) laid paper, vertical chainlines 28 mm. apart; unwatermarked; uncoated, rough; deep red (between Centroid 12 and 13) fine linen-cloth (304) cloth boards measure 8 7/8 x 5 3/4 in. (227 x 144 mm.); front: unstamped; spine: stamped in gold, '[vert. from top to bottom] EBERHART *Undercliff Chatto & Windus*'; back: unstamped; top and fore-edges trimmed, bottom edges rough trimmed; yellowish white (Centroid 92) wove, unwatermarked endpapers.

Dust Jacket: total measurement 8 7/8 x 16 15/16 mm. (227 x 432 mm.); grayish tan (no Centroid equiv.) laid paper, vert. chainlines 24 mm. apart, watermarked '[crown device] I [in open-face semi-Gothic] Abbey Mills I Greenfield'; inner side smooth, outer side rough; printed in dark red (approx. Centroid 16); front: 'Undercliff I *Poems 1946-1953* I [8-ornamental star device] I Richard Eberhart'; spine: '[vert. from top to bottom] UNDERCLIFF [ornament] *Poems 1946-1953* [ornament like first; horiz. at base] *C & W*'; back: '[within a pair of swelled rules] *Poetry* I *by Richard Eberhart* I [33 lines in roman and ital., including a list of books by RE (*Burr Oaks and Selected Poems*, with excerpts from *Poetry Review* and *Time and Tide*), Douglas Le Pan, Patric Dickinson, Wilfred Owen, and Isaac Rosenberg] I [within swelled rules] *Chatto & Windus*'; front flap: '[32 lines in roman and ital., about RE and his work, including excerpts from reviews by Edith Sitwell and Conrad Aiken] I [lower right corner] 10 s. 6d. I net' back flap: unprinted.

Text Contents: Section I: "Indian Pipe," "Go to the Shine That's on a Tree," "What If Remembrance," "Chant of the Forked Lightning," "Sometimes the Longing for Death," "One Way Dialogue," "At Night," "Reality! Reality! What Is It?" "A Love Poem," "Wisdom," "God and Man," "The Poet-Weathervane," "The Horse Chestnut Tree," "The Tobacconist of Eighth Street," "Sea Scape With Parable," "Seals, Terns, Time," "The Cancer Cells," "The Look," "Baudelaire," "Oedipus," "Indian Summer," "Order and Disorder," "Forms of the Human," "That Final Meeting," "Soul's Reach,"

"Chialism"; Section II: "Fragment of New York, 1929," "Aesthetics After War," "On Shooting Particles Beyond the World," "War and Poetry," "Choosing a Monument," "Letter I," "A Legend of Viable Women," "A Man of Sense," "The Verbalist of Summer"; Section III: "An Herb Basket," "Concord Cats," "Phoenixes Again," "Lines to an Old Man," "To My Son, Aged Four," "On the Fragility of the Mind," "Order Again," "Elusive Concretions," "Furtive Marks on Paper," "To One, Who, Dead, Sees His Poems in Print One Hundred Years Later," "Motion as Grace," "Pleasures of the Morning," "Grape Vine Shoots," "Great Praises," "The Great Stone Face," "The Dry Rot," "The Skier and the Mountain," "Imagination," "The Dream of Time," "Calligraphy," "The Lost Poem," "The Human Being Is a Lonely Creature," "Interior Events," "The Book of Nature."

Publication: Published 2 Nov. 1953 at 6s; 1,000 copies printed, of which 500 were for distribution in Great Britain; 500 sets of sheets with Oxford University Press imprint were for distribution in the United States. A second printing of 825 copies was prepared in the summer of 1954, of which 250 bound and jacketed copies were sold to Oxford University Press in Sept. 1954, with an option on the remaining 500 copies. Publisher's records are unclear as to the acceptance of this option.

Locations: NhD, SW

First Publication: The following poems are herein first published; collected and reprinted appearances are regularly noted:

"One Way Dialogue"
"Seals, Terns, Time": in *CP60, SP65, CP76, CP88*; rept. in *Modern American and Modern British Poetry*, ed. Untermeyer, shorter ed. (1955), p. 341;, and in new and enl. ed. (1962), p. 580; *Fifteen Modern American Poets*, ed. Elliott (1956), p. 34; *A Quarto of Modern Literature*, ed. Leonard Brown, 5th ed. (New York: Scribner's, 1964), pp. 469-470; *The Achievement of Richard Eberhart*, ed. Engel (1968), p. 33; *Patterns in Poetry*, ed. Brown and Milstead (1968), p. 132; Judson Jerome, *Poetry: Premeditated Art* (Boston: Houghton, Mifflin, 1968), pp. 113-14; *A College Book of Modern Verse*, ed. C.F. Main (Belmont, Ca.: Wadsworth, 1970), pp. 236-37; *A Little Treasury of Modern Poetry, English and American*, ed. Williams, 3d ed. (1970), pp. 436-37.
"Soul's Reach"
"Chialism": rept. in *The Earth Is the Lord's: Poems of the Spirit*, ed. Helen Plotz (New York: Crowell, 1965), p. 770.
"Concord Cats": in *CP60, CP76, CP88*; rept. in *The Achievement of Richard Eberhart*, ed. Engel (1968), pp. 63-64.

"Elusive Concretions"
"Furtive Marks on Paper"
"Pleasures of the Morning"
"Great Praises": in *CP60, SP65, CP76, CP88*; rept. in brochure for *The Second Annual Wallace Stevens Program* (Hartford Insurance Co., Hartford, Ct.), 6 May 1965, p. 7.
"Imagination"
"Calligraphy"
"Interior Events"

A13b. *First edition, American issue, first printing* (English sheets) (1953)
All ident. to **A13a** except for:

UNDERCLIFF

POEMS

1946–1953

Richard Eberhart

1953

OXFORD UNIVERSITY PRESS

NEW YORK

Title Page: 8 11/16 x 5 1/4 in. (220 x 133 mm.)

FIRST PUBLISHED 1953

PRINTED IN GREAT BRITAIN

Binding: spine, '[at base, in gold] *Oxford*'.

Dust Jacket: spine: at base, in d. Red (16), '[vert.] OXFORD'; back: '[in dark red] *Modern Poetry* | [ornament] | [ornament] | [10 lines in roman and ital., including a list of six books by four authors, the first of whom is RE, and listing *Selected Poems and Burr Oaks*] | [ornament] | *OXFORD UNIVERSITY PRESS* | *114 Fifth Avenue, New York 11, N.Y.*'; front flap: at lower right, '[in dark red] $4.00'.

Publication: Published 12 Nov. 1953 at $4.00; 500 copies issued from English sheets with Oxford University Press imprint. An additional 177 copies of **A13a** were shipped to Oxford in Feb. 1954 for distribution in the United States.

Locations: DLC, NcGU, NcU, NhD, RE (2), SW (5)

A13c. *First edition, American issue, second printing* (1954)
All ident. to **A13b** except for:

Title Page: '1954' replaces '1953'.

Copyright Page: 'FIRST PUBLISHED 1953 | SECOND IMPRESSION 1954 | PRINTED IN GREAT BRITAIN'.

Dust Jacket: front flap: '[in dark red] Second Impression $2.75'; back flap: at base, '[in dark red] Printed in Great Britain'.

Publication: Published in Sept. 1954 at $2.75; 825 copies printed, of which 250 bound and jacketed copies were sold to Oxford Univ. Press for distribution in the United States. Publisher's records are unclear if Oxford took an option on addtional 500 copies, but the book was declared out-of-print in 1968.

Locations: RE (2), SW (2)

A14 *THE KITE*

Offprint (1956)

Cover Title: '[...] | Richard Eberhart | The Kite |[...]'

Collation: 7 leaves wire-stretched on left side; [165] 166-177 [178].

Contents: p. 165: reprint notice, title, and first page of text; pp. 166-177: text; p. 178: first page of Sonya Rudikoff, "Feminism Reconsidered."

Typography: 42 lines per normal page; 179 (185) x 98 mm.; 20 lines = 91 mm.

Paper: leaf measures 9 3/16 x 6 1/16 in. (234 x 153 mm.); yWhite (92) wove, unwatermarked paper; all edges cut; wire-stitched at left.

Text Contents: "The Kite" (**C358**).

Publication: 25 copies prepared in July 1956 for distribution by the poet; not for sale.

Locations: NhD, RE, SW (2)

Notice of Reprint: at top of p. 165, 'Reprinted from THE HUDSON REVIEW, Vol. IX, No. 2, Summer 1956'.

A15 *THE OAK*

First edition [1957]

Title Pages: each page measures 3 13/16 x 6 3/16 in. (97 x 157 mm.); decoration of oak tree in dark green (approx. 146, but darker).

Copyright Page: '© *1957, by Richard Eberhart & Printed in the United States of America*'.

Collation: [unsigned 1⁶]; 6 leaves; [1-12].

Contents: p. 1: blank; pp. 2-3: title pages p. 4: copyright page; p. 5: half title; pp. 6-9: text; p. 10: blank; p. 11: colophon; p. 12: blank.

Typography: 4 lines of text per page; 27 (46) x 84 mm.; each 4-line section numbered with Roman numeral at top, flanked by two leaf ornaments in dark green; initial 'S' on p. 6 is in dark green, initials 'E', 'S', and 'F', on pp. 7, 8, and 9, respectively, are in black.

Paper, Card Cover, and Jacket: leaf measures 3 13/16 x 6 3/16 in. (97 x 157 mm.); white, wove, unwatermarked paper; all edges cut. Binding 1: hand-sewn with white cord in white card cover, 4 x 12 11/16 in. (102 x 321 mm.), folded once vertically to 4 x 6 5/16 in. (102 x 160 mm.); light pinkish gray (no Centroid equiv.) decorated paper jacket tipped on inner side of card cover; regular leaf-like design in gold and gy. r Br (46); unlettered. Binding 2: hand sewn with white cord in l. Ol Gy (approx. 112) thick, wove card cover, 4 5/16 x 12 15/16 in. (110 x 329 mm.), folded once vertically to 4 5/16 x 6 7/16 in. (110 x 164 mm.); uncoated, rough; front fore-edge deckled, all other edges cut; unlettered.

Text Contents: "The Oak"

Publication: Published in January 1957; not for sale; 50 copies printed.

Locations: NhD, RE (2), SW (2, both bindings)

First Publication: RE's poem, "The Oak"; in *CP60, CP76, CP88*.

Colophon: p. 11, '*The Oak* was set by hand in Caslon Old Face and | was printed at the press of Marcus McCorison in | January 1957. Of an edition of fifty copies, this | constitutes number [arabic numeral supplied in black ink] | [decoration of oak tree in dark green]'.

A16 *GREAT PRAISES*

A16a. *First edition, English issue* (1957)

GREAT PRAISES

———◦✳◦———

Richard Eberhart

1957

CHATTO & WINDUS

LONDON

Title Page: 8 5/8 x 5 1/4 in. (219 a 135 mm.).

PUBLISHED BY

Chatto & Windus Ltd

LONDON

★

Clarke, Irwin & Co. Ltd

TORONTO

PRINTED IN GREAT BRITAIN

BY T. AND A. CONSTABLE LTD EDINBURGH

Collation: [unsigned A⁴] B-E⁸; 36 leaves; [i-vi] vii [viii], 9-72.

Contents: p. i: half title and epigraph, '*Great praises are in the air!* | 'UNDERCLIFF'' p. ii: list of books by RE; p. iii: title page; p. iv: copyright page; p. v: dedication, 'To | MY WIFE'; p. vi: acknowledgements; pp. vii-viii: table of contents; pp. 9-72: text.

Typography: 37 lines per normal page; 163 (167) x 85 mm.; 20 lines = 88 mm.

Paper and Binding: leaf measures 8 11/16 x 5 5/16 in. (220 x 136 mm.); yWhite (92) wove, unwatermarked paper; uncoated rough; bright yellow (no Centroid equiv.) fine linen-cloth (304) boards measure 9 7/8 x 5 5/8 in. (225 x 143 mm.); front: unstamped; spine: stamped in brown, '[vert. from top to bottom] GREAT PRAISES [wavy rule] Richard Eberhart [at base, horiz. with base of 'C' overlapping top of 'W'] CW'; top and fore-edges trimmed, bottom edges rough trimmed; yWhite (92) wove, unwatermarked endpapers.

Dust Jacket: total measurement, 8 13/16 x 20 in. (224 x 508 mm.); 1. Gray (approx. 264) laid paper, vert. chainlines 25 mm. apart; watermarked '[crown device] | [in open-face, semi-Gothic] Abbey Mills | Greenfield'; printed in d. y Br (approx. 78); front: 'G R E A T | P R A I S E S | [drawing of a rose on a leafy stem] | P O E M S B Y | Richard Eberhart'; spine: '[vert., from top to bottom] GREAT PRAISES [ornament] *Richard Eberhart* [horiz., at base] *Chatto | & | Windus*'; back: 'RECENT POETRY | [34 lines prin. in roman, including a list of six poets and seven titles, with excerpts from reviews, including RE's *Selected Poems* and *Undercliff*, and excerpts from *Time and Tide* and *New York Times*]'; front flap: '[20 lines in roman, about the book and author] | [in lower right corner] *10s 6d* | NET'; back flap: '[7 lines in roman at base, publisher's advertisement]'.

Text Contents: "Cousin Florence," "Sestina," "My Golden and My Fierce Assays," "Ur Burial," "Society of Friends," "Seeing Is Deceiving," "Analogue of Unity in Multeity," "Sea-Hawk," "The Roc," "Theme from Haydn," "Sainte Anne de Beaupré," "Mediterranean Song," "What the Senses Tell," "Independence and Resolution," "To Evan," "The Glance," "The Day-Bed," "Formative Mastership," "The Rich Interior Life," "Idols of Imagination," "The Hand and the Shadow," "Words," "On a Squirrel Crossing the Road in Autumn, in New England," "Man Is God's Nature," "Centennial for Whitman," "Soul," "Fables of the Moon," "Salem," "The Return," "The Advantage of the Outside," "On Getting Used to the World," "The Giantess," "The Wisdom of Insecurity," "Sunday in October," "Summer Landscape," "The Whole View," "Cold Fall," "Going to Class Under Greek Statues," "Vast Light," "Only in the Dream," "Remember the

Source," "Nothing But Change," "To Helen, With a Playbill," "Thrush Song at Dawn."

Publication: Published 18 June 1957 at 10s 6d; 1,550 copies printed, of which 500 were for distribution in Great Britain; 1000 copies, with Oxford University Press imprint, were for distribution in the United States.

Locations: NcU, NhD, RE (3), SW (5)

First Publication: The following poems are herein first published; collected and reprinted appearances are regularly noted.

"My Golden and My Fierce Assays": in *CP60, CP76, CP88*
"Ur Burial": in *CP60, CP76, LR, CP88*
"Sea-Hawk": in *CP60, SP65, CP76, CP88*; rept. in *The Achievement of Richard Eberhart*, ed. Engel (1968), p. 37; *Maine Lines: 101 Contemporary Poems About Maine*, ed. Richard Aldridge (Philadelphia: Lippincott, 1970), p. 76; *The Norton Anthology of Poetry*, ed. Eastman (1970), pp. 528-29; *A Book of Animal Poems*, ed. William Cole (New York: Viking, 1973); *Poetry Is For People*, ed. Tory Westermark and Bryan Gooch (Toronto: Macmillan of Canada, 1973), p. 159; *Mirrors: An Introduction to Literature*, ed. John R. Knott, Jr., and Christopher R. Reaske (New York: Harper and Row, 1975), p. 203.
"What the Senses Tell"
"Independence and Resolution"
"Formative Mastership": *CP60, SP65, CP76, CP88*
"The Rich Interior Life": rept. in *Modern Religious Poems*, ed. Trapp (1964), pp. 250-51.
"Man Is God's Nature": rept. in *Modern Religious Poems*, ed. Trapp (1964), pp. 287-88; *The Earth Is the Lord's: Poems of the Spirit*, ed. Helen Plotz (New York: Crowell, 1965), p. 133.
"On Getting Used to the World"
"Remember the Source"
"Nothing But Change": in *CP60, SP65, CP76, CP88*

Note: Review slips inserted in advance copies of *Great Praises* indicate the publication date as 27 June 1957, but publisher's records declare it as 18 June 1957.

A16b. *First edition, American issue* (English sheets) (1957)
All ident. to **A16a** except for:

GREAT
PRAISES

Richard Eberhart

NEW YORK

OXFORD UNIVERSITY PRESS

1957

Title Page: 8 5/8 x 5 1/4 in. (219 x 135 mm.).

Copyright Page: 'FIRST PUBLISHED 1957 | © BY RICHARD EBERHART 1957 | PRINTED IN GREAT BRITAIN'.

Binding: spine: at base, in brown, '[vert., from top to bottom] *Oxford*'.

Dust Jacket: front: 'G R E A T | P R A I S E S | P O E M S B Y | Richard Eberhart | [fancy type ornament of 8-sided regular geometric design] | Oxford'; spine: horiz., at base, '*Oxford*'; back: '*Modern Poetry* | [ornament] | [11 lines in roman and ital, including a list of 3 authors and 7 books, the first of which is RE, with *Undercliff, Selected Poems*, and *Burr Oaks*] | [ornament] | *OXFORD UNIVERSITY PRESS* | *114 Fifth Avenue, New York 11, N.Y.*; front flap: '[22 lines prin. in roman, about RE and his work (different copy from **A16a**)] | [lower right corner] $4.00'; back flap: at base, 'Printed in Great Britain'.

Publication: Published 26 June 1957 at $4.00; 1,000 copies from English sheets, with Oxford University Press imprint, for distribution in the United States.

Locations: DLC, NcGU, NhD, RE (2), SW (4)

A17 *AUSTERE POEM* and *LIGHT VERSE*

Offprint (1958)

Cover: 'THE GRECOURT REVIEW I Volume 1 Number 3 March, 1958'.

Collation: [unsigned 1^2]; 2 leaves; pp. [1-4].

Contents: pp. 1-3: text; p. 4: blank.

Paper and Card Cover: leaf measures 9 x 6 in. (229 x 153 mm.); yWhite (92) wove paper, watermarked 'WARREN'S I OLDE STYLE'; uncoated smooth; all edges cut; wire-stitched in pale tan (no Centroid equiv.) card cover, 18 x 12 in. (558 x 306 mm.), folded once vertically to 9 x 6 in. (229 x 153 mm.); uncoated rough; front printed in black.

Text Contents: First separate publication of "Austere Poem" (**C406**) and "Light Verse" (**C407**).

Publication: Unknown number of copies prepared for distribution by the poet in March 1958; not for sale.

A18 *COLLECTED POEMS 1930-1960*

A18a. *First edition, English issue* (1960)

COLLECTED
POEMS
1930-1960

❀

Richard Eberhart

INCLUDING
51 NEW POEMS

1960

CHATTO & WINDUS
LONDON

Title Page: 8 1/2 x 5 1/4 in. (216 x 134 mm.)

Published by
Chatto & Windus Ltd.
London

★

Clarke, Irwin & Co. Ltd.
Toronto

© RICHARD EBERHART 1960
PRINTED AT
THE BLACKMORE PRESS
GILLINGHAM, DORSET
BY T. H. BRICKELL AND SON, LTD.

Collation: [unsigned A^8] B-P^8; 120 leaves; [i-vi] vii-xii, 1-228.

Contents: p. i: half title; p. ii: list of other books by RE; p. iii: title page; p. iv: copyright page; p. v: dedication, To | BETTY | RICK and GRETCHEN'; p. vi: acknowledgments; pp. vii-xii: table of contents; pp. 1-228: text.

Typography: 37 lines per normal page; 156 (161) x 86 mm.; 20 lines = 84 mm.

Paper and Binding: leaf measures 8 1/2 x 5 3/8 in. (216 x 137 mm.); yWhite (92) wove, unwatermarked paper; uncoated smooth; s. Red (12) fine bead-cloth (202b) boards measure 8 3/4 x 5 3/4 in. (223 x 147 mm.); spine: stamped in gold, '[horiz.; row of triple rules of decreasing thickness, 27 mm. each] | Collected | Poems | 1930 - 1960 | [ornament] | Richard | Eberhart | [row of triple rules like first] | [at base] CHATTO | & WINDUS'; all edges trimmed; yWhite (92) wove, unwatermarked endpapers.

Dust Jacket: total measurement, 8 3/4 x 20 in. (222 x 509 mm.); pale bluish gray (no Centroid equiv.) wove paper, watermarked, '[in fancy type] BASINGWERK PARCHMENT [rule, 12 mm.] BASINGWERK PARCHMENT'; printed in black and s. Red (12); front: '[in black] Richard Eberhart | [fancy swelled rule, 39 mm.] [fancy bearded-head ornament in strong red] [in black; fancy swelled rule, like first] | Collected | Poems | [in strong red] 1930-1960 | [in black] INCLUDING 51 NEW POEMS | [fancy swelled rules flanking bearded-head ornament, like before] | [in black] CHATTO & WINDUS'; spine: '[horiz.; double rules, 26 mm.] | Collected | Poems | [in strong red] 1930 - | 1960 | [in black; double rules, 26mm.] | Richard | Eberhart | [at base] CHATTO | & | WINDUS'; back: '[39 lines prin. in roman, about the author; photograph of RE at right side, 83 x 51 mm., approx. the height of the first 20 lines]'; front flap: '[42 lines prin. in roman, including blurbs by Edith Sitwell, William Carlos Williams, Edwin Muir, Robert Lowell, and Kenneth Rexroth] | [lower right corner} 25S. NET'; back flap: '[at base, 6-line publisher's advertisement]'.

Contents: contents divided into titled sections from previously published books, with new poems: *A Bravery of Earth*: "This Fevers Me," "O Wild Chaos!," "The Bells of a Chinese Temple"; *Reading the Spirit*: "Maze," "For a Lamb," "Caravan of Silence," "Four Lakes' Days," "Ode to Silence," "The Return of Odysseus," "Where Are Those High and Haunting Skies," "Suite in Prison," "The Groundhog," "The Rape of the Cataract," "1934," "In a Hard Intellectual Light," "My Bones Flew Apart," "The Transfer," "Request for Offering," "Necessity"; *Song and Idea*: "The Scarf of June," "Experience Evoked," "Two Loves," "Burden," "In Prisons of Established Craze," "The Largess," "When Doris Danced," "The Critic With His Pained Eye," "The

Young Hunter," "When Golden Flies Upon My Carcass Come," "Now Is the Air Made of Chiming Balls," "The Child," "Let the Tight Lizard on the Wall," "I Went to See Irving Babbitt," "Recollection of Childhood," "Orchard," "The Soul Longs to Return Whence It Came," "Grave Piece," "The Humanist," "The Virgin," "Man's Greed and Envy Are So Great," "The Goal of Intellectual Man," "If I Could Only Live at the Pitch That Is Near Madness," "I Walked Out to the Graveyard to See the Dead," "A Meditation," "The Full of Joy Do Not Know; They Need Not"; *Burr Oaks*: "Rumination," "Cover Me Over," "The Recapitulation," "Imagining How It Would Be to Be Dead," "I Walked Over the Grave of Henry James," "The Ineffable," "Mysticism Has Not the Patience to Wait for God's Revelation," "The Dream," "The Moment of Vision," "Retrospective Forelook," "The Lyric Absolute," "I Will Not Dare to Ask One Question," "New Hampshire, February," "Triptych," "Ode to the Chinese Paper Snake," "Burr Oaks," "Dam Neck, Virginia," "The Fury of Aerial Bombardment," "An Airman Considers His Power," "At the End of War," "A Ceremony by the Sea"; *Poems: New and Selected*: "World War"; *Selected Poems*: "Brotherhood of Men"; *Undercliff*: "Indian Pipe," "Go to the Shine That's On a Tree," "Sometimes the Longing for Death," "At Night," "A Love Poem," "God and Man," "The Horse Chestnut Tree," "The Tobacconist of Eighth Street," "Seals, Terns, Time," "The Cancer Cells," "Forms of the Human," "Oedipus," "Fragment of New York, 1929," "Aesthetics After War," "On Shooting Particles Beyond the World," "A Legend of Viable Women," "The Verbalist of Summer," "Concord Cats," "On the Fragility of the Mind," "Great Praises," "The Dry Rot," "The Skier and the Mountain," "The Human Being Is a Lonely Creature," "The Book of Nature"; *Great Praises*: "Cousin Florence," "Sestina," "My Golden and My Fierce Assays," "Ur Burial," "Seeing Is Deceiving," "Analogue of Unity in Multeity," "Sea-Hawk," "Sainte Anne de Beaupré," "Mediterranean Song," "To Evan," "The Day-Bed," "Formative Mastership," "The Hand and the Shadow," "Words," "On a Squirrel Crossing the Road in Autumn, in New England," "Centennial for Whitman," "Soul," "Fables of the Moon," "Salem," "The Return," "The Giantess," "The Wisdom of Insecurity," "Sunday in October," "Summer Landscape," "Only in the Dream," "Nothing But Change," "Thrush Song at Dawn"; *New Poems*: "The Voyage," "Off Spectacle Isle," "The Seasons," "The Noble Man," "The Forgotten Rock," "Attitudes," "An Old Fashioned American Business Man," "A Young Greek, Killed in the Wars," "Protagonists," "A Soldier Rejects His Times Addressing His Contemporaries," "Blessed Are the Angels in Heaven," "Villanelle," "Life As Visionary Spirit," "Fortune's Mist," "Yonder," "Autumnal," "The Sacrifice," "Lucubration," "In After Time," "A Testament," "Request," "Love Among the Ruins," "Anima," "The Supreme Authority of the

Imagination," "Perception as a Guided Missle," "By the Stream," "What Gives," "The Oak," "In the Garden," "The Lost Children," "A Commitment," "Apple Buds," "Throwing the Apple," "The Garden God," "Light From Above," "Austere Poem," "Hoot Owls," "Tree Swallows," "The Clam Diggers and Diggers of Sea Worms," "A Ship Burning and a Comet All In One Day," "The Hard Structure of the World," "The Parker River," "At the Canoe Club," "Ospreys In Cry," "Half-Bent Man," "Spring Mountain Climb," "The Passage," "The Gods of Washington, D.C.," "Equivalents of Gnats and Mice," "Birth and Death," "The Incomparable Light."

Publication: Published 15 Sept. 1960 at 25s; 1,750 copies printed, of which 710 were for distribution in Great Britain; 1,040 copies with Oxford University Press imprint were for distribution in the United States. The original date of publication was announced by the press and in review copies as 1 Sept. 1960.

Locations: NcGU, NcU, NhD, RE (3), SW (5)

First Publication: The following poems are herein first published; collected and reprinted appearances are regularly noted.

"Off Spectacle Isle": in *CP76, CP88*; rept. in *Today's Poets: American and British Poetry Since the 1930's*, ed. Chad Walsh (New York: Scribner's, 1964), p. 43; *Maine Lines*, ed. Aldridge (1970), p. 78; *Whales: A Celebration*, ed. Greg Gatenby (Boston: Little, Brown, 1983), p. 72.

"An Old Fashioned American Business Man": in *CP76, CP88*; rept. in *Words Among America*, ed. Glen Gersmehl (Keene, Ca.: Non-Violence Center, 1971), p. 32.

"Blessed Are the Angels In Heaven": in *CP76, CP88*

"Life As Visionary Spirit": in *CP76, CP88*; rept. in *The Achievement of Richard Eberhart*, ed. Engel (1968), p. 69; *Appleseeds and Beercans: Man and Nature in Literature*, ed. C. Michael Wells et al. (Pacific Palisades, Ca.: Goodyear, 1974), pp. 275-76.

A18b. *First edition, American issue* (English sheets) (1960, [i.e., 1961])
All ident to **A18a** except for:

COLLECTED
POEMS
1930-1960

———— ❀ ————

Richard Eberhart

INCLUDING
51 NEW POEMS

NEW YORK
OXFORD UNIVERSITY PRESS
1960

Title Page: 8 1/2 x 5 1/4 in. (216 x 134 mm.).

Copyright Page: 'FIRST PUBLISHED 1960'.

Binding: spine: '[horiz., at base] OXFORD'.

Dust Jacket: total measurement, 8 3/4 x 19 13/16 in. (223 x 504 mm.); inner side and flaps are white, outer side printed l. y Br (approx. 76); inner side coated smooth, outer side coated glossy; printed in d. r Br (44); front:'RICHARD I EBERHART I [in semi-script] Collected Poems 1930 - 1960 I [in roman] INCLUDING FIFTY-ONE NEW POEMS I [leaf ornament]'; spine: '[vert., from top to bottom] EBERHART [horiz., in semi-script] Collected I Poems I 1930 I - I 1960 I [vert., in roman] OXFORD'; back: '[photograph of RE, 140 x 88 mm.] I [lower right side of photograph, vert. from bottom to top] *The Washington Post* I [9 lines in roman, about the author]'; front flap: 'RICHARD EBERHART I [in semi-script] Collected Poems I 1930—1960 I [in roman] INCLUDING I FIFTY-ONE NEW POEMS I [28 lines prin. in roman, about the author and his work, including blurbs by William Carlos Williams and Robert Lowell (continued on back flap)]'; back flap: '[36 lines in roman, including conclusion of Lowell blurb, with blurbs by Edith Sitwell, Conrad Aiken, Edwin Muir, and Kenneth Rexroth] I OXFORD UNIVERSITY PRESS I New York'.

Publication: Published 23 Feb. 1961 at $6.00; 1,040 copies of English sheets with Oxford University Press imprint for distribution in the United States.

Locations: DLC, RE (3), SW (3)

A18c. *First edition, second printing* (photo-offset from **A18b**)
All ident. to **A18b** except for:

Title Page: 8 1/4 x 5 1/4 in. (209 x 134 mm.).

Copyright Page: '*Second American Printing, 1966*' added below Library of Congress catalog number.

Paper and Binding: leaf measures 8 1/4 x 5 3/8 in. (209 x 136 mm.); signature letters have been deleted; gy. r Br (46) bead-cloth (202) boards measure 8 1/2 x 5 5/8 in. (212 x 144 mm.).

Dust Jacket: total measurement, 8 1/2 x 19 13/16 in. (216 x 504 mm.); back: '[10 lines in roman, rewritten note about the author]'; front flap: '[at lower right corner] $6.00'; back flap: last two lines of jacket copy of **A18b** deleted and a 6-line blurb by R.W.B. Lewis has been added]'.

Publication: Published 31 Jan. 1966 at $6.00; 1,500 copies printed. A third printing of 1,000 copies was issued 31 March 1969; all ident. to **A18c**.

A19a. *First edition, trade issue* (1962)

Collected Verse Plays

By

RICHARD EBERHART

Chapel Hill

THE UNIVERSITY OF NORTH CAROLINA PRESS

Title Page: 8 7/16 x 5 1/8 in. (215 x 134 mm.).

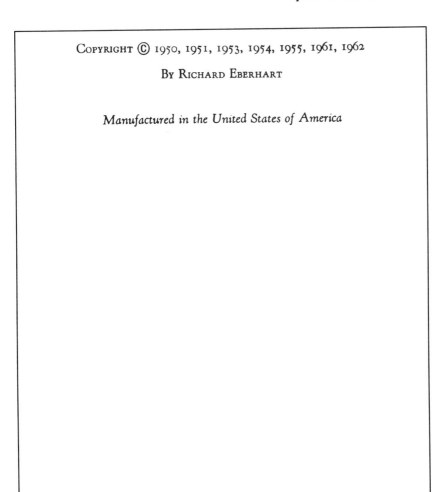

Collation: [unsigned 1-9^8 10^4 11-12^8]; 92 leaves; [i-vi] vii-xv [xvi], [1-2] 3-13 [14-16] 17-24 [25-26] 27-41 [42-44] 45-56 [57-58] 59-102 [103-104] 105-129 [130-132] 133-160 [161-162] 163 [164] 165-167 [168].

Contents: p. i: half title; p. ii: list of books by RE; p. iii: title page; p. iv: copyright page; p. v: dedication, 'To I THE POETS' THEATRE, INC. I Cambridge, Massachusetts; p. vi: blank; p. vii-xiv: introduction by RE; p. xv: table of contents; p. xvi: blank; pp. 1-160: text; p. 161: part title; p. 162: blank; p. 163: notes about previous publication; p. 164: blank; pp. 165-166: notes about first productions; p. 167: colophon; p. 168: blank.

Typography: 43 lines per normal page; 167 (173) x 98 mm.; 20 lines = 78 mm.

Paper and Binding: leaf measures 8 7/16 x 5 3/8 in. (215 x 137 mm.); yWhite (92) wove paper, watermarked, 'WARREN'S I OLDE STYLE'; uncoated smooth; med. Gy (approx. 265) linen-cloth (304) boards measure 8 11/16 x 5 5/8 in. (221 x 144 mm.); spine: contains solid black panel, 114 x 21 mm., stamped in gold, '[horiz.; double rules, 21 mm.] I EBERHART I [rule, 21 mm.] I [vert., from top to bottom] Collected Verse Plays I [horiz.; rule, 21 mm.] I CHAPEL HILL I [double rules, 21 mm.]'; all edges cut, unstained; cloth head and tail bands have alternating yellow and red stripes; yWhite (92) wove, unwatermarked endpapers.

Dust Jacket: total measurement, 8 3/4 x 19 1/2 in. (223 x 496 mm.); wove, unwatermarked paper; inner side coated smooth, outer side coated glossy; inner side, flaps, and back are white; front and spine contain panels in medium grayish blue (no Centroid equiv.), med. gray (between 264 and 265), and light grayish blue (no Centroid equiv.); front: '[against med. grayish blue and med. gray panels, illus. of devil and angel in light grayish blue and rev. out in white] I [in black] COLLECTED I [rev. out in white] VERSE I [in black] PLAYS I RICHARD I EBERHART'; spine: '[vert., from top to bottom; in light bluish gray] EBERHART COLLECTED [rev. out in white] VERSE PLAYS [in black, at base] CHAPEL HILL'; back: '[in black] THE UNIVERSITY OF NORTH CAROLINA PRESS I SERIES IN CONTEMPORARY POETRY I [33 lines in roman and ital, including list of three titles by George Garrett, Thomas Vance, and Elizabeth Sewell, with blurbs] I CHAPEL HILL I The University of North Carolina Press'; front flap: '$5.00 I [34 lines prin. in roman, about the book] I *(continued on back flap)* I [dust jacket designer's logo]'; back flap: '*(continued from front flap)* I [37 lines prin. in roman, about the book and author]'.

Text Contents: Introduction by RE, "Triptych" (**C159**), "Preamble I" (**B40**), "Preamble II" (**C308**), "The Apparition" (**C260**), "The Visionary Farms" (**B31** and **C340**), "Devils and Angels" (**C475**), "The Mad Musician" (**C476**), and RE's notes about previous publication and first productions.

Publication: Published 25 August 1962 at $5.00; 1,149 copies printed, of which 1,036 constitute the trade issue.

Locations: DLC, NcGU, NcU, NhD, RE, SW (5), ViU

First Publication: "The Visionary Farms" contains additional material not included in earlier versions.

Colophon: p. 167, '[all within a frame of broken bars] The text of this book was composed in 10 | point Kennerly, leaded one point, and the | Introduction in 12 point Kennerly, leaded | two point. The book was printed by letter- | press on 60 pound Warren's Olde Style, | wove finish, made by the S.D. Warren | Company. The book was manufactured by | The Seeman Printery, Incorporated, Durham | North Carolina'.

A19b. *First edition, limited and signed issue*
All ident. to **A19a** except for:

Collation: [unsigned 1^8+1 $2-9^8$ 10^4 $11-12^8$]; 93 leaves.

Contents: unnumbered limitation leaf tipped in between pp. ii-iii.

Binding: quarter-bound in putty-colored (no Centroid equiv.) bead-cloth (202) and grayish green (no Centroid equiv.) decorated paper boards, 8 13/16 x 5 3/4 in. (222 x 145 mm.); panel on spine in dark grayish green (no Centroid equiv.).

Dust Jacket: thin protective plastic jacket with horiz. ribbon-like design; unlettered.

Publication: Published simultaneously with **A19a**; 113 copies issued at $10.00 each; see *Notes*.

Locations: NhD, RE, SW (3)

Limitation Leaf: tipped in between pp. ii-iii: '*This is Number* _____ [arabic numeral machine-printed in blue above rule] *of a limited edition of* | *100 copies, specially bound and autographed by the author.* | [RE's autograph in blue ink over black rule, 63 mm.]'.

Notes: Although the limitation calls for only 100 machine-numbered copies, there was a small overrun of 13 copies. In the compiler's collection is copy 104; the copy numbered 105 was offered for sale by a specialist in modern first editions in 1983. References have been made to an English edition from Oxford University Press (1963), but no copies have been located. Neither the University of North Carolina Press nor the Oxford University Press (London) has any record of such an edition.

A20 *THE QUARRY*

A20a. *First edition, American issue* (1964)

The Quarry

New Poems

RICHARD EBERHART

NEW YORK

OXFORD UNIVERSITY PRESS

1964

Title Page: 8 3/4 x 5 3/4 in. (210 x 146 mm.).

Collation: [unsigned 1-4¹⁶]; 64 leaves; [i-xii], [1-2] 3-46 [47-48] 49-114 [115-116].

Contents: p. i: half title; p. ii: list of books by RE; p. iii: title page; p. iv: copyright page; p. v : dedication, '*To Betty, Rick and Gretchen*'; p. vi: blank; p. vii: acknowledgements; p. viii: blank; pp. ix-xii: table of contents; pp. 1-114: text; pp. 115-116: blank.

Typography: 32 lines per normal page; 159 (175) x 115 mm.; 20 lines = 109 mm.

Paper and Binding: leaf measures 8 1/4 x 5 7/8 in. (210 x 149 mm.); yWhite (92) wove, unwatermarked paper; uncoated, smooth; gy. r O (approx. 39 but darker) bead-cloth (202) boards measure 8 1/2 x 6 3/16 in. (216 x 158 mm.); front: stamped in white, '[lower right side, in fancy type] new poems'; spine: stamped in black, '[vert., from top to bottom; in fancy type] Eberhart THE QUARRY [at base] Oxford'; top edges cut, fore- and bottom edges trimmed; white cloth head and tail bands; dark gray (no Centroid equiv.) wove endpapers; uncoated, rough.

Dust Jacket: total measurememt, 8 1/2 x 21 1/16 in. (217 x 537 mm.); wove, unwatermarked paper; inner side and flaps are white; front, spine and back contain black and white photographic design of a quarry wall; inner side coated smooth, outer side coated glossy; front: '[in s.r O (35) fancy type] THE QUARRY | [rev. out in white] new poems | [in strong reddish orange] Richard Eberhart'; spine: '[vert., from top to bottom; in fancy type; black] Eberhart [in strong reddish orange] THE QUARRY | [at base in black] Oxford'; back: unlettered, front flap: 'T H E   Q U A R R Y | *new poems* | BY RICHARD EBERHART | [40 lines prin. in roman, about the book and author] | [lower right corner] $4.75; back flap: '[black and white photograph of RE, 58 x 72 mm.] | *Photograph by Charles R. Schulze* | [28 lines prin. in roman, about RE, including a statement by R.W.B. Lewis, excpt. from sleeve of **G10**] | OXFORD UNIVERSITY PRESS | NEW YORK | *Jacket design by Suniva Ingero*'.

Text Contents: Section I: "The Kite," "The Spider," "The Place," "Sea-Ruck," "The Hamlet Father," "Four Exposures," "LaCrosse at Ninety Miles an Hour," "Impatience As a Gesture of Divine Will," "Loss (To V.R. Lang)," "Contemplation," "Clocks," "To Auden On His Fiftieth," "To Bill Williams," "Nexus," "Examination of Psyche: Thoughts of Home," "The Record," "Divorce," "The Project," "The Mother Part," "Matador," "Prometheus"; Section II: "Old Tom," "The Height of Man," "The Inward Rock," "An Evaluation Under a Pine Tree, Lying On Pine Needles," "Kaire," "The Struggle," "The World Situation," "A New England Bachelor," "A Maine Roustabout," "Sea Burial From the Cruiser *Reve*," "A New England View: My Report," "Flux," "Ruby Daggett," "Hardening Into Print," "The Lament of the New England Mother," "Father and Son," "Father and Daughter," "The Lost," "Moment of Equilibrium Among the Islands," "Hark Back," "Am I My Neighbor's Keeper?", "Christmas Tree," "Looking at the Stars," "Rainscapes, Hydrangeas, Roses and Singing Birds," "Dream Journey of the Head and Heart," "The Water-Pipe," "Winter Kill," "The Seal," "Later or Sooner," "Eagles," "The Gesture," "The Master Image," "The Diver," "To a Poet Who Has Had a Heart Attack," "Ultimate Song," "Vision," "May Evening," "Death By Drowning," "Ways and Means," "Meditation One," "Meditation Two."

Publication: Published 30 April 1964 at $4.75; 3,875 copies printed, of which 3355 were for distribution in the United States; 520 sets of folded and gathered sheets with the Chatto & Windus imprint were bound for distribution in Great Britain.

Locations: DLC, NcGU, NcU, RE (2), SW (5), ViU

First Publication: The following poems are herein first published; collected and reprinted appearances are regularly noted.

"The Hamlet Father": in *CP76, CP88*
"Contemplation": rept. in *Expansive Light* (New York: The Sacred Fire, 1977), pp. 33-34.
"Examination of Psyche: Thoughts of Home": in *CP76, CP88*
"Prometheus": in *CP76, CP88*; rept. in *The Achievement of Richard Eberhart*, ed. Engel (1968), pp. 51-52.
"The Height of Man": in *CP76, CP88*; rept. in *The Distinctive Voice*, ed. Martz (1966), p. 151; *The Achievement of Richard Eberhart*, ed. Engel (1968), p. 53.
"Christmas Tree": in *CP76, CP88*
"The Diver"
"Ways and Means": in *CP76, CP88*; rept. in *The Achievement of Richard Eberhart*, ed. Engel (1968), p. 55.

A20b. *First edition, English issue* (American sheets) (1964)
All ident. to **A20a** except for:

The Quarry

New Poems

RICHARD EBERHART

1964

CHATTO & WINDUS

LONDON

Title Page: 8 1/2 x 5 3/4 in. (216 x 146 mm.).

Copyright Page: 'Published by | Chatto & Windus Ltd | London'.

Paper and Binding: leaf measures 8 1/2 x 5 7/8 in. (216 x 149 mm.); purplish brown (no Centroid equiv.) paper-covered boards (imitation bead-cloth) measure 8 3/4 x 6 1/4 in. (222 x 158 mm.); front: unstamped; spine: stamped in gold, '[vert., from top to bottom] THE QUARRY [wavy rule] Richard Eberhart [in two lines; right] CHATTO [left] & WINDUS'; all edges cut, unstained; no head and tail bands; yWhite (92) wove, unwatermarked endpapers.

Dust Jacket: total measurement, 8 3/4 x 21 1/8 in. (222 x 538 mm.); spine: '[at base; vert., from top to bottom] Chatto & Windus'; front flap: at lower right side, '21s. net.'; back flap: at base, 'CHATTO & WINDUS | LONDON'.

Publication: Published in October 1964 at 21s; 520 copies from Oxford University Press sheets, with Chatto & Windus imprint, for distribution in Great Britain. A later issue of **A20b** is price-clipped and contains a tipped-on gummed label at base of front flap, printed in black, ' £1•05 net'.

Locations: DLC, NhD, RE (3), SW (5)

A21 *THE VASTNESS AND INDIFFERENCE OF THE WORLD*

First separate edition (1965)

[in s. B (178)] THE VASTNESS AND INDIFFERENCE | OF THE WORLD

Collation: broadside, 12 13/16 x 9 3/16 in. (326 x 233 mm.).

Contents: recto: '[in s. Blue (178)] THE VASTNESS AND INDIFFERENCE | OF THE WORLD | [in black, 35 lines in roman, text] | *Richard Eberhart* | [author's autograph in blue ink] | [in strong blue] *300 copies of this poem have been | printed at the Ferguson Press | Milford, N.H.* | [in black, left side] © 1965 by Richard Eberhart [right side] February 5, 1965'; verso: blank.

Typography: 37 lines; 186 (281) x 108 mm.; 20 lines = 96 mm.

Paper: yWhite (92) wove, unwatermarked paper, uncoated rough; top and side edges cut, bottom edge deckled.

Text Contents: "The Vastness and Indifference of the World" (**C538**).

Publication: Published 5 Feb. 1965; approx. 300 copies printed; not for sale.

Locations: NhD, RE (2), SW (6)

A22 *FISHING FOR SNAKES*

First separate edition (1965)

FISHING FOR SNAKES

Collation: broadside, 12 1/4 x 7 1/4 in. (311 x 185 mm.).

Contents: recto: '[reprod. of drawing by Laurence Scott] | *Fishing for Snakes* | [20 lines in roman, text] | *Richard Eberhart* | [author's autograph in blue ink] | *This first printing has been issued by the | Adams & Lowell Printers, in Harvard Yard. | Drawing by Laurence Scott | March, 1965*'; verso: blank.

Typography: 20 lines; 115 (187) x 69 mm.; 20 lines = 95 mm.

Paper: white, wove, unwatermarked paper; uncoated, smooth; all edges cut.

Text Contents: First separate publication of "Fishing for Snakes" (**C522**); in *SP65*.

Publication: Published in March 1965; approx. 50 copies printed; not for sale.

Locations: DLC, NhD, RE, SW (3)

A23 *ROBERTS RULES OF ORDER*

First separate edition (1965)

ROBERTS RULES OF ORDER

Collation: broadside, 8 1/2 x 11 in. (280 x 216 mm.).

Contents: recto: '[left side, reprod. from orig. holograph script] Penny |
Poems | from | Midwestern | University | [remainder reprod. from typescript]
Volume IV Number 1 | April 30, 1965 | Price: One Penny | [13 lines, about
RE] | [14 lines, about the Penny Poems series] | [wavy vert. rule, 268 mm.]
[right side] Roberts Rules of Order | [24 lines, text] | Richard Eberhart | [7
lines, editor's note]'; verso: blank.

Typography: reprod. from typescript and holograph script original.

Paper: yWhite (92) wove, unwatermarked paper; uncoated, smooth.

Text Contents: "Robert's Rules of Order" (C528).

Publication: Published 30 April 1965 at 1 cent; unknown number of copies.
N.B. The Penny Poems series was published by the English Department of
Midwestern University, Wichita Falls, Texas.

Locations: NhD, RE, SW

A24 *SELECTED POEMS 1930-1965*

First edition [1965]

Richard Eberhart

Selected Poems

1930–1965

New Directions

Title Page: 7 15/16 x 5 in. (202 x 130 mm.)

Collation: [unsigned 1-4^{16}]; 64 leaves; [i-x], 1-115 [116-118].

Contents: p. i: about the author; p. ii: list of books by RE; p. iii: title page; p. iv: copyright page; p. v: foreword by RE; p. vi: blank; p. vii-x: table of contents; pp. 1-112: text; pp. 113-115: index of first lines; pp. 116-118: list of other New Directions titles.

Typography: 37 lines per normal page; 157 (165) x 100 mm.; 20 lines = 85 mm.

Paper and Binding: leaf measures 7 15/16 x 5 1/8 in. (202 x 130 mm.); yWhite (92) wove, unwatermarked paper; uncoated, smooth; glued in thick white card cover, total measurement, 7 15/16 x 5 5/16 in. (202 x 135 mm.); front measures 7 15/16 x 5 5/16 in. (202 x 135 mm.); inner side uncoated, outer side coated smooth; front: '[against a photograph of RE in shades of gray; in black] Richard Eberhart: Selected Poems I 1930-1965 I [in lower left corner] a new directions paperbook'; spine: '[vert., from top to bottom] Richard Eberhart: Selected Poems 1930 - 1965 [at base] NDP198'; back:'POETRY I Richard Eberhart I Selected Poems 1930—1965 I [26 lines prin. in roman, about the book and including blurbs by Robert Penn Warren, Conrad Aiken, and Kenneth Rexroth] I *Cover photograph by Henri Cartier-Bresson. Design by David Ford.* I A New Directions Paperbook NDP198 $1.75.

Text Contents: "This Fevers Me," "The Bells of a Chinese Temple," "For a Lamb," "In a Hard Intellectual Light," "The Groundhog," "Maze," "Where Are Those High and Haunting Skies," "1934," "When Doris Danced," "Experience Evoked," "Two Loves," "Burden," "What If Remembrance," "In Prisons of Established Craze," "Now Is the Air Made of Chiming Balls," "When Golden Flies Upon My Carcase Come," "Recollection of Childhood," "The Critic With His Pained Eye," "Orchard," "The Humanist," "I Went to See Irving Babbitt," "The Goal of Intellectual Man," "Imagining How It Would Be to Be Dead," "If I Could Only Live At the Pitch That Is Near Madness," "Cover Me Over," "I Walked Over the Grave of Henry James," "Rumination," "Mysticism Has Not the Patience to Wait For God's Revelation," "I Walked Out to the Graveyard to See the Dead," "The Soul Longs to Return Whence It Came," "Retrospective Forelook," "New Hampshire, February," "The Horse Chestnut Tree," "At Night," "Dam Neck, Virginia," "The Fury of Aerial Bombardment," "World War," "The Cancer Cells," "Indian Pipe," "Forms of the Human," "Seals, Terns, Time," "A Legend of Viable Women," "A Ship Burning and a Comet All in One Day," "Great Praises," "The Tobacconist of Eighth Street," "On Shooting Particles Beyond the World," "The Human Being Is a Lonely Creature," "Sestina," "On the Fragility of the Mind," "The Book of Nature," "Cousin Florence," "Analogue of Unity in Multeity," "To Evan," "Formative Mastership," "The Day-Bed," "Sea-Hawk," "On a Squirrel Crossing the Road in Autumn, in New England," "In After Time," "The Wisdom of Insecurity," "Only in the Dream," "Anima," "The Forgotten Rock," "The Return," "Attitudes," "Light From Above," "Nothing But Change," "The Oak," "The Incomparable Light," "Ospreys in Cry," "Birth and Death," "Apple Buds," "A Commitment," "The Kite," "LaCrosse at Ninety Miles an Hour," "The Place," "Kaire," "The Struggle," "Nexus," "A Maine Roustabout," "Sea Burial From the Cruiser *Reve*," "The Inward Rock," "Flux," "Ruby Dagnet," "Hark Back," "The Lost," "Winter Kill," "A New England Bachelor," "A New England View: My Report," "Am I My Neighbor's Keeper?," "Dream Journey of the Head and Heart," "Moment of Equilibrium Among the Islands," "Rainscapes, Hydrangeas, Roses and Singing Birds," "Hardening

Into Print," "Meditation One," "Meditation Two," "The Water Pipe," "Eagles," "May Evening," "The Gesture," "The Face, the Axe, and Time," "The Killer," "Action and Poetry," "Fishing for Snakes," "At McSorley's Bar," "The Illusion of Eternity," "The Rush," "The Echoing Rocks," "Off Pemaquid," "The Matin Pandemoniums," "Ordeal," "Tones of Spring."

Publication: Published 30 Sept. 1965 at $1.75 as New Directions Paperbook 198; 5,000 copies printed. Subsequent printings of **A24** are clearly identified; for example: *Second Printing*: 'Second Printing' on copyright page and on back of card cover; **'Pulitzer Prize for Poetry'** added to front; p. 116 is blank, and pp. 117-18 contain the list of New Directions paperbooks; the Rexroth blurb has been dropped; *Third Printing*: 'THIRD PRINTING' added to copyright page and on back of card cover; Pulitzer Prize notice dropped from front and **'a new directions paperbook'** reinserted; list of New Directions paperbooks now on pp. 116-17, and p. 118 is blank; *Fourth Printing*: 'FOURTH PRINTING' added to copyright page and on back of card cover; p. 116 is blank, and list of New Directions paperbooks is on p. 117-18; and so on. The publishing history is as follows: 2d printing: 5,000 copies issued on 4 May 1966; 3d printing: 5,000 copies issued on March 1968; 4th printing: 2,000 copies issued on 2 July 1970; 5th printing: 1,500 copies issued in January 1974; 6th printing: 1,000 copies issued on 22 October 1976; 7th printing: 2,000 copies issued on 1 September 1978.

Locations: DLC, NcGU, NcU, NhD, RE (3), SW (7), ViU

A25 *THE IDES OF MARCH*

First separate edition (1967)

THE IDES OF MARCH

Collation: broadside, 9 1/16 x 7 1/4 in. (484 x 185 mm.).

Contents: recto: '[woodcut by K. Klopp in black, green (no Centroid equiv.), and white] I [in artist's holograph; brownish black ink] 5/67 KKlopp I [in black fancy type] *The Ides of March* I [28 lines in roman, text] I *Richard Eberhart* I [author's autograph in blue ink] I *This edition of* The Ides of March *is limited to 95 copies of which this is* I No. [arabic numeral supplied in black ink]. *Hand-printed in Harvard Yard by* I The Lowell House Printers, *March,* 1967. I *Copyright 1967 by Richard Eberhart*.' Verso: blank.

Typography: 28 lines; 195 (276) x 99 mm.; 20 lines = 113 mm.

Paper: thick, wove, unwatermarked brownish orange (between 53 and 54) paper; uncoated rough, all edges cut.

Text Contents: First separate publication of "The Ides of March" (C555); in *SB*; rept. in *The Achievement of Richard Eberhart*, ed. Engel (1968), p. 77; *This Is My Best in the Third Quarter of the Century*, ed. Whit Burnett (Garden City: Doubleday, 1970), pp. 91-92.

Publication: Published in May 1967; 95 copies printed. Correspondence between RE and the printer suggests the publication price was $5.00, but this could not be confirmed.

Locations: DLC, RE (2), SW (5)

A26 *THIRTY-ONE SONNETS*

A26a. *First edition, regular issue* [1967]

THIRTY ONE

SONNETS

RICHARD

EBERHART

THE EAKINS PRESS

NEW YORK · PUBLISHERS

Title Page: 6 1/4 x 4 7/8 in. (160 x 125 mm.); RE's name in deep r O (approx. 36).

Collation: [unsigned 1-2⁴ 3⁶ 4-5⁴]; 22 leaves; [1-44].

Contents: pp. 1-2: blank; p. 3: title page; p. 4: copyright page; p. 5: half title; p. 6: blank; pp. 7-37: text; pp. 38-39: note to the reader by RE, dated April 1966; p. 40: blank; p. 41: list of other books by RE; p. 42: blank; p. 43: colophon; p. 44: blank.

Typography: 14 lines per page; 87 (97) x 78 mm.; 10 lines = 62 mm.

Paper and Binding: leaf measures 6 1/4 x 4 7/8 in. (160 x 125 mm.); white, wove, unwatermarked paper; uncoated rough; dark red (between 15 and 16) coarse linen-cloth (304c) boards measure 6 1/2 x 5 1/4 in. (165 x 133 mm.); front: '[blind-stamped] THIRTY ONE | SONNETS | RICHARD | EBERHART'; spine: stamped in gold, '[vert., from top to bottom] EBERHART SONNETS [at base] EAKINS'; back: unstamped; all edges cut, unstained; white cloth head and tail bands; gray (betweeen 264 and 265) laid endpapers, vert. chainlines 24 mm. apart; watermarked 'FABRIANO'.

Dust Jacket: total measurement, 6 1/2 x 18 3/8 in. (166 x 467 mm.); strong red (between 12 and 15) laid paper, vert. chainlines 26 mm. apart; watermarked 'FABRIANO'; uncoated rough; printed in black; front: 'THIRTY ONE | SONNETS | RICHARD | EBERHART'; spine: '[vert., from top to bottom] EBERHART SONNETS [at base] EAKINS'; back: unlettered; front flap: '$4.95 | [19 lines in roman, about the book] | DESIGNED BY EDITH MCKEON | PRINTED BY THE STINEHOUR PRESS'; back flap: 'OTHER PUBLICATIONS OF | *The Eakins Press* | [11 lines in roman and ital, including a list of six titles and authors] | ORDER FROM YOUR BOOKSELLER OR FROM | THE EAKINS PRESS | 155 East 42 Street, New York, New York 10017'.

Text Contents: "Thirty One Sonnets"; see *Note*.

Publication: Published 15 June 1967 at $4.95; according to RE's correspondence with the publisher, approx. 1,000 copies printed.

First Publication: All except sonnets II, VI, XV, XVI, XXII, XXIV, XXVI, (C547-C543).

Locations: DLC, NhD, RE (2), SW (4)

Colophon: p. 43, '*Designed by Edith McKeon.* | *Set in Monotype Bembo italic* | *and printed on Wookey Mould* | *by The Stinehour Press,* | *Lunenburg, Vermont. Bound* | *by Russell-Rutter Company,* | *New York, New York.*'

Note: These sonnets were written between 11 May and 11 June 1932 for Louise Hawkes Padelford ("Maia"); see Roache, *Richard Eberhart: The Progress of an American Poet*, pp. 72-77.

A26b. *First edition, numbered and signed issue*
All ident. to **A26a.** except for:

Contents: p. 43, colophon and statement of limitation.

Jacket and Publisher's Box: clear plastic protective jacket, unlettered; book enclosed in open-face publisher's box of cloth ident. to binding, 6 13/16 x 5 5/16 in. (173 x 135 mm.); unstamped.

Publication: Published simultaneously with **A26a** at $25.00; 99 signed and numbered copies issued.

Colophon and Statement of Limitation: p. 43, '*Designed by Edith McKeon. Set in* | *Monotype Bembo italic and printed* | *on Wookey Mould by The Stinehour* | *Press, Lunenburg, Vermont.* | *Bound by Russell-Rutter Company,* | *New York, New York. Ninety-nine* | *copies specially bound and signed* | *by the author. Number* [hand-numbered with arabic numeral in black ink, by RE] | [RE's autograph in black ink]'.

A27 *SHIFTS OF BEING*

A27a. *First edition, American issue* (1968)

Shifts

of

Being

Poems by

Richard

Eberhart

New York   OXFORD UNIVERSITY PRESS   1968

Title Page: 8 3/4 x 5 1/8 in. (222 x 131 mm.).

Collation: [unsigned 1^{16} + 1 2-3^{16}]; 49 leaves; [i-x], [1-2] 3-88.

Contents: p. i: half title; p.ii: list of other books by RE; p. iii: title page; p. iv: copyright page; p. v: dedication, '*To Betty, Rick and Gretchen*'; p. vi: blank; p. vii: acknowledgements; p. viii: blank; p. ix-x: table of contents; p. 1: second half title; p. 2: blank; *or* as p. vii: acknowledgements; p. viii: blank; p. ix: second half title; p. x: blank; pp. 1-2: table of contents; p. 3-88: text; *N.B.*: The leaf containing the table of contents, pp. ix-x, or pp. 1-2, is tipped in all copies examined, but is variously found following the acknowledgements leaf or second half title. No priority can be established from the publisher's records, but it may be assumed that the proper placement of the table of contents leaf would be after the acknowledgements and before the second half title.

Typography: 34 lines per normal page; 156 (176) x 101 mm.; 20 lines = 92 mm.

Paper and Binding: leaf measures 8 3/4 x 5 1/4 in. (222 x 133 mm.); yWhite (92) wove, unwatermarked paper; uncoated smooth; moderate grayish greenish blue (no Centroid equiv.) paper covered boards measure 9 x 5 5/8 in. (230 x 144 mm.); front: unstamped; spine: stamped in gold, '[vert. from top to bottom] Eberhart [leaf ornament] Oxford'; back: unstamped; top and bottom edges cut, fore- edges rough cut; very pale grayish blue (no Centroid equiv.) laid endpapers, vert. chainlines 21 m. apart; watermarked 'TWEEDWEAVE'; uncoated rough.

Dust Jacket: total measurement, 9 x 19 in. (230 x 483 mm.); paper ident. to endpapers; front: '[in moderate grayish blue (no Centroid equiv.)] Shifts | of | Being | [in black] *Poems by* | [in moderate grayish blue] Richard | Eberhart'; spine: spine printed moderate grayish blue with lettering rev. out, '[vert., from top to bottom] Eberhart SHIFTS OF BEING Oxford'; back: '[black and white photograph of RE, 139 x 110 mm.] | [in moderate grayish blue] © *Mary Randlett ASMP* | Richard Eberhart'; front flap: '[in moderate grayish blue] Shifts of Being | [in black] Poems by | RICHARD EBERHART | [24 lines prin. in roman, about the book, including blurbs by Edwin Muir, R.W.B. Lewis, Robert Lowell, and James Wright (from *New York Times Book Review*)] | [in moderate grayish blue] $3.75'; back flap: '[20 lines in roman and ital, about RE] | *Jacket design by Sunniva Joyce*'.

Text Contents: "Words," "The Standards," "The Birth of the Spirit," "Extremity," "My Brains Are Slipping in the Fields of Eros," "Refrains," "To Harriet Monroe," "New Love," "When Nature Lies Asleep," "Whenever I See Beauty I See Death," "The Come-On," "The Ascent," "The Tomb by the Sea With Cars Going By," "Recognition," "Gestures Rich in Purpose," "The Rolling Eye," "Against the Wood Thrush," "Opulence," "Memory," "The Vastness and Indifference of the World," "Cliff," "White Night of the Soul," "Hill Dream of Youth, Thirty Years Later," "Why?," "The Symbol," "The Immortal Type," "R.G.E.," "Boston," "To the Field Mice," "Mexico Phantasmagoria," "The Winds," "To My Student, Killed In a Car Crash," "To the Mad Poets," "An Open Gate," "Ball Game," "The Enigma," "The Swans of Inverane," "The Haystack," "Santa Claus in Oaxaca," "Thoor Ballylee," "Looking Head On," "Solace," "Evil," "Marrakech," "Lions Copulating," "The Mastery," "The Ides of March," "A Wedding on Cape Rosier," "On Returning to a Lake in Spring," "The Explorer on Main Street," "Love Pieces," "Swiss New Year," "Trying To Read Through My Writing," "Sanders Theatre," "Outwitting the Trees."

Publication: Published 9 May 1968 at $3.75; 2,000 copies printed. A second printing of 1,500 copies was issued on 28 Nov. 1968 at $3.95; all ident. to A27a except for: dust jacket printed in blackish blue (approx. 188) and black; new price '$3.95' printed in lower right corner of front flap of dust jacket.

Locations: DLC, NcU, NhD, RE (3), SW (5), ViU

First Publication: The following poems are herein first published; collected and reprinted appearances are regularly noted.

"The Standards"

"My Brains Are Slipping in the Fields of Eros": in *CP76, CP88*

"Refrains": in *CP76, CP88*

"When Nature Lies Asleep"

"Whenever I See Beauty I See Death": in *CP76, CP88*

"The Come-On"

"Recognition": in *CP76, CP88*

"The Rolling Eye"

"Against the Wood Thrush"

"Memory": in *CP76, CP88*

"Why?": in *CP76, CP88*

"An Open Gate"

"The Wild Swans of Inverane"

"Thoor Ballylee"

"Solace": in *CP76, CP88*

"Evil": in *CP76, CP88*; rept. in *This Is My Best in the Third Quarter of the Twentieth Century*, ed. Whit Burnett (Garden City, N.Y.: Doubleday, 1970), pp. 93-94; *The Diamond Anthology*, ed. Charles Angoff et al. (South Brunswick, N.J.: A.S. Barnes, 1971), pp. 102-3.

"Love Pieces": rept. in *A Time To Love: Love Poems for Today*, ed. Joan Victor (New York: Crown, 1971), pp. 8-9.

"Outwitting the Trees": rept. in the *Chicago Tribune Magazine*, 26 May 1968, p. 15.

A27b. *First edition, English issue* (photo-offset from **A27a**) (1968)
All ident. to **A27a** except for:

Shifts
of
Being

Poems by

Richard
Eberhart

London   CHATTO & WINDUS   1968

Title Page: 8 1/2 x 5 1/4 in. (216 x 133 mm.).

Copyright Page: '[. . .] I Printed in Great Britain by William Lewis (Printers) Ltd. I Cardiff.

Collation: [unsigned 1-6^8 7^4]; 52 leaves; [i-x], [1-2] 3-88 [89-94]. *N.B.:* the penultimate and terminal leaves are used respectively as the rear flyleaf and pastedown.

Contents: pp. ix-x: table of contents; p. 1: second half title; p. 2: blank.

Paper and Binding: leaf measures 8 1/2 x 5 3/8 in. (216 x 137 mm.); white, wove, unwatermarked paper; uncoated smooth; brill g B (168) paper-covered boards (imitation bead-cloth) measures 8 3/4 x 5 11/16 in. (223 x 145 mm.); spine: stamped in gold, '[vert., from top to bottom] Eberhart [ornament] SHIFTS OF BEING [ornament] Chatto & Windus'; all edges cut, unstained; front endpaper white, wove, unwatermarked; penultimate leaf of 7^4 used as rear endpaper.

Dust Jacket: total measurement, 8 3/4 x 19 7/8 in. (223 x 506 mm.)' white, wove, unwatermarked paper; both sides coated smooth; printed in s. B (178) and black; front: '[vine-like design in strong blue] | [in black open-face type] SHIFTS OF | BEING | [in strong blue] *Poems by* | [in black] RICHARD EBERHART | [vine-like ornament in strong blue]'; spine: '[vert., from top to bottom; in strong blue] SHIFTS OF BEING | [in black] *Poems by* [in strong blue] RICHARD EBERHART [horiz. at base, in black] CHATTO | AND | WINDUS'; back: all ident. except for, '[at base] SBN 7011 1421 5'; front flap: '[16 lines in roman, about the book, including blurbs by Edwin Muir and Robert Lowell] | [at lower right corner] 21S | *net*'; back flap: '[11 lines in roman, about RE]'.

Publication: Published 7 Nov. 1968 at 21s; 1,006 copies printed by photo-offset from **A27a** for distribution in Great Britain.

Locations: NhD, RE (4), SW (3)

A28 *THREE POEMS*

First limited and signed edition (1968)

Three Poems

by

Richard Eberhart

On the occasion of
The English Department Dinner
at the Coolidge Hotel
White River Junction, Vermont
June 1, 1968

Title Page: 8 1/2 x 6 in. (215 x 153 mm.).

© *1968 by Richard Eberhart*

Collation: [unsigned 1^4]; 4 leaves; [1-8].

Contents: p. 1: title page; p. 2: copyright page; pp. 3-5: text; p. 6: statement of limitation; pp. 7-8: blank.

Typography: 25 lines (p. 5); 153 (171) x 102 mm.; 20 lines = 101 mm.

Paper and Binding: leaf measures 8 1/2 x 6 in. (215 x 153 mm.); white, wove, unwatermarked paper; uncoated rough; top and bottom edges cut, fore-edges deckled; handsewn with black cord in m. b G (164) wove wrapper, total measurement 8 15/16 x 12 7/16 in. (227 x 324 mm.), folded once vertically to 8 15/16 x 6 5/16 in. (227 x 162 mm.); all edges cut; front printed in black: 'Three Poems | *by* | Richard Eberhart | *On the occasion of* | *The English Department Dinner* | *at the Coolidge Hotel* | *White River Junction, Vermont* | *June 1, 1968*'.

Text Contents: "To Arthur Dewing," "Light, Free Movements," "Van Black, An Old Farmer in His Dell."

Publication: Published 1 June 1968 at $5.00; 200 copies printed.

Locations: NhD, RE (3), SW (6)

First Publication: all. "Van Black, An Old Farmer in His Dell": in *FG, CP76, CP88*.

Statement of Limitation: p. 8, '*This first edition of* Three Poems | *consists of two hundred copies numbered and* | *signed by the author. Designed and printed by William* | *Ferguson for the Pym-Randall Press, Cambridge,* | *Massachusetts, June 1, 1968* | *This is copy* [arabic numeral supplied in black ink] | [RE's autograph in blue ink]'.

A29 *GO TO THE SHINE THAT'S ON A TREE*

First separate edition [1968]

Cover Title: 'A POEM BY RICHARD EBERHART'.

Collation: [unsigned 1^2]; 2 leaves; [1-4].

Contents: pp. 1-2: blank; p. 3: text; p. 4: statement of limitation.

Typography: 12 lines (p. 3); 98 (112) x 98 mm.

Paper and Binding: leaf measures 10 1/16 x 7 in. (255 x 178 mm.); white, wove, unwatermarked paper; uncoated smooth; all edges cut; handsewn with white cord in medium brown (no Centroid equiv.) wove wrapper; total measurement 10 3/8 x 14 1/8 in. (263 x 360 mm.); folded once vertically to 10 3/8 x 7 in. (263 x 179 mm.); top and fore-edges cut, bottom edges deckled; front printed in black, 'A POEM BY RICHARD EBERHART'.

Text Contents: "Go To the Shine That's On A Tree" (C108).

Publication: Published 20 July 1968; 10 copies printed; not for sale.

Location: SW

Statement of Limitation: p. 4, 'This edition of 10 leaflets was printed by | Michael McCurdy at the Halcyon Press workshop | in Boston, as a gift for the poet. It is not intended for | public distribution. | *July 1968*'.

A30 *HARDY PERENNIAL*

First separate edition [1970 (i.e., 1971)]

Hardy Perennial

Collation: broadside, 19 x 11 in. (484 x 279 mm.).

Contents: recto, 'Richard Eberhart | Hardy Perennial | [20 lines in roman, text]'; verso: blank.

Typography: 20 lines total; 157 (208) x 111 mm.; 20 lines = 157 mm.

Paper: white, wove paper, watermarked '[in open-face] RIVES'; uncoated rough; top edge deckled, other edges cut.

Folder: laid in grayish tan (no Centroid equiv.) folder, 19 3/8 x 11 5/8 in. (490 x 295 mm.); laid paper, vert. chainlines 33 mm. apart, watermarked with a reverse 'P' crossed at the bottom by a horiz. rule and traversed by a reverse 'Z'; printed in black on front: 'The Carrousel Press | Number One | Fall, 1970 | Poems by | Richmond Lattimore | Richard Eberhart | Robert Siegel | James Kuhn | Dorothy Beck | Lee Kanes | Etchings by | Fritz Janschka | [9 lines in roman, acknowledgements] | © 1971 Anne W. Kuhn'.

Text Contents: "Hardy Perennial" (**C612**).

Publication: Published in January 1971 at $15.00 for the set; approx. 100 sets prepared.

Locations: NhD, RE, SW

Note: Also included in this broadside folio is "The Secret Heart"; see **A31**.

A31 *THE SECRET HEART*

First separate edition [1970 (i.e., 1971)]

The Secret Heart

Collation: broadside, 19 x 11 in. (484 x 279 mm.).

Contents: recto, 'Richard Eberhart I The Secret Heart I [30 lines in roman, text]'; verso: blank.

Typography: 30 lines total; 240 (260) x 136 mm.; 20 lines = 142 mm.

Paper: ident. to **A30**.

Folder: ident. to **A30**.

Text Contents: "The Secret Heart" (**C600**).

Publication: Published in January 1971 at $15.00 for the set; approx. 100 sets prepared.

Locations: NhD, RE, SW

Note: Also included in this broadside folio is "Hardy Perennial"; see **A30**.

A32 *FROM LOVE SEQUENCE WITH VARIATIONS*

A32a. *First edition, numbered and signed issue* (1972)

from I LOVE SEQUENCE WITH VARIATIONS

Collation: broadside, 18 x 12 in. (458 x 304 mm.).

Contents: recto, '[right side; in deep G (142), woodcut of three interlocked jonquils with two leaves] [right side; in d. Gray (266)] *from* I LOVE SEQUENCE WITH VARIATIONS I I. I [14 lines in ital, text] I Richard Eberhart| [RE's autograph in blue ink] I [5 lines in ital., statement of limitation]'.

Typography: 16 lines total; 162 (206) x 118 mm.

Paper: thick, tan (no Centroid equiv.) wove paper; unwatermarked; uncoated rough; bottom edge deckled, other edges cut.

Text Contents: First publication of the first stanza of "Love Sequence With Variations" (**C655**).

Publication: Published 15 May 1972; 50 copies printed on special Italian hand-made paper; not for sale.

Locations: NhD, RE, SW

Statement of Limitation: recto, at base, '[in dark gray] *The first stanza of ten to be published in the Summer 1972 issue of the Harvard Advocate, I printed in an edition of 2,000. Copies number I-L have been I printed on hand-made Italian wove paper, I and have been signed by the poet. I This is copy number*: [arabic numeral supplied by RE in blue ink]'. *N.B.*: Although the colophon states that the signed issue is numbered I-L, RE in fact numbered these copies in arabic numerals.

A32b. *First edition, regular issue*

Ident. to **A32a** except printed on yWhite (92) wove, unwatermarked paper; uncoated smooth; all edges cut; copies not signed or numbered by the poet. Published simultaneously with the limited and signed issue.

Locations: NhD, RE (3), SW

A33 *FIELDS OF GRACE*

A33a. *First edition, English issue* (1972)

FIELDS OF GRACE

By

RICHARD EBERHART

1972

CHATTO & WINDUS

LONDON

Title Page: 8 1/2 x 5 7/16 in. (216 x 139 mm.).

Published by
Chatto & Windus Ltd
42 William IV Street
London W.C.2

★

Clarke, Irwin & Co. Ltd
Toronto

ISBN 0 7011 1880 6

© Richard Eberhart 1972

Printed in Great Britain by
Redwood Press Limited
Trowbridge, Wiltshire

Collation: [unsigned 1-4^8]; 32 leaves; [1-8] 9-64.

Contents: p. 1: half title; p. 2: list of other books by RE; p. 3: title page; p. 4: copyright page; p. 5: dedication, 'To I BETTY I DIKKON and STEPHANIE I GRETCHEN and ALEX'; p. 6: blank; pp. 7-8: table of contents; pp. 9-64: text.

Typography: 36 lines per normal page; 158 (167) x 101 mm.; 20 lines = 85 mm.

Paper and Binding: leaf measures 8 1/2 x 5 7/16 in. (216 x 139 mm.); yWhite (92) wove, unwatermarked paper; uncoated smooth; d. r O (approx. 38) paper-covered boards (imitation bead-cloth) measure 8 3/4 x 5 1/2 in. (222 x 140 mm.); spine: stamped in gold, '[vert., from top to bottom] FIELDS OF GRACE [diamond-shaped ornament] Richard Eberhart [at base] CHATTO & WINDUS'; all edges cut, unstained; yWhite (92) wove endpapers, uncoated smooth.

Dust Jacket: total measurement, 8 3/4 x 18 15/16 in. (223 x 482 mm.); v. p. G (148) laid paper, vert. chainlines 26 mm. apart; watermarked '[crown ornament] I [in open-face semi-Gothic] Abbey Mills I Greenfield'; printed in d. b G (165) and deep Red (13); front: '[in dark bluish green] F I E L D S I [right side, the height of 'O F'; in deep red] RICHARD I EBERHART I [in dark bluish green] O F I G R A C E'; spine: '[vert., from top to bottom; in dark bluish green] FIELDS OF GRACE [in deep red] Richard Eberhart [at base; in dark bluish green] CHATTO & WINDUS'; back: '[in deep red] *Some poets' comments on the poetry of* I RICHARD EBERHART I [in dark bluish green; 22 lines in roman, including comments by Richard Wilbur, Robert Lowell, Edwin Muir, Kenneth Rexroth, John Fuller, and A. Alvarez]'; front flap: '[in dark bluish green; 12 lines in roman, about RE and *Fields of Grace*] I [at base] ISBN 0 7011 1880 6 £1•50 *net*'; back flap: '[in bluish green; photograph of RE, 94 x 64 mm.] I *Photo by LaVerne H. Clark* I [20 lines prin. in roman, about RE] I CHATTO & WINDUS LTD I *40/42 William IV Street London WC2N 4DF*'.

Text Contents: "The Young and the Old," "Old Question," "John Ledyard," "Van Black, An Old Farmer in His Dell," "Froth," "The Swallows Return," "The Incredible Splendour of the Magnificent Scene," "The Wedding," "To Kenya Tribesmen, The Turkana," "Kinaesthesia," "Inability to Depict an Eagle," "The Anxiety I Felt in Guanajuato," "Track," "The Bower," "Outgoing, Incoming," "Despair," "Suicide Note," "Meditation of God," "Evening Bird Song," "The Soul," "The Secret Heart," "Time Passes," "Broken Wing Theory," "The Loosening," "The Fisher Cat," "Reading Room, The New York Public Library," "Meaningless Poem," "Icicle," "Homage to the North," "As If You Had Never Been," "The Breathless," "Stealth and Subtleties of Growth," "Emily Dickinson," "Hardy Perennial,"

"Where I Want to Go," "Absolute Silence," "Emerging," "The Presentation," "Idleness," "Quarrel With a Cloud," "Gnat On My Paper," "The Truncated Bird," "Man's Type," "Lenses," "Long Term Suffering," "You Think They Are Permanent But They Pass."

Publication: Published in Oct. 1972 at £1.50; 1,250 copies printed.

Locations: NhD, RE (4), SW (2)

First Publication: The following poems are herein first published; collected and reprinted appearances are regularly noted.

"Meditation of God"
"The Presentation"
"Quarrel With a Cloud": in *CP76, CP88*
"Man's Type": in *CP76, CP88*; rept. in *Poet*, 24 (June 1983), 56.

A33b. *First edition, American issue* (photo-offset from **A33a**)
All ident. to **A33a** except for:

FIELDS OF GRACE

By

RICHARD EBERHART

NEW YORK
OXFORD UNIVERSITY PRESS
1972

Title Page: 8 1/4 x 5 1/2 in. (210 x 140 mm.).

ACKNOWLEDGMENTS

I am grateful to the Editors of the following publications
in which some of the poems in this book first appeared:
Antaeus; The Antioch Review; The Atlantic; The
Chicago Tribune; The Charles Street Journal; Concerning
Poetry; Genesis: Grasp; The London Times Literary
Supplement; Mill Mountain Review; The Nation; New
American Review; New England Galaxy; New York
Poetry; New York Quarterly; The New Republic;
Poetry; Poems from the Hills; The Quest; Quarterly
Review of Literature; Saturday Review; Shenandoah;
The South Florida Poetry Journal; The Southern Review;
Three Poems, 1968; The Virginia Quarterly Review.

The following poems first appeared in *The New Yorker:*
"As If You Had Never Been", "Despair", "The Fisher
Cat", "Homage to the North", "Suicide Note", "Track".

Paper and Binding: leaf measures 8 1/4 x 5 1/2 in. (210 x 140 mm.); yWhite
(92) wove paper, watermarked 'WARREN'S | OLDE STYLE'; uncoated
smooth; light tannish pink (no Centroid equiv.) paper-covered boards measure 8 9/16 x 5 11/16 in. (217 x 144 mm.); printed in d. y Br (78) and black;
front: contains triple-rules frame in dark yellowish brown; spine: '[all within
a dark yellowish brown double-rules frame; in black] *Eberhart* FIELDS OF
GRACE *Oxford*'; back: contains triple-rules frame in dark yellowish brown,
like front; all edges cut, unstained; reddish brown (between 39 and 43) wove,
unwatermarked endpapers; uncoated rough.

Dust Jacket: total measurement, 19 x 8 1/2 in. (483 x 212 mm.); wove, unwatermarked paper; inner side, flaps, and back are white; front and spine printed grayish pink (approx. 33 but darker) and moderate grayish brown (no Centroid equiv.); front: '[all above black and white photograph of field with flowers and trees; rev. out in white] Fields of Grace [in black] / [in dark grayish pink (no Centroid equiv.)] Pocms l by [in black] Richard Eberhart'; spine: '[vert., from top to bottom; rev. out in white] Fields of Grace [in black] Eberhart [at base] Oxford'; back: 'Poets Praise RICHARD EBERHART l [37 lines in roman, including a chronological list of tributes from 13 poets, 1930-1972] l OXFORD UNIVERSITY PRESS, NEW YORK'; front flap: '[in grayish brown] Fields of Grace / Poems l by Richard Eberhart l [25 lines in roman, about the book, including a blurb from Daniel Hoffman] l [in lower right corner] $5.95'; back flap: '[black and white photograph of RE, 74 x 63 mm.] l Photograph by LaVerne Clark l [21 lines in roman, about RE] l **Jacket design by Sigrid Spaeth** l ISBN 0-19-519710-0'.

Publication: Published 9 Nov. 1972 at $5.95; 2,625 copies printed photo-offset from **A33a** with Oxford University Press title page and new copyright page.

Locations: DLC, NcGU, NcU, NhD, RE (3), SW (5), ViU

A34 *THE GROUNDHOG REVISITING*

A34a. *First edition, signed issue* (1972)

THE GROUNDHOG REVISITING

Collation: broadside, 20 x 12 7/8 in. (508 x 330 mm.).

Contents: recto: '[woodcut by Karyl Klopp in dull red (no Centroid equiv.) and blackish blue (approx. 188), approx. 102 x 208 mm.] I [in black; arabic numeral and artist's autograph] XII / 1972 K Klopp I [remainder in black] THE GROUNDHOG REVISITING I [27 lines in ital, text] I Richard Eberhart I [RE's autograph in blue ink] I [statement of limitation]'; verso: blank.

Typography: 27 lines total; 290 (360) x 156 mm.; 20 lines = 215 mm.

Paper: dark yellowish gray (no Centroid equiv.) wove unwatermarked paper; uncoated rough; top and fore-edge deckled, other edges cut.

Text Contents: "The Groundhog Revisiting."

Publication: Published in Dec. 1972 at $15.00; 100 copies, numbered 1-100, signed by the poet and artist, of a total edition of 250 printed.

Locations: NhD, RE, SW

First Publication: "The Groundhog Revisiting"; in *CP76, CP88*.

Statement of Limitation: 'This poem is here printed for the first time, in an edition of 250 copies, of which this is No. [arabic numeral supplied in black ink]. Issued December 1972 by I The Pomegranate Press. Text Copyright 1972 by Richard Eberhart. Illustration Copyright 1972 by The Pomegranate Press.'

A34b. *First edition, regular issue*
All ident. to **A34a** except printed on yWhite (92) wove paper (Weyerhauser Kilmorey); uncoated rough; not signed by the artist or RE.

Publication: Published simultaneously with **A34a**; copies numbered 101-250.

Locations: NhD, RE (3), SW (2)

A35 *SALUTE*

Offprint (1973)

Collation: 2 leaves wire-stitched at left side, 9 x 5 15/16 in. (229 x 150 mm.); one leaf printed on recto only and a second leaf numbered 5-6.

Contents: recto of first (unnumbered) leaf: '*From* | I.A. RICHARDS | ESSAYS IN HIS HONOR | Edited by REUBEN BROWER | HELEN VENDLER | JOHN HOLLANDER | Copyright © 1973 by Oxford University Press'; verso of first (unnumbered) leaf blank; pp. 5-6: text.

Paper: each leaf measures 9 x 5 15/16 in. (229 x 150 mm.); yWhite (92) wove, unwatermarked paper; uncoated smooth; all edges cut.

Text Contents: "Salute" (**B75**).

Publication: 25 copies prepared for distribution by RE in August 1973; not for sale.

Locations: NhD, RE (2), SW (3)

A36 *THE BEGINNING*

First edition (1973)

Cover Title: 5 x 14 5/16 in. (128 x 364 mm.); reprod. from artist's original, in black: 'THE BEGiNNiNG'.

Copyright: none present.

Collation: 15 double leaves, each folded once and glued to the recto or verso respectively of the adjacent leaf; recto of first double leaf and verso of final double leaf each has a single leaf tipped on; [1-30].

Contents: p. 1: cover title; pp. 2-3: reprod. from artist's holographic design, 'Richard Eberhart'; pp. 4-5: poem; pp. 6-7: poem and drawing; pp. 8-9: poem and drawing; pp. 10-11: poem and drawing; p. 12: blank; p. 13: poem; pp. 14-15: poem and drawing; pp. 16-17: poem and drawing; pp. 18-19: leaf is printed black with poem rev. out in white; pp. 20-21: poem and drawing; pp. 22-23: poem and drawing; pp. 24-25: poem and drawing; p. 26: blank; p. 27: poem; p. 28: blank; p. 29 epigraph, '[reprod. from calligraphic original] I began on nonsense and I end on sense, | Which is the wish of man to cultivate the world's garden | Give the Devil his due, praise God for invented Heaven, | And hold to the end every last thing in vein.'; p. 30: blank.

Typography: all reprod. from artist's calligraphic original; irregular number of lines throughout.

Paper: white, wove paper; coated smooth; all edges cut; self-wrapper.

Text Contents: "I Walked Out to the Graveyard to See the Dead," "The Critic Has a Pained Eye" [*sic*], "A Maine Roustabout," "Anima," "Attitudes (Irish Catholic)," "Cover Me Over," "On the Fragility of the Mind," "To Evan," "Only in the Dream," "Forms of the Human," "The Human Being Is a Lonely Creature," "For a Lamb," "Rumination."

Publication: Approx. 10 copies prepared by Shelia Wolk in Sept. or Oct. 1983; not for sale.

Location: SW

Note: The Beginning was prepared as a special project by New York University art student Shelia Wolk. Her calligraphic designs and text, as well as her drawings, were printed by photo-offset on single leaves of white coated paper. The double leaves were glued to each other along the top edges so that the pages of this "book" open from front to back rather than from right to left.

A37 *TWO POEMS*

A37a. *First edition, numbered issue* (1975)

Two Poems

by

Richard Eberhart

Aralia Press—1975

Title Page: 8 1/2 x 6 in. (215 x 152 mm.).

Copyright Page: ' © 1975 by Richard Eberhart'.

Collation: [unsigned 1^4]; 8 leaves; [1-8].

Contents: p. 1: title page; p. 2: copyright page; p. 3: half title; pp. 4-6: text; p. 7: statement of limitation; p. 8: blank.

Typography: 35 lines per normal page; 150 (161) x 78 mm.; 20 lines = 86 mm.

Paper and Binding: leaf measures 8 1/2 x 6 in. (215 x 152 mm.); yWhite (92) wove, unwatermarked paper; uncoated rough; wire-stitched in brill. Y (approx. 83) thick, wove wrapper; total measurement, 8 15/16 x 13 in. (227 x 330 mm.), folded once vertically to 8 15/16 x 6 1/2 in. (227 x 165 mm.); front printed in black, '*Two Poems* | *by* | Richard Eberhart'.

Text Contents: "Stopping a Kaleidoscope" and "To a Dead Man."

Publication: Published 1 Oct. 1975 at $10.00; 326 copies printed, of which 300 were numbered and 26 were lettered A-Z.

Locations: NhD, RE (2), SW (5)

First Publication: Both. "Stopping a Kaleidoscope" in *WL*; also publ. separately as **A54**.

Statement of Limitation: p. 7, '*This first edition of* Two Poems | *is limited to twenty-six copies* | *lettered A to Z and signed, not for sale,* | *and three hundred copies, numbered and signed.* | *Designed by M.A. Peich for the Aralia Press,* | *West Chester, Pennsylvania, 1 October 1975.* | *This is copy number* | [arabic numeral supplied in reddish brown ink]'.

A37b. *First edition, lettered issue*
All ident. to **A37a** except for wrapper, which is m. O Y (71); not for sale; letter supplied on p. 7 in reddish brown ink.

A38 *POEMS TO POETS*

A38a. *First edition, regular issue* (1975)

POEMS TO POETS
Richard Eberhart
ENGRAVINGS by MICHAEL McCURDY

THE PENMAEN PRESS LINCOLN

Title Page: 8 13/16 x 6 in. (224 x 152 mm.); title, author's name, and single-rules frame in s. g B (169).

Collation: [unsigned 1-5^4]; 20 leaves; [1-6] 7-8 [9-10] 11-12 [13-14] 15-17 [18-20] 21-16 [27-28] 29-32 [33-34] 35 [36-40].

Contents: p. 1: half title; p. 2: blank; p. 3: title page; p. 4: copyright page; p. 5: table of contents; p. 6: blank; pp. 7-8: preface by RE; p. 9: second half title; p. 10: blank; pp. 11-35: text and full-page illustrations; pp. 36-38: blank; p. 39: colophon and statement of limitation; p. 40: blank.

Typography: 30 lines per normal page; 146 (170) x 98 mm.; 20 lines = 98 mm.

Paper and Binding: leaf measures 8 13/16 x 6 in. (224 x 152 mm.); yWhite (92) wove, unwatermarked paper; uncoated smooth; glued in stiff, yWhite (92) card cover, 8 13/16 x 6 in. (224 x 152 mm.); all edges trimmed, unstained; no endpapers.

Dust Jacket: greenish blue (between 168 and 169) wove, unwatermarked paper, dust jacket glued to spine; uncoated rough; printed in black and s. Blue (approx. 178); front: '[in strong blue] POEMS TO POETS | Richard Eberhart | [in black] ENGRAVINGS by MICHAEL McCURDY | [within strong blue single-rules frame, 131 x 105 mm., wood engraving of Robert Frost (from title page) in black]'; spine: '[vert., from top to bottom; in strong blue] POEMS TO POETS RICHARD EBERHART PENMAEN PRESS'; back: '[in strong blue, 16 lines prin. in roman, about the book, RE, and Michael McCurdy] | [publisher's device] | *THE PENMAEN PRESS* | LINCOLN, MASSACHUSETTS'; front flap: '[in strong blue] $6.00 | PENMAEN POETRY BOOKS | [double-rules, 62 mm.] | [15 lines prin. in roman, advertisement for books by Gerard Malanga, X.J. Kennedy, and William Ferguson] | [thick rule, 64 mm.] | The Penmaen Press | OLD SUDBURY ROAD | LINCOLN, MASS. 01773 | *Telephone 617-259-0842*'; back flap: unprinted.

Text Contents: preface by RE; "To Harriet Monroe," "At the Conoe Club (*To Wallace Stevens*)," "To Bill Williams," "The Young and the Old (*For W.B. Yeats*)," "Request (*for Dame Edith Sitwell*)," "Worldly Failure (*To Robert Frost*)," "Emily Dickinson," "To Auden On His Fiftieth," "Trying to Hold It All Together (*To W.H. Auden*)," "Lorca," "Portrait of Rilke," "Life and Death / Jean Garrigue (1914-1972)," "Face, Ocean (*To Stephen Spender*)."

Publication: Published 4 Dec. 1975 at $6.00; 1,000 copies printed, of which 700 were bound in stiff card cover with dust jacket.

Locations: DLC, NcU, RE, SW (5), ViU

First Publication: all are here republished.

Colophon and Statement of Limitation: p. 39, '*Poems to Poets* was designed and printed by the publisher | Michael McCurdy at the Penmaen Press in Lincoln, Mas- | sachusetts during the autumn of 1975. Michael Bixler set | the Times Roman and and Perpetua type, which was printed on Mohawk Superfine. The binding of both hardcover | and wrapper editions was executed at Robert Burlen and | Son. Of an edition of 1,000, 300 were hardbound, num- | bered 1-300 and signed by the poet and artist. The remain- | ing 700 books were bound in paper wrappers over stiffen- | ers. | This is number [arabic numeral supplied in blue ink]'.

A38b. *First edition, special issue*
All ident. to **A38a** except for:

Title Page: 9 x 6 in. (229 x 152 mm.).

Binding: black, fine bead-cloth (202b) boards measure 9 5/16 x 6 1/4 in. (237 x 159 mm.); stamped in gold; front: 'P O E M S   T O   P O E T S' spine: '[vert., from top to bottom] POEMS TO POETS RICHARD EBERHART

PENMAEN PRESS'; all edges cut, unstained; greenish blue endpapers (like dust jacket of **A38a**); clear plastic protective jacket.

Publication: Issued simultaneously with **A38a** at $20.00; 300 copies (of 1,000 printed).

Locations: NhD, RE (2), SW (2)

Colophon and Statement of Limitation: p. 39, '[below arabic numeral; author's autograph in black ink] | [artist's autograph in black ink]'.

A39 *COLLECTED POEMS 1930-1976*

A39a. *First edition, American issue* (1976)

Richard Eberhart

COLLECTED
POEMS
1930-1976

INCLUDING 43 NEW POEMS

1976

OXFORD UNIVERSITY PRESS

NEW YORK

Title Page: 7 15/16 x 4 5/8 in. (201 x 118 mm.).

Collation: Smythe-sewn; [1-12^{16}]; 192 leaves; [i-vi] vii-xvi [xvii-xviii], 1-364 [365-366].

Contents: p. 1: half title; p. ii: list of other books by RE; p. iii: title page; p. iv: copyright page; p. v: acknowledgements; p. vi: blank; pp. vi-xvi: table of contents; p. xvii: second half title; p. xviii: blank; pp. 1-364: text; pp. 365-366: blank.

Typography: 37 lines per normal page; 156 x 162 mm.; 20 lines = 84 mm.

Paper and Binding: leaf measures 7 15/16 x 4 13/16 in. (201 x 123 mm.); yWhite (92) wove, unwatermarked paper; uncoated smooth; grayish pink (between 31 and 32) fine bead-cloth (202b) boards measure 8 3/16 x 5 1/4 in. (208 x 133 mm.); spine: lettered in s. OY (68), '[vert., from top to bottom; in two lines, right] EBERHART OXFORD | [left] COLLECTED POEMS 1930-1976'; all edges cut, unstained; white cloth head and tail bands; yWhite (92) wove, unwatermarked endpapers; uncoated smooth.

Dust Jacket: total measurements, 8 13/16 x 19 1/2 in. (208 x 496 mm.); inner side, spine, and flaps are white; front and back printed in deep O (51); inner side coated smooth, outer side coated glossy; front: '[all within a black frame of single-rules, 201 x 120 mm., against a deep orange panel; rev. out in white, fancy script] Collected | Poems | [black and white photograph of RE filling out lower part of panel; right of photograph] 1930 1976 | [at base of panel, against photograph of RE] Richard Eberhart'; spine: '[vert., from top to bottom; in black] Eberhart | [in deep orange fancy script; in 3 lines; right] Collected [middle] 1930 1976 [left] Poems | [in black; horiz. at base; in roman] OXFORD'; back: '[against a deep orange panel; rev. out in white] Also by Richard Eberhart | Fields of Grace | Shifts of Being | The Quarry | About Richard Eberhart | Richard Eberhart | The Progress of an American Poet | Joel H. Roache | OXFORD UNIVERSITY PRESS | NEW YORK'; front flap: '[in deep orange fancy script] Collected | 1930 1976 | Poems | [remainder in black] Richard Eberhart | [24 lines prin. in roman, about the book, including statements by Dame Edith Sitwell, Robert Penn Warren, and Stanley Kunitz] | 0-19-519849-2 $13.95'; back flap: [17 lines in roman, about RE] | [at base] *Cover Design by [logo] Moose Graphics*'.

Text Contents: "This Fevers Me," "O Wild Chaos!," "The Bells of a Chinese Temple," "Maze," "For a Lamb," "Caravan of Silence," "Four Lakes' Days," "Ode to Silence," "The Return of Odysseus," "Where Are Those High and Haunting Skies," "Suite in Prison," "The Groundhog," "The Rape of a Cataract," "1934," "In a Hard Intellectual Light," "My Bones Flew Apart," "The Transfer," "Request for Offering," "Necessity," "The Scarf of June," "Experience Evoked," "Two Loves," "Burden," "In Prisons of Established Craze," "The Largess," "When Doris Danced," "The Critic With His Pained Eye," "The Young Hunter," "When Golden Flies Upon My Carcass Come," "Now Is the Air Made of Chiming Balls," "The Child," "Let the

Tight Lizard on the Wall," "I Went to See Irving Babbitt," "Recollection of Childhood," "Orchard," "The Soul Longs to Return Whence It Came," "Grave Piece," "The Humanist," "The Virgin," "Man's Greed and Envy Are So Great," "The Goal of Intellectual Man," "If I Could Only Live at the Pitch That Is Near Madness," "I Walked Out to the Graveyard to See the Dead," "A Meditation," "The Full of Joy Do Not Know; They Need Not," "Rumination," "Cover Me Over," "The Recapitulation," "Imagining How It Would Be to Be Dead," "I Walked Over the Grave of Henry James," "The Ineffable," "Mysticism Has Not the Patience to Wait For God's Revelation," "The Dream," "The Moment of Vision," "Retrospective Forelook," "The Lyric Absolute," "I Will Not Dare to Ask One Question," "New Hampshire, February," "Triptych," "Ode to the Chinese Paper Snake," "Burr Oaks," "Dam Neck, Virginia," "The Fury of Aerial Bombardment," "An Airman Considers His Power," "At the End of War," "A Ceremony By the Sea," "World War," "Brotherhood of Men," "Indian Pipe," "Go To the Shine That's On a Tree," "Sometimes the Longing for Death," "At Night," "A Love Poem," "God and Man," "The Horse Chestnut Tree," "The Tobacconist of Eighth Street," "Seals, Terns, Time," "The Cancer Cells," "Forms of the Human," "Oedipus," "Fragment of New York, 1929," "Aesthetics After War," "On Shooting Particles Beyond the World," "A Legend of Viable Women," "The Verbalist of Summer," "Concord Cats," "On the Fragility of the Mind," "Great Praises," "The Dry Rot," "The Skier and the Mountain," "The Human Being Is a Lonely Creature," "The Book of Nature," "Cousin Florence," "Sestina," "My Golden and My Fierce Assays," "Ur Burial," "Seeing Is Deceiving," "Analogue of Unity in Multeity," "Sea-Hawk," "Sainte Anne de Beaupré," "Mediterranean Song," "To Evan," "The Day-Bed," "Formative Mastership," "The Hand and the Shadow," "Words," "On a Squirrel Crossing the Road in Autumn, in New England," "Centennial for Whitman," "Soul," "Fables of the Moon," "Salem," "The Return," "The Giantess," "The Wisdom of Insecurity," "Sunday in October," "Summer Landscape," "Only in the Dream," "Nothing But Change," "Thrush Song at Dawn," "The Voyage," "Off Spectacle Isle," "The Seasons," "The Noble Man," "The Forgotten Rock," "Attitudes," "An Old Fashioned American Business Man," "A Young Greek, Killed in the Wars," "Protagonists," "A Soldier Rejects His Times Addressing His Contemporaries," "Blessed Are the Angels in Heaven," "Villanelle," "Life As Visionary Spirit," "Fortune's Mist," "Yonder," "Autumnal," "The Sacrifice," "Lucubration," "In After Time," "A Testament," "Request," "Love Among the Ruins," "Anima," "The

Supreme Authority of the Imagination," "Perception as a Guided Missile," "By the Stream," "What Gives," "The Oak," "In the Garden," "The Lost Children," "A Commitment," "Apple Buds," "Throwing the Apple," "The Garden God," "Light From Above," "Austere Poem," "Hoot Owls," "Tree Swallows," "The Clam Diggers and the Diggers of Sea Worms," "A Ship Burning and a Comet All in One Day," "The Hard Structure of the World," "The Parker River," "At the Canoe Club," "Ospreys Cry," "Half-Bent Man," "Spring Mountain Climb," "The Passage," "The Gods of Washington, D.C.," "Equivalence of Gnats and Mice," "Birth and Death," "The Incomparable Light," "Mais l'Amour Infini Me Montera Dans l'Âme," "On Seeing an Egyptian Mummy in Berlin, 1932," "The Spider," "Sea-Ruck," "The Hamlet Father," "Four Exposures," "LaCrosse at Ninety Miles an Hour," "Loss," "To Auden on His Fiftieth," "To William Carlos Williams," "Nexus," "Examination of Psyche: Thoughts of Home," "The Project," "Matador," "Premetheus," "Old Tom," "The Height of Man," "An Evaluation Under a Pine Tree, Lying on Pine Needles," "Kaire," "A New England Bachelor," "A Maine Roustabout," "Sea Burial from the Cruiser *Reve*," "Flux," "Ruby Daggett," "Hardening Into Print," "The Lament of a New England Mother," "The Lost," "Moment of Equilibrium Among the Islands," "Am I My Neighbor's Keeper?," "Christmas Tree," "Looking at the Stars," "Dream Journey of the Head and Heart," "Winter Kill," "Later or Sooner," "The Gesture," "Ultimate Song," "Vision," "May Evening," "Ways and Means," "Meditation Two," "The Illusion of Eternity," "The Standards," "The Birth of the Spirit," "Extremity," "My Brains Are Slipping in the Fields of Eros," "Refrains," "To Harriet Monroe," "Whenever I See Beauty I See Death," "Recognition," "Opulence," "Memory," "The Vastness and Indifference in the World," "Hill Dream of Youth, Thirty Years Later," "Why?," "R.G.E.," "To the Field Mice," "The Assassin," "Ball Game," "The Enigma," "The Haystack," "Santa Claus at Oaxaca," "Looking Head On," "Solace," "Evil," "Marrakech," "Lions Copulating," "The Ides of March," "A Wedding on Cape Rosier," "On Returning to a Lake in Spring," "The Explorer On Main Street," "Sanders Theater," "The Young and the Old," "Old Question," "John Ledyard," "Van Black, An Old Farmer in His Dell," "Froth," "The Swallows Return," "The Wedding," "To Kenya Tribesmen, The Turkana," "Kinaesthesia," "The Anxiety I Felt in Guanajuato," "Track," "The Bower," "Despair," "Suicide Note," "Evening Bird Song," "The Secret Heart," "Time Passes," "Broken Wing Theory," "The Fisher Cat," "Reading Room, The New York

Public Library," "Meaningless Poem," "Homage to the North," "As If You Had Never Been," "The Breathless," "Stealth and Subtleties of Growth," "Emily Dickinson," "Hardy Perennial," "Quarrel With a Cloud," "Gnat on My Paper," "The Truncated Bird," "Man's Type," "Long Term Suffering," "You Think They Are Permanent But They Pass," "Hatred of the Old River," "Vermont Idyll," "The Scouring," "The Cage," "The Poet," "Man and Nature," "Old Tree By the Penobscot," "Placation of Reality," "Emblem," "Worldly Failure," "A Man Who Was Blown Down By the Wind", "The Hop-Toad," "United 555," "Light, Time, Dark," "Death in the Mines," "Adam Cast Forth (Borges)," "Redemption," "Undercliff Evening," "Portrait of Rilke," "Sphinx," "The Groundhog Revisiting," "Big Rock," "American Hakluyt," "Life and Death," "Flow of Thought," "Mind and Nature," "Wild Life and Tamed Life," "Inchiquin Lake, Penobscot Bay," "Face, Ocean," "Three Kids," "Trying to Hold It All Together," "A Way Out," "Incidence of Flight," "Slow Boat Ride," "The Poem as Trajectory," "Snow Cascades," "Coast of Maine," "Usurper," "Vision Through Timothy," "Once More, O Ye . . . "

Publication: Published 17 June 1976 at $13.95; 3,650 copies printed, of which 2,598 were for distribution in the United States; 692 copies with the Chatto & Windus imprint were for distribution in Great Britain.

Locations: DLC, NcGU, NcU, NhD, RE (3), SW (3), ViU

A39b. *First edition, second American printing* (photo-offset from **A39a**) [1978] All ident. to **A39a** except for:

Title Page: 7 7/8 x 4 3/4 in. (200 x 121 mm.).

Copyright Page: 'Second Printing, 1978'.

Paper and Binding: leaf measures 7 7/8 x 4 13/16 in. (200 x 122 mm.); tanninsh pink (deeper than **A39a**) fine bead-cloth (202b) boards measure 8 1/4 x 5 1/4 in. (210 x 135 mm.); top edges cut, fore- and bottom edges rough cut.

Dust Jacket: total measurement, 8 1/4 x 19 11/16 in. (210 x 501 mm.); back: '[rev. out in white] *Collected Poems* I was winner of the I 1976 National Book Award I OXFORD UNIVERSITY PRESS I

NEW YORK'; front flap: price changed to '$15.00'; back flap: at base, 'Jacket photograph by Layle Silbert'.

Publication: 1,582 copies issued in May 1978 at $15.00; photo-offset from **A39a**.

A39c. *First edition, English issue* (American sheets) (1976)
All ident. to **A39a** except for:

Richard Eberhart

COLLECTED
POEMS

1930-1976

INCLUDING 43 NEW POEMS

1976

CHATTO & WINDUS

LONDON

Title Page: 7 15/16 x 4 3/4 in. (201 x 121 mm.).

Published by
Chatto & Windus Ltd
42 William IV Street
London W.C.2

＊

Clarke, Irwin & Co. Ltd
Toronto

ISBN 0 7011 2165 3

© Richard Eberhart 1930, 1936, 1940, 1944, 1947, 1951,
1953, 1957, 1960, 1964, 1965, 1968, 1972, 1976
Printed in the U.S.A.

Paper and Binding: leaf measures 7 15/16 x 4 7/8 in. (201 x 124 mm.); grayish pink (no Centroid equiv.) boards measure 8 3/16 x 5 5/16 in. (209 x 135

mm.); spine: '[in strong orange yellow, at base; in two lines; right] CHATTO I [left] & WINDUS'.

Dust Jacket: total measurement, 8 1/4 x 18 11/16 in. (210 x 475 mm.); putty-colored (no Centroid equiv.) laid paper, vert. chainlines 26 mm. apart; contains dark blue threads; printed in black and m. G (145); front: '[in moderate green] RICHARD I EBERHART I [in black; drawing of man in moonlight leaning against a tree] I [in moderate green] COLLECTED I POEMS I 1930-1976'; spine:'[horiz.; in moderate green] COLLECTED I POEMS I 1930-1976 I [at base] CHATTO I & I WINDUS'; back: '[in moderate green] *Poets and Critics in praise of* I *Richard Eberhart* I COLLECTED POEMS (1960) I [18 lines prin. in roman, including statements by John Wain, John Davenport, Bernard Bergonzi, Edith Sitwell, Conrad Aiken, William Carlos Williams, Robert Lowell] I CHATTO & WINDUS LTD I 40 William IV Street I London WC2N 4DF'; front flap: '[in moderate green, 17 lines prin. in roman, about RE] I [at base, left side] ISBN 0 7011, 2165 3 [right side] £8.00 I *net*' back flap: '[in moderate green; 7 lines in roman, about RE] I [at base] Chatto & Windus Ltd. I 40 William IV Street I London WC2N 4DF'.

Publication: Published in Sept. 1976 at £8.00; 692 copies from American sheets, with Chatto & Windus imprint, for distribution in Great Britain.

Locations: NhD, RE (3), SW (2)

A40 *THE FORT AND THE GATE*

First separate edition (1976)

THE FORT AND THE GATE

Collation: broadside, 8 5/16 x 5 3/8 in. (211 x 137 mm.).

Contents: recto: 'The Fort and the Gate I For Machi Razi reading Cavafy I [37 lines in ital, text] I Richard Eberhart I [right side, TLS logo] I 10 September 1976'; verso: blank.

Typography: reprod. by photo-offset from **C740**.

Paper: white, wove, unwatermarked paper; both sides coated smooth; all edges cut.

Text Contents: "The Fort and the Gate" (**C740**).

Publication: approx. 100 copies privately printed for G. Michael Razi for distribution as a Christmas greeting in December 1976; not for sale.

Locations: RE, SW

A41 *THE GODS OF WASHINGTON, D.C.*

First separate edition (1977)

THE GODS OF WASHINGTON, D.C.

Collation: broadside, 14 X 9 in. (356 X 229 mm.).

Contents: recto: '[reprod. from typescript orig.] THE GODS OF WASHINGTON, D.C. | [28 lines, text] | from *Collected Poems 1930 - 1976* | Oxford University Press | New York 1976 p 225 | [in roman] **a** | **folger poetry broadside** | **inaugural series 1977**'; verso: blank.

Typography: all reprod. from typescript original except 3 lines at base.

Paper: yWhite (92) wove, unwatermarked paper; uncoated rough, all edges trimmed.

Text Contents: "The Gods of Washington, D.C."

Publication: Published in Jan. 1977; approx. 200 copies printed; not for sale (distributed at RE's Folger Shakespeare Library poetry reading).

Locations: NhD, RE (3), SW (7)

A42 *OPULENCE*

First separate edition (1977)

OPULENCE

Collation: broadside, 11 x 28 in. (280 x 710 mm.).

Contents: recto: '[left side; reprod. of painting by Philip Pearlstein, prin. in reddish orange, gray, light blue, and shades of green and black] [right side; rev. out in white against black panel] Opulence I [7 lines in roman, text] I [at right edge] Poet: Richard Eberhart I Artist: Philip Pearlstein I [4 lines in roman and ital, credit and copyright notice for poem] I Supported, in part, by a grant I from the Commonwealth of I Pennsylvania Council on the Arts I and the National Endowment I for the Arts. Copyright © 1977 I Three Rivers Press, C.M.U.'

Typography: 7 lines of text; 120 (240) x 335 mm.

Paper: thick, white, wove paper; both sides coated smooth; all edges cut.

Text Contents: "Opulence."

Publication: Published in Jan. 1977; 500 copies printed; not for sale. Produced as part of a Federal Department of Transportation grant for poetry on buses, subways, and commuter trains.

Locations: NhD, RE, SW

A43 *THE PLAY*

First edition (1977)

[reprod. from RE's holograph orig.] The Play

Collation: broadside, 13 15/16 x 9 in. (354 x 228 mm.).

Contents: recto: '[reprod. from RE's holograph orig.] The Play | [17 lines, text] | [RE's autograph] | © 1977 | [reprod. from calligraphic orig.] **the** | **Folger Evening** | **Poetry series** | **1977/78** | [device] | **Broadside**'; verso: blank.

Typography: text reprod. form RE's holograph original; remainder from calligraphic original.

Paper: white, wove, unwatermarked paper; uncoated rough; all edges trimmed.

Text Contents: "The Play."

Publication: Published in October 1977; approx. 200 copies printed; not for sale (distributed at RE's Folger Shakespeare Library poetry reading).

Locations: NhD, RE, SW (5)

First Publication: "The Play"; in *WL*; rept. in *TLS*, 19 May 1978, p. 550.

A44 *HOUR:::GNATS*

First signed and limited edition (1977)

HOUR:::GNATS
New Poems by
Richard Eberhart
Putah Creek Press
1977

Richard Eberhart

© Richard Eberhart, 1977

Cover Title and Copyright: 'HOUR:::GNATS I New Poems by I Richard Eberhart I Putah Creek Press I 1977 I [RE's autograph in blue ink] I © Richard Eberhart, 1977 I [arabic numeral supplied in lower right corner in blue ink]'.

Collation: [unsigned 1⁸]; 16 leaves; [1-16].

Contents:t p. 1: cover title; pp. 2-4; blank; p. 5: poem; pp. 6-8: blank; p. 9: illus. by Carolyn Shine; pp. 10-12: blank; p. 13: poem; pp. 14-15: blank; p. 16: colophon and statement of limitation.

Typography: 20 lines per normal page; 111 (126) x 87 mm.; 20 lines = 111 mm.

Paper: leaf measures 9 x 6 in. (230 x 153 mm.); pale, grayish white (no Centroid equiv.) wove, handmade Japanese paper; uncoated smooth; handsewn on left side with white cord in self-wrapper.

Text Contents: "Hour" (**C754**) and "Gnats."

Publication: Published in Dec. 1977 at $5.50; 200 copies printed.

First Publication: "Gnats"; in *WL*.

Locations: NhD, RE (2), SW (5)

Colophon and Statement of Limitation: p. 16, '200 copies, designed, handset, and printed on I a Royal Columbian press by Sid Berger for I the Library Associated, University of Calif- I ornia, Davis. Number 3 in the Library Associates Fine Arts Series. I Bembo type; Hosho and Kozo papers. I Signed and numbered by the poet, and signed I by the artist, Carolyn S. Shine.'

A45 *OF POETRY AND POETS*

First edition [1979]

OF POETRY   Richard
AND POETS   Eberhart

University of Illinois Press   *Urbana Chicago London*

Title Page: 9 x 5 7/8 in. (229 x 149 mm.).

© 1979 by the Board of Trustees of the University of Illinois
Manufactured in the United States of America

Library of Congress Cataloging in Publication Data

Eberhart, Richard, 1904–
Of poetry and poets.

1. Poetry—Addresses, essays, lectures.
2. Eberhart, Richard, 1904–   —Interviews.
I. Title.
PS3509.B456035   809.1   78–11597
ISBN 0–252–00630–5

Collation: [unsigned 1-5^{16} 6^4 7-11^{16}]; 164 leaves; [i-viii] ix-xiii [xiv], [1-2] 3-107 [108-110] 111-215 [216-218] 219-312 [313-314].

Contents: p. i: half title; p. ii: blank; p. iii: title page; p. iv: copyright page; p. v: dedication, '*To* Ivor and Dorothea, Jack and Moira, I Betty, Dikkon, Channa, Lena, Malya, I Alex, Gretchen, and Benjamin'; p. vi: blank; pp. vii-viii: table of contents; pp. ix-xii: foreward by James Dickey; p. xiii: preface by RE; p. xiv: blank; pp. 1-312: text; pp. 313-314: blank.

Typography: 42 lines; 177 (195) x 109 mm.; 20 lines = 84 mm.

Running Titles: head, 'Of Poetry and Poets I ['Foreword' or individual section title in roman]'.

Paper and Binding: leaf measures 9 x 5 7/8 in. (229 x 149 mm.); yWhite (92) wove paper watermarked 'WARREN'S I OLDE STYLE'; grayish brown (between 60 and 61) fine bead-cloth (202b) boards measure 9 1/4 x 6 3/16 in. (236 x 158 mm.); spine: stamped in silver, '[vert., from top to bottom] OF POETRY AND POETS Eberhart [horiz.] University I of Illinois I Press'; top and bottom edges cut, fore-edges rough cut; all edges unstained; cloth head and tail bands have alternating red and yellow stripes; yWhite (92) wove, unwatermarked endpapers; uncoated smooth.

Dust Jacket: total measurement, 9 1/4 x 21 1/8 in. (235 x 538 mm.); wove, unwatermarked paper; inner side and flaps are white; front, spine and back are printed d. r O (38); inner side coated smooth; outer side coated glossy; front: '[in grayish brown (no Centroid equiv.)] Of I [rev. out in white] Poetry I [in grayish brown] and I [rev. out in white] Poets I [in grayish brown, row of three feather-like ornaments] I Richard I [rev. out in white] Eberhart'; spine: ' [vert., from top to bottom; rev. out in white] Of Poetry and Poets [in grayish brown] Eberhart [rev. out in white, in two lines; right] UNIVERSITY OF I [left] ILLINOIS PRESS'; back: '[photograph of RE, 110 x 154 mm.] I [in grayish brown, at base; left side] *Photo: Tom Jones* [right side] ISBN 0-252-00630-5'; front flap: '[in dark reddish orange] $15.00 I OF POETRY AND POETS I [in grayish brown] Richard Eberhart I *Foreword by James Dickey* I [23 lines prin. in roman, about the author]'; back flap: '[in grayish brown] *Of poets and poetry* . . . I [52 lines prin. in roman, including description of 3 titles and books; titles in dark reddish orange, text in grayish brown]'.

Text Contents: Part 1: "Notes on Poetry," "Poetry As a Creative Principle," "Pure Poetry," "Why I Write Poetry," "How I Write Poetry," "The Poet As Teacher," "Will and Psyche in Poetry," "The Theory of Poetry," "Poetry and Politics," "Literary Death," "A Haphazard Poetry Collecting"; Part 2:"Empson's Poetry," "Pound's New Cantos," "Some Memories of Dylan Thomas," "West Coast Rhythms," "Memory of Meeting Yeats, AE, Gogarty,

James Stephens," "On Theodore Roethke's Poetry," "Robert Frost: His Personality," "Remarks on Auden," "Robert Frost in the Clearing," "Reflections on Wallace Stevens"; Part 3: "An Interview with Richard Eberhart" (*Shenandoah*, 1964), "An Interview with Richard Eberhart" (*William and Mary Review*, 1964), "An Interview with Richard Eberhart" (*Pulse*, 1973), "An Interview with Richard Eberhart" (*American Poetry Review*, 1977), "An Interview with Richard Eberhart" (*New York Quarterly*, 1978); Epilogue: "National Book Award Acceptance Speech."

Publication: Published 24 April 1979 at $15.00; 2,545 copies printed; a second printing of 1,521 copies was issued on 12 May 1980.

Locations: DLC, NcGU, NcU, RE (3), SW (3), ViU

A46 *SURVIVORS*

A46a. *First edition, regular issue* (1979)

SURVIVORS
RICHARD
EBERHART

BOA EDITIONS • BROCKPORT NEW YORK • 1979

Title Page: 8 3/4 x 6 in. (222 x 152 mm.); RE's name in med. Gy (265).

BOA PAMPHLETS, SERIES A

No. 1: *The Bridge of Change*
      John Logan
No. 2: *The Toy Bone*
      Donald Hall
No. 3: *Sunlight: A Sequence for my Daughter*
      Poems by David Ignatow
      Drawings by Rose Graubert Ignato
No. 4: *Survivors*
      Richard Eberhart

"Time's Clickings" originally appeared in *The Virginia Quarterly Review* and "Learning from Nature" was in proof at the *Times Liberary Supplement* (London) when it suspended publication. Grateful acknowledgement is made to the editors.

"Blue Spring," "Time's Clickings," "Survivors," "Learning from Nature" and "The Rose" will be included in Richard Eberhart's forthcoming book of poems, *Ways of Light*, to be published by Oxford University Press, New York, in the Spring of 1980.

Publication of books and pamphlets by BOA Editions is made possible with the assistance of grants from:

The Literature Program of the New York State Council on the Arts.
The Literature Program of the National Endowment for the Arts.

Designed and printed at the Visual Studies Workshop
Typeset by City Newspaper
Special binding by Gene Eckert, Inc.
Distributed by The Book Bus, 31 Prince Street,
Rochester, New York 14607

BOA Editions
Publisher: A. Poulin, Jr.
92 Park Avenue
Brockport, N.Y. 14420

Collation: [unsigned 1^8]; 16 leaves; [1-3] 4-15 [16].

Contents: p. 1: title page; p. 2: copyright page; p. 3: half title; pp. 4-15: text; p. 16: statement of limitation.

Typography: 34 lines; 157 (178) x 101 mm.; 20 lines = 27 mm.

Paper and Binding: leaf measures 8 3/4 x 6 in. (222 x 152 mm.); yWhite (92) wove paper, watermarked 'WARREN'S I OLDE STYLE'; uncoated smooth; wire-stitched in card cover, total measurement, 8 3/4 x 12 in., folded once vertically to 8 3/4 x 6 in. (222 x 153 mm.); both sides coated smooth; all edges trimmed; unlettered.

Dust Jacket: total measurement, 8 3/4 x 20 1/16 in. (222 x 509 mm.); inner side, back, and flaps are white; front contains a printed black panel; both sides coated smooth; front: '[against black panel, 185 x 127 mm.; in s. Red (12)] SURVIVORS I [in dark y G approx. 132)] Richard Eberhart I [row of type ornaments in strong red and dark yellowish green]'; back: unlettered; front flap: '[in dark yellowish green; upper right corner] $3.00'; back flap: unlettered.

Text Contents: "Blue Spring," "Time's Clickings," "Nostalgia for Edith Sitwell," "The Impersonal," "Maine Summer High Color Luncheon," "Survivors," "Learning from Nature," "The Rose."

Publication: Published in Sept. 1979 at $3.00; 500 copies printed, of which 400 were issued in card cover with dust jacket.

Locations: DLC, NhD, RE (4), SW (7)

First Publication: The following poems are here first published; collected appearances are regularly noted.

    "Blue Spring": in *WL*
    "Survivors": in *WL*
    "Learning from Nature": in *WL, CP88*
    "The Rose": in *WL*

Statement of Limitation: p. 16, '*Survivors* has been issued in a first printing of 500 I copies, of which 400 copies are bound in I wrappers. I Seventy-five copies have been signed by the poet I and retained by the publisher to be subsequently I issued as part of boxed sets of ten pamphlets. I Twenty-five copies are bound in French papers I over boards by Gene Eckert, numbered I to XXV, I signed by the poet, and include a poem in I holograph by Richard Eberhart. Five of these I copies have been retained by the publisher for I presentation purposes.'

A46b. *First edition, special issue*
All ident. to **A46a** except for:

Binding: quarter-bound in black fine bead-cloth (202b) and French marbled-paper boards (prin. in dark pink, orangish yellow, light blue, and dark blue), in swirl pattern; total measurement, 8 15/16 x 6 1/8 in. (228 x 115 mm.); stamped in gold on front, '[left side; vert., from bottom to top] BOA EDITIONS RICHARD EBERHART SURVIVORS'.

Publication: Published simultaneously with **A46a**; 25 copies, numbered I-XXV, issued at $25.00 each.

Statement of Limitation: p. 16, contains roman numeral, I-XXV, RE's autograph and holograph poem in blue ink.

A47 *OF TRUTH*

First edition (1980)

OF TRUTH

Collation: broadside, 14 x 9 in. (356 x 229 mm.).

Contents: recto: '[in deep R (13)] Of Truth I [in black] —*for* Robert Penn Warren I [30 lines prin. in roman, text] I [in deep red] Richard Eberhart I [author's autograph in blue ink] I [in black]] LIMITED TO SEVENTY-FIVE NUMBERED COPIES OF WHICH THIS IS NUMBER [arabic numeral supplied in black ink] I COPYRIGHT © 1980 BY RICHARD EBERHART'; verso: blank.

Typography: 30 lines total; 191 (265) x 98 mm.; 20 lines = 110 mm.

Paper: white, wove, unwatermarked paper; uncoated smooth; all edges trimmed.

Portfolio and Box: laid in moderate gray (between 265 and 266) coarse bead-cloth (202) portfolio, 14 1/8 x 9 1/4 in. (359 x 235 mm.); white paper label on front, '[within a frame of deep red intersecting horiz. and vert. rules; in grayish greenish blue (no Centroid equiv.)] R P W I 24 • IV • 80'; portfolio laid in openface box, 14 1/2 x 9 3/8 in. (368 x 238 mm.), quarter-bound in gray coarse bead-cloth (like portfolio) and hand marbled paper prin. in dull grayish green, pale greenish gray, and gray; or pale greenish gray, dull orangish yellow, green and dull red (1112ad Spanish), each with vert. rule stamped in gold along fore-edge of cloth; spine label: white paper label, 113 x 19 mm., tipped on spine: '[all within frame of cross-hatched horiz. and vert. rules, in grayish greenish blue] *for* ROBERT PENN WARREN : PALAEMON PRESS'.

Text Contents: "Of Truth (for Robert Penn Warren)."

Publication: Published 24 April 1980 at $125.00 (for the entire portfolio); of 75 sets prepared, 55 were for public sale; see *Note*.

Locations: RE, SW (4)

First Publication: "Of Truth (for Robert Penn Warren)"; in *LR*.

Limitation Leaf: laid in portfolio; white, wove paper, 10 x 8 in. (258 x 203 mm.); printed on recto only, '[in black] FOR ROBERT PENN WARREN [deep red wavy rule; in black] 24 • IV • 80 [deep red wavy rule; in black] OF SEVENTY- I FIVE SETS PUBLISHED, FIFTY-FIVE ARE FOR PUBLIC SALE. I FIFTEEN ADDITIONAL COPIES OF THE WOODCUT ARE FOR I THE USE OF THE ARTIST. THIS IS SET NO. [arabic numeral supplied in red ink.]. I [autograph of publisher in black ink] I . . . *wer kann aber auch einem grossen Dichter genug dan-* I *ken, dem kostbarsten Kleinod einer Nation?*— I Ludwig van Beethoven to Bettina von Arnim, April 1811'.

Note: Also included in this special 75th birthday tribute to Robert Penn Warren are an original woodcut by Ann Carter Pollard, and poems by A.R. Ammons, Fred Chappell, James Dickey, George Garrett, John Hollander, William Meredith, Reynolds Price, Rosanna Warren, and Richard Wilbur.

A48 *WAYS OF LIGHT*

First edition (1980)

Ways of Light

Poems 1972-1980

RICHARD EBERHART

NEW YORK   OXFORD

OXFORD UNIVERSITY PRESS

1980

Title Page: 8 1/4 x 5 1/4 in. (210 x 133 mm.).

Copyright © 1980 by Richard Eberhart

Library of Congress Cataloging in Publication Data
Eberhart, Richard, 1904-
Ways of light.
I Title
PS3509.B456W38   811'.5'2   79-25150
ISBN 0-19-502737-X

Printed in the United States of America

Collation: Smythe-sewn; 40 leaves; [i-xii], [1-2] 3-15 [16] 17-67 [68].

Contents: p. i: half title; p. ii: list of books by RE; p. iii: title page; p. iv: copyright page; p. v: dedication, 'To | *My wife,* | *My children* | *And grandchildren*'; p. vi: blank; p. vii: acknowledgements; p. 1: epigraph from Richard Crashaw; p. 2: blank; pp. 3-68: text.

Typography: 32 lines per normal page; 156 (176) x 93 mm.; 20 lines = 99 mm.

Paper and Binding: leaf measures 8 1/4 x 5 1/4 in. (210 x 133 mm.); yWhite (92) wove, unwatermarked paper; uncoated rough; pale yellowish pink (between 31 and 32) paper-covered boards measure 8 1/2 x 5 1/4 in. (216 x 146 mm.); printed in m. Br (58); front: contains a fancy frame of cross-hatched single rules, with flower-like ornaments in all corners; all within thick, single rules frame, 197 x 117 mm.; unlettered; spine: '[short double-rules and flower-like ornament; vert., from top to bottom] EBERHART Ways of Light OXFORD [horiz., flower-like ornament and double-rules like first]'; back: frame like front; all edges cut, unstained; grayish brown (between 61 and 64) wove, unwatermarked endpaper; uncoated rough.

Dust Jacket: total measurement, 8 7/16 x 19 in. (215 x 484 mm.); laid paper, vert. chainlines 20 mm. apart; both sides uncoated rough; inner side, flaps and back are white; front and spine printed deep yellowish pink (between 29 and 32); front: '[against black abstract design of a figure moving into intense light; rev. out in white] Ways of Light | [in med. Gy (approx. 265)] Richard Eberhart'; spine: '[in very dark grayish black; vert., from top to bottom] Eberhart Ways of Light Oxford'; back: '[photograph of RE, 178 x 113 mm.] | *William Packard* | Oxford University Press'; front flap: '[in very dark grayish black] Ways of Light | Richard Eberhart | [24 lines prin. in roman, about RE] | ISBN 0-19-502737-X $11.95'; back flap: '[in very dark grayish black, 17 lines prin. in roman, about the author (cont. from front flap)] | Also by

Richard Eberhart | [list of 4 titles] | About Richard Eberhart | RICHARD EBERHART | *The Progress of an American Poet* | Joel H. Roache | [at base] *Jacket design by Joy Taylor'*.

Text Contents: "Rifkin Movement," "Under the Hill," "Angels and Man," "In the Air," "Interior Winter Sequence," "Los Arcos," "Love Sequence with Variations," "Stopping a Kaleidoscope," "Then and Now," "Winter Squirrels in Pine Trees," "Blue Spring," "The Rose," "Time's Clickings," "Nostalgia for Edith Sitwell," "Word-Prowess," "Robert's Rules of Order," "Opposition," "Ichetucknee," "Fat Spider," "Gnats," "Quarry-Stone," "Sagacity," "A Snowfall," "Trip," "Wet June," "What You Keep on Your Mantelpiece," "Coloma," "The Bones of Coleridge," "The Fort and the Gate," "A Loon Call," "Speculative Nature Note," "Offering to the Body," "Survivors," "The Swinging Bridge," "Death in a Taxi," "Stone Words for Robert Lowell," "In Situ," "The Play," "Night Thoughts," "Autumn," "Learning from Nature."

Publication: Published 29 May 1980 at $11.95; 2,313 copies printed.

Locations: DLC, NcGU, NhD, RE (4), SW (4), ViU

First Publication: The following poems are here first published; collected appearances are noted.

> "Under the Hill"
> "Interior Winter Sequence"
> "Then and Now"
> "Nostalgia for Edith Sitwell": in *CP88*
> "Opposition": in *LR, CP88*
> "Ichetucknee": in *FP, LR, CP88*
> "Trip"
> "Wet June"
> "Coloma"
> "Stone Words for Robert Lowell"
> "Night Thoughts"

A49 *BETTER MANAGEMENT*

First edition [1980]

Better Management

Collation: broadside, 11 15/16 x 8 in. (304 x 202 mm.).

Contents: recto: '[in deep O (51)] Better Management I [remainder in black; 16 lines in roman, text] I Richard Eberhart I THIRTY COPIES PRIVATELY PRINTED FOR STUART WRIGHT'; verso: blank.

Typography: 16 lines total; 144 (238) x 94 mm.

Paper: pale grayish green (no Centroid equiv.) laid paper, vert. chainlines 32 mm. apart; watermarked with hand-and-flower device and intersecting initials 'G' and 'B' in fancy open-face, with date '1976'; uncoated rough.

Text Contents: "Better Management."

Publication: Published 30 May 1980; 30 copies printed for private distribution by RE and Stuart Wright; not for sale.

Locations: NhD, RE (5), SW (3)

First Publication: "Better Management"; in *4P, LR*.

Note: RE signed 10 of Wright's copies in blue ink below his printed name.

A50 *JOHN FINLEY*

First edition [1980]

JOHN FINLEY

Collation: broadside, 14 7/8 x 8 7/8 in. (378 x 226 mm.).

Contents: recto: '[in deep O (51)] John Finley | [in black, 25 lines in roman; text in two numbered sections] | [in deep orange] Richard Eberhart | [in black] FORTY COPIES HAVE BEEN PRINTED FOR STUART WRIGHT | Copyright © 1980 by Richard Eberhart'; verso: blank.

Typography: 25 lines total; 228 (322) x 108 mm.

Paper: pale grayish green (no Centroid equiv.) laid paper, vert. chainlines 32 mm. apart; watermarked with hand-and-flower device and intersecting initials 'G' and 'B' in fancy open-face, with date '1976'; uncoated rough.

Text Contents: "John Finley."

Publication: Published 30 May 1980; 40 copies printed for private distribution by RE and Stuart Wright; not for sale.

Locations: NhD, RE (2), SW (5)

First Publication: "John Finley"; in *4P, LR, CP88*; rept. in *Poetry Now* 6, no. 5 (1982), 3.

Note: RE signed 15 of Wright's copies in black ink below his printed name.

First edition [1980]

FOUR
POEMS

by Richard Eberhart

PUBLISHED BY STUART WRIGHT : WINSTON-SALEM, N.C.

Title Page: 8 7/16 x 5 7/16 in. (214 x 138 mm.); title and ornament in deep R (13).

Copyright © 1980 by Richard Eberhart

Collation: [unsigned 1⁸]; 16 leaves; [1-16].

Contents: pp. 1-2: blank; p. 3: title page; p. 4: copyright page; pp. 5-13: text (poem titles in deep red); p. 14: blank; p. 15: statement of limitation; p. 16: blank.

Paper and Binding: leaf measures 8 7/16 x 5 7/16 in. (214 x 138 mm.); yWhite (92) wove, unwatermarked paper; uncoated smooth; single signature handsewn with white cord and bound in dark gray (approx. 266) paper-covered boards, 8 3/4 x 5 11/16 in. (223 x 145 mm.); all edges cut, unstained; front contains white paper label, 37 x 70 mm., printed in black and deep red, '[all within a frame of black cross-hatched vert. and horiz. rules, straight and wavy; in deep red] FOUR POEMS | [ornament in black] | [in deep red] Richard Eberhart'; no endpapers.

Text Contents: "Better Management," "Transformation," "John Finley," and "A Dream."

Publication: Published 9 June 1980 at $30.00; 165 copies printed; see *Note*.

First Publication: The following poems are here first published; reprinted appearances are noted:

   "Transformation": in *LR, CP88*; rept. in *New England Review*, 3 (Spring 1981), 343-44.
   "A Dream": in *LR, CP88*; rept. in *New England Review*, 3 (Spring 1981), 342-43.

Statement of Limitation: p. 15, 'FOUR POEMS by Richard Eberhart | is limited to 165 copies; 125, numbered | 1-125, are for public sale, and | forty, numbered *i-xl*, are for | distribution by the poet and publisher. | All four poems are here | first published; *A Dream* was written | in 1949 and "discovered" by the | poet in 1980. This is no. [arabic or roman numeral supplied in black or red ink] | LAVS DEO | [RE's autograph in blue ink]'.

Note: Although the statement of limitation indicates that all four poems are here first published, "Better Management" (A49) and "John Finley" (A50) were in fact previously published as broadsides for distribution by the poet and publisher.

A52 *NEW HAMPSHIRE: NINE POEMS*

A52a. *First edition, regular edition* (1980)

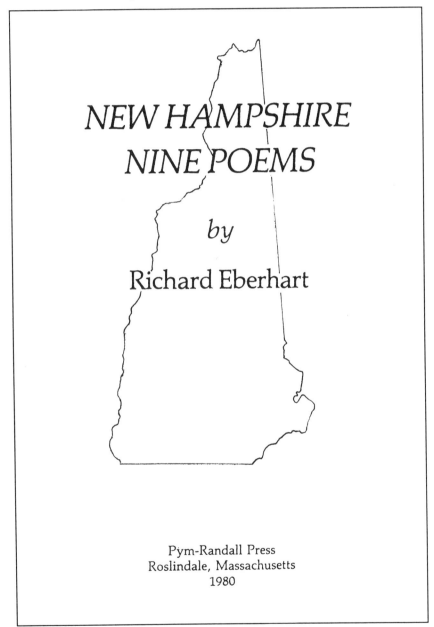

NEW HAMPSHIRE
NINE POEMS

by

Richard Eberhart

Pym-Randall Press
Roslindale, Massachusetts
1980

Title Page: 8 1/2 x 4 15/16 in. (215 x 126 mm.); map of New Hampshire in l.
Gray (264).

This Pym-Randall Poetry and the Arts Foundation, Inc. publication was made possible with support from the Massachusetts Council on the Arts and Humanities, a state agency whose funds are recommended by the Governor and appropriated by the State Legislature.

Pym-Randall Press
73 Cohasset Street
Roslindale, Massachusetts 02131

Collation: [unsigned 1^8]; 16 leaves; [1-16].

Contents: p. 1: title page; p. 2: copyright page; p. 3: epigraph, signed '*Richard Eberhart*'; p. 4: blank; pp. 5-15: text; p. 16: statement of limitation.

Typography: 35 lines; 148 (156) x 92 mm.; 20 lines = 85 mm.

Paper and Binding: leaf measures 8 1/2 x 5 15/16 in. (215 x 126 mm.); yWhite (92) laid paper, vert. chainlines 27 mm. apart; unwatermarked; uncoated rough; wire-stitched in card cover, total measurement 8 1/2 x 4 15/16 in. (215 x 126 mm.), folded once vertically to 8 1/2 x 4 5/16 in. (215 x 126 mm.); inner side white, outer side printed light gray (between 264 and 265), light orangish yellow (between 70 and 73); both sides coated smooth; front: divided into five panels by five thick black rules; panels are in light gray and light orangish yellow: '[in black] *NEW HAMPSHIRE | NINE POEMS | by* Richard Eberhart'; back: divided into four panels by six thick black rules;

two are light gray, one is light orangish yellow, and one contains a black and white photograph of RE, 150 x 78 mm.: '[at top left corner, in black] $3.00 | [against heavy black rule above photograph of RE; rev. out in white] Richard Eberhart | [against vert. rule on right side of photograph; rev. out in white; vert., from top to bottom] Photograph by William Packard'.

Text Contents: "Hardening Into Print," "Winter Kill," "Spring Mountain Climb," "The Explorer on Main Street," "The Fisher Cat," "Storm and Quiet," "On Returning to a Lake in Spring," "Ruby Daggett," "New Hampshire, February."

Publication: Published in Oct. 1980 at $3.00; 500 copies printed, of which 450 unnumbered copies constitute the regular issue.

Locations: DLC, NhD, RE (2), SW (5)

Statement of Limitation: p. 16, 'This pamphlet is limited | to an edition of 500 copies | of which copies numbered 1-50 | have been signed by the author. | Designed by Joanne Randall in | October 1980. | [at base] Printed by The Wallace Press, Milford, New Hampshire.'

A52b. *First edition, numbered and signed issue*
All ident. to **A52a** except for:

Statement of Limitation: p. 16, 'This pamphlet is limited | to an edition of 500 copies | of which copies numbered 1-50 | have been signed by the author. | Designed by Joanne Randall in | October 1980. | This is copy number | [arabic numeral supplied in black ink] | [RE's autograph in blue ink] | Printed by The Wallace Press, Milford, New Hampshire.'

A53 *CHOCORUA*

First limited and signed edition [1981]

Chocorua

Nadja

Richard Eberhart

Title Pages: each page measures 10 x 6 7/8 in. (254 x 175 mm.)

Copyright Page: 'Copyright 1981 by Richard Eberhart'.

Collation: [unsigned 1¹⁶]; 32 leaves; [1-32].

Contents: pp. 1-3: blank; pp. 4-5: title page; p. 6: copyright page; pp. 7-9: preface by RE; p. 10: blank; pp. 11-27: text, printed in black and blackish green; p. 28: blank; p. 29: colophon and statement of limitation; pp. 30-32: blank.

Typography: irregular number of lines per page; p. 15, 158 (169) x 97 mm.; 10 lines = 55 mm.

Paper and Binding: leaf measures 10 x 6 7/8 in. (254 x 175 mm.); tannish white (no Centroid equiv.) wove paper, watermarked '[crown ornament] I UMBRIA I ITALIA I C.M. I P.'; uncoated smooth; top edges trimmed, fore- and bottom edges deckled; handsewn with white cord in pale gray (no Centroid equiv.) thick, wove paper wrapper; total measurement, 20 1/2 x 14 1/14 in. (520 x 363 mm.); folded once vertically to 10 1/4 x 14 1/4 in. (520 x 363 mm.); front measures 10 1/4 x 7 1/8 in. (520 x 181 x mm.); front: printed in dark green (no Centroid equiv.) in upper left, 'Chocorua'.

Text Contents: "Chocorua."

Publication: Published in May 1981 at $75.00; 76 copies printed, of which 50 copies, numbered 1-50, were for sale; 26 lettered copies were distributed to friends and supporters of the press.

Locations: DLC, NhD, RE (2), SW (3)

First Publication: RE's poem, "Chocorua": in *LR*.

Colophon and Statement of Limitation: p. 29, 'Chocorua I was printed in the months of March and April. I The handmade papers are I HMP Kingston and Fabriano Umbria. I The type is handset ATF Garamond. I 50 numbered copies are for sale I and 26 are lettered and reserved by Nadja. I [arabic numerals supplied in pencil, 1/50, 2/50, and so on; or letter A-Z] I [RE's autograph in pencil]'.

A54 *STOPPING A KALEIDOSCOPE*

First separate edition [1981]

Cover Title: 11 x 8 1/2 in. (280 x 216 mm.).

Copyright Page: none present.

Collation: one leaf, folded once vertically; [unsigned 1²]; [1-4].

Contents: p. 1: cover title, '[in deep O (51)] The Campaign for | DARTMOUTH | [in deep grayish brown (no Centroid equiv.)] Convocation 1981'; pp. 2-3: text and colophon; p. 4: blank.

Typography: irregular number of lines; p. 2, 145 (171) x 96 mm.

Paper: yWhite (92) wove, unwatermarked paper; uncoated rough; all edges cut.

Text Contents: "Stopping a Kaleidoscope."

Publication: approx. 2,000 copies printed for distribution to Dartmouth College students, faculty and administrators, in June 1981; not for sale.

Locations: NhD, RE (7), SW (4)

Colophon: p. 3, 'This signed copy of the poem | *Stopping a Kaleidoscope* by Richard Eberhart | is presented to you by | the students, faculty, and administrators of | Dartmouth College | with sincere thanks for your efforts | on behalf of the | Campaign for Dartmouth | [RE's autograph in black ink]'.

A55 *FLORIDA POEMS*

A55a. First edition, regular issue (1981)

Florida Poems

by Richard Eberhart

Drawings by Karen Tucker Kuykendall

Konglomerati Press · Gulfport, Florida · 1981

Title Pages: each page measures 6 9/16 x 8 3/8 in. (166 x 213 mm.); decorative borders, rule, and ornament on right page in gy. y G (approx. 122).

Some of these poems previously appeared in *The Virginia Quarterly Review, The Prosery,* and in Richard Eberhart's *Ways of Light,* Oxford University Press, 1980.

This publication has been sponsored by Konglomerati Florida Foundation for Literature and the Book Arts, Inc., and the State of Florida, Department of State, with the assistance of the National Endowment for the Arts, a federal agency. This project prohibits discrimination on the grounds of race, color, national origin, sex, handicap or age in accordance with Federal law.

Konglomerati Press, P. O. Box 5001, Gulfport, Florida 33737

Collation: [unsigned 1-5⁴]; 20 leaves; [1-40].

Contents: pp. 1-2: blank; p. 3: half title; pp. 4-5: title pages; p. 6: copyright page; p. 7: blank; pp. 8-35: text; p. 36: reprod. of drawing by Karen Kuykendall; p. 37: about the author; p. 38: about the artist; p. 39: colophon; p. 40: blank; text printed in black and grayish yellowish green.

Typography: irregular number of lines; p. 17: 15 lines, 75 (85) x 99 mm.; 10 lines = 50 mm.

Paper and Binding: leaf measures 6 9/16 x 8 3/8 in. (166 x 213 mm.); yWhite (92) wove, unwatermarked paper; uncoated smooth; all edges cut, unstained; gy Y G (approx. 122) wove endpapers with reprod. of drawing by Kuykendall in black; uncoated rough; tipped in card cover along spine and left edge; light grayish blue (between 171 and 172) thick, wove paper; uncoated rough; front measures 6 11/16 x 8 1/2 in. (170 x 216 mm.); cover label: white paper, 40 x 65 mm., tipped on front, '[all within ornamental frame, in black] FLORIDA POEMS I Richard Eberhart'; spine label: white paper label, 166 x 6 mm., tipped on spine, '[vert., from top to bottom, in black] Florida Poems Richard Eberhart Konglomerati'.

Text Contents: "Opposition," "Blue Spring," "Incidence of Flight," "Dark Memories," "Gainesville Sun," "Classification," "The Swinging Bridge," "Key West," "Mistaken Identity," "Wet June," "Transformation," "The Great Trees," "The Long Swing," "Sunset Over Florida," "Ichetucknee."

Publication: Published 15 August 1981 at $7.00; 1,000 copies printed, of which 600 copies constituted the regular issue.

Locations: DLC, NhD, RE (5), SW (5)

First Publication: The following poems are here first published; collected appearances are noted.

"Gainesville Sun": in *LR*
"The Great Trees": in *LR*
"Sunset Over Florida": in *LR*

Note: "Opposition" was printed on a special flyer advertising *Florida Poems*; one leaf, folded three times vertically; front measures 5 11/16 x 4 1/4 in. (145 x 108 mm.).

A55b. *First edition, special issue*
All ident. to **A55a** except for:

Binding: quarter-bound in light gray (no Centroid equiv.) and greenish blue (between 173 and 174) fine bead-cloth (202b) boards, 6 3/4 x 8 9/16 in. (170 x 218 mm.); light gray cloth on spine has design by Kuykendall printed in black; cloth head and tail bands have alternating green and white stripes; cover label like **A55a**; spine label: white paper, 29 x 6 mm., printed in black, '[vert., from top to bottom] Florida Poems'; all edges cut, unstained.

Publication: 400 copies issued simultaneously with **A55a** at $12.50.

Locations: DLC, NhD, RE, SW (2)

A56 *RAIN*

First edition (1982)

RAIN

Collation: one leaf, folded once; [1-4].

Contents: p. 1: '[in deep R (13); fancy type] Rain I [remainder in black; 12 lines, text] I RICHARD EBERHART'; p. 2: blank; p. 3: invitation to reading by Eberhart; p. 4: statement of limitation.

Paper: leaf measures 6 x 7 in. (152 x 176 mm.); folded once vertically to 6 x 3 1/2 in. (152 x 88 mm.); yWhite (92) wove, unwatermarked paper; fore-edge of p. 1 deckled, all other edges trimmed.

Typography: text, 87 (107) x 70 mm.; 12 lines total.

Text Contents: "Rain."

Publication: 50 copies printed as an invitation to RE's reading at Reynolda House, Winston-Salem, N.C., 7 Oct. 1982; not for sale.

Locations: RE, SW (3)

First Publication: "Rain": in *LR*; rept. in *The Motive for Metaphor*, ed. Francis C. Blessington and Guy Rotella (Boston: Northeastern Univ. Press, 1983), p. 63.

Statement of Limitation: p. 4, '[in deep red] *Rain is here first published in an edition of fifty I copies only. Copyright, 1982, by Richard Eberhart*'.

Note: Ten copies were numbered in black ink, I-X. on p. 4, and signed by RE in blue ink on p. 1, below his printed name.

A57 *THROWING YOURSELF AWAY*

A57a. *First edition, separate issue* (1983)

THROWING YOURSELF AWAY

Collation: broadside, 16 1/16 x 12 in. (409 x 305 mm.).

Contents: recto: '[left side, reprod. of line drawing by Bernard Taylor in l. Blue (181)] [right side; in s. Pink (2)] *Throwing Yourself Away* | [remainder in black; 16 lines in roman, text] | Richard Eberhart | [RE's autograph in blue ink] | *Throwing Yourself Away* by Richard Eberhart. The original line drawing is by Barnard Taylor. | Stone House Press. *Portfolio One* / 1983. Number 5. Copy [arabic numeral supplied in red ink, within fancy brackets]'; verso: contains colophon (see *Colophon*).

Typography: text, 16 lines; 174 (250) x 138 mm.

Paper: white, wove paper, watermarked '[in script] Arches'; uncoated smooth; fore- and bottom edges deckled, other edges trimmed.

Text Contents: "Throwing Yourself Away."

Publication: Published 1 Dec. 1983 at $30.00; 150 copies printed, of which 115 were for sale separately.

Locations: NhD, RE (2), SW (2)

Colophon: verso, '[in black] The Stone House Press, Box 196, Roslyn, New York 11576 | Handset in Goudy Oldstyle, with title in Goudy Italic, & printed by hand on Arches | Text paper by M.A. Gelfand, in an edition of 150 signed and numbered copies, | with 115 for sale. First publication of this poem. Text copyright © 1983, | by Richard Eberhart. Illustration © 1983, by Barnard Taylor.'

A57b. *Portfolio One, joint issue*

Broadside ident. to **A57a** except issued in publisher's portfolio with other broadsides, as follows:

Portfolio: broadside laid in dark blue (approx. 183) fine bead-cloth (202b) folder, 16 1/4 x 12 1/8 in. (417 x 310 mm.); white spine label, 143 x 9 mm., printed in s. P (2): '[vert., from top to bottom] PORTFOLIO ONE / 1983 [leaf ornament] THE STONE HOUSE PRESS'; open-face publisher's box of ident. blue cloth; unlettered, no label.

Limitation Leaf: laid in folder, yWhite (92) wove, unwatermarked paper, printed in black, '[publisher's device] I PORTFOLIO ONE / 1983 I This portfolio has been printed from type handset at the Stone House Press and ma- I chine (Monotype) set by the Out of Sorts Letter Foundery, Mamaroneck, New York, I and, in the case of the wood engravings, from wood blocks. [ornament] Folder and slipcase are I by Alpha-Pavia, New York City. [ornament] All broadsides are signed by their author and num- I bered. [ornament] Edition limited to 100 copies, of which 25 are reserved. The remaining copies I are numbered 26-100. (Apart from those in the portfolio, 50 copies of each broadside I have been printed. Ten copies are reserved for the authors & artists; 40 copies are num- I bered 111-150.) I This is portfolio copy [arabic numeral supplied in black ink, within fancy brackets] I [publisher's autograph in black ink] I Morris A. Gelfand, Printer & Publisher I The Stone House Press, Box 196, Roslyn, New York 11576'.

Publication: Published simultaneously with **A57a**; 100 sets prepared at $250.00 each.

Locations: NhD, RE, SW

Note: Portfolio One contains an original wood engraving by John De Pol, a title leaf and with copyright on verso; a table of contents leaf; introduction (2 leaves printed on recto only); and illustrated broadside poems by Susan Astor, Robert Bly, Constance Carrier, Vince Clemente, William Heyen, Norbert Kraft, Joyce Carol Oates, William Stafford, and May Swenson; and the limitation leaf described above.

A58 *THE LONG REACH*

A58a. *First edition, cloth issue* (1984)

Richard Eberhart
THE LONG REACH
New & Uncollected Poems
1948-1984

A NEW DIRECTIONS BOOK

Title Page: 7 15/16 x 5 1/4 in (202 x 133 mm.).

Grateful acknowledgment is made to the editors and publishers of books and magazines in which some of the poems in this collection first appeared: *Ameri- can Poetry Review; From A to Z: 200 Contemporary American Poets* (The Swallow Press/Ohio University Press); *The Bellingham Review; The Chicago Tribune; Conjunctions; Cumberland Poetry Review; Chocorua* (Nadja Press); *The Devil's Millhopper; Florida Poems* (Konglomerati Press); *Forum; Four Poems* (Palaemon Press, Ltd.); *Gryphon; Harvard Magazine; High Country News; Kentucky Poetry Review; A Local Muse; The London Times Literary Supplement; Mid-Century American Poets* (Copyright 1950 by John Ciardi); *Nadja Press; National Forum; Negative Capability; New American Review; New England Review; New Poems by American Poets* (Ballantine Books); *New Hampshire/Nine Poems* (Pym-Randall Press); *New Republic; The New York Times; New York Quarterly; Paideuma; PN Review; Ploughshares; Poems to Poets* (Pomegranate Press); *Penmark Rising; Poetry Now; The Prosery; The Pomegranate Press* (broadside); *Pulse (The Lamar Review); For Rexroth (The Ark 14,* Festschrift); *I. A. Richards: Essays in His Honor* (Copyright © 1973 by Oxford University Press); *The Southern Review; Survivors* (Boa Editions); *Tamarisk; The Tiger's Eye; Vanderbilt Poetry Review; Wonders: Writing and Drawings for the Child in Us All* (Copyright © 1980 by Rolling Stone Press).

The following poems were included in the collection *Florida Poems* (Copyright © 1981 by Richard Eberhart), published by Konglomerati Press, P. O. Box 5001, Gulfport, Florida 33737: "Transformation," "Opposition," "Incidence of Flight," "The Swinging Bridge," "Mistaken Identity," "The Great Trees," "Ichetucknee," "Gainsville Sun," "Key West."

Manufactured in the United States of America
First published clothbound and as New Directions Paperbook 565 in 1984
Published simultaneously in Canada by George J. McLeod, Ltd., Toronto

Library of Congress Cataloging in Publication Data
Eberhart, Richard, 1904–
    The long reach.
    (A New Directions Book)
    I. Title.
PS3509.B456L6   1983   811'.52   83-23746
ISBN 0-8112-0885-0
ISBN 0-8112-0886-9 (pbk.)

New Directions Books are published for James Laughlin
by New Directions Publishing Corporation,
80 Eighth Avenue, New York 10011

Collation: [unsigned 1-3^{15} 4-5^{12} 6-8^{16}]; 120 leaves; [i-iv] v-viii, [1-2] 3-47 [48-50] 51-93 [94-96] 97-166 [167-168] 169-231 [232].

Contents: p. i: half title; p. ii: list of books by RE; p. iii: title page; p. iv: copyright page; pp. v-viii: table of contents; pp. 1-231: text; p. 232: blank.

Typography: 40 lines; 169 (174) x 95 mm.; 20 lines = 85 mm.

Paper and Binding: leaf measures 7 15/16 x 5 5/16 in. (202 x 135 mm.); yWhite (92) wove, unwatermarked paper; uncoated smooth; m. b G (164) fine bead-cloth (202b) boards measure 8 1/4 x 5 7/16 in. (211 x 140 mm.); spine: stamped in gold, '[vert. from top to bottom] Richard Eberhart THE LONG REACH NEW DIRECTIONS'; top and bottom edges trimmed, fore-edges cut; all edges unstained; yWhite (92) wove, unwatermarked endpapers; uncoated smooth.

Dust Jacket: total measurement, 8 1/4 x 19 5/8 in. (212 x 499 mm.); both sides white; inner side uncoated, outer side coated glossy; printed in black; front: 'Richard Eberhart | [initial 'T'] THE LONG [initial 'H'] REACH | [rule, 83 mm.] | New & Uncollected Poems | 1948-1984 | [black and white photograph of RE, 142 x 139 mm.]'; spine: '[vert., from top to bottom] Richard Eberhart THE LONG REACH NEW DIRECTIONS'; back: 'Some Other Poetry Books | from New Directions | [16 lines in roman and ital, including a list of 11 authors and 18 titles] | NEW DIRECTIONS 80 EIGHTH AVENUE NEW YORK 10011'; front flap: '[reprod. from computer type] FPT 0-8112-0885-0 > $16.00 | [remainder in roman] Richard Eberhart | [initial 'T'] THE LONG [initial 'H'] REACH | [rule, 55 mm.] | New & Uncollected Poems | 1948-1984 | [21 lines prin. on roman, about RE and this collection] | (*continued on back flap*) | *Jacket photograph by Susan Mullally*; | *design by Hermann Strohbach* | A NEW DIRECTIONS BOOK'; back flap: '(*continued from front flap*) | [22 lines prin. in roman, about RE and this book] | NEW DIRECTIONS | 80 Eighth Avenue, New York 10011'.

Text Contents: Section 1: "Chant of the Forked Lightning," "Passage," "Ur Burial," "There Is an Evil in the Air," "A Man of Sense," "Dusty Answer," "Old Memory," "Slant Angle," "Midwinter," "Discovery," "The Block," "Mind," "Somewhere Else," "Grip of the Cold," "Rain," "The Ideal and the Real," "Shiftings," "Love Poetry," "Episode," "A 3 x 5 Poem," "Poem of the Least," "The Scale," "To Alpha Dryden Eberhart: On Being Seventy-Five," "To the Mad Poets," "Target," "The Fig that Floats," "The Whole View," "Ben Franklin," "Lorca," "A Line of Verse of Yeats," "Edgar Lee Masters," "A Whack at Empson," "Eagles," "Invective with Suggestions," "The Place,"

"Old Dichotomy: Choosing Sides"; Section 2: "Two Translations from *Justice Without Revenge* (*El Castigo sin Venganza*), by Lope de Vega,"Protection," "Mother Swallow," "Fear of Death by Water," "Better Management," "Storm and Quiet," "Hysteria of Communication," "Transformation," "Opposition," "Incidence of Flight," "The Swinging Bridge," "Mistaken Bridge," "The Great Trees," "Ichetucknee," "News of the World," "Harvard Stadium," "The Airy Vent," "Dark Memories," "Feat," "Gainesville Sun," "Words," "The Words," "Specifications," "Reading an Old Poem," "The Poem," "The Year," "Thinking: Being," "Lying Still," "John Finley," "Emerson's Concord," "Poetry and Games," "Maine Summer High Color Luncheon," "The Truth," "Address to Time," "Address to God," "Prayer to the God of Harm, The Song of the Poet"; Section 3: "Still," "Of Truth," "The Invitation of the Evening," "News," "A Certain Distance from Man," "Youth and Age," "Sunset Over Florida," "The Impersonal," "Winter," "Waiting for Something to Happen," "Face in the Clouds Larger than Life Size," "The Flag," "Song," "Sea Storm," "Hopelessness of Achieving the Past," "Bats," "Belief," "Far Out," "Good Place," "Inexplicable," "Island Message," "Key West," "Order," "Salute," "A Telling," "Time," "The Visionary," "Fog I," "Fog II," "Accommodating Oneself to September," "Fate's Election," "Great Principles Are Thrown Down by Time," "Harmony," "Hour," "The Melancholy Fit," "New York Prospect," "Pitch of Grief," "Talking Back to Nature," "To a Dead Man," "Spirits Appearing," "Waiting," "Grandson," "Depths," "Pulling Out the Vines," "The Fisher Cat," "Vignettes"; Section 4: "Memory and Desire," "Spirit Descends in Man," "The Interrogator," "The Long Swing," "Division," "The Challenge of the Air," "No Control," "Classification," "Throwing Yourself Away," "How to Make Something of the Rocks," "The Fight Against the Inert," "How Do I Further Spend My Glory?," "A Rich Kiss," "Lilac Feeling," "Co-operation Is No Competition," "A Token," "How It Is," "Louise," "As We Go," "Understanding the Impossible," "Touch and Go," "Going to Maine," "Spite Fence," "Survivors," "Sea Bells," "Man and Nature," "Fog I," "Fog II," "Transformation," "To the Moon," "Commas in Wintertime," "Fantasy of the Impersonal," "Fantasy of a Small Idea," "A Dream," "Testimony," "The Killer," "Chocorua."

Publication: Published 6 April 1984 at $16.00; 4,000 copies printed, of which 1,000 were issued in cloth boards with dust jacket.

Locations: DLC, NcU, NhD, RE (5), SW (2), ViU

First Publication: The following poems are herein first published:

"Love Poetry": rept. in *Touchstone*, 21 (Fall 1984), 10.
"Edgar Lee Masters": in *CP87*; rept. in *Touchstone*, 21 (Fall 1984), 10.
"Accommodating Oneself to September": rept. in *Touchstone*, 21 (Fall 1984), 10.

A58b. *First edition, card cover issue*
All ident. to **A58a** except for:

Title Page: 7 15/16 x 5 1/16 in. (201 x 129 mm.).

Binding: perfect bound in card cover like dust jacket of **A58a**, 7 15/16 x 5 3/16 in. (201 x 132 mm.); white, wove paper; inner side uncoated, outer side coated glossy; spine: '[at base, vert., from top to bottom] NDP565'; back: ' [upper left corner] POETRY I Richard Eberhart I '[initial 'T'] THE LONG [initial 'H'] REACH I [rule, 54 mm.] I New & Uncollected Poems I 1948-1984 I [26 lines prin. in roman, comprising material from flaps of dust jacket of **A59a**] I [within brackets] Also by Richard Eberhart: *Selected Poems 1930-1965*, NDP198. [close brackets] I *Cover photograph by Susan Mullally; design by Hermann Strohbsch* I A NEW DIRECTIONS PAPERBOOK NDP565 I [reprod. from computer type] FPT ISBN 0-8112-0886-9 >> $8.95'.

Publication: Published 6 April 1984 (simultaneously with **A58a**) at $8.95; 3,000 copies issued in card cover (of 4,000 printed).

Locations: NhD, RE (7), SW (4)

First edition (1984)

TEN POEMS

by

Richard Eberhart

The great eye strains and blinks
Searching the sky
For an answer.

PRIVATELY PRINTED FOR STUART WRIGHT

Title Page: 8 7/8 x 5 5/8 in. (226 x 144 mm.); title in deep Red (13).

Copyright Page: none present.

Collation: [unsigned 1^4 2-5^2 6^4]; 32 leaves; [1-32].

Contents: pp. 1-8: blank; p. 9: title page; p. 10: blank; pp. 11-21: text; p. 22: blank; p. 23: statement of limitation; p. 24: blank; pp. 25-32; blank; *n.b.:* the first and final leaves are used as pastedowns.

Typography: 37 lines; 159 (171) x 92 mm.; 20 lines = 86 mm.

Paper and Binding: text: thick, white, wove paper; unwatermarked; uncoated rough; top edges cut, fore- and bottom edges deckled; 1^4 and 6^4 are binder's leaves and serve as pastedowns as well as front and end leaves; thinner white, wove paper, watermarked '[in script] Arches'; uncoated smooth; quarter-bound by hand in s. Br (55) leather and marbled-paper (1202 nonpareil) boards, 9 11/16 x 6 5/16 in. (233 x 162 mm.); marbled paper prin. in brown, grayish brown, dull yellowish orange, and bluish gray; spine: stamped in gold, '[vert., from top to bottom] EBERHART - TEN POEMS'.

Text Contents: "This Fevers Me," "For a Lamb," "On a Squirrel Crossing the Road in Autumn, in New England," "The Horse Chestnut Tree," "The Tobacconist of Eighth Street," "Cousin Florence," "Dam Neck, Virginia," "The Fury of Aerial Bombardment," "The Groundhog," "Great Praises."

Publication: Privately printed for Stuart Wright on the occasion of RE's 80th birthday, 5 April 1984; 13 copies printed, of which ten were bound. Five copies were for presentation purposes, and five copies were for sale at $300.00. The three overrun sets of sheets were signed by RE and numbered in pencil on the title page, 'I/3', 'II/3', or 'III/3'.

Locations: RE, SW (2)

Statement of Limitation: p. 23, 'TEN COPIES HAVE BEEN PRINTED TO HONOR | RICHARD EBERHART ON THE OCCASION OF HIS | EIGHTIETH BIRTHDAY, 5 APRIL 1984 | [letter A-J supplied in black ink]'.

Note: The epigraph on the title page is from RE's poem "Searcher" (**B3, C5**). All copies signed on title page in blue ink by RE.

A60 *RECAPITULATION OF A POEM TAKEN BY THE NEW YORKER*

First edition (1984)

RECAPITULATION OF A POEM TAKEN BY THE NEW YORKER

Collation: broadside, 12 1/2 x 9 in. (313 x 229 mm.)

Contents: recto, '[in s. Red (12)] Recapitulation of a Poem Taken by The New Yorker I [remainder in black; 26 lines in roman, text] I Richard Eberhart I [author's autograph in blue ink] I PALAEMON PRESS LIMITED I Copyright, 1984, by Richard Eberhart'; verso: blank.

Typography: text, 26 lines; 124 (174) x 88 mm.; 20 lines = 85 mm.

Paper: white, wove, unwatermarked paper; uncoated smooth; bottom edge deckled, other edges trimmed.

Portfolio: laid in (with other broadsides) in marbled paper portfolio, 12 9/16 x 9 1/16 in. (324 x 230 mm.); 1112ad Spanish, prin. in gray, brown, dull brownish orange, and white; cover label: '[all within a black single-rules frame, 126 x 84 mm.; in brownish orange (no Centroid equiv.)] *Fifty Years of American Poetry* I [in black] A Tribute to Marie Bullock I 11 April 1984 I [swelled rule in brownish orange, 26 mm.] I [in black, list of 22 poets in two columns of 11 each] I [brownish orange swelled rule like first] I [in black] PALAEMON PRESS LIMITED'.

Text Contents: "Recapitulation of a Poem Taken by The New Yorker."

Publication: Published 11 April 1984 by Palaemon Press for the Academy of American Poets, in honor of its director, Marie Bullock; 50 sets prepared, of which 25 were for the contributors or for presentation, and 25 sets were for public sale at $225.00 per set. *N.B.*: An overrun of 10 copies of RE's poem was numbered '1/10' through '10/10'; these copies, with other overrun copies, were reserved for the use of the publisher.

Locations: RE, SW (4)

First Publication: "Recapitulation of a Poem Taken by The New Yorker."

Note: Other poets included in this broadside folio tribute to Marie Bullock are John Ashbery, Philip Booth, Louis O. Coxe, J.V. Cunningham, Robert Fitzgerald, Anthony Hecht, Daniel Hoffman, John Hollander, Stanley Kunitz, James Merrill, W.S. Merwin, John F. Nims, Howard Nemerov, James Schuyler, W.D. Snodgrass, Mark Strand, May Swenson, Mona Van Duyn, David Wagoner, Robert Penn Warren, and Richard Wilbur.

A61 *SPITE FENCE*

A61a. *First separate edition, first issue* (1984)

SPITE FENCE

Collation: broadside, 16 5/8 x 10 5/8 in. (423 x 271 mm.).

Contents: '[within a decorative frame reprod. from artist's orig., broken on left, and including haystacks, pumpkins, berries on vine, etc.] Spite Fence | [initial 'A' in first line; 17 lines in roman, text] | Richard Eberhart | [left side, author's autograph in blue ink] | [below decorative frame] 1984 | In Celebration of His Eightieth Birthday | [10 lines, about RE and statement of limitation] | Published by Mt. State Press, 1984.'; verso: blank.

Typography: text, 17 lines; 202 (365) x 114 mm.

Paper: pale tannish yellow (no Centroid equiv.) wove, unwatermarked paper; uncoated rough; all edges cut.

Text Contents: "Spite Fence" (from **A58**).

Publication: Published in May 1984; 80 copies printed; not for sale.

Locations: NhD, RE (5), SW (3)

Statement of Limitation: '"Spite Fence" first appeared in the *London Times Literary Supplement* (1981) and will be included in | "my new long book *The Long Reach* being published by New Directions Spring 1984." Seventy-eight pieces | are issued by Mountain State Press, by permission of Richard Eberhart, and are numbered and signed. The | poem may not be reproduced without permission of Richard Eberhart who holds the copyright.'

Note: Although the statement of limitation indicates that the 78 signed and numbered "pieces" were issued, the compiler has not been able to locate a numbered copy; all copies located were signed, however. Either the issue was somewhat larger than 78 "pieces," or the copies were issued unnumbered.

A61b. *First edition, second issue* (reduced format by photo-offset)
All ident. to **A61a** except for:

Collation: 11 x 8 1/2 in. (280 x 217 mm.).

Typography: 136 (245) x 80 mm.

Publication: Unknown number of copies in reduced format, on stock ident. to **A61a** issued in the summer of 1984 (after July); not for sale.

Locations: NhD, RE (2), SW (2)

Note: Copies of **A61b** were not signed by RE but contain his signature re-prod. from original.

A62 *COLLECTED POEMS 1930-1986*

A62a. *First edition* (1987, [i.e. 1988])

Richard Eberhart

COLLECTED POEMS

1930–1986

NEW YORK   OXFORD

OXFORD UNIVERSITY PRESS

1988

Title Page: 7 15/16 x 4 3/4 in. (202 x 122 mm.).

Oxford University Press
Oxford   New York   Toronto
Delhi   Bombay   Calcutta   Madras   Karachi
Petaling Jaya   Singapore   Hong Kong   Tokyo
Nairobi   Dar es Salaam   Cape Town
Melbourne   Auckland

and associated companies in
Beirut   Berlin   Ibadan   Nicosia

Published by Oxford University Press, Inc.,
200 Madison Avenue, New York, New York 10016

Oxford is a registered trademark of Oxford University Press

Library of Congress Cataloging-in-Publication Data
Eberhart, Richard, 1904–
Collected poems, 1930–1986.
1. Title.
PS3509.B456A6   1987   811'.52   87-15236
ISBN 0-19-504055-4

Previously published poems in this book first appeared in the following collec-
tions: A Bravery of Earth, Reading the Spirit, Song and Idea, Poems New and
Selected, Burr Oaks, Selected Poems, Under Cliff, Great Praises, Collected Poems
1930–1960, The Quarry, Selected Poems 1930–1965, Shifts of Being, Fields of
Grace, Ways of Light, The Long Reach, Four Poems, Florida Poems, Breadloaf
Anthology.

1 3 5 7 9 8 6 4 2
Printed in the United States of America
on acid-free paper

Collation: Smythe-sewn; 236 leaves; [i-v] vi-xvi [xvii-xviii], 1-444 [445-446].

Contents: p. i: half-title; p. ii: list of books by RE; p. iii: title page; p. iv: copyright page; p. v: acknowledgements; pp. vi-xvi: contents; p. xvii: second half title with quoted statement about poetry by RE (1983); p. xviii: blank; p. 1-444: text; pp. 445-446: blank.

Typography: 37 lines per normal page; 156 x 94 mm.; 20 lines = 84 mm.

Paper and Binding: leaf measures 7 15/16 x 4 7/8 in. (202 x 124 mm.); yWhite (Centroid 92) wove, unwatermarked paper; binding: quarter-bound in black bead-cloth (202b) and d. Gray (Centroid 266) boards, 8 3/16 x 5 1/4 in. (208 x 135 mm.); stamped in silver; spine: 'EBERHART | COLLECTED | POEMS | 1930 | TO | 1986 | [at base] OXFORD'; back: at bottom, 'ISBN: 0-19-504055-4'; all edges trimmed; cloth head and tail bands have checkered pattern in blue and white; yellowish white (Centroid 92) wove, unwatermarked endpapers, coated smooth.

Dust Jacket: total measurement, 8 3/16 x 19 1/16 in. (208 x 484 mm.); thick, white, wove paper, unwatermarked; inner side coated smooth, outer side coated glossy; printed in gy. p B (Centroid 204) and S.G (Centroid 14); front: '[in grayish purplish blue] COLLECTED | [in strong green, rule, 99 mm.] | [letters of 'POEMS' in grayish purplish blue, and interlocking, with strong green irregular areas at points of intersection] POEMS | [strong green rule, 99 mm.] | [in grayish purplish blue] 1930 [in strong green, block ornament] [in grayish purplish blue] 1986 | [in strong green, block ornament] [in grayish purplish blue] RICHARD [in strong green, block ornament] | [in grayish purplish blue] EBERHART'; spine: '[vert., from top to bottom; 'COLLECTED' and '1930 [block ornament] 1986' within strong green vert. rules; in grayish purplish blue] COLLECTED ['POEMS' like on front] POEMS 1930 [in strong green, block ornament] 1986 [in grayish purplish blue] EBERHART [horiz., at base] OXFORD'; back: '[in grayish purplish blue, photograph of RE surrounded by single rules frame] | [at bottom, right side] ISBN 0-19-504055-4'; front flap: '[in strong green] COLLECTED | [rule, 59 mm.] | 1930 1986 | RICHARD EBERHART | [in grayish purplish blue, 22 lines prin. in roman, about RE and his work, including quoted statements from Robert Penn Warren and Dame Edith Sitwell] | [right side] $29.95'; back flap: '[in grayish purplish blue] **About the Author** | [19 lines prin. in roman] | [at bottom] *Back cover photograph by | Hawthorn/Olson, Photographers, Inc. | Jacket design by Jenkins and Page*'.

Text Contents: Text contents ident. to **A39** with the addition of the following poems, published since 1976: "Rifkin Movement," "Stopping a Kaleidoscope," "Nostalgia for Edith Sitwell," "Gnats," "Sagacity," "A

Snowfall," "The Bones of Coleridge," "A Loon Call," "The Play," "Learning from Nature," "There Is an Evil in the Air," "Somewhere Else," "The Ideal and the Real," "To the Mad Poets," "Lorca," "A Line of Verse from Yeats," "Edgar Lee Masters," "The Place," "Old Dichotomy: Choosing Sides," "Transformation," "Opposition," "The Swinging Bridge," "Mistaken Identity," "Ichetucknee," "Harvard Stadium," "John Finley," "Emerson's Concord," "Poetry and Games," "The Truth," "News," "The Flag," "Sea Storm," "Key West," "Great Principles Are Thrown Down by Time," "The Long Swing," "How It Is," "Going to Maine," "Spite Fence," "Commas in Wintertime," "Fantasy of a Small Idea," "A Dream," "Testimony," "The Killer," "Sailing to Buck's Harbor," "Ceremonial," "The Sacrifice," "The Lament of a New England Mother," "Ives," "Mystery of the Abstract," "White Pines, Felled 1984," "A Clerihew for Alan Gaylord," "Throwing Yourself Away," "River Water Music," "The Wild Swans of Inverane," "Snowy Owl," "Going Backward Going Forward," "Listing," "The Hand," "The Mystical Beast in the Shadows," "The Angels," "Dead Skunk," "Question Mark," "Waiting to Lean to the Master's Command," "The Broken Pen," "Deep Fishing," "The Difficulty of Ideas," "On the Subtle Man," "Gulled," "Configuration," "Velvet Rocks," "Memory," "Laocoön," "Quanta," "Hornets by the Sill," "Statue of Liberty," "Going," "New Entrepreneurial Man," "21st Century Man."

Publication: Published 21 Jan. 1988 at $29.95; 2,200 copies printed; issued in cloth only. See *Note.*

Note: Collected Poems 1930-1986 was scheduled for December publication, and bound copies were received by the publisher during the middle of that month. RE received a complimentary copy and noticed that the leaf containing pp. 365-66 had been partially printed. He notified Oxford Univ. Press, and it was discovered that the entire edition had been thus misprinted. According to RE's editor, Mimi Melek (ltr. to SW, 18 Feb. 1988), the entire edition was recalled and cancelled leaves containing the corrected text were tipped in. Melek maintains that only the one copy was sent out, and that no others were circulated in December. Of 14 copies examined, including three that were sent out for review in early February 1988, all copies contained the cancelled leaf. It is likely, however, that other copies may have been inadvertently distributed in December 1987.

First Publication: The following poems are here first published:

"News"
"Sailing to Buck's Harbor"
"The Wild Swans of Inverane"
"Snowy Owl"
"Waiting to Lean to the Master's Command"
"The Broken Pen"
"The Difficulty of Ideas"
"On the Subtle Man"
"Gulled"
"Configuration"
"Quanta"
"Statue of Liberty"
"New Entrepreneurial Man"

B
Contributions to Books and Pamphlets

B1 *AUSTINIAN* 1921

[in fancy type] AUSTINIAN | PUBLISHED BY | SENIOR CLASS | OF | 1921 | AUSTIN HIGH SCHOOL | AUSTIN MINN. K.H.

Copyright Page: none present.

Binding: light grayish brown paper (imitation leather) glued at spine and tied front to back with gold ribbon through two punches, with envelope edges; total measurement, 11 1/4 x 7 15/16 in. (284 x 202 mm.); front: stamped in gold, '[in fancy type] AUSTINIAN | [Austin High School logo, with '21' at base]'.

Contents: First publication of RE's poem, "The Shell Vase," p. 16, and a facetious letter, "Dear Me:—," pp. 15-16.

Publication: Published in Oct. 1921.

Note: RE was editor-and-chief of the 1921 *Austinian*. His poem, "The Shell Vase," is his first published. By any standard, Eberhart was an exceptionally well-rounded and popular student. Among senior kudos, he received "most popular boy," "best looking boy," and "best all-around boy." During his years at Austin High School, he played football and was captain of the team his senior year; he also played baseball and basketball, and ran track. Eberhart was a class officer each of his four years in high school, and was a debater; he acted in a number of class plays, and played in the school orchestra and sang in its chorus. He was president of the debating league and captain of the debate team. The inscription below his class picture reads: "Well directed energy, with invincible determination, will do anything that can be done in the world."

B2 *THE DUODECIM ANNUAL 1923*

[all within single rules frame] The | Duodecim | Annual | [double-rule, 80 mm.] | [left side] VOL. VI [center] 1923 [right side] NO. 1 | [double-rules, like first, except for ornament below bottom rule] PUBLISHED AT | Austin, Minn. | June 15, 1923

Copyright Page: none present.

Binding: wire-stitched in coated white paper wrapper, 9 3/16 x 10 in. (233 x 254 mm.), folded once vertically to 9 3/16 x 5 in. (233 x 127 mm.); printed in black; front: the only copy examined was wire-stitched in wrapper for the 1922 annual, as follows: '[double-rule, top of which is fancy, 89 mm.] | [left side] Volume V [right side] Number 1 | [rule, 89 mm.] | The | 1922 | Duodecim Annual | [double-rule, 89 mm., below which is an ornament] | PUBLISHED AT | Austin, Minn. | June 15, 1922'; back: contains 'Afterword' signed 'THE EDITORS'.

Contents: "The Man with Green Glasses," an article about the Duodecim Society, signed 'Richard G. Eberhart, 21', on p. 19.

Publication: Published 15 June 1923.

B3 *THE ARTS ANTHOLOGY* 1925

THE ARTS ANTHOLOGY | DARTMOUTH VERSE 1925 | WITH INTRODUCTION | BY ROBERT FROST | [publisher's device in brownish orange] | [remainder in black] PORTLAND MAINE | THE MOSHER PRESS | MDCCCCXXV

Copyright Page: 'COPYRIGHT 1925 BY THE ARTS | *All Rights Reserved*'.

Binding: quarter-bound in white paper (imitation vellum) and grayish blue paper boards, 7 x 4 1/2 in. (178 x 115 mm.); yellowish white laid endpapers; top and bottom edges rough cut, fore-edges untrimmed; spine printed in black and brownish orange; issued in unprinted glassine jacket.

Contents: First book publication of "Searcher" (**C5**), p. 8; and first publication of:

> "Moosilauke Phantasy," p. 9.
> "The Village Daily," p. 10; rept. in *Poetry*, 31 (Nov. 1927), 82-83.
> "And All Shade Fade Away," p. 11.

Publication: Published in June 1925; 500 copies printed.

Colophon: p. 59: 'FIVE HUNDRED COPIES OF THIS BOOK | PRINTED ON VAN GELDER PAPER BY THE | MOSHER PRESS PORTLAND

MAINE FOR | THE ARTS HANOVER NEW HAMPSHIRE | AND THE TYPE DISTRIBUTED IN THE MONTH OF MAY MDCCCCXXV | NO. [arabic numeral supplied in black ink] | [publisher's device].

Note: In his introduction, Robert Frost mentions Eberhart's poem, "The Village Daily," with three others, as getting "up the salt water." "Their realism," Frost remarks, "represents an advance," and they "show acceptance of the fact that the way to better is often through the worse." Eberhart continues to cite Frost's encouraging comments at this early stage in his career and what they meant to him.

B4 *YOUNG PEGASUS* 1926

[all within a double-rules frame, the outer of which is fancy] YOUNG | PEGASUS | PROSE AND VERSE | *Edited by the* | INTERCOLLEGIATE LITERARY | MAGAZINE CONFERENCE | [publisher's device] LINCOLN MAC VEAGH | THE DIAL PRESS | NEW YORK MCMXXVI

Copyright Page: 'COPYRIGHT, 1926 | THE DIAL PRESS, INC.'

Binding and Dust Jacket: quarter-bound in blue cloth and orange and blue decorated paper boards, 7 3/4 x 5 1/2 in. (195 x 138 mm.); spine stamped in gold; top edges trimmed, fore- and bottom edges rough trimmed; thick gray wove endpapers; mottled blue and light blue dust jacket printed in black.

Contents: First book publication of "Nirvana" (C31; later titled "Cover Me Over") on p. 309.

Publication: Published in Sept. 1926 at $2.50.

B5 *CAMBRIDGE POETRY, 1929*

CAMBRIDGE POETRY | 1929 | EDITED BY | CHRISTOPHER SALTMARSHE | JOHN DAVENPORT & BASIL WRIGHT | [publisher's device] | *Published by Leonard & Virginia Woolf at The* | *Hogarth Press, 52 Tavistock Square, London, W.C. 1* | 1929

Copyright Page: 'Printed in Great Britain by | NEILL & CO., LTD., EDINBURGH'.

Binding: gray paper boards measure 7 7/16 x 5 in. (189 x 126 mm.); printed on front and spine in black; all edges trimmed; yellowish white, wove, unwatermarked endpapers.

Contents: First publication of three poems:

"Maze," p. 28: in *RS, PNS, SP51, CP60, SP65, CP76, CP88*; rept. in *Dartmouth Verse 1922-1932* ("The Arts Chapbook No. 1") (Hanover, N.H.: The Arts, 1932), p. 10; *An Anthology of American Poetry*, ed. Alfred Kreymborg, 2d rev. ed. (New York: Tudor Publishing, 1941), p. 630; *The Norton Anthology of Poetry*, ed. Arthur M. Eastman (New York: Norton, 1970), p. 528.
"Nannette," p. 29
"Caravan of Silence," pp. 30-32; in *RS, SP51, CP60, CP76, CP88*.

Publication: Published in March 1929; erratum slip loosely inserted.

B6 *NEW SIGNATURES: POEMS BY SEVERAL HANDS* 1932

NEW SIGNATURES I POEMS BY SEVERAL HANDS I COLLECTED BY I MICHAEL ROBERTS I [publisher's device] I *Published by Leonard & Virginia Woolf at The I Hogarth Press, 52 Tavistock Square, London, W.C. 1* I 1932.

Copyright Page: '*First Published* 1932'.

Binding: blue paper boards measure 7 1/2 x 4 7/8 in (190 x 125 mm.); front and spine stamped in gold; all edges trimmed; yellowish white wove endpapers.

Contents: First book publication of "Request for Offering" (**C52**), p. 64; "Necessity" (**C72**), pp. 58-69; "Fragments" (**C57**), pp. 61-62. The following poems are here first published:

"Cellar," p. 63.
"Cynic Song," p. 65; in *RS*.

Publication: Published 25 Feb. 1932; 600 copies printed. Rept. in March 1932 (750 copies); and rept. photolithographically in Sept. 1934 (1,025 copies), and again in 1935 (1,025 copies).

B7 *POEMS OF TOMORROW: AN ANTHOLOGY*
OF CONTEMPORARY VERSE 1935

POEMS | OF TOMORROW | AN ANTHOLOGY | OF CONTEMPORARY | VERSE | CHOSEN FROM | *THE LISTENER* | *By* | Janet Adam Smith | LONDON | *CHATTO & WINDUS* | 1935

Copyright Page: 'PRINTED IN GREAT BRITAIN | BY R. AND R. CLARK LTD. | ALL RIGHTS RESERVED'.

Binding and Dust Jacket: light blue cloth boards measure 7 7/16 x 4 3/4 in. (189 x 121 mm.); spine stamped in gold; top and fore-edges trimmed, bottom edges rough trimmed; top edges stained light blue; white, wove, unwatermarked endpapers; yellow dust jacket printed in blue.

Contents: First book publication of "The Groundhog" (**C76**), pp. 38-39; 'Dissertation by Wax Light" (**C77**), pp. 40-41; and "1934" (**C78**), pp. 42-43.

Publication: Published in June 1935 at 5s.

B8 *NEW LETTERS IN AMERICA* [1937]

NEW LETTERS | IN AMERICA | EDITOR | HORACE GREGORY | ASSOCIATE EDITOR | ELEANOR CLARK | W • W • NORTON & COMPANY | PUBLISHERS • NEW YORK

Copyright Page: '*First Edition*'.

Binding and Dust Jacket: light tannish gray cloth boards measure 9 3/4 x 5 3/4 in. (223 x 149 mm.); front and spine contain panels stamped in red and lettered in black; all edges trimmed, top edges stained dark reddish pink; yellowish white, wove, unwatermarked endpapers; white dust jacket printed in red and black.

Contents: First publication of three poems:

"Poem in Construction," pp. 74-75; in two numbered parts, I: "I Like a Pump, That Dirty Water Draws"; and II: "Grotesque-handed Engine, Foolfaced, Servitor"; rept. in *Furioso*, 1 (Summer 1939), 14-16.
"Poem" [later titled "I Walked Out to the Graveyard to See the Dead,"] p. 75; as "I Walked Out to the Graveyard to See the Dead" in *SI, SP51,*

CP60, SP65, CP76, CP88; rept. in *Southern Review*, 7 (Spring 1942), 861; *Mid-Century American Poets*, ed. Ciardi (1950), p. 238; *Modern Poetry American and British*, ed. Friar and Brinnin (1951), p. 281; *Perspectives U.S.A.*, no. 10 (Winter 1955), 27; *The American Tradition in Literature*, ed. Bradley et al., rev. ed. (1961), v. 2, p. 1542, and in 3d ed (1967), p. 1623; *Poetry in English*, ed. Taylor and Hall (1963), p. 638, and in 2d ed. (1970); *An Approach to Literature*, ed. Cleanth Brooks et al., 4th ed. (New York: Appleton-Century-Crofts, 1964), p. 380, and in 5th ed. (1975), p. 456; *The Voice That Is Great Within Us*, ed. Hayden Carruth (New York: Bantam, 1970), p. 246; *American Literature: The Makers and the Making*, ed. Cleanth Brooks et al., v. 2 (New York: St. Martin's, 1972), p. 2920, and in shorter ed. (1974), p. 1739.

"The Virgin," pp. 75-76; in *SI, CP60, CP76, CP88*

Publication: Published 9 Sept. 1937 at $2.00; approx. 800 to 900 copies printed.

B9 *NEW DIRECTIONS IN PROSE & POETRY 1937*

NEW DIRECTIONS | IN PROSE & POETRY | 1937 | [publisher's device] | NEW DIRECTIONS | NORFOLK - CONN

Copyright Page: 'COPYRIGHT 1937 BY NEW DIRECTIONS'.

Binding and Dust Jacket: pictorial paper boards prin. in light blue, gray, black and white measure 9 1/4 x 6 1/8 in. (235 x 158 mm.); lettered in black, white, and shades of gray; all edges trimmed, unstained; yellowish white, wove, unwatermarked endpapers; white dust jacket printed on outer side like paper boards.

Contents: First publication of "Three Poems":

"My Desire to Write Poetry," p. 219; in *SI*.
"Grave Piece," pp. 219-21; in *SI, CP60, CP76, CP88*; rept. with RE's explanatory note in *Explicator*, 6 (Feb. 1948), 1-4.
"Song ['I see her in her feeble age']," p. 221; in *SI*.

Publication: Published in Nov. 1937 at $2.50; 1,000 copies printed.

B10 *FROM "THE HUMAN BEING"* [1939]

Offprint

Collation: one leaf folded twice to 10 7/8 x 8 in.(276 x 202 mm.); 8 leaves; [1-8]; top edges uncut.

Contents: p. 1: '[black and white photograph of W.H. Auden, 154 x 84 mm.] | WYSTAN HUGH AUDEN'; pp. 2-3: blank; pp. 4-5: "Ode" by Auden, signed with his pseudonym, "The Feather Merchant"; pp. 6-7: blank; p. 8: "From 'The Human Being'" by RE.

Paper: white, wove, unwatermarked paper; coated smooth; fore- and bottom edges cut, top edges uncut.

Contents: "From 'The Human Being'" (**C104**).

Publication: Unknown number of copies of this offprint from the St. Mark's *Vindex* were prepared in June 1939 for distribution by RE and Auden. It should be noted that this offprint does in fact constitute a separate printing of the poems, although the leaf containing the photograph and poems was printed in an overrun, possibly also for distribution. The overrun copies may be distinguished from the true offprint in that they are folded only once, and all edges are trimmed. The reprint was printed on one side only, whereas the overrun was printed two up.

B11 *NEW DIRECTIONS IN PROSE & POETRY 1939*

NEW DIRECTIONS | IN PROSE & POETRY | 1939 | [publisher's device] | NEW DIRECTIONS • NORFOLK • CONN.

Copyright Page: 'COPYRIGHT 1939 BY NEW DIRECTIONS'; no statement of first edition.

Binding and Dust Jacket: white paper boards printed blue and lettered in red and white, 9 1/4 x 6 33/8 in. (236 x 162 mm.); all edges cut, unstained; yellowish white, wove, unwatermarked endpapers; white dust jacket printed like paper boards.

Contents: First publication of "Foundation," pp. 239-42.

Publication: Published 1 Nov. 1939 at $3.00.

B12 *WE MODERNS* [1939]

[cover title, within irregularly shaped 8-sided box, rev. out in white against a reprod. of Carl Van Vechten's photograph of a painting by Ruth Bower; in black] WE MODERNS I GOTHAM BOOK MART I 1920-1940 I [within panel at base, rev. out in white] The Life of the Party at FINNEGAN'S WAKE in our Garden I on Publication Day I *Painting by Ruth Bower Photograph by Carl Van Vechten*

Copyright Page: none present.

Card Cover: glued in pictorial card cover, 8 x 5 1/2 in. (204 x 140 mm.) also issued in stiff white card cover printed ident. to above but with spiral loose leaf binding.

Contents: RE's brief introductory biographies of W.H. Auden, p. 12, and Frederic Prokosch, p. 56; signed with RE's college pseudonym, 'R.E. Ghormley'.

Publication: Issued as Gotham Book Mart Catalogue 42, 17 Dec. 1939; 3,500 copies printed, of which 500 were issued in loose-leaf binding at $1.00.

B13 *THE LYRIC PSALTER* [1940]

[all within ornamental frame; in semi-Gothic] The I Lyric Psalter I [in roman] THE MODERN READER'S I BOOK OF PSALMS I *Edited by* I HARRY H. MAYER I [publisher's device] LIVERIGHT PUBLISHING CORPORATION I NEW YORK

Copyright Page: 'COPYRIGHT 1940 I BY LIVERIGHT PUBLISHING CORPORATION'.

Binding: blue cloth boards measure 9 1/2 x 6 1/2 in. (242 x 167 mm.); front and spine contain dark blue panels stamped in gold; all edges cut, top edges stained dark pink; dark blue cloth head and tail bands; yellowish white, wove, unwatermarked endpapers; dust jacket not seen.

Contents: First publication of two adaptations of biblical Psalms:

"Psalm 103 ['Bless the Lord O My Soul'] (A Free Paraphrase)," pp. 196-97.
"Psalm 124 ['The Way to Wisdom and Redemption'] (A Modern's Marginalia to This Psalm)," pp. 253-54.

Publication: Published 25 May 1940; 3,000 copies printed.

B14 *FOUR DARTMOUTH POEMS* 1940

Four Dartmouth Poems | [ornament] | *1 9 4 0* [ornament] | WITH A PREFACE BY | *SIDNEY COX* | BAKER LIBRARY PRESS

Copyright Page: 'COPYRIGHT 1940 BY DANIEL OLIVER ASSOCIATES'.

Binding: 3 leaves handsewn in light gray laid paper wrapper, vert. chainlines 28 mm. apart, watermarked '[in script] Georgian'; printed in black, on front: '*Four* | *Dartmouth* | *Poems*'.

Contents: First publication of "Recollection of Childhood," p. 8; in *SI, SP51, CP60, SP65, CP76, CP88*; rept. in *A Reading Apprenticeship: Literature*, ed. Norman A. Brittin (New York: Holt, Rinehart & Winston, 1971), pp. 447-48.

Publication: Probably printed during the summer, 1940; not for sale.

Statement of Limitation: '*One hundred twenty-five copies of this pamphlet,* | *none of which is for sale, have been printed by the* | *Daniel Oliver Associates of Dartmouth College.* | *This is No.* [arabic numeral supplied in black ink]'.

Note: The other poets included are William Bronk, Samuel French Morse, and Reuel Denney.

B15 *AMERICAN SIGNATURES* [1941]

[in red] AMERICAN | SIGNATURES | [remainder in black] A COLLECTION OF MODERN LETTERS | *edited by RAE BEAMISH* | THE BLACK FAUN PRESS | ROCHESTER, NEW YORK PRAIRIE CITY, ILLINOIS

Copyright Page: 'Copyright, 1941, by The Black Faun Press'; no statement of first edition.

Binding and Dust Jacket: dark green cloth boards measure 8 7/8 x 6 in. (225 x 152 mm.); front and spine stamped in gold; all edges cut, unstained; yellowish white, wove endpapers; pale greenish gray dust jacket printed in black and green.

Contents: First publication of RE's poem, "The Cathedral at Palma," p. 69; and first book publiction of "Two Loves" (**C121**), p. 70.

Publication: Published in Nov. 1941.

Statement of Limitation: p. 70, 'AMERICAN SIGNATURES I *has been printed from handset Deepdene type, in an I edition of 250 numbered copies, designed by I Romney Winter I This is number* [arabic numeral supplied in black ink]'.

B16 *VERTICAL* [1941]

[in black; left side, design by Alexander Calder the hgt. of 'VERTICAL' on right side] [in red; right side, vert., from top to bottom] V E R T I C A L I [remainder in black, horiz.] A YEARBOOK FOR ROMANTIC- I MYSTIC ASCENSIONS. I EDITED I EUGENE JOLAS. PUBLISHED BY THE I GOTHAM BOOKMART PRESS • NEW YORK

Copyright Page: 'COPYRIGHT 1941 BY EUGENE JOLAS'.

Binding: regular issue: quarter-bound in black cloth and white paper boards, 9 1/4 x 6 in. (235 x 155 mm.); front contains the title page design by Calder printed in black on paper portion; spine contains a white paper label printed in red; vert., from top to bottom, 'V E R T I C A L'; all edges cut, top edges stained dark reddish pink; yellowish white wove, unwatermarked endpapers; special issue: black cloth boards measure 9 3/8 x 6 in. (240 x 153 mm.); front stamped in gold with Calder design from title page; spine label ident. to regular issue; top edges stained dark reddish pink; clear glassine dust jacket (special issue only) printed in red on inner side of front and back, to the left and right, respectively, of the spine folds, '[vert., from top to bottom] V E R T I C A L'.

Contents: First publication of "The Recapitulation," pp. 33-35; in *BO, CP60, CP76, CP88*; rept. in *Modern Religious Poems: A Contemporary Anthology,* ed. Jacob Trapp (New York: Harper & Row, 1964), pp. 284-285; *The Achievement of Richard Eberhart*, ed. Bernard Engel (Glenview, Ill.: Scott, Foresman, 1968), p. 59.

Publication: Published in Dec. 1941 at $2.75 for the regular issue and $4.50 for the special issue; 500 copies printed, of which 400 constitute the regular issue and 100 the special issue.

Statement of Limitation: regular issue, p. 203, 'OF THIS EDITION, SET IN ELECTRA TYPES | AND PRINTED ON SPECIAL ANTIQUE PAPER | FOUR HUNDRED COPIES HAVE BEEN PRINTED | AT THE WALPOLE PRINTING OFFICE | MOUNT VERNON, NEW YORK'; special issue: p. 203, 'OF THIS EDITION, SET IN ELECTRA TYPES | AND PRINTED ON SPECIAL RAG PAPER | ONE HUNDRED COPIES HAVE BEEN PRINTED | AT THE WALPOLE PRINTING OFFICE | MOUNT VERNON, NEW YORK | [Jolas's autograph in blue ink]'.

B17 *NEW POEMS 1942* [1942]

[within double-rules frame, reversed out in white against a red panel, within a single-rules frame] NEW | POEMS | 1942 | [below panel, in black] An Anthology of | British and | American Verse | *EDITED BY* | Oscar Williams | [below double-rules frame] *PETER PAUPER PRESS • MOUNT VERNON • N.Y*

Copyright Page: 'COPYRIGHT 1942 BY THE PETER PAUPER PRESS'.

Binding and Dust Jacket: regular issue: dark blue cloth boards with orangish red paper labels on front and spine, with lettering in white, measure 8 3/8 x 6 1/4 in. (214 x 160 mm.); all edges cut, top edges stained light red; yellowish white, wove, unwatermarked endpapers; white dust jacket printed in red, blue, and black; special autographed issue: contains four additional leaves with the autographs of the contributors; RE's autograph appears on the third leaf; half-bound in ivory linen and French marbled-paper boards, 9 7/16 x 6 3/8 in. (241 x 160 mm.); green paper spine label printed in ivory; all edges trimmed, top edges gilt; white wove endpapers; glassine jacket; dark green binder's board slipcase.

Contents: First publication of two poems and first book publication of "The Dream" (**C147**), pp. 80-81; "The Largess" is rept. on pp. 84-85. First publication:

"Kafka's America," pp. 80-81.
"Hand-View," pp. 82-84.

Publication: Published 17 April 1942 at $3.00 (regular issue) and $25.00 (special issue). Twenty-six copies of the special issue were for sale, and at least 33 additional copies were presented to the contributors (each containing the recipient's name on the limitation page).

B18 *NEW DIRECTIONS NUMBER SEVEN 1942*

NEW DIRECTIONS | *NUMBER SEVEN* | 1942 | [publisher's device] | PUBLISHED BY NEW DIRECTIONS | NORFOLK • CONNECTICUT

Copyright Page: 'COPYRIGHT 1942 BY NEW DIRECTIONS'; no statement of first edition.

Binding and Dust Jacket: green cloth boards measure 9 1/4 x 6 1/4 in. (235 x 158 mm.); spine contains white paper label printed in green; all edges cut, unstained; yellowish white, wove, unwatermarked endpapers; yellow dust jacket printed in green and black.

Contents: "Poems in Construction," pp. 47-72, some of which are here first published, others of which are reprinted, as follow:

"The Perturbation," a poem in four numbered parts, pp. 47-49; first publication.
"The Inspissation," pp. 49-53; first publication; in three numbered parts.
"Ingathering," pp. 53-56, a poem in six numbered and one titled part; first book publication of pt. I, "I Wrote Helen a Letter But Got No Reply" (**C118**), pp. 53-57; first publication of pt. 2, "Compulsion Is Hid in the Blood: Conflicts," pp. 57-58; first book publication of "Song ['There Is a Place in Stoical Autumn, a Glass']" (**C137**), pp. 58-59; first book publication of pt. III, "And at Lake Geneva, Which Is in Wisconsin" (**C130**), pp. 59-62; first publication of pt. IV, "There Is Something to be Said for Everything," pp. 62-63; first publication of pt. V, "By the Physical Act of Lying By a Stream," pp. 64-67.
"World-View" (**C131**), rept. on pp. 67-72.

Publication: Published 9 Aug. 1942 at $3.50.

B19 *NEW POEMS 1943* [1943]

NEW POEMS | 1943 An Anthology of | British and American Verse | *Edited by* OSCAR WILLIAMS | [rule, 92 mm.] | HOWELL, SOSKIN, PUBLISHERS

Copyright Page: 'COPYRIGHT, 1943, BY OSCAR WILLIAMS'; no statement of first edition.

Binding and Dust Jacket: light gray cloth boards measure 8 3/16 x 5 1/2 in. (208 x 140 mm.); spine lettered in black; all edges cut, unstained; yellowish white, wove unwatermarked endpapers; white dust jacket printed in light olive green and black.

Contents: First publication of "Speech from a Play: Enter the Poet, Alone," pp. 80-83; rept. as "Speech from a Play," in *Kenyon Review*, 6 (Spring 1944), 191. First book publication of "Of Truth: The Protagonist Speaking" (**C144**), pp. 83-84.

Publication: Published 17 Aug. 1943 at $2.75.

B20 *AMERICAN WRITING 1943* [1944]

AMERICAN WRITING | 1943 | *The Anthology and Yearbook of the American* | *Non-Commercial Magazine* | *Edited by* | ALAN SWALLOW | [publisher's device] | Boston | BRUCE HUMPHRIES, INC. | Publishers

Copyright Page: 'Copyright, 1944, by | BRUCE HUMPHRIES, INC.'; no statement of first edition.

Binding and Dust Jacket: light gray cloth boards measure 8 x 5 7/16 in. (202 x 140 mm.); spine lettered in green; all edges cut, top edges stained green; yellowish white, wove, unwatermarked endpapers; white dust jacket printed in bluish green and black.

Contents: First book publication of "Dublin Afternoon" (**C145**), p. 106.

Publication: Published in June 1944 at $2.50.

B21 *NEW POEMS 1944*

['N' and 'P' in script] NEW POEMS 1944 | AN ANTHOLOGY OF AMERICAN AND | BRITISH VERSE, WITH A SELECTION | OF POEMS FROM THE ARMED FORCES | Edited by OSCAR WILLIAMS | [three ornaments] | *New York* | HOWELL, SOSKIN, PUBLISHERS

Copyright Page: 'COPYRIGHT, 1944, BY OSCAR WILLIAMS'; no statement of first edition.

Binding and Dust Jacket: light orangish brown cloth boards measure 7 11/16 x 5 3/8 in. (196 x 136 mm.); spine lettered in black; all edges cut, unstained; yellowish white, wove, unwatermarked endpapers; white dust jacket printed in black, brownish orange, and orange.

Contents: First book publication of "Dam Neck, Virginia" (**C162**), pp. 219-20, and "The Fury of Aerial Bombardment" (**C161**), p. 220.

Publication: Published 15 Aug. 1944 at $3.00.

B22 *AMERICAN WRITING 1944* [1945]

AMERICAN WRITING | 1944 | *The Anthology and Yearbook of the American* | *Non-Commercial Magazine* | *Edited by* | HELEN FERGUSON CAUKIN | and ALAN SWALLOW | [publisher's device] | Boston | BRUCE HUMPHRIES, INC. | Publishers

Copyright Page: 'Copyright, 1945, by | BRUCE HUMPHRIES, INC.'; no statement of first edition.

Binding and Dust Jacket: deep tan cloth boards measure 8 1/16 x 5 9/16 in. (205 x 140 mm.); spine lettered in red; all edges cut, top edges stained red; yellowish white, wove, unwatermarked endpapers; white dust jacket printed in red and blue.

Contents: First book publication of "The Game," (**C153**), p. 175.

Publication: Published in Feb. 1945 at $2.50.

B23 *WAR AND THE POET* 1945

War and the Poet | AN ANTHOLOGY OF POETRY | EXPRESSING MAN'S ATTITUDES TO WAR | FROM | ANCIENT TIMES TO THE PRESENT | *Edited by* | Richard Eberhart | LT. COMDR., U.S.N.R. | *and* | Seldom Rodman | M/SGT., A.U.S. | [ornament] | *New York* | T H E D E V I N - A D A I R C O M P A N Y | 1945

Copyright Page: 'COPYRIGHT 1945 BY THE DEVIN-ADAIR CO.'; no statement of first edition.

Binding and Dust Jacket: gray cloth boards measure 8 7/16 x 5 1/2 in. (215 x 140 mm.); front and spine stamped in gold and red; all edges cut, unstained; yellowish white, wove, unwatermarked endpapers; white dust jacket printed in grayish blue and red.

Contents: Co-edited by RE, with his "Preface: Attitudes to War," pp. v-xv.

Publication: Published in Dec. 1945 at $3.00; 1,000 copies printed.

Note: In one of the compiler's copies of *War and the Poet*, Karl Shapiro has written, "I also worked on this book—in Selden's office at the O.S.S. in Washington, D.C. . . . Selden can give details."

B24 *ACCENT ANTHOLOGY* [1946]

A c c e n t | A N T H O L O G Y | Selections from *Accent*, | A Quarterly of New | Literature, 1940-1945 | *Edited by* | KERKER QUINN *and* | CHARLES SHATTUCK | HARCOURT, BRACE AND COMPANY, NEW YORK

Copyright Page: '*first edition*'.

Binding and Dust Jacket: brown cloth boards measure 8 3/16 x 5 5/8 in. (210 x 145 mm.); spine stamped in black and gold; all edges trimmed, unstained; yellowish white, wove, unwatermarked endpapers; white dust jacket printed in dull brownish orange and black.

Contents: First book publication of "Empson's Poetry" (**C163**), pp. 571-88.

Publication: Published 19 Aug. 1946 at $4.00; 4,000 copies printed.

B25 *A LITTLE TREASURY OF AMERICAN POETRY* 1948

[against a grayish green panel, rev. out in white semi-script] A | Little Treasury | of | American Poetry | [in roman] THE CHIEF POETS | *from colonial times to the present day* | [in black] *Edited with an Introduction by* | *Oscar Williams* | [remainder rev. out in white; ornament] | NEW YORK | CHARLES SCRIBNER'S SONS | 1948

Copyright Page: 'COPYRIGHT, 1948, BY | CHARLES SCRIBNER'S SONS | [...] | A'.

Binding and Dust Jacket: black cloth boards measure 6 3/4 x 4 3/8 in. (180 x 123 mm.); spine stamped in yellow; all edges cut and stained very pale orange; cloth head and tail bands have alternating black and white stripes; yellowish white, wove, unwatermarked endpapers; white dust jacket printed in black and yellow.

Contents: First publication of "On Shooting Particles Beyond the World," pp. 692-93; in rev. ed. (1952), pp. 435-36; and in 3d ed. (1970), pp. 434-35; in *Un, CP60, SP65, CP76, CP88*; rept. in: *American Literature: A Brief Anthology*, ed. Charles S. Bonslog and Alfons L. Korn (Honolulu: Univ. of Hawaii, 1949), p. 141; *F.T. Palgrave's The Golden Treasury of the Best Songs and Lyrical Poems, Centennial Edition*, ed. Oscar Williams (New York: New American Library, 1953), pp. 460-61; *Poems: Wadsworth Handbook and Anthology*, ed. C.F. Main and Peter J. Seng, 2d ed. (Belmont, Ca.: Wadsworth, 1965), pp. 234-35; *The Achievement of Richard Eberhart*, ed. Engel (1968), pp. 35-36; *The Realities of Literature*, ed. Dietrich (1971), pp. 174-75; *Appleseeds and Beercans, Man and Nature in Literature*, ed. C. Michael Wells et al. (Pacific Palisades, Ca.: Goodyear, 1974), pp. 268-69; *The Modern Age*, ed. Leonard Lief and James F. Light, 3d ed. (New York: Holt, Rinehart and Winston, 1976), p. 650: *Tygers of Wrath: Poems of Hate, Anger, and Invective*, ed. X.J. Kennedy (Athens: Univ. of Georgia Press, 1981), pp. 332-33.

The following poems are herein reprinted: "The Groundhog," pp. 686-87; "The Largess," pp. 687-88; "Imagining How It Would Be to Be Dead," pp. 688-89; "At Lake Geneva," pp. 689-91; "The Fury of Aerial Bombardment," p. 693; "Dam Neck, Virginia," pp. 694-95; " Meditation," pp. 695-98.

Publication: Published in June 1948 at $2.50; 10,000 copies printed.

Note: Also issued quarter-bound in gray and blue cloth; spine stamped in red and gold; clear plastic protective jacket; and laid in publisher's box printed in red, blue, and gray.

B26 *NEW DIRECTIONS 10* 1948

[reprod. from calligraphic original; initials 'N', 'D', and 'l' intersect at left margin] NEW | DIRECTIONS | 10 | [in script] in prose and poetry | [in roman] AN ANNUAL EXHIBITION GALLERY OF NEW | AND DIVERGENT TRENDS IN LITERATURE'

Copyright Page: 'COPYRIGHT 1960 BY NEW DIRECTIONS'; no statement of first edition.

Binding and Dust Jacket: tannish gray cloth boards measure 9 1/4 x 6 1/8 in. (236 x 158 mm.); spine lettered in deep red; all edges trimmed; yellowish white, wove, unwatermarked endpapers; yellowish white dust jacket printed in black, with Lee Mullican jacket design on front and part of spine in shades of gray.

Contents: First publication of two poems:

"Sestina," pp. 42-43; in *GP, CP60, SP65, CP76, CP88*; rept. in *Interim*, 4 (Nos. 1-2, 1954), 25-26.
"The Helldiver Gunner," pp. 43-45; rept. as "Johnny Dare: The Helldiver Gunner," in *Chicago Tribune Magazine*, 18 June 1968, p. 12.

Publication: Published 3 Dec. 1948 at $4.50; 3,900 copies printed, of which 3,000 were issued in cloth dust jacket, and 900 in card cover (not seen).

B27 *MID-CENTURY AMERICAN POETS* [1950]

[all within a double-rules frame] E D I T E D *by* J O H N C I A R D I | *Mid-Century | American | Poets* | | [rule, 92 mm.] | *Twayne Publishers, Inc. New York 4*

Copyright Page: '*Copyright* 1950 *by John Ciardi*'; no statement of first edition.

Binding and Dust Jacket: moderate blue cloth boards measure 8 11/16 x 5 1/4 in. (220 x 142 mm.); front and spine stamped in light blue; top and bottom edges cut, fore-edges rough trimmed; yellowish white, wove, unwatermarked endpapers; strong yellowish pink dust jacket printed in blue.

Contents: First publication of RE's essay, "Notes on Poetry," pp. 225-29; and two poems:

"The Cancer Cells," pp. 238-39; in *Un, CP60, SP65, CP76, CP88*; rept. in John Ciardi, *How Does a Poem Mean?* (Boston: Houghton, Mifflin, 1959), p. 806; *An Anthology of Modern Poetry*, ed. John Wain (London: Hutchinson, 1963), pp. 63-64; *Today's Poets*, ed. Walsh (1964), pp. 41-42; *Literature for Understanding*, ed. B. Bernard Cohen (Chicago: Scott, Foresman, 1966), p. 111; *A College Treasury: Fiction, Drama, Poetry*, ed. Paul Jorgensen and Frederick B. Shroyer. 2d ed. (New York: Scribner's, 1967), p. 563; *The Discovery of Poetry*, ed. Thomas E. Sanders (Glenview, Ill.: Scott, Foresman, 1967), pp. 32-33; *The Unity of Literature*, ed. Michael W. Alssid and William Kenney (Reading, Mass.: Addison-Wesley, 1968), p. 276; *A Little Treasury of Modern Poetry*, ed. Williams, 3d ed. (1970), pp. 435-36; *Dartmouth Alumni Magazine*, 69 (May 1977), 42; *The Harper Anthology of Poetry*, ed. John Frederick Nims (New York: Harper & Row, 1981), pp. 615-16; *The Student* (Wake Forest Univ., Winston-Salem, N.C.), Autumn 1982, 39.
"A Man of Sense," pp. 239-43; in *Un*.

The following poems are herein reprinted: "A Legend of Viable Women," pp. 230-33; "For a Lamb," p. 233; "The Groundhog," pp. 234-35; "If I Could Only Live at the Pitch That Is Near Madness," p. 235; "From Four Lakes' Days," p. 236; "The Fury of Aerial Bombardment," p. 237; "I Walked Out to the Graveyard to See the Dead," p. 238; "The Tobacconist of Eighth Street," p. 243.

Publication: Published in April 1950 at $4.00; 2,000 copies printed. A second printing was issued in January 1952 at $4.00, prepared by photo-offset in reduced format: moderate blue cloth boards measure 8 x 5 1/2 in. (203 x 141 mm.); white dust jacket printed in blue.

B28 *NEW DIRECTIONS IN PROSE AND POETRY 12* 1950

[in bold] N [in open-face] 12 | [centered below 'N' and '12'; in gray] D | new directions in prose & poetry

Copyright Page: 'COPYRIGHT 1950 BY NEW DIRECTIONS'.

Binding and Dust Jacket: quarter-bound in black and rust colored cloth boards, 9 1/4 x 6 1/4 in. (235 x 158 mm.); spine lettered in red; all edges cut, unstained; yellowish white, wove, unwatermarked endpapers; white dust jacket printed in orange, black, and gray.

Contents: "Two Poems": first book publication of "Letter I" (**C229**), pp. 105-114; "A Legend of Viable Women" (**C205**) rept. on pp. 114-17.

Publication: Published 15 Dec. 1950 at $5.00; 3,400 copies printed, of which 2,000 were bound; according to publisher's records, "the balance were lost."

B29 *POETRY AWARDS 1951*

[pair of type ornaments] *Poetry Awards* | *1951* | [ornament] | A COMPILATION OF ORIGINAL POETRY | PUBLISHED IN MAGAZINES OF THE | ENGLISH-SPEAKING WORLD | IN 1950 | [publisher's device] | PHILADELPHIA | UNIVERSITY OF PENNSYLVANIA PRESS | 1951

Copyright Page: 'Copyright 1951'; no statement of first edition.

Binding and Dust Jacket: yellowish tan boards measure 8 3/4 x 5 5/8 in. (222 x 144 mm.); spine stamped in deep purple; all edges cut, unstained; yellowish white, wove, unwatermarked endpapers; tan dust jacket printed in deep purple.

Contents: First book publication of "That Final Meeting" (**C245**), p. 25.

Publication: Published in Dec. 1951 at $2.50; 1,500 copies printed.

B30 *NEW WORLD WRITING: SECOND MENTOR SELECTION* [1952]

New | WORLD | WRITING | SECOND MENTOR SELECTION | PUBLISHED BY | [publisher's device] | THE NEW AMERICAN LIBRARY

Copyright Page: '*First issued, November 1952*'.

Binding: perfect bound in white card cover, 7 1/8 x 4 15/16 in. (182 x 110 mm.); all edges cut and stained yellow; printed in blue, orange and black.

Contents: First publication of the following poems:

"Pleasures of the Morning," p. 211; in *Un.*
"Society of Friends," pp. 211-13; in *GP.*

Publication: Published in Nov. 1952 at 50 cents; approx. 150,000 copies printed.

B31 *NEW WORLD WRITING: THIRD MENTOR SELECTION* [1953]

New | WORLD | WRITING | THIRD MENTOR SELECTION | PUBLISHED BY | [publisher's device] | THE NEW AMERICAN LIBRARY

Copyright Page: *'First issued, May, 1953'.*

Binding: perfect bound in white card cover, 7 1/8 x 4 3/16 in. (182 x 107 mm.); all edges cut and stained yellow; printed in brownish gold, black, and grayish green.

Contents: First publication of "The Visionary Farms (Scenes I-XIV)," pp. 63-96. In *CVP* (with concluding Scene XV). "A Note on the Production at the Poets Theatre," May 1952, by Jeanne Tufts and Frank Cassidy, is contained on p. 97.

Publication: Published in May 1953 at 50 cents; 152,215 copies printed.

B32 *NEW POEMS BY AMERICAN POETS* 1953

NEW | POEMS | *By American Poets* | [rule] Edited by ROLFE HUMPHRIES | BALLANTINE BOOKS • NEW YORK 1953

Copyright Page: 'COPYRIGHT, 1953, BY BALLANTINE BOOKS, INC.'

Binding: hardcover issue: grayish green paper boards measure 8 x 5 1/4 in. (213 x 148 mm.); stamped in yellowish orange on front and spine; all edges cut, unstained; yellowish white, wove, unwatermarked endpapers; white dust jacket printed in yellowish orange, grayish blue, and black; card cover issue: perfect bound in card cover like dust jacket of hard cover issue, 7 1/4 x 4 1/4 in. (181 x 109 mm.).

Contents: First book publication of "The Human Being Is a Lonely Creature" (**C295**), p. 53, and "The Horse Chestnut Tree" (**C254**), pp. 55-56. First publication of two poems:

"Sainte Anne de Beaupré," pp. 54-55; in *GP, CP60, CP76, CP88.*
"Ur Burial," p. 55; in *GP, CP60, CP76, CP88.*

Publication: Published 21 Sept. 1953 at $2.00 (hardcover) and 35¢ (card cover); 103,000 copies printed, of which 3,000 were issued in hardcover and 100,000 in card cover.

B33 *THE POCKET BOOK OF MODERN VERSE* [1954]

THE POCKET BOOK OF | m o d e r n v e r s e | [row of 32 bullets] | ENGLISH AND AMERICAN POETRY OF | THE | LAST HUNDRED YEARS FROM | WALT WHITMAN TO DYLAN THOMAS | EDITED BY | o s c a r w i l l i a m s | [publisher's device] | POCKET BOOKS, INC. NEW YORK

Copyright Page: '1st printing [. . .] February, 1954'.

Binding: perfect bound in white card cover, 6 7/16 x 4 3/16 in. (163 x 107 mm.), printed in gold, blue, red, yellow, and black; all edges cut and stained yellow.

Contents: First book publication of "The Noble Man" (**C298**), pp. 460-61. The following poems are herein reprinted: "The Groundhog," pp. 457-58; "The Fury of Aerial Bombardment," pp. 458-59; "Dam Neck, Virginia," p. 459; "The Horse Chestnut Tree," p. 461; "The Soul Longs to Return Whence It Came," p. 462-63.

Publication: Published in April 1954 at 50¢ as Cardinal Giant CG-16.

B34 *HIGHLIGHTS OF MODERN LITERATURE* [1954]

Highlights of | MODERN LITERATURE | *A Permanent Collection of Memorable Essays from* | [in gothic] The New York Times Book Review [end gothic] | *Edited by Francis Brown* | [publisher's device] | A MENTOR BOOK | Published by THE NEW AMERICAN LIBRARY

Copyright Page: 'FIRST PRINTING, MARCH, 1954'.

Binding: perfect bound in card cover, 7 1/8 x 4 1/4 in. (180 x 109 mm.); printed in purplish blue, black, yellow, and deep red; all edges cut.

Contents: First book publication of "Why I Say It in Verse" (C304), pp. 160-62.

Publication: Published in March 1954 at 35¢ as Mentor Books M104.

B35 *NEW WORLD WRITING: FIFTH MENTOR SELECTION* [1954]

New | WORLD | WRITING | FIFTH MENTOR SELECTION | PUBLISHED BY | [publisher's device] | THE NEW AMERICAN LIBRARY

Copyright Page: '*First issued, April, 1954*'.

Binding: perfect bound in white card cover, 7 1/8 x 4 3/16 in. (182 x 107 mm.); printed in purplish blue, yellow, and reddish orange; all edges cut and stained deep pink.

Contents: RE selected the poems included on pp. 73-98 and wrote the notes on the authors.

Publication: Published in April 1954 at 50¢ .

B36 *CONTEMPORARY POETRY* [1954]

[circle of red, hollow 5-pointed stars] | [remainder in black; in open-face type breaking circle of stars on right side] Contemporary | Poetry | [below circle] *EDITED BY MARY OWINGS MILLER* | [rule, 89 mm.] | *Volume Fourteen … Nineteen Fifty-Four* | *Published by Contemporary Poetry* | *Baltimore, Maryland*

Copyright Page: '*Copyright, Mary Owings Miller, 1954*'; no statement of first edition.

Binding and Dust Jacket: light green cloth boards measure 8 3/4 x 5 3/4 in. (223 x 147 mm.); front and spine stamped in gold; top and bottom edges cut, fore-edges untrimmed; yellowish white, wove, unwatermarked endpapers; white dust jacket printed in red, with protective glassine wrapper around dust   jacket.

Contents: First publication of two poems:

"Analogue of Unity in Multeity," pp. 11-12; in *GP, CP60, SP65, CP76, CP88*; rept. in *The Norton Anthology of Poetry*, ed. Eastman (1973), pp. 665-66.
"The Hand and the Shadow," p. 13: in *GP, CP60, CP76, CP88*.

Publication: Published in Oct. 1954 at $2.50; 500 copies printed.

Colophon: p. 51, 'COLOPHON I This book has been designed, set in Fairfield type I and printed by the J.H. Furst Company, I Baltimore, Maryland. The paper is I Linweave Laid Deckle Edge.'

B37 *WALT WHITMAN: A CENTENNIAL CELEBRATION* [1954]

[rev. out in white against a solid black panel, 39 x 106 mm.; in script] *Walt Whitman* I [within a single-rules frame] A CENTENNIAL CELEBRATION I [below black panel; in black] THE BELOIT POETRY JOURNAL I Chapbook Number Three

Copyright Page: '. . . Copyright, 1954, by The Beloit Poetry Journal.'

Binding: wire-stitched in white paper card cover, 8 1/2 x 4 7/8 in. (212 x 125 mm.); printed in black and light olive green; all edges cut.

Contents: First publication of "Centennial for Whitman (Amimetobion, not Synapothanumenon)," pp. 7-10 (later titled "Centennial for Whitman"), pp. 7-10; in *GP, CP60, CP76, CP88*; rept. in *London Magazine*, 2 (Oct. 1955), 37-40; *West Hills Review*, 1 (Fall 1979), 16-19.

Publication: Published in late Sept. or early Oct. 1954 at 75 cents.

B38 *READING MODERN POETRY* [1955]

[two-page title; left] PAUL ENGLE, Professor of English, Director of Writers' Workshop, [right] State University of Iowa READING I [left] WARREN CARRIER, Assistant Professor of English, Bard College [right] MODERN I [left] SCOTT, FORESMAN AND COMPANY Chicago, Atlanta, Dallas [right] New York, San Francisco POETRY

Copyright Page: 'Copyright, 1955 by Scott, Foresman and Company'; no statement of first edition.

Binding: light bluish green paper boards measure 7 3/4 x 5 5/16 in. (196 x 135 mm.); both sides and spine contain design of regular pattern of rows of parallel dots, rev. out in white; printed in red; all edges cut, untrimmed, unstained; yellowish white, wove, unwatermarked endpapers.

Contents: First book publication of RE's prose introduction, "Eberhart's Grave Piece" (**C194**), pp. 273-74; the poem is rept. on pp. 271-72.

Publication: Published 3 Jan. 1955 at $2.50.

B39 *THE NEW POCKET ANTHOLOGY OF AMERICAN VERSE* [1955]

[ornamental rule] The *New* POCKET ANTHOLOGY OF | American VERSE | *from Colonial Days to the Present* | *Edited by* | OSCAR WILLIAMS | [device] | [ornamental rule] | THE POCKET LIBRARY

Copyright Page: 'POCKET LIBRARY edition published August, 1955 | 1st printing [. . .] June, 1955'.

Binding: perfect bound in white card cover, 6 3/8 x 4 1/4 in. (173 x 115 mm.); printed in black, red, and blue, and contains photographs of some of the poets included; all edges cut and stained yellow.

Contents: First publication of "The Advantage of the Outside," pp. 168-69; in *GP*. First book publication of "On a Squirrel Crossing the Road in Autumn, in New England," p. 169.

Publication: Published in Aug. 1955 at 50¢ ; 6,000 copies printed.

B40 *DISCOVERY NO. 6* [1955]

[two-page title; left] editor: **vance bourjaily** | associate : robert kotlowitz | managing editor : anne bernays kaplan | assisting : arnold dolin | : suzanne sundheim | poetry editor : robert pack | **pocket books, inc., new york** [bold vert. rule, 16 mm.; right of rule] a | cardinal | edition | [right side] **discovery** [bold vert. rule, 23 mm.] **no. 6** | [double column listing 20 contributors]

Copyright Page: 'Cardinal edition published September, 1955 | 1st printing ....July, 1955'.

Binding: perfect bound in white card cover, 6 3/8 x 4 3/16 in. (162 x 107 mm.); printed in red, purple, yellow, blue and black; all edges cut and stained yellow.

Contents: First publication of "A Dialogue" (later titled "Preamble I"), pp. 77-86; in *CVP* as "Preamble I."

Publication: Published in Sept. 1955 at 35¢ as Cardinal Editions C-185.

B41 *TWENTIETH CENTURY AUTHORS: FIRST SUPPLEMENT* [1955]

TWENTIETH CENTURY | AUTHORS | FIRST SUPPLEMENT | A Biographical Dictionary of Modern Literature | *Edited by Stanley J. Kunitz* | *Assistant Editor* | VINETA COLBY | [publisher's device] | NEW YORK | THE H. W. WILSON COMPANY | NINETEEN HUNDRED FIFTY-FIVE

Copyright Page: 'Copyright 1955 | by the H. W. Wilson Company'; no statement of first edition.

Binding: black cloth boards measure 10 1/2 x 7 1/4 in. (260 x 185 mm.); spine stamped in gold; all edges trimmed, unstained; cloth head and tail bands have alternating gray and white stripes; yellowish white, wove, unwatermarked endpapers.

Contents: First publication of RE's untitled autobiographical and artistic statement on pp. 296-98.

Publication: Published in Nov. 1955 at $8.00.

B42 *FIFTEEN MODERN AMERICAN POETS* [1956]

FIFTEEN | MODERN AMERICAN POETS | *Edited by* GEORGE P. ELLIOTT | *New York* | *Toronto* | RINEHART & COMPANY, INC.

Copyright Page: '[. . .] © 1956 by George P. Elliott'.

Binding: perfect bound in white card cover, 7 5/16 x 4 7/8 in. (196 x 135 mm.); front and spine printed in black; all edges cut, unstained.

Contents: First book publication of "Idols of Imagination" (**C309**), p. 36; "Cold Fall" (**C335**), p. 37; and "The Day-Bed" (**C327**), pp. 38-39. The following poems are herein reprinted: "This Fevers Me," p. 21; "For a Lamb," pp. 21-22; "In a Hard Intellectual Light," pp. 22-23; "Two Loves," p. 23; "When Golden Flies Upon My Carcass Come," pp. 23-24; "If I Could Only Live at the Pitch That Is Near Madness," p. 24; "Rumination," pp. 24-25; "Cover Me Over," p. 25; "A Meditation," pp. 25-29; "Imagining How It Would Be to Be Dead," p. 29; "New Hampshire, February," p. 30; "Go to the Shine That's On a Tree," pp. 30-31; "What If Remembrance?," p. 31; "Reality! Reality! What Is It?," pp. 31-33; "The Horse Chestnut Tree," pp. 33-34; "Seals, Terns, Time," p. 34; "Forms of the Human," p. 35; "The Human Being Is a Lonely Creature," pp. 35-36; and "Sestina," pp. 37-38.

Publication: Published in April 1956 as Rinehart Edition 79.

B43 *RIVERSIDE POETRY 2* [1956]

Riverside | Poetry 2 | 48 New Poems by 27 Poets | Selected by | MARK VAN DOREN | MARIANNE MOORE | RICHARD EBERHART | With an Introduction by | STANLEY R. HOPPER | TWAYNE PUBLISHERS, NEW YORK

Copyright Page: 'Copyright 1956 by Twayne Publishers, Inc.'; no statement of first edition.

Binding and Dust Jacket: black cloth boards measure 8 3/4 x 5 11/16 in. (223 x 145 mm.); front and spine stamped in silver; all edges cut, unstained; yellowish white, wove, unwatermarked endpapers; yellow dust jacket lettered in white.

Contents: RE served as co-editor.

Publication: Published 10 July 1956 at $2.75.

B44 *A FRIENDLY VISIT: POEMS FOR ROBERT FROST* [1957]

A FRIENDLY VISIT | poems for Robert Frost | Illustrated by John McNee | [drawing of 3 apples] | [6 lines prin. in ital, statement by Marianne Moore] | BELOIT POETRY JOURNAL | CHAPBOOK NUMBER FIVE

Copyright Page: verso of front of card cover, 'Coypright [*sic*], 1957, by The Beloit I Poetry Journal'; no statement of first edition.

Binding: card cover issue: wire-stitched in thick, white, wove card cover, 8 3/8 x 10 1/8 in. (212 x 258 mm.), folded once vertically to 8 3/8 x 5 1/16 in. (212 x 129 mm.); lettered in black, illus. by McNee in grayish pink; all edges cut, unstained; hardcover issue: putty-colored cloth boards stamped in gold on spine, '[vert., from top to bottom] A FRIENDLY VISIT: poems for Robert Frost'; yellowish white, wove, unwatermarked endpapers.

Contents: First publication of a "Memoir," pp. 18-19.

Publication: Published in June or July 1957 at 75¢ for the card cover issue; the hardcover issue was not for sale.

B45 *NEW POEMS BY AMERICAN POETS #2* 1957

N E W I P O E M S I BY AMERICAN POETS I No. 2 I *edited by Rolfe Humphries* I Ballantine Books • New York • 1957 I [rule, 89 mm.]

Copyright Page: '©, 1957, by Ballantine Books, Inc.' no statement of first edition.

Binding: hardcover issue: yellowish gray cloth boards measure 8 x 5 1/4 in. (209 x 142 mm.); spine stamped in deep orange; top and bottom edges cut, fore-edges rough trimmed; yellowish white, wove, unwatermarked end-papers; white dust jacket printed in deep yellow, orangish red, and black; card cover issue: perfect bound in white card cover, 7 1/8 x 4 1/4 in. (181 x 109 mm.); printed in red, light blue, and black; all edges stained pale orange.

Contents: First publication of three poems:

"A Stone," p. 46.
"In the Garden," p. 46: in *CP60, CP76, CP88*.
"The Lost Children," p. 47; in *CP60, CP76, CP88*; rept. in *The Cry of Rachel: An Anthology of Elegies on Children*, ed. Sister Mary Immaculate (New York: Random House, 1966), p. 115; *The Achievement of Richard Eberhart*, ed. Engel (1968), p. 71.

Publication: Published 16 Sept. 1957 at $3.00 (hardcover issue) and 35¢ (card cover issue); 66,356 copies printed, of which 3,136 were issued in hard-cover and 63,220 in card cover.

B46 *BEST POEMS OF 1956* 1957

BEST POEMS | of 1956 | BORESTONE MOUNTAIN | POETRY AWARDS | 1957 | *A Compilation of Original Poetry | published in | Magazines of the English-speaking World | in 1956 | Ninth Annual Issue* | [publisher's device] | STANFORD UNIVERSITY PRESS • STANFORD, CALIFORNIA | 1957

Copyright Page: '© 1957 by Robert Thomas Moore, Trustee'; no statement of first edition.

Binding and Dust Jacket: medium brown cloth boards measure 8 3/4 x 5 5/8 in. (223 x 145 mm.); spine stamped in dark brown; all edges cut, unstained; yellowish white, wove, unwatermarked endpapers; white dust jacket printed in green and light grayish green.

Contents: First book appearance of "Thrush Song at Dawn" (**C361**), p. 31.

Publication: Published 17 Oct. at $3.50; 1,000 copies printed.

B47 *NEW POEMS 1957* 1957

N e w P o e m s | [swelled rule] [within a fancy oval] 1957 [swelled rule] | *Edited by* | KATHLEEN NOTT | C. DAY LEWIS | THOMAS BLACKBURN | [publisher's device] | *London* | MICHAEL JOSEPH

Copyright Page: First published by | MICHAEL JOSEPH LTD | [. . .] | 1957'.

Binding and Dust Jacket: quarter-bound in yellow cloth and white decorated paper printed in black; all edges cut, unstained; yellowish white, wove, unwatermarked endpapers; light blue dust jacket printed in dark blue.

Contents: First book publication of "Attitudes" (**C359**), p. 41; and first publication of "Lucubration," pp. 41-42; in *CP60, CP76, CP88*.

Publication: Published 21 Oct. 1957 at 15s; 2,600 copies printed.

B48 *THIRTEEN DARTMOUTH POEMS* 1958

Thirteen Dartmouth Poems | SELECTED BY | RICHARD EBERHART | *The Charles Butcher Fund* | HANOVER N.H. | *1958*

Copyright Page: '© COPYRIGHT 1958 BY RICHARD EBERHART'; no statement of first edition.

Binding: sewn with white cord in thick, yellowish white card cover and wrapper, 7 9/16 x 5 1/2 in. (192 x 141 mm.); gray, wove paper wrapper watermarked 'DELLA ROBBIA'; bottom edges deckled; printed in black on front.

Contents: Foreword by RE, pp. 8-9; RE selected the poems for inclusion.

Publication: Published in June 1958; 150 copies printed; price unknown.

Statement of Limitation: p. 26, 'ONE HUNDRED FIFTY COPIES PRINTED | AT THE STINEHOUR PRESS IN MAY 1959 | COVER AND BINDING | BY WILLIAM DICKSON AND ERNEST HOLM | THIS IS COPY | [arabic numeral supplied in black ink on black printed rule]'.

B49 *WE BELIEVE IN PRAYER* [1958]

[Greek cross formed by thin vert. and horiz. rules, the former of which is broken by 'W' of WE] WE BELIEVE IN PRAYER | *A Compilation of Personal Statements by American and | World Leaders About the Value and Efficacy of Prayer | by* | LAWRENCE M. BRINGS | [publisher's device] | *Publishers* | T.S DENISON & COMPANY | Minneapolis

Copyright Page: 'Copyright ©, 1958 by | T.S. DENISON & COMPANY'; no statement of first edition.

Binding: light grayish tan cloth boards measure 8 5/8 x 5 11/16 in. (220 x 145 mm.); front stamped in gold, spine stamped in red and gold; all edges cut, unstained; cloth head and tail bands have alternating tan and red stripes; white, wove endpapers; dust jacket not seen.

Contents: First publication of a brief essay, "Prayer Is Intensely Individual," pp. 178-79.

Publication: Published in Dec. 1958 at $5.00.

B50 *ANTHOLOGY OF MAGAZINE VERSE FOR 1958* 1959

Anthology of Magazine Verse I For 1958 I Edited by I William Stanley Braithwaite I and Anthology of Poems I From the Seventeen Previously Published I Braithwaite Anthologies I Edited by Margaret Haley Carpenter I The Schulte Publishing Company I New York City I 1959

Copyright Page: 'COPYRIGHT © 1959'; no statement of first edition.

Binding and Dust Jacket: quarter-bound in brown cloth and yellowish brown paper boards, 8 1/2 x 5 3/4 in. (217 x 145 mm.); front and spine contain paper and labels printed in black; all edges cut, unstained; yellowish white, wove, unwatermarked endpapers; white dust jacket printed in dark and light blue.

Contents: First book publication of "The Garden God" (**C405**), pp. 56-57; "Fortune's Mist" (**C412**), pp. 58-59; "To Bill Williams" (**C253**), p. 59; "Half-Bent Man" (**C413**), p. 60; "The Clam Diggers and Diggers of Sea Worms" (**C415**), pp. 61-62; "A Ship Burning and a Comet All in One Day" (**C417**), pp. 62-63.

Publication: Published 23 April 1959 at $5.95.

B51 *THE GUINNESS BOOK OF POETRY 1957/58* 1959

THE GUINNESS | BOOK OF POETRY | 1957/58 | [publisher's device] *| PUTNAM | 42 GREAT RUSSELL STREET | LONDON MCMLIX*

Copyright Page: ' © *1959*'; no statement of first edition.

Binding and Dust Jacket: medium blue cloth boards measure 8 11/16 x 5 3/4 in. (222 x 146 mm.); spine stamped in gold; all edges cut, top edges stained grayish blue; yellowish white, wove, unwatermarked endpapers; white dust jacket printed in black and medium grayish blue.

Contents: First book publication of "Tree Swallows" (**C411**), pp. 60-62.

Publication: Published 4 May 1959 at 10s 6d; 3,000 copies printed.

B52 *THE CHICAGO REVIEW ANTHOLOGY* [1959]

THE I CHICAGO I REVIEW I ANTHOLOGY I EDITED BY DAVID RAY I
THE [publisher's device] UNIVERSITY OF CHICAGO PRESS

Copyright Page: '*Copyright 1947, 1948, 1949, 1950, 1951, 1952, 1953,* I
1954, 1955, 1956, 1957, 1958. © *1959 by The Univer-* I *sity of Chicago.*
Published 1959.' No statement of first edition.

Binding and Dust Jacket: dark blue cloth boards measure 9 1/2 x 6 1/4 in.
(241 x 160 mm.); all edges cut, top edges stained gray; yellowish white,
wove, unwatermarked endpapers; white dust jacket printed in black, medium
blue, pale gray.

Contents: First book publication of "Yonder" (**C317**), pp. 184-85, and "Some
Men Have It Early" (**C316**), p. 185.

Publication: Published in June 1959 at $5.00.

B53 *THIRTY DARTMOUTH POEMS* 1959

THIRTY I DARTMOUTH POEMS I SELECTED BY I RICHARD
EBERHART I THE CHARLES BUTCHER FUND I HANOVER • NEW
HAMPSHIRE I 1959

Copyright Page: 'Copyright, 1959, by Richard Eberhart'; no statement of
first edition.

Binding: handsewn with white cord in thick yellowish white card cover and
wrapper, 8 15/16 x 6 1/4 in. (226 x 157 mm.); light gray or tan (no priority)
laid paper wrapper, bottom edges deckled; printed in black on front; cover
drawing by James A. Herbert.

Contents: Foreword by RE, p. 5; RE also made the selection of poems
included.

Publication: Published in June 1959; 150 copies printed; price unknown.

Statement of Limitation: p. 40, 'One hundred fifty copies printed I at the
Stinehour Press in May 1959 I of which this copy is I *No.* [arabic numeral
supplied in black ink]'.

B54 *YOUR AASA IN 1958-59* 1959

Your AASA I in 1958-59 I Offical Report, American Association of I School Administrators, for the Year 1958 I Including a Record of the Annual Meeting and I Work Conference on "education and the Creative I Arts," held at Atlantic City, February 14-18, 1959

Copyright Page: 'COPYRIGHT 1959 BY THE I AMERICAN ASSOCIATION OF SCHOOOL ADMINISTRATORS'; no statement of first edition.

Binding: perfect bound in light green card cover, 9 x 6 in. (228 x 152 mm.); front and spine lettered in dark green.

Contents: First publication of an essay, "His Own Poetry," pp. 162-76. The following poems are rept. in the essay: "For a Lamb," "Now Is the Air Made of Chiming Balls," "If I Could Only Live at the Pitch That Is Near Madness," "New Hampshire, February," "The Cancer Cells," "Seals, Terns, Time," "The Horse Chestnut Tree," "Cousin Florence," "Sea-Hawk," "Salem," "Nothing But Change."

Publication: Published in July 1959 at $3.00.

B55 *NEW POEMS 1960*

[ornament] NEW POEMS I 1960 I [ornament] *Edited by* I ANTHONY CRONIN I JON SILKIN I TERENCE TILLER I *With a Preface by* I ALAN PRYCE-JONES I HUTCHINSON OF LONDON

Copyright Page: '*First published 1960*'.

Binding and Dust Jacket: quarter-bound in blue paper and decorated paper (in gray, black, white, and yellow) boards, 8 1/16 x 5 1/2 in.; spine stamped in gold and white; all edges cut, unstained; yellowish white, wove, unwatermarked endpapers; white dust jacket printed in yellow, black, and gray.

Contents: First book publication of "Ospreys in Cry" (C399), p. 49.

Publication: Published in March 1960 at 16s.

B56 *THE GUINNESS BOOK OF POETRY 1958/59* 1960

THE GUINNESS | BOOK OF POETRY | 1958/59 | [publisher's device] | PUTNAM | 42 GREAT RUSSELL STREET | LONDON

Copyright Page: ' © *1960*'; no statement of first edition.

Binding and Dust Jacket: medium blue cloth boards measure 8 3/4 x 5 3/4 in. (222 x 148 mm); spine stamped in gold; all edges cut, top edges stained medium blue; yellowish white, wove, unwatermarked endpapers; white dust jacket printed in orange and black.

Contents: Presumed first publication of "Old Tom," pp. 53-54; in *Qu, CP76, CP88*. See *Note*.

Publication: Published 11 April 1960 at 10s 6d; 3,000 copies printed.

Note: The acknowledgements indicate that "Old Tom" first appeared in the *Observer* and *Author*, but no periodical appearance could be located. RE's publication log indicates that he submitted the poem to the *Observer*, but it does not seem to have been published there.

B57 *WRITING POETRY* [1960]

Writing Poetry | [ornament] | By JOHN HOLMES | *Boston* | THE WRITER, INC. | *Publishers*

Copyright Page: 'COPYRIGHT ©1960, BY JOHN HOLMES'.

Binding: tan cloth boards measure 8 1/2 x 5 3/4 in. (215 x 149 mm.); spine stamped in blue; all edges cut, unstained; cloth head and tail bands have alternating blue and white stripes; yellowish white, wove, unwatermarked endpapers.

Contents: First publication of "Why I Say It In Verse" pp. 87-90.

Publication: Published 15 June 1960 at $5.00; reprinted in 1966, with appropriate notice on copyright page.

B58 *DYLAN THOMAS: THE LEGEND AND THE POET* [1960]

Dylan Thomas: | The Legend and the Poet | A COLLECTION OF BIOGRAPHICAL | AND CRITICAL ESSAYS | EDITED BY E.W. TEDLOCK | [publisher's device] | HEINEMAN | LONDON MELBOURNE TORONTO

Copyright Page: 'First published 1960'.

Binding and Dust Jacket: brown paper (imitation bead-cloth) boards measure 8 11/16 x 5 5/8 in. (221 x 145 mm.); spine stamped in silver; thick, yellowish white, wove, unwatermarked endpapers; light gray dust jacket printed in black and red.

Contents: First book publication (here untitled) of "Some Memories of Dylan Thomas" (**C323**), pp. 55-57.

Publication: Published in Sept. 1960 at 25s.

B59 *THE GUINNESS BOOK OF POETRY 1959/60* [1961]

THE GUINNESS | BOOK OF POETRY | 1959/60 | [publisher's device] | *PUTNAM | 42 GREAT RUSSELL STREET | LONDON*

Copyright Page: '© *1961*'; no statement of first edition.

Binding and Dust Jacket: medium blue cloth boards measure 8 3/4 x 5 5/8 in. (222 x 144 mm.); spine stamped in gold; all edges cut, top edges stained medium blue; yellowish white, wove, unwatermarked endpapers; white dust jacket printed in deep red, black, and pink.

Contents: First book publication of "Equivalence of Gnats and Mice" (**C442**), p. 55.

Publication: Published 8 May 1961 at 10s 6d; 3,000 copies printed.

B60 *THE MOMENT OF POETRY* [1962]

The Moment | of | Poetry | EDITED BY | *Don Cameron Allen* | THE JOHNS HOPKINS PRESS: BALTIMORE

Copyright Page: '© 1962, The Johns Hopkins Press, Baltimore 18, Maryland'; no statement of first edition.

Binding and Dust Jacket: grayish blue cloth boards measure 8 7/16 x 5 3/4 in. (215 x 145 mm.); front and spine stamped in silver; all edges cut, unstained; cloth head and tail bands have alternating grayish blue and yellow stripes; yellowish white, wove, unwatermarked endpapers; white dust jacket printed in black, grayish blue, and blue.

Contents: First publication of RE's essay, "Will and Psyche in Poetry," pp. 48-72. In *OPP*; rept. in *A Celebration of Poets*, ed. Don Cameron Allen (Baltimore: Johns Hopkins, 1967), pp. 152-76; *n.b.*: this volume, issued as Johns Hopkins Paperbacks JH-34, contains the earlier collections, *Four Poets on Poetry* (1959) and *The Moment of Poetry*.

Publication: Published in April 1962 at $3.50; 3,112 copies printed.

B61 *THE WIND AND THE RAIN* [1962]

THE WIND | AND | THE RAIN | AN EASTER BOOK FOR 1962 | *Edited by* | NEVILLE BRAYBROOKE | LONDON | *Secker & Warburg*

Copyright Page: 'First published in England 1962 by | Martin Secker & Warburg Limited'.

Binding and Dust Jacket: reddish brown cloth boards measure 8 3/4 x 5 11/16 in. (221 x 146 mm.); spine stamped in silver; all edges cut, unstained; yellowish white, white, unwatermarked endpapers; white pictorial dust jacket printed in green, grayish green, and black.

Contents: First publication of "An Evaluation Under a Pine Tree, Lying on Pine Needles," pp. 268-69; in *Qu, CP76, CP88*.

Publication: Published 2 April 1962 at 25s.

B62 *FORTY DARTMOUTH POEMS* 1962

FORTY | DARTMOUTH | POEMS | *Selected, and with an* | *introduction, by* | RICHARD EBERHART | HANOVER | *Dartmouth Publications* | 1962

Copyright Page: 'COPYRIGHT • 1962 • BY TRUSTEES OF DARTMOUTH COLLEGE'; no statement of first edition.

Binding: handsewn with white cord in thick yellowish white laid paper card cover, 9 x 6 in. (230 x 152 mm.); glued in grayish green, wove paper wrapper, watermarked 'USA'; printed in black and red on front; woodcut by Frank Miya; all edges cut.

Contents: Introduction by RE, p. 5; RE also selected the poems for inclusion.

Publication: Published in May or June 1962; 300 copies printed.

Statement of Limitation: p. 52, '300 copies | printed in May 1962 | at The Stinehour Press | Lunenburg, Vermont | cover woodcut by | Frank Miya'.

B63 *MODERN AMERICAN POETRY:*
NEW AND ENLARGED EDITION [1962]

[medallion picturing two Pegasuses] NEW AND ENLARGED EDITION | *Modern American Poetry* | EDITED BY *Louis Untermeyer* | [publisher's device] | HARCOURT, BRACE & WORLD, INC. | NEW YORK • BURLINGAME

Copyright Page: '© 1962, BY HARCOURT, BRACE & WORLD, INC.'; no statement of first edition.

Binding and Dust Jacket: strong red cloth boards measure 9 1/4 x 6 9/16 in. (235 x 167 mm.); front stamped in gold and white; white cloth head and tail bands; yellowish white, wove, unwatermarked endpapers; white dust jacket printed in light blue, black, and gold.

Contents: First book publication of "A New England Bachelor" (**C451**), pp. 580-81; "Rainscapes, Hydrangeas, Roses and Singing Birds" (**C457**), p. 581. The following poems are herein reprinted: "The Horse Chestnut Tree," pp. 578-79; "The Groundhog," pp. 579-580; "Seals, Terns, Time," p. 580.

Publication: Published 8 Aug. 1962 at $8.25.

B64 *POET'S CHOICE* 1962

POET'S | CHOICE | [ornamental rule] | EDITED BY | Paul Engle and Joseph Langland | [publisher's device] | THE DIAL PRESS NEW YORK 1962

Copyright Page: 'Copyright © 1962 by Paul Engle and Joseph Langland'; no statement of first edition.

Binding and Dust Jacket: deep red cloth boards measure 9 3/8 x 6 3/8 in. (237 x 160 mm.); spine stamped in gold; top edges trimmed, fore- and bottom edges rough trimmed; dark reddish orange, wove endpapers; cream-colored dust jacket printed in orange, gold, and black.

Contents: First publication of RE's commentary on his poem, "On a Squirrel Crossing the Road in Autumn, in New England," p. 61; the poem is rept. on p. 60.

Publication: Published 29 Oct. 1962 at $6.00 (after 31 Dec. 1962, $6.75). Issued in card cover like dust jacket of **B64** on 22 April 1963 at $1.45.

Note: Rept. in 1966 by Dell Publishing as Delta Paperbook 6982 at $1.95; also in 1966 by Time, Inc.

B65 *PAUL SAMPLE RETROSPECTIVE* 1963

[in black] HOPKINS CENTER | THE JAFFE-FRIEDE GALLERY | [in grayish blue] PAUL | SAMPLE [in black] RETROSPECTIVE | DARTMOUTH COLLEGE | JUNE 1963 • HANOVER, NEW HAMPSHIRE

Copyright Page: none present.

Binding: wire-stitched grayish blue card cover, 8 15/16 x 6 in. (227 x 152 mm.); outer side contains black, white, and gray reprod. of item no. 22 from exhibition; inner side unlettered; all edges cut.

Contents: Foreword by RE, p. 3.

Publication: Printed for distribution at Paul Sample exhibition, June 1963; 1,000 copies printed; not for sale.

B66 *PROGRESSIONS* 1963

[all within a single-rules frame] PROGRESSIONS | *and other* | POEMS | *by* | ALBERT COOK | *artist* | CAROLYN HUFF KINSEY | [publisher's device] | THE UNIVERSITY OF ARIZONA PRESS | TUCSON 1963

Copyright Page: 'Copyright © 1963'; no statement of first edition.

Binding and Dust Jacket: light grayish blue cloth boads measure 9 1/4 x 6 5/16 in. (236 x 160 mm.); spine printed in blue; all edges trimmed; cloth head and tail bands have alternating blue and white stripes; yellowish white, wove, un-watermarked endpapers; light blue laid paper dust jacket printed in strong grayish blue.

Contents: Introduction by RE, pp. x-xi.

Publication: Published in July 1963 at $4.50 (price later raised to $5.50); 500 copies printed.

Colophon: p. 129, 'The type in this volume is Fairfield, chosen for its relia-bility and | beauty. It was designed in 1940 by artist-designer Rudolph Ruzicka. | The composition was performed by Morneau Typographers as di- | rected by Douglas Peck. Tyler Printing Company reproduced | the book by offset lithography on Warren's University Eggshell. The | binding was done by Arizona Trade Bindery in Joanna parchment, | sky-blue linen.'

B67 *THIRTY FIVE DARTMOUTH POEMS* 1963

THIRTY FIVE | DARTMOUTH | POEMS | *Selected, and with an* | *introduc-tion, by* | RICHARD EBERHART | HANOVER | *Dartmouth Publications* | 1963

Copyright Page: 'COPYRIGHT • 1963 • BY THE TRUSTEES OF DARTMOUTH COLLEGE'.

Binding: handsewn with white cord in tan, laid card cover, 9 x 6 1/16 in. (228 x 155 mm.); glued in grayish green, wove paper wrapper; printed in black on front; all edges trimmed; front contains woodcut by Robert Evans.

Contents: First publication of a verse introduction by RE, p. 5; RE also se-lected the poems for inclusion.

Publication: Published in Oct. 1963 at $2.00; 200 copies printed.

Statement of Limitation: p. 46, '200 copies I printed in September 1963 I at the Stinehour Press I Lunenburg, Vermont I cover woodcut by I Robert Evans'.

B68 *CEA CHAP BOOK* [1963]

[cover title; in semi-gothic] C E A Chap Book I [woodcut the height of next 4 lines; remainder in roman] WHAT TO SAY I ABOUT I A POEM I By W. K. Wimsatt, Jr. I *with* I [list of 8 contributors] I *in a summer symposium*

Copyright Page: 'Copyright © 1963 by the College English Association, Inc.'; no statement of first edition.

Binding: wire-stitched in laid paper wrapper, watermarked '[in script] Hamilton I Kilmory'; printed in black on front; all edges cut.

Contents: First publication of RE's essay, "The Fine Reaches of Enthusiasm," pp. 23-25.

Publication: Published in Dec. 1963 at 75¢ , as a supplement to *The CEA Critic,* 26 (Dec. 1963).

B69 *THE NEW ORLANDO POETRY ANTHOLOGY* [1963]

[in open-face] The I NEW ORLANDO I Poetry Anthology I [in roman] GREENWICH VILLAGE I [open-face] Volume II I [remainder in roman] Editors I ANCA VRBOVSKA I ALFRED DORN I ROBERT LUNDGREN I Foreign Sales I JAMES BOYER MAY I Published by I NEW ORLANDO PUBLICATIONS I New York, N.Y.

Copyright Page: 'Copyright 1963 by I New Orlando Publications I [. . .] I *THIS IS A FIRST EDITION*'.

Binding: perfect bound in thick, wove, orangish yellow card cover, 8 9/16 x 5 3/8 in. (217 x 140 mm.); front and spine printed in black.

Contents: First publication of "Water-Pipe," p. 27; in *Qu, SP65.* First book publication of "Hark Back" (**C481**), pp. 26-27; "Memory and Desire" rept. on p. 26.

Publication: Published in Dec. 1963 at $2.50.

B70 *JOHN CROWE RANSOM* 1964

John Crowe Ransom I Gentleman, Teacher, Poet, Editor I Founder of The Kenyon Review I A Tribute from the I Community of Letters I Edited by I D. David Long and Michael R. Burr I [in fancy type] *The Kenyon* I [in gothic] Collegian I A Supplement to Vol. LXXXX, NO. 7 I Gambier, Ohio I 1964

Copyright Page: 'Copyright © 1964 I Kenyon College'; no statement of first edition.

Binding: wire-stitched in thick, white, wove wrapper, 11 x 8 1/2 in. (282 x 216 mm.); front stamped in gold; all edges cut, unstained.

Contents: First publication of "May Evening," p. 19; in *Qu, SP65, CP76, CP88*; rept. in *The Achievement of Richard Eberhart*, ed. Engel (1968), p. 47.

Publication: Published 24 Jan. 1964; 800 copies printed; not for sale; rept. in 1964 (2,000 copies), and again in 1965 (2,000 copies).

B71 *NATIONAL POETRY FESTIVAL* 1964

National I Poetry I Festival I HELD IN THE LIBRARY OF CONGRESS I OCTOBER 22-24, 1962 I *PROCEEDINGS* I [seal of the Library of Congress] I GENERAL REFERENCE AND BIBLIOGRAPHY DIVISION I REFERENCE DEPARTMENT I WASHINGTON : 1964

Copyright Page: '[within a single-rules frame] L. C. card 64-60048'; no statement of first edition.

Binding: perfect bound in yellowish white card cover, 9 1/8 x 5 11/16 in. (231 x 147 mm.); printed in black.

Contents: "Introduction of Sir Herbert Read," pp. 343-46.

Publication: Published in July 1964 at $1.50.

B72 *84TH COMMENCEMENT, HOLDERNESS SCHOOL* 1964

[cover title] 84th [school seal] | COMMENCEMENT | HOLDERNESS SCHOOL | JUNE 7, 1964

Copyright Page: none present.

Binding: wire-stitched in gray pictorial card cover, 8 7/8 x 6 in. (225 x 153 mm.); all edges cut; front printed in blue and black, back printed in black.

Contents: First publication of RE's commencement address, pp. 1-7; in *OPP.*

Publication: Published in July 1964 for distribution to friends and alumni of Holderness School; approx. 200 copies printed; not for sale.

B73 *THE CONTEMPORARY POET AS ARTIST AND CRITIC* [1964]

[two-page title; across both pages, list of 25 poets] | [left] *Eight Symposia* | *edited by* | ANTHONY OSTROFF | [right] THE CONTEMPORARY *Poet* | AS *Artist* | AND *Critic* | [publisher's device] *Boston and Toronto* | LITTLE, BROWN AND COMPANY

Copyright Page: 'FIRST PRINTING'.

Binding and Dust Jacket: strong red cloth boards measure 8 15/16 x 9 9/16 in. (227 x 168 mm.); front blindstamped with publisher's device, spine stamped in black; top and bottom edges trimmed; yellowish white, wove, un-watermarked endpapers; white pictorial dust jacket printed in red and black.

Contents: First publication of RE's untitled comments on Richard Wilbur's "Love Calls Us to the Things of This World," pp. 4-5; and his comments on his own poem, "Am I My Neighbor's Keeper," pp. 158-66; the poem is rept. on p. 142.

Publication: Published in 14 July 1964 at $5.00.

B74 *OF POETRY AND POWER* [1964]

[two-page title; left] O F P O E T R Y [right] A N D P O W E R | [left] P O E M S O C C A S I O N E D [right] B Y T H E P R E S I D E N C Y |

[left] AND BY THE DEATH [right] OF JOHN F. KENNEDY |
[left] *Foreword by Arthur Schlesinger, Jr.* [right] EDITED WITH AN
INTRODUCTION | *by Erwin A. Glikes and Paul Schwaber* | B A S I C
B O O K S , I N C. | P U B L I S H E R S / N E W Y O R K

Copyright Page: '© 1964 by Basic Books, Inc.'; no statement of first edition.

Binding and Dust Jacket: black cloth boards measure 9 1/2 x 5 11/16 in. (242
x 146 mm.); spine stamped in red and blue; all edges cut, top edges stained
light blue; yellowish white, wove, unwatermarked endpapers; white pictorial
dust jacket printed in black, orange, yellow, blue, green, and strong red.

Contents: First publication of two poems:

"The Killer ['There I go, with an inscrutable face,'] (On the
Assassination of President Kennedy)," p. 90: in *SP65*.
"The Spirit of Poetry Speaks," p. 91.

Publication: Published 6 Nov. 1964 at $5.95.

B75 *FESTSCHRIFT FOR MARIANNE MOORE'S SEVENTY SEVENTH BIRTHDAY* 1964

Festschrift | FOR | MARIANNE | MOORE'S | Seventy Seventh Birthday | *by
various hands* | Edited by | Tambimuttu | [publisher's device] |
TAMBIMUTTU & MASS | *1964*

Copyright Page: 'Copyright 1964 by Tambimuttu'; no statement of first edition.

Binding and Dust Jacket: quarter-bound in black cloth and decorated paper
boards prin. in grayish blue and pale violet, 8 13/16 x 5 3/4 in. (223 x 148
mm.); spine stamped in gold; all edges trimmed; cloth head and tail bands
have alternating grayish blue and white stripes; yellowish white, wove, unwatermarked endpapers; grayish white pictorial dust jacket printed in dark pink
and black.

Contents: First publication of "A Memoir," pp. 72-73, and three poems:

"Salute," pp. 72-73: in *LR*; rept. in *I.A. Richards: Essays in His Honor*,
ed. Reuben Brower et al. (New York: Oxford, 1973), pp. 5-6.
"To Harriet Monroe," p. 74: in *PP*.
"Opulence," p. 75: in *SB*.

Publication: Published in Nov. 1964 at $4.95.

B76 *TODAY'S POETS* [1964]

T O D A Y ' S I P O E T S [aldine leaf] I AMERICAN AND BRITISH POETRY SINCE I THE 1930's [3 aldine leaves] I EDITED BY *C H A D W A L S H* I BELOIT COLLEGE I CHARLES SCRIBNER'S SONS I NEW YORK

Copyright Page: 'Copyright © 1964 Charles Scribner's Sons I [. . .] I A-10.64[V] I [. . .]'.

Binding: perfect bound in thick yellowish white card cover, 8 1/4 x 5 1/2; inner side white, outer side grayish violet; lettered in purple, orange, pink, and grayish violet.

Contents: First publication of "To Laughter, To Leering," pp. 46-47; rept. in *Yorkshire Post*, 13 July 1967, p. 9; and rept. appearances of "The Groundhog," pp. 35-36; "Now Is the Air Made of Chiming Balls," pp. 36-37; "The Soul Longs to Return Whence It Came," pp. 37-39; "If I Could Only Live at the Pitch That Is Near Madness," p. 39; "The Fury of Aerial Bombardment," pp. 39-40; "The Horse Chestnut Tree," pp. 40-41; "The Tobacconist of Eighth Street," p. 41; "The Cancer Cells," pp. 41-42; "Cousin Florence," pp. 42-43; "Off Spectacle Isle," p. 43; "Attitudes," p. 44; "A Ship Burning and a Comet All in One Day," pp. 44-45; "Am I My Neighbor's Keeper?," pp. 45-46; "Hark Back," p. 46; "The Spider," pp. 47-48.

Publication: Published in Nov. 1964 at $3.50. *N.B.*: RE's poems are not rept. in the 2d ed. (1972).

B77 *TWENTY ONE DARTMOUTH POEMS* 1964

TWENTY ONE I DARTMOUTH I POEMS I *Selected by* I RICHARD EBERHART I HANOVER I *Dartmouth Publications* I 1964

Copyright Page: 'COPYRIGHT • 1964 • BY TRUSTEES OF DARTMOUTH COLLEGE'; no statement of first edition.

Binding: wire-stitched in white card cover, 9 x 6 1/16 in. (229 x 154 mm.); glued in tan, wove paper wrapper, printed in red and black on front; all edges cut; woodcut by Terry Lee on front.

Contents: Postscript by RE on p. 29; RE also selected the poems for inclusion.

Publication: Published in Dec. 1964; 200 copies printed; price unknown.

Statement of Limitation: p. 32, '200 copies | Printed at The Stinehour Press | November 1964'.

B78 *MEDITATIONS ON A GREAT MAN GONE* [1965]

Meditations on a Great Man Gone | *and other poems* | Salem Slobodkin | With a Preface by RICHARD EBERHART | THE BOND WHEELWRIGHT COMPANY | [publisher's device] FREEPORT, MAINE

Copyright Page: 'Copyright, 1965, by Martin Slobodkin'; no statement of first edition.

Binding and Dust Jacket: red cloth boards measure 9 3/16 x 6 1/8 in. (234 x 156 mm.); spine stamped in gold; all edges trimmed; yellowish white, wove, unwatermarked endpapers; light gray pictorial dust jacket printed in black.

Contents: Preface by RE, p. vii.

Publication: Published in Jan. 1965 at $3.50.

B79 *AFTER THIS EXILE* 1965

[two-page title; right] MANUEL A. VIRAY | [left] *A f t e r* [right] *T h i s E x i l e* | [left] with essays by | Richard Eberhart | Leonard Casper | Bienvenido N. Santos | [right] PHOENIX PUBLISHING HOUSE, INC. | PUBLISHING DIVISION OF ALEMAR'S | QUEZON CITY | 1965

Copyright Page: 'Copyright 1965 by | Manuel A. Viray and Phoenix Publishing House, Inc.'; no statement of first edition.

Binding: perfect bound in white card cover, 8 15/16 x 6 in. (227 x 152 mm.), printed in deep yellowish pink, orangish yellow, and black; front printed in black, spine reversed out in white.

Contents: Prefatory note by RE, "Searching Honesties of the Heart," p. xiii.

Publication: Published in Nov. 1965 at $1.50.

B80 *THIRTY TWO DARTMOUTH POEMS* 1965

THIRTY TWO | DARTMOUTH | POEMS | *Selected by* | RICHARD EBERHART | HANOVER | *Dartmouth Publications* | 1965

Copyright Page: 'COPYRIGHT • 1965 • BY THE TRUSTEES OF DARTMOUTH COLLEGE'; no statement of first edition.

Binding: handsewn with white cord in light brown card cover, 9 x 6 in. (229 x 155 mm.); light brown jacket like stock of card cover, printed on front in black; wood-engraving on front by David Godine.

Contents: Foreword by RE, p. 5; RE also selected the poems for inclusion.

Publication: Published in Nov. 1965 at $2.00; 200 copies printed.

Statement of Limitation: p. 40, '200 copies | printed in October 1965 | at The Stinehour Press | Lunenburg, Vermont'.

B81 *POETS ON POETRY* [1966]

POETS | ON | POETRY | *Edited by HOWARD NEMEROV* | B A S I C B O O K S , I N C ., P U B L I S H E R S | *New York London*

Copyright Page: '© 1966 by Howard Nemerov'; no statement of first edition.

Binding and Dust Jacket: grayish tan cloth boards measure 8 1/2 x 5 7/8 in. (215 x 150 mm.); spine lettered in purple; all edges cut, unstained; white cloth head and tail bands; yellowish white, wove, unwatermarked endpapers; white dust jacket printed in dark yellowish brown, tan, and reddish pink.

Contents: First publication of RE's essay, "How I Write Poetry," pp. 17-39; in *OPP*. The following poems are herein reprinted: "Indian Pipe," pp. 17-18; For a Lamb," pp. 20-21; "The Groundhog," pp. 21-22; "If I Could Only Live at the Pitch That Is Near Madness," p. 24; "New Hampshire, February," pp. 25-26; "The Fury of Aerial Bombardment," p. 27; "The Horse Chestnut Tree," p. 29; "The Cancer Cells," pp. 30-31; "Seals, Terns, Time," pp. 32-33; "Cousin Florence," pp. 33-34; "A Ship Burning and a Comet All in One

Day," pp. 35-36; "On a Squirrel Crossing the Road in Autumn, in New England," p. 37; "Am I My Neighbor's Keeper?," pp. 38-39.

Publication: Published 21 Jan. 1966 at $4.95.

B82 *ROBERT WORTH BINGHAM POETRY ROOM* 1966

Robert Worth Bingham | *Poetry Room* | University of Louisville | *Library* | *Thursday, February ten* | *Nineteen Hundred Sixty-six* | *Louisville, Kentucky*

Copyright Page: none present.

Binding: wire-stitched in white, wove, pictorial card cover, 10 15/16 x 6 15/16 in. (278 x 177 mm.); front lettered in black; all edges cut.

Contents: First publication of "Marrakech," pp. 11, 13; in *SB, CP76, CP88*; rept. in *Southern Review*, n.s. 3 (Jan. 1967), 115-16; *The New Orlando Poetry Anthology*, ed. Anca Vrbovska et al. (New York: New Orlando Publications, 1968), pp. 47-48; *The Achievement of Richard Eberhart*, ed. Engel (1968), pp. 74-75; *This Is My Best in the Third Quarter of the Century*, ed. Burnett (1970), pp. 94-96; *A Little Treasury of Modern Poetry English and American*, ed. Williams, 3d ed. (1970), pp. 440-41.

Publication: Published 10 Feb. 1966; not for sale.

B83 *MASTER POEMS OF THE ENGLISH LANGUAGE* 1966

M A S T E R | P O E M S | OF THE ENGLISH LANGUAGE | [swelled rule, 98 mm.] | *Over one hundred poems* | *together with Introductions* | *by leading poets and critics* | *of the English-speaking world* | EDITED BY | Oscar Williams | [publisher's device] | T R I D E N T   P R E S S | *New York 1966*

Copyright Page: '*Copyright, ©, by Trident Press*'; no statement of first edition.

Binding and Dust Jacket: black cloth boards measure 9 1/4 x 5 3/4 in. (234 x 148 mm.); spine stamped in gold; all edges cut, top edges stained light blue; yellowish parchment-like wove endpapers; unlettered glassine protective jacket; laid in open-face brownish gold binder's board box, printed in black and pale grayish green.

Contents: First publication of RE's essay, "Wordsworth Tintern Abbey," pp. 424-27.

Publication: Published 17 Jan. 1966 at $10.00; reissued in card cover by Washington Square Press in 1967; RE's essay is contained on pp. 436-39.

B84 *TWENTY FIVE DARTMOUTH POEMS* 1966

TWENTY FIVE I DARTMOUTH I POEMS I SELECTED, WITH NOTES ON POETRY, I AND A POSTSCRIPT, BY I RICHARD EBERHART I HANOVER I *Dartmouth Publications* I 1966

Copyright Page: 'COPYRIGHT • 1966 • BY TRUSTEES OF DARTMOUTH COLLEGE'; no statement of first edition.

Binding: handsewn with white cord in reddish brown card cover, 9 x 6 in. (229 x 152 mm.); reddish brown jacket like stock of card cover, printed in black on front; all edges trimmed; cover woodcut by Harry Teague.

Contents: "Notes on Poetry," pp. 5-7; in *OPP*; and a postscript, on p. 37; RE also selected the poems for inclusion.

Publication: Published in Dec. 1966 at $2.00; 200 copies printed.

Statement of Limitation: p. 40, '200 copies I printed in November 1966 I at The Stinehour Press I Lunenburg, Vermont'.

B85 *WINTERFEST* 1967

[all in shades of dark gray; circle of six designs esp. for 1967 Boston Winterfest] I [fancy] Winterfest I [rule] I February 19 thru 26 / 1967 I [rule]

Copyright Page: no notice of copyright contained.

Binding: wire-stitched in white card cover, 11 x 17 in. (280 x 433 mm.), folded once to 11 x 8 1/2 in. (280 x 217 mm.); inner side and back are white, front is printed reddish violet; lettered in black and shades of dark gray; all edges cut, unstained.

Contents: First publication of "Boston," pp. 44-45. In *FG*; rept. in *Doors into Poetry*, ed. Chad Walsh, 2d ed. (Englewood Cliffs, N.J.: Prentice-Hall, 1970), pp. 271-74.

Publication: Published in Feb. 1967 as souvenir bulletin for Boston's 1967 Winterfest, at 25¢.

B86 *AUTHORS TAKE SIDES ON VIETNAM* [1967]

First edition
[short vert. rule] AUTHORS I TAKE SIDES ON VIETNAM I Two questions on the war in Vietnam I answered by the authors of several nations I EDITED BY I CECIL WOOLF AND JOHN BAGGULEY I [publisher's device] I PETER OWEN • LONDON

Copyright Page: ' © 1967 Peter Owen and Simon & Schuster Inc.'; no statement of first edition.

Binding and Dust Jacket: binding 1: black paper (imitation bead-cloth) boards measure 8 3/4 x 5 5/8 in. (223 x 144 mm.); spine stamped in silver; all edges cut; first and last leaves used as paste-downs; white dust jacket printed in red and black; binding 2: 300 copies bound in dark purplish blue cloth boards; spine lettered in gold; top edges stained dark blue or violet; unlettered glassine jacket; laid in yellowish green laid paper leaf printed on recto in black, 'Please accept this copy of I *Authors Take Sides on Vietnam* I with the compliments and thanks of Cecil Woolf and John Bagguley I [at base] 24 Victoria Square, London SW1 I September 1967'.

Contents: Statement by RE on p. 97.

Publication: Published 18 Sept. 1967 at 37s 6d; 2,300 copies printed; 2,000 in binding 1, and 300 in binding 2 (not for sale).

Note: A substantive error occurs in RE's contribution; it is corrected as follows, from RE's copy (in the compiler's collection): 97.18 angel] animal

First American Edition

AUTHORS I TAKE I SIDES I ON VIETNAM I Two Questions I on the War in Vietnam I Answered by the Authors I of Several Nations I Edited by I CECIL WOOLF and I JOHN BAGGULEYI [publisher's device] I SIMON AND SCHUSTER, NEW YORK

Binding: perfect bound in white card cover, 11 x 8 1/2 in. (280 x 216 mm.); printed in black and red.

Publication: Published 31 Oct. 1967 at $1.95; 10,000 copies printed; rept. in April 1968, 3,500 copies.

Note: RE's contribution is contained on p. 33; the error noted above was not corrected in the American edition.

B87 *AMERICAN CHRISTMAS*, 2d ed. 1967

[in black] Edited by I Webster Schott & Robert J. Myers I [in red open-face] AMERICAN CHRISTMAS I [in black; roman] Second Edition I Hallmark Cards, Incorporated I Kansas City, Missouri, 1967

Copyright Page: 'Second Edition'.

Binding and Dust Jacket: red cloth boards measure 10 1/2 x 6 5/8 in. (272 x 180 mm.); front blindstamped, spine and back stamped in gold; all edges cut, unstained; yellowish white, wove, unwatermarked endpapers; white pictorial dust jacket printed in purple, yellow, mustard, light green, green, deep pink, light blue, and black.

Contents: First publication of "Santa Claus in Oaxaca," p. 50; in *SB, CP76, CP88*; rept. in *The Achievement of Richard Eberhart*, ed. Engel (1968), p. 83.

Publication: Published in Nov. 1967 at $3.95.

Note: RE's poem does not appear in the first edition (1965).

B88 *GOLDEN HORN 1967*

Golden Horn | 1967

Copyright Page: none present.

Binding: glued in white, pictorial card cover, 9 1/4 x 6 5/8 in. (235 x 168 mm.); printed in black and light grayish brown.

Contents: First publication of "To the Field Mice," p. 45; in *SB*.

Publication: Published in late Dec. 1967 or early Jan. 1968; 300 copies printed.

Note: Golden Horn was published by The Humanities Department, Robert College, Bebeck P.K. 8, Istanbul.

B89 *ZINEB* 1968

[in fancy type] ZINEB | [in roman] POEMS FROM MOROCCO | *by* | BADREDDINE M. BENNANI | *with a preface by* | RICHARD EBERHART | ROGER BURT PRESS | HANOVER, N.H. | 1968

Copyright Page: 'Copyright © 1968 by | Badreddine M. Bennani'; no statement of first edition.

Binding: wire-stitched in white pictorial card cover, 8 1/4 x 5 1/2 in. (210 x 138 mm.); printed in black; all edges trimmed.

Contents: Preface by RE, p. 7.

Publication: Published 10 Jan. 1968 at $1.00; 500 copies printed.

B90 *THE ACHIEVEMENT OF RICHARD EBERHART* [1968]

THE ACHIEVEMENT OF RICHARD EBERHART | A COMPREHENSIVE SELECTION OF HIS POEMS WITH A CRITICAL INTRODUCTION | BERNARD F. ENGEL | Michigan State University | SCOTT, FORESMAN AND COMPANY

Copyright Page: 'Copyright © by Scott, Foresman and Company, Glenview, Illinois 60025'; no statement of first edition.

Binding: perfect bound in white card cover, 9 x 6 in. (228 x 152 mm.); printed in black and dark pink; front contains a black and white photograph of RE.

Contents: First book publication of the following poems:

"The Mastery" (**C554**), p. 76.
"The Ides of March" (**C555**), p. 77.
"The Enigma" (**C575**), p. 78.

"On Returning to a Lake in Spring" (**C558**), p. 79.
"The Explorer on Main Street" (**C556**), p. 79-80.
"Hill Dream of Youth, Thirty Years Later" (**C532**), p. 81.
"A Wedding on Cape Rosier" (**C557**), p. 82.
"The Vastness and Indifference of the World" (**C538**), p. 84.

The following poems are rept. herein: "Go To the Shine That's On a Tree," p. 4; "The Groundhog," pp. 23-24; "When Golden Flies Upon My Carcass Come," p. 24; "Orchard," p. 25; "Cover Me Over," p. 26; "The Soul Longs to Return Whence It Came," pp. 27-28; "New Hampshire, February," p. 29; "The Horse Chestnut Tree," p. 30; "At Night," p. 31; "Dam Neck, Virginia," pp. 31-32; "The Fury of Aerial Bombardment," p. 32; "Seals, Terns, Time," p. 33; "The Tobacconist of Eighth Street," p. 34; "On Shooting Particles Beyond the World," pp. 35-36; "The Human Being Is a Lonely Creature," p. 36; "Sea-Hawk," p. 37; "On a Squirrel Crossing the Road in Autumn, in New England," p. 38; "The Wisdom of Insecurity," pp. 39-40; "La Crosse at Ninety Miles an Hour," p. 41; "The Place," pp. 42-43; "Sea-Burial from the Cruiser *Reve*," p. 44; "A New England Bachelor," p. 45; "Moment of Equilibrium Among the Islands," p. 46; "May Evening," p. 47; "Off Pemaquid," p. 48; "The Spider," pp. 48-49; "The Project," pp. 49-50; "Matador," p. 50; "Prometheus," p. 51; "Old Tom," pp. 51-52; "The Height of Man," p. 53; "Vision," pp. 53-55; "Ways and Means," p. 55; "The Rape of the Cataract," pp. 56-57; "Request fot Offering," p. 58; "The Recapitulation," p. 59; 'Ode to the Chinese Paper Snake," pp. 60-62; "The Attic," p. 63; "Concord Cats," pp. 63-64; "The Skier and the Mountain," pp. 64-65; "Words," p. 66; "Sunday in October," pp. 66-67; "Protagonists," p. 67; "Villanelle," p. 68; "Life As Visionary Spirit," p. 69; "The Supreme Authority of the Imagination," p. 70; "The Lost Children," p. 71; "The Hard Structure of the World," pp. 72-73; "Half-Bent Man," pp. 73-74; "Marrakech," pp. 74-75.

Publication: Published 29 Jan. 1968 at $1.75.

B91 *NINETEEN DARTMOUTH POEMS* 1967 [i.e., 1968]

NINETEEN | DARTMOUTH | POEMS | SELECTED BY | RICHARD EBERHART | HANOVER | *Dartmouth Publications* | 1967

Copyright Page: 'COPYRIGHT • 1967 • BY TRUSTEES OF DARTMOUTH COLLEGE'; no statement of first edition.

Binding: handsewn with white cord in tan, wove card cover, 9 x 6 in. (229 x 153 mm.); all edges trimmed; tan jacket like stock of card cover printed in black on front; wood engraving by Stanley L. Rice on front.

Contents: Acknowledgement by RE, p. 5; RE also selected the poems for inclusion.

Publication: Published in late Feb. or early March 1968 at $2.00; 200 copies printed.

Statement of Limitation: p. 32, '200 copies | printed in February 1968 | at The Stinehour Press | Lunenburg, Vermont'.

B92 *THE NEW ORLANDO POETRY ANTHOLOGY* [1968]

[in open-face] The | NEW ORLANDO | Poetry Anthology | [in roman] GREENWICH VILLAGE | [in open-face] Volume III | [remainder in roman] Editors | ANCA VRBOVSKA | ALFRED DORN | ROBERT LUNDGREN | Foreign Sales | JAMES BOYER MAY | Published by | NEW ORLANDO PUBLICATIONS | New York, N.Y.

Copyright Page: 'THIS IS A FIRST EDITION'.

Binding: perfect bound in white card cover, 8 9/16 x 5 1/2 in. (217 x 140 mm.); printed in black and yellow.

Contents: First book publication of the poems:

> "Music Over Words" (**C565**), pp. 46-47.
> "The Winds" (**C559**), p. 49.
> "Swiss New Year" (**C579**), pp. 50-51.
> "Marrakech" (**B82**) is rept. on pp. 47-48.

Publication: Published in Dec. 1968 at $2.50.

B93 *ROBERT LOWELL: A COLLECTION OF CRITICAL ESSAYS* [1968]

R O B E R T | L O W E L L | A COLLECTION OF CRITICAL ESSAYS | Edited by *Thomas Parkinson* | Prentice-Hall, Inc. [publisher's device] *Englewood Cliffs, N.J.*

Copyright Page: 'Copyright © 1968 [. . .] I 10 9 8 7 6 5 4 3 2 1 '; no statement of first edition.

Binding: hardcover issue: black cloth boards measure 8 1/4 x 5 13/16 in. (210 x 150 mm.); spine and back stamped in gold; all edges cut, unstained; yellowish white, wove, unwatermarked endpapers; white dust jacket printed in black and purple; card cover issue: also issued in card cover like dust jacket of hardcover issue, 8 x 5 3/8 in. (203 x 138 mm.).

Contents: First book publication of "Review of *Lord Weary's Castle*" (**C183**), pp. 48-52.

Publication: Published in Dec. 1968 at $4.95 (hardcover) and $1.95 (card cover).

B94 *A DIRTY HAND: THE LITERARY NOTEBOOKS OF WINFIELD TOWNLEY SCOTT* [1969]

[in black] The Literary Notebooks of I [in blue] Winfield Townley Scott I [in black] "a I d i r t y I h a n d" I Foreword by Merle Armitage I [publisher's device in blue] I [in black] UNIVERSITY OF TEXAS PRESS, AUSTIN & LONDON

Copyright Page: 'Copyright © 1969 by Mrs. Winfield Townley Scott'; no statement of first edition.

Binding and Dust Jacket: medium blue cloth boards measure 9 1/4 x 6 1/8 in. (235 x 156 mm.); spine stamped in gold; all edges cut, top edges stained pale gray; cloth head and tail bands have alternating orange and yellow stripes; bright yellow laid endpapers, watermarked '[in script] Ticonderoga I Text'; yellow dust jacket ident. to endpapers, printed in black, dark blue and red.

Contents: First publication of quoted and paraphrased comments by RE on pp. 96 and 122.

Publication: Published 1 Jan. 1969 at $4.75.

B95 *FIFTY DARTMOUTH POEMS* 1968 [i.e., 1969]

FIFTY | DARTMOUTH | POEMS | SELECTED | AND WITH AN INTRODUCTION BY | RICHARD EBERHART | HANOVER | *Dartmouth Publications* | 1968

Copyright Page: 'COPYRIGHT • 1968 • BY THE TRUSTEES OF DARTMOUTH COLLEGE'; no statement of first edition.

Binding: handsewn with white cord in thick, light grayish blue card cover, 9 x 6 in. (229 x 153 mm.); glued in light grayish blue jacket (like stock of card cover), printed on front in black; wood- engraving on front by Kari Prager.

Contents: Introduction by RE, pp. 7-8; RE also selected the poems for inclusion.

Publication: Published in March or April 1969 at $2.00; 200 copies printed.

Statement of Limitation: p. 55, '200 copies | printed in February 1969 | at The Stinehour Press | Lunenburg, Vermont'.

B96 *JOHN MILTON* [1969]

Trade Issue

[all within a frame of double-rules; in fancy type] JOHN MILTON | [rule, 93 mm., connecting sides of frame] PARADISE LOST | PARADISE REGAINED | AND | SAMSON AGONISTES | [ornament] | INTRODUCTION BY | RICHARD EBERHART | [rule, 93 mm.] | DOUBLEDAY & COMPANY, Inc. | Garden City, New York

Copyright Page: 'INTRODUCTION COPYRIGHT © 1969 By | NELSON DOUBLEDAY, INC.'; no statement of first edition.

Binding and Dust Jacket: dark blue cloth boards measure 8 7/16 x 5 11/16 in. (215 x 145 mm.); spine stamped in gold and black; top and bottom edges cut, fore-edges rough trimmed; cloth head and tail bands have alternating grayish blue and yellow stripes; light olive green, wove, unwatermarked endpapers; white dust jacket printed in purple, light olive green, and light grayish blue.

Contents: Introduction by RE, pp. 1-13.

Publication: Published 21 March 1969 at $5.95.

International Collector's Library Issue

Ident. to trade issue except for:

Binding: full simulated leather boards ("The Marie Antoinette Binding") measure 8 1/2 x 5 3/4 in. (215 x 144 mm.); front and spine stamped in gold; top and bottom edges cut, fore-edges rough trimmed; top edges gilt; cloth head and tail bands have alternating red and yellow stripes; brown, wove, unwatermarked endpapers; text printed on tannish, laid "antique" paper.

Publication: 1,000 copies prepared by photo-offset from the trade issue for subscribing members to the International Collector's Library; publication date and price are unknown.

B97 *VOCES IN DESERTO* 1969

[in fancy type] the quest I [in roman] VOCES IN DESERTO I Poetry Pamphlet Number Three 1969 I [. . .]

Copyright Page: 'Copyright © 1969, **the quest**'; no statement of first edition.

Binding: wire-stitched in thick, grayish green, wove paper wrapper, 8 1/2 x 11 in. (216 x 282 mm.), folded once vertically to 8 1/2 x 5 1/2 in. (216 x 141 mm.); printed in black; all edges cut, unstained.

Contents: First publication of "Kinaesthesia," on back of wrapper; in *FG, CP76, CP88*; rept. in the *Chicago Tribune*, 11 Oct. 1969, p. 6.

Publication: Published in Sept. 1969 at 75¢ ; 250 copies printed.

B98 *QUALITY: ITS IMAGE IN THE ARTS* [1969]

[two-page title; left, photograph of a wreath] [right] Q U A L I T Y I [rule] ITS IMAGE IN THE ARTS I [in script] Louis Kronenberger [in roman] EDITOR I [left] A BALANCE HOUSE BOOK I [remainder right] CONCEIVED AND PRODUCED BY [in script] Marshall Lee I [in roman] NEW YORK ATHENEUM

Copyright Page: 'F I R S T   E D I T I O N'.

Binding and Dust Jacket: black quarter-cloth (sized black cloth spine, fine bead-cloth on front and back) boards measure 11 1/8 x 8 5/8 in. (283 x 218 mm.); front blindstamped 'Q U A L I T Y', spine stamped in gold and violet; all edges rough cut, top edges stained pink; cloth head and tail bands have alternating red and yellow stripes; dark brownish yellow, wove, unwatermarked endpapers; white pictorial dust jacket printed prin. in brown, black, gold, and blue.

Contents: First publication of RE's essay, "Poetry," pp. 327-40; in *OPP* as "Pure Poetry."

Publication: Published in Nov. 1969 at $24.95.

B99 *SIXTY DARTMOUTH POEMS* 1969

SIXTY | DARTMOUTH | POEMS | SELECTED | AND WITH A FOREWORD BY | RICHARD EBERHART | HANOVER | *Dartmouth Publications* | 1969

Copyright Page: 'COPYRIGHT • 1969 • BY TRUSTEES OF DARTMOUTH COLLEGE'; no statement of first edition.

Binding: handsewn with white cord in pale blue card cover, 9 x 6 in. (230 x 150 mm.); glued in dust jacket like card cover; front printed in red and black; front contains woodcut in red.

Contents: Foreword by RE, pp. 7-11; RE also selected the poems for inclusion.

Publication: Published 10 Dec. 1969 at $2.00; 200 copies printed.

Statement of Limitation: p. 67, '200 copies | printed in December 1969 | at The Stinehour Press | Lunenburg, Vermont'.

B100 *THIS IS MY BEST IN THE THIRD QUARTER OF THE CENTURY* [1970]

America's 85 Greatest Living Authors Present | THIS IS MY BEST | IN THE THIRD QUARTER OF THE CENTURY | [rule, 61 mm.] | Edited by Whit Burnett | DOUBLEDAY & COMPANY, INC. GARDEN CITY, NEW YORK

Copyright Page: 'COPYRIGHT © 1970 BY WHIT BURNETT'; no statement of first edition.

Binding and Dust Jacket: grayish tan cloth boards measure 8 1/2 x 5 7/8 in. (215 x 150 mm.); spine lettered in black and gold; top and bottom edges cut, fore-edges trimmed; tan cloth head and tail bands; pale grayish yellow wove, unwatermarked endpapers; white dust jacket printed grayish yellow, black, and blue.

Contents: First publication of an untitled letter, "Dear Whit," pp. 90-91; and first book publication of two poems: "John Ledyard" (**C593**), pp. 96-97, and "Will" (**C618**), pp. 97-98. The following poems are herein reprinted: "The Ides of March," pp. 91-92; "Outwitting the Trees," pp. 92-93; "Evil," pp. 93-94; and "Marrakech," pp. 95-96.

Publication: Published 6 July 1970 at $10.00.

B101 *TRANSLATIONS BY AMERICAN POETS* [1970]

[in script] Translations by | American Poets | [in roman] EDITED BY JEAN GARRIGUE | OHIO UNIVERSITY PRESS • ATHENS

Copyright Page: 'Copyright © 1970 by Ohio University Press'; no statement of first edition.

Binding and Dust Jacket: blue cloth boards measure 9 3/4 x 6 5/8 in. (248 x 168 mm.); front and spine stamped in gold; all edges cut, unstained; brownish gold, wove, unwatermarked endpapers; white dust jacket printed in green, red, and black.

Contents: First publication of RE's translations of Andre Bouchet:

"The Wind Hugs the Blood," p. 97.
"The Day," p. 97.
"High Tide," p. 99.

Publication: Published 22 Feb. 1970 at $15.00; 3,000 copies printed.

B102 *POEMS FROM THE HILLS* [1970]

poems | **from** | **the** | **hills,** | **1970** | edited by | William Plumley | [school seal and cartouche] | MHC Publications

Copyright Page: '*Copyright © 1970 by MHC Publications*'; no statement of first edition.

Binding: perfect bound in white card cover, 8 7/6 x 6 in. (225 x 153 mm.); printed in red and black.

Contents: First publication of two poems:

"Night Song," p. 18
"Where I Want to Go," p. 19; in *FG*; rept. in *Poet*, 25 (April 1984), 10.

Publication: Published in late February or March 1970 at $2.50, by Morris Harvey College, Charleston, W.Va.; 2,500 copies printed.

B103 *EMILY DICKINSON: LETTERS FROM THE WORLD* [1970]

emily dickinson: | letters from the world | [rule, 54 mm.] | compiled, edited & designed by | Marguerite Harris

Copyright Page: '*Copyright © 1970 Marguerite Harris*'; no statement of first edition.

Binding: perfect bound in white card cover, 9 x 6 in. (230 x 154 mm.); front, spine and back are printed in black.

Contents: First publication of RE's "A Note," p. 52, and first book publication of "Emily Dickinson" (**C609**), pp. 44-45.

Publication: Published in Aug. 1970 at $2.50.

B104 *SEVENTY DARTMOUTH POEMS* 1970

SEVENTY | DARTMOUTH | POEMS | SELECTED | AND WITH A PREFACE AND | AN ESSAY ON "WAR POETRY" | BY RICHARD EBERHART | HANOVER | *Dartmouth Publications* | 1970

Copyright Page: 'COPYRIGHT © BY TRUSTEES OF DARTMOUTH COLLEGE'; no statement of first edition.

Binding: handsewn with white cord in tan, wove card cover, 9 x 6 in. (230 x 154 mm.); tan dust jacket like card cover, printed in green and black; front contains a woodcut in green by Christopher Keith.

Contents: First book publication of RE's preface, pp. 7-8 (originally titled "For the Dartmouth Poetry Symposium, January 1970," (**C602**); and first publication of "War Poetry," pp. 82-97 (first delivered as a commencement address at Middlesex School, Concord, Mass., 4 June 1970); RE also selected the poems for inclusion.

Publication: Published in Dec. 1970 at $2.00; 200 copies printed.

Statement of Limitation: p. 88, '200 copies | printed in December 1970 | at The Stinehour Press | Lunenburg, Vermont'.

B105 *ROBERT LOWELL: A PORTRAIT OF THE ARTIST IN HIS TIME*
[1970, i.e. 1971]

[two-page title; left] Edited by Michael London | and Robert Boyers | DAVID LEWIS NEW YORK | [right] ROBERT LOWELL: | A Portrait of the Artist | in His Time | [black and white photograph of Lowell, 108 x 90 mm.]

Copyright Page: 'First printing'.

Binding and Dust Jacket: quarter-bound in blue and grayish tan cloth boards, 9 3/4 x 7 1/4 in. (235 x 186 mm.); front printed in blue, spine stamped in gold; all edges trimmed, unstained; tan cloth head and tail bands; tan, wove, unwatermarked endpapers; white pictorial dust jacket printed in blue, light grayish blue, gray, and black.

Contents: First book publication of "The Gold Standard," pp. 28-30, an excpt. from "Five Poets" (**C269**).

Publication: Published in Jan. 1971 at $15.00.

B106 RICHARD EBERHART: THE PROGRESS
OF AN AMERICAN POET 1971

[ornamental rule, 85 mm.] | RICHARD EBERHART | *The Progress* | *of an American Poet* | [ornamental rule like first] | JOEL ROACHE | New York OXFORD UNIVERSITY PRESS 1971

Copyright Page: 'Copyright © 1971 by Joel Roache'; no statement of first edition.

Binding and Dust Jacket: full yellowish green cloth boards measure 8 7/16 x 5 3/4 in. (215 x 145 mm.); spine printed in grayish green and pale orange; all edges cut, unstained; cloth head and tail bands have alternating yellow and grayish green stripes; yellowish white, wove, unwatermarked endpapers; white pictorial jacket containing photograph of RE on front; printed in yellow, black, and greenish grayish yellow.

Contents: First publication or first book publication of numerous diary excerpts, unpublished letters, poetry, and prose, throughout.

Publication: Published 4 Feb. 1971 at $8.50; 2,000 copies printed.

B107 POEMS FROM THE HILLS, 1971

Poems | From The Hills | 1971 | Edited by William Plumley | [college seal and cartouche] | MHC Publications

Copyright Page: '*Copyright © 1971 by MHC Publications*'; no statement of first edition.

Binding: perfect bound in white card cover, 9 1/6 x 6 in. (230 x 153 mm.); printed in light olive brown and black.

Contents: First publication of "The Truncated Bird," p. 20; in *FG*; rept. in *Poet*, 23 (Oct. 1982), 14.

Publication: Published in April 1971 at $2.50 by Morris Harvey College, Charleston, W.Va.; 5000 copies printed.

B108 *ATLANTIC BRIEF LIVES* [1971]

Atlantic | BRIEF LIVES | *A Biographical Companion to the Arts* | *Edited by* LOUIS KRONENBERGER | *Associate Editor* | EMILY MORISON BECK | [publisher's device] | *An Atlantic Monthly Press Book* | LITTLE, BROWN AND COMPANY • BOSTON • TORONTO

Copyright Page: 'FIRST EDITION | TO9 /71'.

Binding and Dust Jacket: brownish red cloth boards measure 9 1/2 x 6 1/2 in. (251 x 175 mm.); front stamped in gold, spine stamped in gold and black; top edges cut, fore- and bottom edges rough cut; top edges stained dull red; cloth head and tail bands have alternating dull red and yellow stripes; brownish red, wove, unwatermarked endpapers; light gray wove dust jacket printed in brownish red, black, and blue.

Contents: First publication of "Gerard Manley Hopkins," RE's brief critical essay on the poet, pp. 382-84.

Publication: Published 13 Sept. 1971 at $15.00.

B109 *ATTACKS OF TASTE* 1971

[within black single-rules frame and dull red ornamental frame; in dull red] ATTACKS | OF TASTE | [remainder in black; ornamental rule, 34 mm.] | *Compiled and Edited* | *by* | EVELYN B. BYRNE | & | OTTO M. PENZLER | ON TEENAGE READING: | *"You must remember that youngsters (as* | *youngsters for some reason never remem-* | *ber) have attacks of taste like at-* | *tacks of* | *measles."* —ARCHIBALD MACLEISH | [below frames] New York GOTHAM BOOK MART 1971

Copyright Page: 'Copyright © 1971 by | EVELYN B. BYRNE and OTTO M. PENZLER'; no statement of first edition.

Binding and Dust Jacket: tannish white cloth boards measure 9 1/2 x 6 3/8 in. (241 x 161 mm.); all edges trimmed; dark orangish brown laid endpapers; white cover and spine labels printed in dull red and black; unlettered white dust jacket.

Contents: First publication of RE's brief, untitled account of his childhood reading, p. 20.

Publication: Published 25 Dec. 1971 at $15.00; 500 copies printed.

Colophon: p. 65, 'Printed in Trump Mediaeval and Caslon types at the Noel Young I Press, Santa Barbara, Calif., by Noel Young & Graham Macintosh. I This first edition is limited to 500 copies numbered and signed by I the editors, of which 100 copies are for presentation & not for sale. I '#' and arabic numeral supplied in black ink] I ['Evelyn B. Byrne' in blue ink] I ['Otto Penzler' in black ink] I Printed in the United States of America I [in presentation copes only, recipient's name supplied in black ink]'.

B110 *FIFTY SIX DARTMOUTH POEMS* 1971 (i.e., 1972)

FIFTY SIX I DARTMOUTH I POEMS I SELECTED I AND WITH A NOTE ON "PROTEST" I AND AN AFTERWORD ON "SEALS, TERNS, TIME" I BY RICHARD EBERHART I HANOVER • NEW HAMPSHIRE I 1971

Copyright Page: 'COPYRIGHT © 1971 BY TRUSTEES OF DARTMOUTH COLLEGE I *privately printed*'; no statement of first edition.

Binding: handsewn with white cord in light bluish green card cover, 9 x 6 in. (230 x 154 mm.); jacket like card cover and printed on front in black; front contains a woodcut by Christopher Keith.

Contents: First publication of "Note on *Protest*," p. 7; and RE's commentary "Eberhart's 'Seals, Terns, Time'" , pp. 73-74; RE also selected the poems for inclusion.

Publication: Published in March 1972 at $2.00; 200 copies printed.

Statement of Limitation: p. 76, '200 copies I printed in February 1972 I at The Stinehour Press I Lunenburg, Vermont'.

B111 *NORTHERN LIGHTS: WRITERS FROM THE UPPER VALLEY OF VERMONT AND NEW HAMPSHIRE* [1972]

[reprod. from calligraphic orig.] Northern Lights I [reprod. from typescript] (Writers of the Upper Valley on the Connecticut River) I Edited by DOROTHY BECK I A GRANITE Publication, Chap Book No. 1

Copyright Page: 'Copyright 1972 by Granite Publications, Inc.'; no statement of first edition.

Binding: perfect bound in putty-colored card cover, 9 x 5 15/16 in. (229 x 151 mm.); front printed in blue and black.

Contents: First publication of RE's poem, "Self-Spinner Speaking," p. 34.

Publication: Published in June 1972 at $5.00; 500 copies printed.

B112 *EZRA POUND: THE CRITICAL HERITAGE* [1972]

EZRA POUND | *THE CRITICAL HERITAGE* | *Edited by* | ERIC HOMBERGER | School of English and American Studies | University of East Anglia | [rule, 102 mm.] | ROUTLEDGE & KEGAN PAUL : LONDON AND BOSTON

Copyright Page: '*First published 1972*'.

Binding and Dust Jacket: grayish blue cloth boards measure 8 3/4 x 5 3/4 in. (222 x 147 mm.); spine stamped in gold; all edges cut, unstained; yellowish white, wove, unwatermarked endpapers; white pictorial dust jacket printed in orange and light green.

Contents: First book publication of "Richard Eberhart on the Character of Pound's Work," pp. 375-87, a rept. of RE's essay-review, "Pound's New Cantos" (**C204**).

Publication: Published in Sept. 1972 at £6.50.

B113 *BEST POEMS OF 1971* 1972

Best Poems of 1971 | [in open-face] Borestone Mountain | Poetry Awards 1972 | [rule, 139 mm.] | [remainder in roman] A Compilation of Original Poetry | Published in Magazines of the | English- Speaking World in 1971 | **Twenty-fourth Annual Issue** | **Volume XXIV** | **Pacific Books, Publishers,** Palo Alto, California | 1972

Copyright Page: 'Copyright © 1972 by Borestone Mountain Poetry Awards.' No statement of first edition.

Binding and Dust Jacket: grayish tan cloth boards measure 8 3/4 x 5 5/8 in. (223 x 143 mm.); spine stamped in gold; all edges cut, unstained; cloth head and tail bands have alternating light brown and white stripes; yellowish white, wove, unwatermarked endpapers; white dust jacket printed in light green, bluish green, and grayish blue.

Contents: First book publication of "Death in the Mines" (**C636**), p. 30.

Publication: Published 27 Nov. 1972 at $4.50; 1,500 copies printed.

B114 *THE BEASTS & THE ELDERS* 1973

The Beasts & the Elders I **by Robert Siegel** I Published for I **The University Press of New England** I Hanover, New Hampshire 1973

Copyright Page: 'Copyright © 1973 by Trustees of Dartmouth College'; no statement of first edition.

Binding and Dust Jacket: orangish red cloth boards measure 8 3/4 x 6 3/16 in. (221 x 157 mm.); front and spine stamped in white; all edges trimmed; black, wove, unwatermarked endpapers; white dust jacket printed in orangish red and black; or, perfect bound in white card cover like dust jacket of hard cover issue, 8 1/2 x 5 7/8 in. (215 x 148 mm.).

Contents: Foreword by RE, pp. ix-x.

Publication: Published in Oct. 1979 at $7.00 (hardcover) and $3.50 (card cover); 1,289 copies printed, of which 546 were issued in cloth and 743 in card cover.

B115 *MISCELLANY TWO* 1974

MISCELLANY I TWO I Edited by I Reginald Cook I VERMONT ACADEMY OF ARTS AND SCIENCES I *Occasional Paper No. 13* I 1974

Copyright Page: '© by the Vermont Academy of Arts and Sciences'; no statement of first edition.

Binding: wire-stitched in thick, wove, orange card cover, 8 7/8 x 6 in. (225 x 153 mm.); all edges cut; front printed in black.

Contents: First publication of an essay, "Robert Frost in the Clearing," pp. 7-12; rept. in *Southern Review*, n.s. 11 (April 1975), pp. 260-68. In *OPP.*

Publication: Published in Feb. 1974 at $2.50; 500 copies printed.

B116 *THE LYRIC POTENTIAL* [1974]

THE LYRIC | POTENTIAL | Arrangements and Techniques in Poetry | JAMES E. MILLER, JR. | [5 lines in roman and ital, about Miller] | ROBERT HAYDEN | [6 lines in roman and ital, about Hayden] | ROBERT O'NEAL | [4 lines in roman and ital, about O'Neal] | SCOTT, FORESMAN AND COMPANY

Copyright Page: 'Copyright © 1974 Scott, Foresman and Company | Glenview, Illinois.'

Binding: perfect bound in white pictorial card cover, 9 x 6 in. (230 x 152 mm.), printed in bluish gray, shades of reddish pink, and black.

Contents: First publication of RE's prose statement concerning his poem, "This Fevers Me," on p. 193; the poem is rept. on p. 192. "The Groundhog" is rept. on pp. 256-57.

Publication: Published 12 March 1974 at $2.46.

B117 *FROM THE HILLS* [1974]

[cover title; rev. out in white and highlighted in blue] From the Hills | [in brown] Special pictorial issue, featuring the real-life | JOHN BOY AND THE WALTON STAR | [above photographs] Earl Hammer Richard Thomas | [in light grayish blue] *William Plumley, Editor MHC Publications | Shirley Young Campbell, Assistant Editor $3.95*

Copyright Page: p. 1, '*Copyright © 1974 by MHC Publications*'; no statement of first edition.

Binding: wire-stitched in pictorial card cover, 11 x 8 1/2 in. (279 x 218 mm.); all edges cut; printed in light grayish blue and brown on front.

Contents: First publication of "Time," p. 23; in LR. Also included is an excpt. from RE's comments on method in poetry from *Agenda* (Spring 1973), p. 23.

Publication: Published in April 1974 at $3.95 by Morris Harvey College, Charleston, W.Va.; 5,000 copies printed.

B118 *CHILDHOOD'S JOURNEY* 1974

[cover-title] *CHILDHOOD'S JOURNEY* | *BY* | *Richard Eaton* | Copyright 1974

Copyright: on cover title; see above. No statement of first edition.

Binding: wire-stitched in white, wove paper wrapper (ident. to text stock), 9 x 6 in. (229 x 153 mm.); all edges cut; printed in black on front.

Contents: Preface by RE, pp. 2-4.

Publication: Privately printed for distribution by the author in June 1974; approx. 100 copies printed; not for sale.

B119 *CRY OF THE HUMAN* [1975]

Cry of the Human | Essays on Contemporary | American Poetry | *Ralph J. Mills, Jr.* | University of Illinois Press | *Urbana Chicago London*

Copyright Page: '© by the Board of Trustees of the Univeristy of Illinois'; no statement of first edition.

Binding and Dust Jacket: bluish green cloth boards measure 9 1/4 x 6 3/16 in. (235 x 157 mm.); spine stamped in silver; all edges trimmed, unstained; cloth head and tail bands have alternating grayish blue and yellow stripes; yellowish white, wove, unwatermarked endpapers; white dust jacket printed in green and medium blue.

Contents: Foreword by RE, pp. xi-xiii.

Publication: Published 23 April 1975 at $10.95; 2,530 copies printed.

B120 *PARA-DESA* [1975]

[all within a double rules frame, the outer of which is formed by single rules, the inner, fancy; in fancy type] Para-Desa | [remainder in roman] *by* | HENRY BAILEY STEVENS | [publisher's device] | VEGETARIAN WORLD PUBLISHERS | Los Angeles

Copyright Page: 'Copyright, © 1975, by Henry Bailey Stevens'; no statement of first edition.

Binding and Dust Jacket: green imitation leather boards measure 8 15/16 x 5 3/4 in. (228 x 146 mm.); spine stamped in gold; all edges cut, unstained; cloth head and tail bands have alternating orange and yellow stripes; white pictorial endpapers printed in shades of gray and black; white dust jacket printed in dark yellow, green, and black.

Contents: Introduction by RE, p. xi.

Publication: Published in May 1975 at $5.00.

B121 *JOHN KEATS'S PORRIDGE* [1975]

[rule, 75 mm.] | JOHN KEATS'S | PORRIDGE | [rule, 75 mm.] | Favorite Recipes of | American Poets | [rule, 75 mm.] | *Victoria McCabe* | [rule, 75 mm.] | UNIVERSITY OF IOWA PRESS | [rule, 75 mm.]

Copyright Page: '© 1975 by The University of Iowa'; no statement of first edition.

Binding: perfect bound in white decorative card cover, 8 x 5 3/16 in. (202 x 133 mm.), printed in blue, black, orange, and reddish purple.

Contents: First publication of RE's version of his daughter's recipe, "Jerusalem Artichokes," p. 38.

Publication: Published in June 1975 at $2.95; 5,336 copies printed.

B122 *CAFE AT ST. MARKS: THE APALACHEE POETS* [1975]

CAFE at ST. MARKS | The Apalachee Poets | General Editor | Van K. Brock | Editors | David Jordan and Hal Steven Shows | Cover Illustration | Lincoln Stone | Production | David Morrill and Vicki Woodworth | courtesy of Mediatype

Copyright Page: none present; contents on pp. 2-5.

Binding: perfect bound in grayish tan card cover, 8 1/2 x 5 1/2 in. (211 x 139 mm.); printed in reddish orange.

Contents: First publication of "Youth and Age," p. 46; in *LR.* "The Place" (**C418**) rept. on pp. 45-46.

Publication: Published 8 Dec. 1975 at $3.00, by the Anhinga Press, Tallahassee, Fla.; 500 copies printed.

B123 *THE FACE OF POETRY* 1976

THE FACE OF POETRY : | 101 Poets In Two Significant Decades | —the 60's & the 70's | Photographic portraits by | LaVerne Harrell Clark | Foreword by | Richard Eberhart | Edited by | LaVerne Harrell Clark | and | Mary MacArthur | GALLIMAUFRY | Arlington | 1976

Copyright Page: 'THE FACE OF POETRY is copyright © 1976 by | LaVerne Harrell Clark and GALLIMAUFRY.' No statement of first edition.

Binding: perfect bound in white card cover, 9 x 6 in. (228 x 152 mm.); printed in black, with fancy letters in title containing photographic images by Clark.

Contents: Foreword by RE, p. 15; first publication of "Times Offerings," pp. 79-80.

Publication: Published in July 1976 at $6.95. A second printing was prepared by photo-offset in 1979 by Heidelberg Graphics, Chico, Ca., and published at $8.95; perfect bound in white card cover printed in red and black.

B124 *THE WATER OF LIGHT* [1976]

[in light bluish gray] T H E I W A T E R I O F I L I G H T I [remainder in black; rule] I *A Miscellany in Honor of* I *Brewster Ghiselin* I Edited by Henry Taylor I UNIVERSITY OF UTAH PRESS, SALT LAKE CITY

Copyright Page: 'Copyright © 1976 by the University of Utah Press'; no statement of first edition.

Binding and Dust Jacket: brown cloth boards measure 9 13/16 x 8 3/16 in. (250 x 182 mm.); spine stamped in gold; all edges cut, unstained; light grayish blue, wove, unwatermarked endpapers; white, wove, unwatermarked endpapres; white, wove dust jacket printed in light grayish blue and black.

Contents: First publication of RE's untitled statement about Brewster Ghiselin, p. 90; first book appearance of " *The Nets* by Brewster Ghiselin," p. 91.

Publication: Published 2 March 1976 at $10.00; 1,200 copies printed.

B125 *TO EBERHART FROM GINSBERG* 1976

TO EBERHART FROM GINSBERG I A Letter About HOWL 1956 I [in light blue; row of three rules, each 85 mm.] I AN EXPLANATION BY ALLEN GINS- I BERG OF HIS PUBLICATION *HOWL* I AND RICHARD EBERHART'S *NEW* I *YORK TIMES* ARTICLE "WEST COAST RHYTHMS" TOGETHER WITH COM- I MENTS BY BOTH POETS AND RELIEF I ETCHINGS BY JEROME KAPLAN I [row of three rules, like first] I [in black] THE PENMAEN PRESS 1976

Copyright Page: '[publisher's device] I "West Coast Rhythms" copyright ©1956 by *The New York Times* I *Company*. Reprinted by permission. Remaining textual matter and I prints copyright © 1976 by the Penmaen Press. All rights reserved.' No statement of first edition.

Binding: card cover issue: perfect bound in white photographic card cover, 9 3/16 x 6 3/16 in. (232 x 156 mm.); printed in black; front contains photographs of RE and Allen Ginsberg; hard cover issue: quarter-bound in blue cloth and medium blue denim cloth boards, 9 7/16 x 6 3/8 in. (240 x 163 mm.); front and spine stamped in silver; all edges cut; yellowish white, wove, unwatermarked endpapers; clear, unprinted plastic protective jacket.

Contents: First publication of RE's introduction, "How This Book Came Into Being," pp. 7-9; first book publication of "West Coast Rhythms" (**C363**), pp. 41-45.

Publication: Published in March 1976 at $5.00 (card cover issue) and $20.00 (later $25.00); 1,289 copies printed, 300 of which were issued in hardcover and 989 in card cover. *N.B.:* An unsigned hardcover issue of 38 copies was issued at $12.00. There were also two additional hardcover issues which were made up from the softcover issue: 116 copies were bound in blue English Seta cloth, and 160 copies were bound in green Seta cloth. See *Note.*

Colophon: p. 47, 'This first edition of *To Eberhart from Ginsberg* was printed | & published by Michael McCurdy at the Penmaen Press | in Lincoln, Massachusetts, and completed in March, | 1976. Of an edition of 1500, 300 were hardbound, numbered | and signed by Richard Eberhart and Allen Ginsberg. | "West Coast Rhythms" was published originally by *The | New York Times Book Review* in September, 1956. | Typographic design is by Michael McCurdy. The Times | New roman type was set by Michael Bixler, and the paper | is Warren's Olde Style. Robert Burlen & Son bound both | hard and soft cover editions and Robert Hauser created the | binding design for the hardcover edition. Jerome Kaplan's | relief etchings were printed directly from the original plates. | Editorial assistance was provided by Deborah McCurdy. | This is number [arabic numeral supplied in black or blue ink].' | [in the hardbound copies only; RE's autograph in blue ink | [Allen Ginsberg's autograph in black ink]'.

Note: In addition to the hardbound issues that were signed or unsigned, an unknown number of copies were supplied as *hors de commerce* copies to RE and Ginsberg. These are identified respectively on the colophon page in blue ink as 'RE' or 'AG' after 'This is number' .

B126 *THIRD WORLD CONGRESS OF POETS* 1976

[cover title; in blue] THIRD WORLD CONGRESS OF POETS | June 23-27, 1976 | [reprod. of autograph of Edgar Allen Poe, 224 x 151 mm.]

Copyright Page: 'Copyright © 1976 Third World Congress of Poets, Inc.'; no statement of first edition.

Binding: glued in gray card cover, 11 1/4 x 8 1/2 in. (286 x 216 mm.); front printed in blue.

Contents: First publication of a brief untitled statement about poetry by RE, p. 6.

Publication: 1,000 copies prepared for distribution at the Third World Congress of Poets, Baltimore, Md., 23 June 1976; not for sale.

B127 *MOVING OUT* [1976]

M o v i n g   O u t I *David Walker* I University Press of Virginia I Charlottesville

Copyright Page: '*First published 1976*'.

Binding and Dust Jacket: dark orangish yellow cloth boards measure 9 3/16 x 6 in. (233 x 153 mm.); spine stamped in gold; all edges cut; white cloth head and tail bands; yellowish white, wove, unwatermarked endpapers; cream-colored dust jacket printed in brown and orangish brown.

Contents: Foreword by RE, pp. v-vii, an excpt. of which is printed on the back flap of the dust jacket.

Publication: Published 27 July 1976 at $6.95; 1,000 copies printed.

B128 *CROSSING AMERICA* [1976]

[in green] CROSSING AMERICA I [in gray] LEO CONNELLAN I [wood engraving by Michael McCurdy, in black] I [in gray] THE P E N M A E N   P R E S S   L I N C O L N

Copyright Page: 'Copyright 1976 by Leo Connellan'; no statement of first edition.

Binding: hardcover issue: green cloth boards measure 9 1/2 x 6 1/4 in. (241 x 164 mm.); spine stamped in gold; all edges cut, unstained; thick, wove, gray endpapers; issued without jacket; card cover issue: perfect bound in thick white card cover, 9 1/4 x 6 1/8 in. (235 x 155 mm.); printed in black and gray.

Contents: Preface by RE, p. 7.

Publication: Published in October 1976 at $20.00 (hardcover) and $4.00 (cardcover); 898 copies printed of which 200 were issued in hardcover and 698 in card cover.

Colophon: p. 37, 'THIS FIRST EDITION OF *CROSSING AMERICA* | WAS HAND-PRINTED AT THE PENMAEN PRESS | IN LINCOLN, MASSACHUSETTS IN OCTOBER, | 1976 BY MICHAEL McCURDY, SCOTT-MARTIN | KOSOFSKY AND SYDNEY LICHT. THE WOOD | ENGRAVING AND TYPESETTING ARE BY M. | McCURDY. TWO HUNDRED BOOKS ARE HARD- | BOUND WITH AN ORIGINAL BINDING DESIGN | BY ROBERT HAUSER. THESE HAVE BEEN NUM- | BERED 1-200 AND SIGNED BY THE POET. | [in hardcover copies only] THIS IS NUMBER _____ [with number supplied in blue ink] | [author's autograph in blue ink]'.

B129 *THE SANDPIPERS* 1976

The | Sandpipers | S E L E C T E D   P O E M S (1 9 6 5 - 1 9 7 5) | With a Foreword by | Richard Eberhart | and a Portrait of the Poet by | Edward Plunkett | [ornament] | *David Posner* | A Florida Technological University Book | T H E   U N I V E R S I T Y   P R E S S E S   O F   F L O R I D A | Gainesville, 1976

Copyright Page: 'COPYRIGHT © 1959, [. . .] 1976 BY DAVID POSNER'; no statement of first edition.

Binding and Dust Jacket: black cloth boards measure 9 1/4 x 6 1/4 in. (235 x 159 mm.); front contains white paper label printed in black; spine stamped in gold; all edges cut, unstained; cloth head and tail bands have alternating white and gray stripes; yellowish white, wove, unwatermarked endpapers; white dust jacket printed in blue and black.

Contents: Foreword by RE, p. ix, an excpt. of which is printed on the back of the dust jacket.

Publication: Published in Dec. 1976 at $5.00; 1,067 copies printed, of which 102 were numbered and autographed by the author. A second printing of 1,093 copies was issued in Nov. 1977.

B130 *BEST POEMS OF 1975* 1976

Best Poems of 1975 | [in open-face] Borestone Mountain | Poetry Awards 1976 | [rule, 133 mm.] | [remainder in roman] A Compilation of Original Poetry | Published in Magazines of the | English-speaking World in 1975 | **Volume 28** | **Pacific Books, Publishers**, Palo Alto, California | 1976

Copyright Page: 'Copyright © 1976 by Borestone Mountain Poetry Awards.' No statement of first edition.

Binding and Dust Jacket: dark grayish tan cloth boards measure 8 3/4 x 5 3/4 in. (222 x 145 mm.); spine stamped in gold; all edges cut, unstained; cloth head and tail bands have alternating yellow and gray stripes; yellowish white, wove, unwatermarked endpapers; white dust jacket printed in red and blue.

Contents: First book publication of "A Way Out" (**C715**), pp. 28-29, and "Coast of Maine" (**C725**), p. 30.

Publication: Published 31 Dec. 1976 at $5.95; 1,500 copies printed.

B131 *MADEIRA & TOASTS FOR BASIL BUNTING'S 75TH BIRTHDAY*
1975 (i.e., 1977)

[four-page title composed of two leaves folded once each toward center; with illus. by John Furnival contained on all four; right] MADEIRA & TOASTS | FOR BASIL BUNTING'S 75TH BIRTHDAY | *Edited by Jonathan Williams* | The Jargon Society | Dentdale | March 1, 1975

Copyright Page: 'Copyright 1977 by *The Jargon Society* | [. . .] There are 1250 copies | for private distribution'; no statement of first edition.

Binding: perfect bound in white pictorial card cover, 9 x 6 in. (228 x 152 mm.); printed prin. in black, brown, and olive green.

Contents: First publication of "Word-Prowess," p. 24; in *WL*.

Publication: Published in March 1977; for private distribution only; not for sale.

B132 *W.B. YEATS: INTERVIEWS AND RECOLLECTIONS* [1977]

W.B. YEATS | Interviews and Recollections | Volume 1 | *Edited by* | E.H. Mikhail | With a Foreword by | A. Norman Jeffares | [in open-face] M

Copyright Page: '*First published 1977 by* | THE MACMILLAN PRESS, LTD'.

Binding and Dust Jacket: light grayish olive boards measure 8 3/4 x 5 3/4 in. (223 x 145 mm.); spine stamped in gold; all edges trimmed, unstained, yellowish white, wove, unwatermarked endpapers; white pictorial dust jacket printed prin. in green, light grayish green, olive green, bluish green, brownish orange, and black.

Contents: First book publication of "Memory of Meeting Yeats" (**C393**), pp. 193-95.

Publication: Published in June 1977 at £7.95.

B133 *INTO THE ROUND AIR* [1977]

Into the Round Air | Edited by | RAYMOND ROSELIEP | [publisher's device] | Thistle Publications | Derry • Pennsylvania

Copyright Page: 'First Printing, October, 1977'.

Binding: handsewn with black cord in light blue card cover, 8 3/8 x 5 3/8 in. (213 x 139 mm.); front printed in black; all edges cut, untrimmed.

Contents: First publication of "Quarry-Stone," pp. 12-13; in *WL*.

Publication: Published in Oct. 1977 as Thistle Publications Number One, at $3.50; the editor refers to this chapbook as a "surrogate fifth issue" of *Thistle* magazine.

B134 *THE VENTRILOQUIST* [1977]

The Ventriloquist | *New and Selected Poems* | by Robert Huff | University Press of Virginia | Charlottesville

Copyright Page: 'First published 1977'.

Binding and Dust Jacket: deep reddish orange cloth boards measure 9 5/16 x 6 1/16 in. (237 x 153 mm.); spine stamped in gold; all edges cut, unstained; white, wove, unwatermarked endpapers; very pale grayish white pictorial dust jacket printed in brownish orange and black.

Contents: Foreword by RE, p. 5, an excpt. of which is rept. on back flap of the dust jacket.

Publication: Published 21 Oct. 1977 at $6.95; 1,028 copies printed.

B135 *FIFTY CONTEMPORARY POETS:*
THE CREATIVE PROCESS [1977]

Fifty | Contemporary | Poets: | [rule, 109 mm.] | THE CREATIVE PROCESS | [rule, 109 mm.] | Edited by ALBERTA T. TURNER | *The Cleveland State University* | DAVID McKAY COMPANY, INC. | NEW YORK

Copyright Page: 'COPYRIGHT © 1977 BY DAVID McKAY COMPANY, INC.' no statement of first edition.

Binding: hardcover issue: orangish yellow cloth boards measure 9 1/4 x 6 1/4 in. (236 x 159 mm.); spine lettered in black; top and bottom edges cut, fore-edges rough trimmed; cloth head and tail bands have alternating red and yellow stripes; yellowish white, wove, unwatermarked endpapers; white dust jacket printed prin. in shades of orange, yellow, gray, and black; card cover issue: perfect bound in card cover like dust jacket of hardcover issue.

Contents: First book publication of RE's poem, "A Snowfall" (**C734**), pp. 85-86; with a letter to the editor concerning the poem, on pp. 86-89.

Publication: Published in Nov. 1977 at $12.50 (hardcover) and $5.95 (card cover).

B136 *THE POETRY ANTHOLOGY* 1978

THE | *POETRY* | ANTHOLOGY | 1912-1977 | [swelled rule] | *Sixty-five Years of America's Most* | *Distinguished Verse Magazine* | [*Poetry* logo] | EDITED BY | *Daryl Hine & Joseph Parisi* | HOUGHTON MIFFLIN COMPANY | BOSTON 1978

Copyright Page: 'Copyright © 1978 by The Modern Poetry Association | [...] P 10 9 8 7 6 5 4 3 2 1'.

Binding: hardcover issue: red cloth boards measure 8 9/16 x 5 3/4 in. (228 x 155 mm.); front and spine stamped in silver; all edges cut, unstained; cloth head and tail bands have alternating red and black stripes; yellowish white, wove, unwatermarked endpapers; white dust jacket with photographic design printed in red, black, and gray; card cover issue: perfect bound in card cover like dust jacket of hard cover issue, 8 1/8 x 5 1/8 in. (218 x 140 mm.).

Contents: First book publication of "Under the Hill" (**C48**), pp. 106-7.

Publication: Published 30 June 1978 at $20.95 (hard cover) and $12.95 (card cover); rept. in card cover as Sentry Edition 86 at $10.95.

B137 *HER BEAUTY LIKES ME WELL* [1979]

[cover title; rev. out in white] HER | BEAUTY | LIKES ME | WELL | poems by | LUIS FRANCIA | DAVID FRIEDMAN

Copyright: on verso of front card cover, 'POEMS OF LUIS FRANCIA © 1979 LUIS FRANCIA | POEMS OF DAVID FRIEDMAN © 1979 DAVID FRIEDMAN | FOR "KITTY" © 1977 DAVID FRIEDMAN'; no statement of first edition.

Card Cover: wire-stitched in thick, white card cover, 8 3/8 x 5 7/16 in. (213 x 140 mm.); front printed black with letters rev. out in white.

Contents: Foreword by RE, p. 1.

Publication: Published in March 1979 at $2.00.

B138 *IN THE FOURTH WORLD* [1979]

IN THE | FOURTH WORLD | *poems by* | SANDRA M. GILBERT | *with an introduction by Richard Eberhart* | *The University of Alabama Press* | *University, Alabama*

Copyright Page: 'Copyright © 1979 | The University of Alabama Press'; no statment of first edition.

Binding: perfect bound in white card cover, 8 1/2 x 5 3/8 in. (216 x 138 mm.); printed in shades of pink, dull red, and black.

Contents: Introduction by RE, p. ix; an excpt. rept. on back of card cover.

Publication: Published in Sept. 1979 at $3.95.

B139 *WORLD ANTHOLOGY* [1980]

[reprod. from typescript orig.] WORLD ANTHOLOGY | *A VERSE MOSAIC BY LIVING POETS* | *OF AND FOR ALL CONTINENTS* | *Compiled By* | ORVILLE CROWDER MILLER | and | DOROTHY MUNNS MILLER | *Published by* | DELORA MEMORIAL FUND FOR WORLD BROTHERHOOD | Urbana, Illinois, U.S.A.

Copyright Page: '© 1980 by Dorothy Munns Miller'; no statement of first edition.

Binding: perfect bound in brilliant grayish blue card cover, 9 x 6 in. (229 x 153 mm.); printed in black on front.

Contents: First publication of "Learning from Nature," p. 49; in *WL, CP88*.

Publication: Published in March 1980 at $5.00.

B140 *FOR REXROTH: THE ARK 14* [1980]

For | **REXROTH** | [illus.] | **The Ark** | *Edited by Geoffrey Gardner* | The Ark | New York | [right side, the hgt. of last three lines] *14*

Copyright Page: 'Copyright © 1980 by The Ark'; no statement of first edition.

Binding and Dust Jacket: light gray cloth boards measure 8 3/4 x 5 5/8 in. (222 x 143 mm.); spine lettered in black; all edges trimmed, unstained; deep orangish red, wove endpapers; gray pictorial dust jacket printed in black.

Contents: First publication of "Two for Rexroth";

"The Year," pp. 182-83; in *LR*.
"Prayer to the God of Harm, The Song of the Poet," p. 184; in *LR*.

Publication: Published in May 1980 at $10.00; 1,200 copies printed.

Colophon: p. 414, 'This book has been set in Garamond by | John Minczeski | 1200 copies have been printed by | Haymarket Press. | 26 of these have been signed and lettered A-Z by | Kenneth Rexroth | and are *hors de commerce*.'

B141 *DESIRE: EROTIC POETRY THROUGH THE AGES* [1980]

DESIRE | Erotic Poetry Through | the Ages | *Edited by William Packard* | *Foreword by Richard Eberhart* | ST. MARTIN'S PRESS | *New York*

Copyright Page: '10 9 8 7 6 5 4 3 2 1 | First Edition'.

Binding and Dust Jacket: quarter-bound in black cloth and black paper boards, 9 7/16 x 5 5/8 in. (241 x 143 mm.); spine stamped in silver; top and bottom edges cut, fore-edges rough untrimmed; cloth head and tail bands have alternating black and white stripes; purple wove endpapers; white pictorial dust jacket printed prin. in pale gray, black, yellow, and reddish pink.

Contents: Foreword by RE, pp. 1-4, a portion of which is rept. on front and back flaps of dust jacket. Two poems are herein rept: "Lions Copulating," pp. 2-3, and "The Reading Room, The New York Public Library," p. 196.

Publication: Published in Sept. 1980 at $12.95; 4,000 copies printed.

B142 *WONDERS: WRITINGS AND DRAWINGS*
FOR THE CHILD IN US ALL [1980]

[row of three rules, 118 mm., the middle of which is thick] | [in fancy type] WONDERS | *Writings and Drawings for* | *the Child in Us All* | [row of three rules like first, broken in middle by device of smiling quarter-moon and three stars] | Edited by | JONATHAN COTT | & MARY GIMBEL | [row of three rules like first] | ROLLING STONE PRESS / SUMMIT BOOKS / NEW YORK | [rule, 118 mm.]

Copyright Page: 'FIRST EDITION | 1 2 3 4 5 6 7 8 9 10'.

Binding and Dust Jacket: quarter-bound in very dark red cloth and dark red paper boards, 9 1/2 x 6 1/2 in. (243 x 166 mm.); front and spine stamped in gold; all edges cut, unstained; white cloth head and tail bands; dark blue wove endpapers; white pictorial jacket printed in dark red and dark blue.

Contents: First publication of "To Alpha Dryden Eberhart, November 26, 1977, on Being Seventy-Five," pp. 168-69; in *LR*; rept. in *The Poet's Choice*, ed. George E. Murphy, Jr. (Green Harbor, Mass.: Tendril Magazine, 1980), p. 52.

Publication: Published in Dec. 1980 at $14.95.

B143 *DO NOT GO GENTLE: POEMS ON DEATH* [1981]

DO NOT I GO GENTLE I *POEMS ON DEATH* I Edited by William Packard I Foreword by Richard Eberhart I ST. MARTIN'S PRESS NEW YORK

Copyright Page: 'Copyright © 1981 by William Packard'; no statement of first edition.

Binding and Dust Jacket: quarter-bound in natural linen-cloth and light olive green paper boards, 7 1/4 x 5 1/4 in. (184 x 134 mm.); spine stamped in gold; top and bottom edges trimmed, fore-edges untrimmed; cloth head and tail bands have alternating brown and white stripes; light grayish green, wove endpapers; deep tan dust jacket printed in purple and green.

Contents: Foreword by RE, pp. xiv-xv; "The Groundhog" is rept. on pp. 97-99.

Publication: Published in May 1981 at $9.95; 1,500 copies printed.

B144 *FIFTH WORLD CONGRESS OF POETS* 1981

FIFTH I WORLD CONGRESS OF POETS I SAN FRANCISCO 1981 I POEMS BY DELEGATES

Copyright Page: 'Copyright © 1981, 5th World Congress of Poets, San Francisco'; no statement of first edition.

Binding: perfect bound in orange pictorial card cover, 8 15/16 x 6 3/4 in. (211 x 171 mm.); printed in black.

Contents: First publication of "Fantasy of a Small Idea," p. 64; in *LR, CP88*; rept. in *Poetry Now*, 6, no. 5, issue 35 (1982), p. 2.

Publication: Published in July 1981 at $5.00; 2,000 copies printed.

B145 *BREAD, HASHISH AND MOON* 1982

Bread, Hashish and Moon I *FOUR MODERN ARAB POETS* I Edited by I BEN BENNANI I INTRODUCTION BY RICHARD EBERHART I CALLIGRAPHY BY KAMAL BOULLATA I *Greensboro:* Unicorn Press, Inc. 1982

Copyright Page: 'COPYRIGHT © 1982 BY UNICORN PRESS'; no statement of first edition.

Binding: hardcover issue: quarter-bound in light brown cloth and light brownish orange paper boards, 8 3/4 x 5 11/16 in. (222 x 145 mm.); front printed in black, green and brown; spine contains brownish orange paper label printed in black; all edges trimmed; brown, wove endpapers; no dust jacket; card cover issue: perfect bound in card cover like binding of hardcover issue, 8 7/16 x 5 7/16 in. (214 x 139 mm.).

Contents: Introduction by RE, pp. 1-2.

Publication: Published 1 Feb. 1982 at $12.00 (hardcover) and $6.00 (card cover); 1,000 copies printed of which 250 were issued in hardcover and 750 were issued in card cover.

Colophon: p. 57, 'Alan Brilliant hand-set this book in Kennerly type; I he also hand-bound the sheets, printed by I Inter Collegiate Press.'

B146 *POETSPEAK* [1983]

Poetspeak: I *In their work, about their work* I A selection by Paul B. Janeczko I BRADBURY PRESS [ornament] SCARSDALE, NEW YORK

Copyright Page: 'Copyright © 1983 by Paul B. Janeczko. I [...] I 10 9 8 7 6 5 4 3 2 1'; no statement of first edition.

Binding and Dust Jacket: quarter-bound in blue and deep tan cloth boards, 9 1/4 x 6 1/4 in. (234 x 160 mm.); spine stamped in copper; all edges trimmed, unstained; strong blue wove endpapers; white pictorial dust jacket printed prin. in grayish blue, shades of pink, green, brown, and black.

Contents: First publication of RE's brief commentary on his poem, "On a Squirrel Crossing the Road in Autumn, in New England," p. 165; the poem is rept. on pp. 164-65; "Flux" is rept. on p. 99.

Publication: Published in July 1983 at $12.95.

B147 *FIRE-TESTED* [1983]

Fire-Tested I By Hans Juergensen I [reprod. of a drawing by Juergensen]

Copyright Page: '© Copyright by Hans Juergensen'; no statement of first edition.

Binding: wire-stitched in orange card cover, 8 5/8 x 5 1/4 in. (221 x 140 mm.); printed in black on front and back; all edges trimmed.

Contents: RE's brief statement about the book, p. 5.

Publication: Published in Sept. 1983.

B148 *WARNINGS* [1984]

[in open-face] WARN- I INGS: I An Anthology I on the I NUCLEAR PERIL

Copyright Page: 'First Edition'.

Binding: perfect bound in orange pictorial card cover, 9 x 5 5/16 in. (227 x 151 mm.); printed in dark reddish orange.

Contents: First publication of "Testimony," pp. 136-38; in *LR, CP88.*

Publication: Published by the *Northwest Review* as a special two-number anthology (v. 22) in Jan. 1984 at $8.00

B149 *SETTLING IN IN HANOVER* [1984]

[in black] Settling In in Hanover I *& Other Essays* I by I Douglas McCreary Greenwood I cartouche in grayish blue] I [in black] The Stinehour Press [ornament] Lunenburg, Vermont

Copyright Page: no statement of copyright; contains dedication.

Binding: perfect bound in yellowish white card cover, 9 x 6 in. (229 x 153 mm.); printed in grayish blue on front and spine.

Contents: Introduction by RE, p. 3.

Publication: Published in April 1984; 1,000 copies printed; not for sale.

Statement of Limitation: p. 36, '*This gathering of essays | was designed by Patricia Stinehour | and printed at The Stinehour Press | in an edition of 1000 copies,* | *of which this is No.* [arabic numeral in blue ink] | [cartouche ident. to title page, in grayish blue]'.

B150 *CRITICAL ESSAYS ON LOUISE BOGAN* 1984

Critical Essays on | Louise Bogan | [rule, 102 mm.] | Martha Collins | G.K. Hall & Co. • Boston, Massachusetts

Copyright Page: 'Copyright © 1984 by Martha Collins'; no statement of first edition.

Binding: quarter-bound in deep blue and grayish tan cloth boards, 9 1/2 x 6 3/8 in. (242 x 163 mm.); spine stamped in gold; all edges trimmed, unstained; cloth head and tail bands have alternating blue and white stripes; yellowish white, wove, unwatermarked endpapers; issued without a dust jacket.

Contents: First book publication of "Common Charms from Deep Sources" (**C315**), pp. 67-68.

Publication: Published 10 April 1984 at $35.00.

B151 *THE PUSHCART PRIZE, IX* [1984]

[two-page title; left] [row of three type ornaments] **THE PUSHCART PRIZE, IX:** [right] **BEST OF THE SMALL PRESSES** | . . . *WITH AN INDEX TO THE FIRST NINE VOLUMES* | **An annual small press reader** | [left, publisher's device; right] EDITED BY BILL HENDERSON | with The Pushcart Prize editors | Introduction by Jayne Anne Phillips | published by THE PUSHCART PRESS | 1984-85 Edition | [left] **BEST OF THE SMALL PRESSES** [right] **THE PUSHCART PRIZE, IX:** [row of three type ornaments]

Copyright Page: 'First printing, July, 1984'.

Binding and Dust Jacket: quarter-bound in dark blue cloth and light blue paper boards, 9 9/16 x 6 5/8 in. (243 x 168 mm.); spine stamped in silver; top and bottom edges trimmed; cloth head and tail bands have alternating blue and white stripes; light blue, wove endpapers; white dust jacket printed in dark blue, yellow, and black.

Contents: First book publication of "Making Poetry a Continuum" (**C819**), pp. 170-202.

Publication: Published in July 1984 at $24.95.

B152 *THE NEW YORK QUARTERLY*
("Reflections and Developments") [1984]

[cover title; upper right corner, in black, publisher's logo of interlocking 'NYQ'] | [lower left side, rev. out in white] the | NEW YORK QUARTERLY

Copyright Page: none present.

Binding: wire-stitched in white card cover with photograph of the Brooklyn bridge on front, 9 x 5 7/8 in. (227 x 150 mm.); front and back printed in black; all edges trimmed.

Contents: First publication of an untitled letter from RE to *New York Quarterly* editor William Packard, p. 9.

Publication: Unknown number of copies issued in late Sept. or October 1984 as promotional brochure; editorial statement of pp. 1-2 titled "NYQ: Reflections and Developments"; remainder consists of tributes and statements about the magazine.

B153 *A POET TO HIS BELOVED* [1985]

A Poet | to His Beloved: | THE EARLY LOVE POEMS | OF W.B. YEATS | INTRODUCTION BY | RICHARD EBERHART | ST. MARTIN'S PRESS / *New York*

Copyright Page: 'First Edition | 10 9 8 7 6 5 4 3 2 1'.

Binding and Dust Jacket: black cloth boards measure 7 1/4 x 5 5/16 in. (184 x 135 mm.); spine stamped in gold; top and bottom edges trimmed, fore-edges untrimmed; top edges stained purple; dark bluish purple wove endpapers; purple cloth place marker bound in; pale tan wove dust jacket printed in black and purple.

Contents: Introduction by RE, pp. ix-xi.

Publication: Published in Nov. 1985 at $8.95; 6,500 copies printed.

B154 *THE BREAD LOAF ANTHOLOGY OF CONTEMPORARY AMERICAN POETRY* [1985]

[two-page title; left] PUBLISHED FOR THE BREAD LOAF WRITERS' CONFERENCE | *Middlebury College* | [publisher's device] | BY UNIVERSITY PRESS OF NEW ENGLAND | *Hanover and London, 1985* [right] THE BREAD LOAF ANTHOLOGY | *of Contemporary American Poetry* | *Edited by Robert Pack, Sydney Lea, and Jay Parini.*

Copyright Page: '© 1985 by Bread Loaf Writers' Conference / Middlebury College'; no statement of first edition.

Binding and Dust Jacket: hardcover issue: black cloth boards measure 8 1/4 x 6 1/4 in. (212 x 159 mm.); spine stamped in gold; all edges cut, unstained; cloth head and tail bands have alternating black and white stripes; tan, wove endpapers; white dust jacket printed in light grayish blue and black; card cover issue: perfect bound in card cover like dust jacket of hard cover issue, 8 x 6 in. (203 x 153 mm.).

Contents: First publication of "The Mystical Beast in the Shadows," pp. 69-70; in *CP88*. First book publication of "River Water Music" (**C818**), p. 69; "Dead Skunk" (**C810**), pp. 70-71; "White Pines, Felled 1984" (**C834**), pp. 71-72; "The Angels" (**C833**), pp. 72-73.

Publication: Published 1 Oct. 1985 at $25.00 (hardcover) and $14.95 (card cover).

B155 *A CELEBRATION OF TEACHERS* [1985]

[abstract diamond-design; slanted from left to right, vert. from top to bottom] NCTE DIAMOND JUBILEE | *A Celebration* | *of Teachers* | National Council of Teachers of English | 1111 Kenyon Road, Urbana, Illinois 61801

Copyright Page: 'Copyright © 1985 by the National Council of Teachers of English.

Binding: wire-stitched in thick white card cover, 9 x 6 in. (228 x 153 mm.); inner side white, outer side printed silver-gray; lettering in dark red and rev. out in white; all edges cut, unstained.

Contents: First publication of RE's untitled tribute to his high school English teacher, pp. 14-15.

Publication: Published in Nov. 1985; a "New Edition" issued in 1986; RE's tribute on pp. 17-18.

B156 *BEST MINDS* 1986

BEST MINDS | A TRIBUTE TO ALLEN GINSBERG | EDITED BY BILL MORGAN | & BOB ROSENTHAL | LOSPECCHIO PRESS | NEW YORK | 1986

Copyright Page: 'Copyright © 1986 by Bill Morgan and Bob Rosenthal'.

Binding: trade issue: red cloth boards measure 10 5/16 x 7 3/16 in. (272 x 193 mm.); front and spine stamped in gold; all edges cut, unstained; cloth head and tail bands have alternating red and black stripes; yellowish white, wove, unwatermarked endpapers; numbered issue: all ident. to trade issue except for: black cloth boards; red, wove endpapers; statement of limitation on copyright page, 'This is Copy | [rule, with number '1/250', '2/250', etc., supplied above in blue ink] | of the Limited Edition | [editors' autographs in blue ink]'; lettered issue: all ident. to numbered issue except a letter A-Z is supplied in black ink on rule, and a signed photograph of Ginsberg is tipped in on the colophon page.

Contents: First publication of "Allen Ginsberg: A Man of Spirit," pp. 94-96, dated 21 July 1983.

Publication: Published 3 June 1986 at $25.00 (trade issue), $75.00 (numbered issue), and $125.00 (lettered issue); approx. 750 copies printed.

Colophon: p. 312, 'This first printing of *Best Minds* is published on 3 June 1986 and is limited to an edition of | 226 copies, 200 of which are numbered and signed by the editors and 26 of which are let- | tered A to Z and signed by the editors and Allen Ginsberg and contain an additional self- | portrait photograph by the poet. In addition, 500 contributors' copies in special binding | have been printed, 250 of which are numbered and 250 of which are *hors commerce* | copies for the writers of these tributes.'

B157 *UNDER OPEN SKY* [1986]

[two-page title; right, wood engraving by John De Pol, which is continued on left side; remainder left] UNDER OPEN SKY | *Poets on William Cullen Bryant* | EDITED BY NORBERT KRAPF | WOOD ENGRAVINGS BY JOHN DE POL | [continuation of wood engraving from left side] | FORDHAM UNIVERSITY PRESS | NEW YORK MCMLXXXXVI

Copyright Page: 'Text copyright: © 1986, by Norbert Krapf | Illustrations copyright: © 1986, by John De Pol'; no statement of first edition.

Binding: three bindings; card cover: perfect bound in white pictorial card cover, 9 x 6 in. (230 x 153 mm.); printed in black and olive green; hardbound: dark olive green cloth boards measure 9 1/4 x 6 1/4 in. (235 x 159 mm.); front and spine stamped in gold; all edges cut, unstained; cloth head and tail bands have alternating green and yellow stripes; decorated endpapers printed in green; white dust jacket like card cover except back contains advertisement for *The Letters of William Cullen Bryant*; special binding: quarterbound in gray linen-cloth and green decorated paper boards, 9 5/8 x 6 5/8 in. (245 x 168 mm.); spine stamped in gold; all edges cut, unstained; cloth head and tail bands have alternating yellow and orange stripes; light olive green laid paper endpapers; clear glassine protective jacket, unprinted.

Contents: First publication of a brief essay, "Memory of Learning 'Thanatopsis' in Youth," pp. 60-61.

Publication: Published 15 Sept. 1986 at $17.50 (card cover), $29.95 (hardbound), and $65.00 (special binding); 1185 copies printed, of which 400 were issued in card cover, 600 in hardcover with dust jacket, and 185 copies in special binding signed by the editor and illustrator.

Colophon: in paperbound and hardcover issue, p. 111: 'COLOPHON | *Under Open Sky* was designed by M.A. Gelfand, and printed by him with as- | sistance from Jim Ricciardi and Lynn Peterson at The Stone House Press. It was | set in Monotype Emerson at Out of Sorts Letter Foundery, Mamaroneck, New | York, with hand composition at the Press. | He has provided the reproduction | proofs from which this edition of 1,000 copies has been printed on Mohawk | Superfine paper. | [seal of Fordham University]'; in special binding: all ident. except for: '[...] with hand composition at the Press. The decorative cover paper, printed | by offset, was created by John De Pol, illustrator of the text. Printed from the | type and blocks on Mohawk Letterpress paper, and bound by Alpha-Pavia, New | York. This edition is limited to 185 signed

& numbered copies, with 140 for sale. | [left side] This is copy [(number supplied in black ink)] [right side; signed in blue ink by the editor and illustrator]'.

B158 *JOHN CIARDI: MEASURE OF THE MAN* 1987

[reprod. from author's autograph] John Ciardi | [remainder in roman] MEASURE OF THE MAN | edited by Vince Clemente | The University of Arkansas Press | Fayetteville 1987 [rule, 33 mm.]

Copyright Page: 'Copyright © 1987 by The Board of Trustees | The University of Arkansas Press, Fayetteville, Arkansas 72701'; no statement of first edition.

Binding: cloth issue: dark blue cloth boards measure 9 1/4 x 6 1/4 in. (236 x 159 mm.); spine lettered in white; all edges cut, unstained; cloth head and tail bands have alternating blue and white stripes; dull white, wove, unwatermarked endpapers; light bluish gray dust jacket printed in blue; card cover: perfect bound in card cover like dust jacket of cloth issue, 9 x 6 in. (230 x 153 mm.).

Contents: First publication of RE's tribute, "Thanks, John, for Being," pp. 32-33.

Publication: Published in March 1987 at $19.95 (cloth issue) and $9.95 (card cover issue); 1,750 copies printed, of which 750 were issued in cloth and 1,000 copies in card cover.

B159 *DICTIONARY OF LITERARY BIOGRAPHY YEARBOOK: 1986* 1987

Dictionary of Literary Biography | Yearbook: 1986 | Edited by | J.M. Brook | A Bruccoli Clark Laymen Book | Gale Research Company • Book Tower • Detroit, Michigan 18226

Copyright Page: '[…] | Copyright © 1987 | GALE RESEARCH COMPANY | […]'; no statement of first edition.

Binding: light blue cloth boards measure 11 1/4 x 8 5/8 in. (287 x 222 mm.); front and spine contain dark blue panels lettered in gold; spine also lettered in blue; all edges cut, unstained; cloth head and tail bands have alternating light blue and white stripes; endpapers contain photographic reproductions in black and white.

Contents: First publication of an untitled statement by RE on his term as consultant in poetry to the Library of Congress, p. 36.

Publication: Published in May 1987 at $95.00.

B160 *THE INAUGURATION OF JAMES OLIVER FREEMAN AS FIFTEENTH PRESIDENT OF DARTMOUTH COLLEGE* [1987]

[all in green; within a single rule frame] [seal of Dartmouth College] The Inauguration | *of* | JAMES OLIVER FREEMAN | *as* | Fifteenth President | *of* | Dartmouth College

Copyright Page: none present.

Binding: wire-stitched in pale gray card cover; front measures 8 15/16 x 6 in. (228 x 153 mm.); top and bottom edges trimmed, fore-edges deckled.

Contents: First publication of RE's poem, "Inauguration," p. 1. *N.B.* text stock ident. to card cover.

Publication: Published 19 July 1987 for distribution at the inauguration of James O. Freeman, Dartmouth College, Hanover, N.H.; approx. 3,000 copies printed.

B161 *CONTEMPORARY NEW ENGLAND POETRY: A SAMPLER* 1987

Contemporary | *New England Poetry:* | *A Sampler* | Edited by | Paul Ruffin | Foreword by George Garrett | Introduction by X.J. Kennedy | Copyright © 1987 by | *Texas Review Press* | Sam Houston State University | All Rights Reserved

Binding: perfect bound in pale green card cover, 8 15/16 x 5 5/16 in. (228 x 152 mm.); front and spine printed in green; all edges cut, unstained.

Contents: First publication of three poems by RE:

    "Brief Candle" p. 38
    "At Archie Peisch's Funeral"
    "Millennia" p. 40

Publication: Published in July 1987 at $5.00; 750 copies.

C
Contributions to Periodicals

C1 "Go Your Own Way." Tower (Dartmouth College, Hanover, N.H., student literary magazine), 1 (17 Oct. 1924), 4. Poem. Sgd. 'R.G. Eberhart'.

Note: RE entered Dartmouth College as a sophomore in September 1923, after having spent his freshman year at the University of Minnesota. This poem was the first he published since high school, although he had written a great many. See Joel Roache, Richard Eberhart: The Progress of an *American Poet* (New York: Oxford Univ. Press, 1971), p. 13ff.

A rare little magazine in the compiler's collection, *Monkey*, no. 1 (17 August 1916), published and hand-printed by Neil Campbell, Dryden Eberhart (RE's older brother), and RE (12 years old) is identified as a semi-monthly. However, no other copies could be located, and RE recollects that only the one number was printed. It contains no signed article by RE, but he recollects he "may have contributed a few short pieces."

C2 "The Inevitable." *Tower*, 1 (17 Oct. 1924), 8. Poem. Sgd. 'R.G. Eberhart'.

C3 "Impressions." *Tower*, 1 (6 Nov. 1924), 9. Poem. Sgd. 'R.G. Eberhart'.

C4 "Beneath Rich Stars." *Dartmouth Bema* (undergraduate literary magazine), 13 (Dec. 1924), 23. Poem. Sgd. 'R.G. Eberhart'.

C5 "Searcher." *Tower*, 1 (15 Dec. 1924), 8. First of "Two Poems," signed 'R.G. Eberhart'. Rept. *The Arts Anthology: Dartmouth Verse 1925*, introd. by Robert Frost (Portland, Me.: The Mosher Press, 1925), p. 8; *Poetry*, 31 (Nov. 1927), 85.

C6 "Barriers." *Tower*, 1 (15 Dec. 1924), 8. Second of "Two Poems" by RE.

C7 "The Lady Styx." *Tower*, 1 (7 Feb. 1925), 8. Poem. Sgd. 'R.G. Eberhart'. Rept. in *Austin Daily Herald* (29 May 1936), p. 2.

C8 "Despair." *Tower*, 1 (21 Feb. 1925), 3. Poem. Sgd. 'R.G. Eberhart'. *Note:* This poem should not be confused with another of the same title, **C615**.

C9 "To a Proud Lady." *Dartmouth Bema*, 13 (March 1925), 26. Poem. Sgd. 'R.G. Eberhart'.

C10 "Silver." *Tower*, 1 (23 March 1925), 11. Poem. Sgd. 'R.G. Eberhart'.

C11 "Truth." *Dartmouth Bema*, 13 (April 1925), 8. Poem. Sgd. 'R.G. Eberhart'.

C12 "The Community Dog Show." *Tower*, 1 (15 April 1925), 7. Humorous editorial in "The Cauldron" (col.), signed 'R.G.E.'.

C13 "Tin Gods." *Tower*, 1 (15 April 1925), 7. Humorous editorial in "The Cauldron," sgd. 'R.G.E.'.

C14 "Veil." *Tower*, 1 (15 April 1925), 7. Poem. Sgd. 'R.G. Eberhart'.

C15 "Another Change in Chapel." *Tower*, 1 (15 April 1925), 8-9. Article. Sgd. 'R.G.E.'.

C16 "Hyacinthus and the Jonquil." *Tower*, 1 (24 April 1925), 9. Story. Sgd. 'R.G. Eberhart'. *Note:* RE is listed as a member of the Editorial Board in this number of Tower.

C17 "A Freshman Orientation Course." Tower, 1 (8 May 1925), 1-3. Editorial, signed 'R.G. Eberhart'.

C18 "Stylistic Wizardry." *Tower*, 1 (8 May 1925), 5. Review of e.e. cummings, *XLI Poems*. Sgd. 'R.G. Eberhart'.

C19 "Worshipper." *Tower*, 1 (8 May 1925), 7. Poem. Sgd. 'R.G. Eberhart'.

C20 "Wonder and Shadow." *Dartmouth Bema*, 13 (June 1925), 37. Poem. Sgd. 'R.G. Eberhart'.

C21 "Ultimate." *Dartmouth Bema*, 13 (June 1925) 41. Poem. Sgd. 'R.G. Eberhart'.

C22 "Altars." *Tower*, 1 (1 June 1925), 9. Poem. Sgd. 'R.G. Eberhart'.

C23 "Ghost—Chaste and White." *Tower*, 1 (1 June 1925), 10. Poem. Sgd. 'R.G. Eberhart'.

C24 "A Greek Returns." *Tower*, 1 (1 June 1925), 10. Rev. of H.D., *Collected Poems*. Sgd. 'R.G. Eberhart'.

C25 "Homo Sapiens aetat 21." *Tower*, 1 (1 June 1925), 10. Poem. Sgd. 'R.G. Eberhart'.

C26 "Renunciation." *Tower*, 2 (25 Sept. 1925), 10. Poem. Sgd. with pseudonym 'R.E. Ghormley'.

C27 "Sculptor." *Tower*, 2 (25 Sept. 1925), 10. Poem. Sgd. with pseudonym 'R.E. Ghormley'.

C28 "Circe." *Tower*, 2 (25 Sept. 1925), 12. Poem. Sgd. 'R.G. Eberhart'.

C29 "Recognition." *Tower*, 2 (25 Sept. 1925), 15. Poem. Sgd. 'R.G. Eberhart'. In *CP88*.

C30 "Bruges." *Tower*, 2 (9 Oct. 1925), 15. Poem. Sgd. 'R.G. Eberhart'.

C31 "Nirvana" (later titled "Song," "Cover Me Over," and "Cover Me Over, Clover"). *Tower*, 2 (6 Nov. 1925), 6. Poem. As "Cover Me Over" in *BO*, *SP51*, *CP60*, *SP65*, *CP76*, *CP88*. Rept. in *New Student* (Harvard Univ.), 17 March 1926, p. 4; *Young Pegasus: Prose and Verse* (New York: Dial, 1926), p. 309 (**B4**); as "Song," in *Poetry*, 31 (Nov. 1927), 85; as "Cover Me Over, Clover," in *Fifteen Modern American Poets*, ed. George P. Elliott (New York: Rinehart, 1956), p. 25; *The Achievement of Richard Eberhart*, ed. Bernard Engel (Glenview, Ill.: Scott Foresman, 1968), p. 26; *Contemporary Poetry in America*, ed. Miller Williams (New York: Random House, 1973), p. 5; *Student* (Wake Forest Univ., Winston-Salem, N.C., student literary magazine), Autumn 1982, 32. *Note:* The following authorial revisions have been identified; page and line numbers refer to the first appearance:

"Nirvana"] "Song" *Poetry* (1927)] "Cover Me Over" *BO*⁺

6.2 over] ~, *Poetry* (1927)

6.6 hands;] ~. *Poetry* (1927)

6.8 Nor...lands.] In...lands. *Poetry* (1927)

C32 "M.D." *Tower*, 2 (19 Nov. 1925), 12. Poem. Sgd. with pseudonym 'R.E. Ghormley'.

C33 "Revolt on Seeing the Ciitro Monumentale di Milano." *Tower*, 2 (19 Nov. 1925), 14. Poem. Sgd. 'R.G. Eberhart'.

C34 Untitled rev. of *A Miscellany of American Poetry 1925*, in *Tower*, 2 (12 Dec. 1925), 16. Signed 'R.G.E.'

C35 "For Rupert Brooke." *Tower*, 2 (6 Feb. 1926), 11. Poem. Sgd. 'R.G. Eberhart'.

C36 "Hierarchy." *Tower*, 2 (1 March 1926), 8. Poem. Sgd. 'R.G. Eberhart'. Rept. *Dartmouth Alumni Magazine*, 17 (April 1926), 546-7. *Note:* This poem won the 1926 Dartmouth Arts Prize.

C37 "The Great Adventure." *Tower*, 2 (1 March 1926), 13. Rev. of Kendall Banning, *The Great Adventure*. Sgd. 'R.G.E.'

C38 "You Are Cold and Lovely, White-Armed One." *Tower*, 2 (19 March 1926), 16. Poem. Sgd. 'R.G. Eberhart'.

C39 "Man and His Fellows." *Tower*, 2 (25 March 1926), 7-8. Rev. of Ernest Martin Hopkins, *Man and His Fellows*. Sgd. 'R.G.E.'

C40 "A Review." *Tower*, 2 (22 April 1926, 14. Rev. of Clarence Dewitt Thorpe, *The Mind of John Keats*. Sgd. 'R.G.E.'

C41 "Schopenhauer." *Tower*, 2 (22 April 1926), 16. Poem. Sgd. 'R.G. Eberhart'. Rept. in *Poetry*, 31 (Nov. 1927), 83. *Note*: The following authorial revisions have been identified; page and line numbers refer to the first appearance.

16.1-2 An...track.] *deleted*

16.3 "The] ∧~

16.3 turns,] ~.

16.5 burns,] ~–

16.7 "There] ∧~

16.11 "The] ∧~

16.14 Pain...wind] Freedom...mind

16.15 "Say] ∧ ~

16.17-18 Comes...real.] *completely revised and rewritten as* Is... real.

16.19-42 Three...die"] *deleted*

C42 "An Evaluation." *Tower*, 2 (22 April 1926), 17-18. Editorial. Sgd. 'R.G. Eberhart'.

C43 "Ilaria del Caretto." *Tower*, 2 (15 May 1926), 13. Poem. Sgd. 'R.G. Eberhart'.

C44 "Day Song." *Tower*, 2 (14 June 1926), 15. Poem. Sgd. 'R.G. Eberhart'.

C45 "Life Necessity" (retitled "Purpose" by RE in his copy of *Tower*). *Tower*, 2 (14 June 1926), 22. Poem. Sgd. 'R.G. Eberhart'.

C46 "Class Ode." *Dartmouth Bema*, 14 (19 June 1926), 24.

C47 "Finalities." *Tower*, 3 (23 Nov. 1926), 10. Poem in two titled parts, "Orchard Burial" and "L.F." Sgd. 'R.G. Eberhart'.

C48 "Under the Hill." *Poetry*, 31 (Nov. 1927), 80-81. First of eight poems under collective title, "Things Known." Rept. in *The Poetry Anthology 1912-1977*, ed. Daryl Hine and Joseph Parisi (Boston: Houghton Mifflin, 1978), pp. 106-7. Of the eight, four are reprinted from earlier appearances: "The Village Daily" (*The Arts Anthology*, **B3**), pp. 82-83; "Schopenhauer" (**C41**), p. 83; and "Song" (originally "Nirvana," **C31**, but later as "Cover Me Over"), p. 85.

C49 "Looking Down." *Poetry*, 31 (Nov. 1927), 81-82. Poem.

C50 "Windy." *Poetry*, 31 (Nov. 1927), 84. Poem.

C51 "Twenty-Two." *Poetry*, 31 (Nov. 1927), 84. Poem.

C52 "Request for Offering." *Experiment*, no. 2 (Feb. 1929), 23. Poem. In *RS*, *SP51*, *CP60*, *CP76*, *CP88*. Rept. in *Transition*, nos. 19-20 (June 1930), 127; *New Signatures: Poems by Several Hands*, ed. Michael Roberts (London: Hogarth Press, 1932), p. 64; *Dartmouth Verse 1922-1932* (The Arts Chapbook No. 1) (Hanover, N.H.: The Arts, 1932), p. 11; *Discovering Poetry*, ed. Elizabeth Drew, rev. ed. (New York: Norton, 1962), p. 88; *The Achievement of Richard Eberhart*, ed. Engel (1968), p. 58.

C53 "Room." *Cambridge Review*, 50 (1 March 1929), 319. Poem. Sgd. 'R.G. Eberhart'.

C54 "Maya and the Hunter." *Cambridge Review*, 50 (1 March 1929), 331. Poem. In *RS*. *Note:* "Maya" (or "Maia", below) is Louise Hawkes (Padelford). See Joel Roache, *Richard Eberhart: The Progress of an American Poet*, pp. 72-77, *et passim*.

C55 "To Maia." *Cambridge Review*, 50 (1 March 1929), 332. Poem. Rept. in *Experiment*, no. 3 (May 1929), 48.

C56 "Sonnet ['When all my victories are worn away']." *Eagle* (St. John's College, Cambridge, literary magazine), 45 no. 203, (March-April 1929), 240. Sgd. 'R.G.E.'

C57 "Fragments." *Experiment*, no. 3 (May 1929), 44. Poem. In *RS*. Rept. in *New Signatures: Poems by Several Hands*, ed. Roberts (1932), pp. 61-62. *Note*: This number of *Experiment* reprints "To Maia" (**C55**), on p. 48. The following authorial revision has been identified between the appearance in *Experiment* and republication in *New Signatures*; page and line numbers refer to the first appearance.

6.8 Allay the fever of] Instil a quietness in

C58 "This Is." *Experiment*, no. 3 (May 1929), 44. Poem.

C59 "I Slept Upon a Green Hill in the Spring." *Cambridge Review*, 50 (5 June 1929), 522. Poem.

C60 "Through the Sallow Window of Cold Ocean." *Cambridge Review*, 50 (5 June 1929), 524. Poem.

C61 "In Sun." *Cambridge Review*, 50 (5 June 1929), 526. Poem.

C62 "Boulder." *London Mercury*, 20 (July 1929), 238-39. First of "Two Poems."

C63 "Hill Climber." *London Mercury*, 20 (July 1929), 239. Second of "Two Poems."

C64 "For a Lamb." *Experiment*, no. 4 (Nov. 1929), 19. Poem. In *RS*, *SP51*, *CP60*, *SP65*, *CP76*, *CP88*. Rept. in *Mid-Century American Poets*, ed. John Ciardi (New York: Twayne, 1950), p. 233; *Fifteen Modern American Poets*, ed. Elliott (1956), pp. 21-22; *The American Tradition in Literature*, ed. Sculley Bradley et al., rev. ed., (New York: Norton, 1961), v. 2, p. 1541, and in 3d ed. (1967), v. 2, p. 1662; *Poets of England and America*, ed. Gerald D. Sanders et al., 4th ed. (New York: Macmillan, 1962), v. 2, p. 402, and in 5th ed. (1970), v. 2, p. 359; *The Distinctive Voice*, ed. William J. Martz (Glenview, Ill.: Scott, Foresman, 1966), p. 147; *Poems to Remember*, ed. Dorothy Petitt (New York: Macmillan, 1967), p. 125; *Three Dimensions of Poetry: An Introduction*, ed. Vincent Stewart (New York: Scribner's, 1969), p. 226; *Sounds and Silences: Poetry for Now*, ed. Richard Peck (New York: Dell, 1970), p. 67; *Norton Anthology of Poetry*, ed. Arthur Eastman et al. (New York: Norton, 1970), p. 1067; *A Little Treasury of Modern Poetry in English and American*, ed. Oscar Williams, 3d ed. (New York: Scribner's, 1970), p. 430; *Poetry Brief: An Anthology of Short, Short Poems*, ed. William Cole (New York, Macmillan, 1971), p. 27; A.T. Tolley, *The Poetry of the Thirties* (New York: St. Martin's, 1975), p. 61; *Dartmouth Alumni Magazine*, 69 (May 1977), 41; *Student* (Wake Forest Univ., Winston-Salem, N.C.), Autumn 1982, 38.

C65 "Wentworth Place." *Poetry*, 35 (Dec. 1929), 122. First of five poems under collective title "The Slope Sun—1927."

C66 "L'aprés-midi d'un faune." *Poetry*, 35 (Dec. 1929), 122-23. Poem.

C67 "The Kiss of Stillness." *Poetry*, 35 (Dec. 1929), 123-24. Poem.

C68 "Nightwatch on the Pacific," *Poetry*, 35 (Dec. 1929), 125. Poem.

C69 "Sumatra Shore Leave." *Poetry*, 35 (Dec. 1929), 125-27. Poem.

C70 "Ocean View Hotel." *Eagle*, 46 (Dec. 1929), 5. Poem.

C71 Untitled review of John Erskine, *Sincerity*. *New Republic*, 61 (8 Jan. 1930), 204. Signed 'R.G.E.'

C72 "Necessity." *Experiment*, no. 5 (Feb 1930), 4-5. Poem. In *RS*, *SP51*, *CP60*, *CP76*, *CP88*. Rept. *New Signatures*, ed. Roberts (1932), pp. 58-60. *Note*: The following authorial revisions have been identified between the first publication in *Experiment* and republication in *New Signatures*; page and line numbers refer to the first appearance.

> 4.12 still.] ~ ? *New Signatures*
>
> 4.16 Tomorrow] To-morrow *New Signatures*

C73 Untitled review of Witter Bynner, *Indian Earth. New Republic*, 62 (26 March 1930), 166. Sgd. 'R.G.E.'

C74 "Quern." *Experiment*, no. 6 (Oct. 1930), 39. Poem. *Note*: This number reprints "Request for Offering" (**C52**), on p. 23.

C75 "The Return of Odysseus." *Scrutiny*, 3 (June 1934), 64. Poem. In *RS, SP51, CP60, CP88*.

C76 "The Groundhog." *Listener*, 12 (22 Aug. 1934), 334. In *RS, PNS, SP51, CP60, SP65, CP76, CP88*. Rept. in *Poems of Tomorrow: An Anthology of Contemporary Verse Chosen from* The Listener, ed. Janet Adam Smith (London: Chatto & Windus, 1935), p. 38; *The Faber Book of Modern Verse*, ed. Michael Roberts (London: Faber & Faber, 1936), pp. 248-49, and in the 2d ed. (1951), pp. 259-60; *Poems of Today* (Third Series), comp. The English Association (London: Macmillan, 1938), pp. 57-59; *A Book of Modern Verse* (London: Chatto & Windus, 1939), pp. 60-61; *A Dialogue on Modern Poetry*, ed. Ruth Baily (London: Oxford, 1939), pp. 46-47; *New Poems 1940: An Anthology of British and American Verse*, ed. Oscar Williams (New York: Yardstick Press, 1941), pp. 91-92; *Twentieth-Century American Poetry*, ed. Conrad Aiken (New York: Modern Library, 1944), pp. 368-69, and in rev. ed. (1963), pp. 350-51; *A Comprehensive Anthology of American Poetry*, ed. Conrad Aiken (New York: Modern Library, 1944), pp. 463-64; *An Anthology of Famous English and American Poetry*, ed. William Rose Benet and Conrad Aiken (New York: Modern Library, 1945), pp. 911-12; *The War Poets: An Anthology of the War Poetry of the 20th Century*, ed. Oscar Williams (New York: John Day, 1945), pp. 121-22; *The Zephyr Book of American Verse*, ed. Ebba Dalin (Stockholm: Continental Book Co., 1945), pp. 268-70; *A Little Treasury of Modern Poetry, English and American*, ed. Oscar Williams (New York: Scribner's, 1946), pp.128-29, and in rev. ed. (1952), pp. 432-33, and in 3d ed. (1970). pp. 430-32; *A Little Treasury of Great Poetry, English and American*, ed. Oscar Williams (New York: Scribner's, 1947), pp. 136-37; *A Little Treasury of American Poetry: The Chief Poets from Colonial Times to the Present Day*, ed. Oscar Williams (New York: Scribner's, 1948), pp. 686-87; *100 American Poems: Masterpieces of Lyric, Epic, and Ballad from Colonial Times to the Present*, ed. Selden Rodman (New York: New American Library, 1948), pp. 172-73; *A Complete College Reader*, ed. John Holmes and Carroll S. Towle (Boston: Houghton, Mifflin, 1950), p. 917; *Mid-Century American Poets*, ed. Ciardi (1950), pp. 234-35; *The American Genius*, ed. Edith Sitwell (London: John Lehmann, 1951), pp. 174-75; *The Faber Book of Modern Verse*, ed. Michael Roberts (London: Faber & Faber,

2d. ed., 1951), with supplement of poems chosen by Anne Ridler, pp. 259-60, and in 3d. ed. (1966), pp. 211-12; *Modern Poetry: American and British*, ed. Kimon Friar and John Malcolm Brinnin (New York: Appleton-Century-Crofts, 1951), pp. 282-83; *F.T. Palgrave's The Golden Treasury of Best Songs and Lyrical Poems*, Centennial Edition, rev. and enl. by Oscar Williams (New York: New American Library, 1953), pp. 445-46; *The Penguin Book of Modern American Verse*, ed. Geoffrey Moore (London: Penguin, 1954), pp. 229-31; *The Pocket Book of Modern Verse: English and American Poetry of the Last Hundred Years*, ed. Oscar Williams (New York: Pocket Books, 1954), pp. 457-58; *Modern American and British Poetry*, ed. Louis Untermeyer, with Karl Shapiro and Richard Wilbur (New York: Harcourt, Brace, 1955), pp. 340-41; *The New Pocket Anthology of American Verse from Colonial Days to the Present* (New York: World, 1955), pp. 167-68; *Reading Modern Poetry*, ed. Paul Engle and Warren Carrier (Chicago: Scott, Foresman, 1955), pp. 275-76; *Perspectives U.S.A.*, no. 10 (Winter 1955), 26-27; *Exploring Poetry*, ed. M.L. Rosenthal and A.J.M. Smith (New York: Macmillan, 1955), pp. 571-72; *Poet's Gold: Poems for Reading Aloud*, ed. David Ross, 2d rev. ed. (New York: Devin-Adair, 1956), pp. 389-90; *Seven Centuries of Verse, English and American*, ed. A.J.M. Smith, 2d rev. ed. (New York: Scribner's, 1957), pp. 684-85; *Modern Verse in English 1900-1950*, ed. David Cecil and Allen Tate (New York: Macmillan, 1958), pp. 474-75; *The Family Album of Favorite Poems*, ed. P. Edward Ernest (New York: Grosset & Dunlap, 1959), pp. 62-63; *American Poetry*, ed. Karl Shapiro (New York: Crowell, 1960), p. 208; *Understanding Poetry*, ed. Cleanth Brooks and Robert Penn Warren, 3d ed. (New York: Holt, Rinehart, and Winston, 1960), p. 194, and in 4th ed. (1976), pp. 378-79; *American Literature: Readings and Critiques*, ed. R.W. Stallman (New York: Putnam's, 1961), pp. 945-46; *Discovering Modern Poetry*, ed. Elizabeth Drew & George Conner (New York: Holt, Rinehart and Winston, 1961), pp. 260-61; *Chief Modern Poets of England and America*, ed. Gerald D. Sanders et al., 4th ed. (1962), v. 2, pp. 402-3, and in 5th ed. (1970), v. 2, pp. 359-60; *Literature for Writing: An Anthology of Major British and American Authors*, ed. Martin Steinmann and Gerald Willen, 2d ed. (Belmont, Ca.: Wadsworth, 1962), p. 680; *Modern American Poetry: Modern British Poetry*, ed. Louis Untermeyer, new and enl. ed. (New York: Harcourt, Brace and World, 1962), pp. 579-80; *A Poetry Sampler*, ed. Donald Hall (New York: Franklin Watts, 1962), pp. 121-22; *Poetry II*, ed. R. Stanley Peterson (New York: Macmillan, 1962), pp. 96-97; *The Colour of Saying: An Anthology of Verse Spoken by Dylan Thomas*, ed. Ralph N. Maud and Aneirin Talfan Davies (London: Dent, 1963), pp. 55-57; *Introduction to Literature*, ed. Lynn Altenbernd and Leslie L. Lewis (New York: Macmillan, 1963), p. 474; *Poetry: A Closer Look*, ed. James M. Reid et al. (New York: Harcourt, Brace and World,

1963), pp. 90-91; *Poetry in English*, ed. Warren Taylor and Donald Hall (New York, Macmillan, 1963), pp. 637-38, and in 2d ed. (1970); *American Lyric Poems from Colonial Times to the Present*, ed. Elder Olson (New York: Appleton-Century-Crofts, 1964), pp. 134-35; *An Anthology Introducing Poetry*, ed. Alice C. Coleman and John R. Theobald (New York: Holt, Rinehart and Winston, 1964), pp. 127-28; *The College Book of British and American Verse*, ed. A. Kent Hiatt and William Park (Boston: Allyn and Bacon, 1964); *Dylan Thomas's Choice: an Anthology of Verse Spoken by Dylan Thomas*, ed. Ralph Maud and Aneirin Talfan Davies (Norfolk, Conn.: New Directions, 1964), pp. 49-50; *Introducing Poetry*, ed. Alice C. Coleman and John R. Theobald (New York: Holt, Rinehart and Winston, 1964), pp. 127-28; *A Second Book of Poetry*, ed. R. Stanley Peterson (New York: Macmillan, 1964), pp. 102-3; *Today's Poets: American and British Poetry Since the 1930's*, ed. Chad Walsh (New York: Scribner's, 1964), pp. 35-36; *Studying Poetry: A Critical Anthology of English and American Poems*, ed. Karl Kroeber and John O. Lyons (New York: Harper and Row, 1965), pp. 376-77; *Twentieth Century American Writing*, ed. William T. Stafford (New York: Odyssey Press, 1965), pp. 673-74; *The Force of Few Words*, ed. Jacob Korg (New York: Holt, Rinehart and Winston, 1966), pp. 355-56; *An Introduction to Literature*, ed. Ralph H. Singleton and Stanton Millet (Cleveland: World, 1966), pp. 261-62; *Literature for Understanding*, ed. B. Bernard Cohen (Chicago: Scott, Foresman, 1966), pp. 110-11; *100 American Poems of the Twentieth Century*, ed. Laurence Perrine and James M. Reid (New York: Harcourt, Brace and World, 1966), pp. 192-93; *A College Treasury: Fiction, Drama, Poetry*, ed. Paul A. Jorgensen and Frederick B. Shroyer, 2d ed. (Englewood Cliffs, N.J.: Prentice-Hall, 1967), pp. 594-95; *Master Poems of the English Language*, ed. Oscar Williams (New York: Trident, 1966), pp. 1007-8; *The Achievement of Richard Eberhart*, ed. Engel (1968), pp. 23-24; *American Literature*, ed. Mark Schorer et al. (New York: Houghton, Mifflin, 1968), p. 706; *American Literature Survey*, ed. Milton R. Stern and Seymour L. Gross, rev. ed. (New York: Viking, 1968), v. 4, pp. 594-95; *College English: The First Year*, ed. Alton C. Morris et al., 5th ed. (New York: Harcourt, Brace and World, 1968), p. 678, and in 7th ed, (1978), p. 575; *Imaginative Literature: Fiction, Drama, Poetry*, ed. Alton C. Morris et al. (New York: Harcourt, Brace and World, 1968), p. 318, and in 3d ed. (1978), p. 345; *Poetry: Premeditated Art*, ed. Judson Jerome (Boston: Houghton, Mifflin, 1968), pp. 393-94; *The Twentieth Century Revised and Expanded*, ed. Milton R. Stern and Seymour L. Gross (New York: Viking, 1968), pp. 594-95; *A Book of Modern American Poetry*, ed. Jane McDermott and Thomas V. Lowery (New York: Harcourt, Brace and Jovanovich, 1970), pp. 184-85; *A College Book of Verse*, ed. C.F. Main (Belmont, Ca.: Wadsworth, 1970), pp. 234-35; *Discovery and Response: Drama, Fiction, and Poetry*, ed. Martha Banta and Joseph

N. Satterwhite (New York: Macmillan, 1970), p. 403; *Icarus: An Anthology of Literature*, ed. John H. Bens and Douglas R. Baugh (New York: Macmillan, 1970), pp. 157-58; *Mandala: Literature for Critical Analysis*, ed. Wilfred L. Guerin et al. (New York: Harper and Row, 1970), pp. 312-13; *The Total Experience of Poetry*, ed. Ruth and Marvin Thompson (New York: Random House, 1970), pp. 55-56; *Toward Composition: Readings for Freshman English*, ed. Univ. of Minnesota Freshman English staff (Dubuque, Iowa: Kendall-Hunt, 1970), pp. 452-53; *Voices of Poetry*, ed. Allen Kirschner (New York: Dell, 1970), pp. 129-30; *Literature in America: The Modern Age*, ed. Charles Kaplan (New York: Free Press, 1971), pp. 359-60; *The Pleasures of Poetry*, ed. Donald Hall (New York: Harper and Row, 1971); *The Norton Introduction to Literature*, ed. Carl E. Bain et al. (New York: Norton, 1970), and in 2d ed. (1977); *American Literature: The Makers and the Making*, ed. Cleanth Brooks et al. (New York: St. Martins, 1973), v. 2, p. 2918, and in shorter ed. (1974), p. 1738; *Contemporary Poetry in America*, ed. Williams (1973), p. 5; *50 Modern American and British Poets, 1920-1970*, ed. Louis Untermeyer (New York: David McKay, 1973), pp. 663-64; *The Norton Introduction to Literature: Poetry*, ed. J. Paul Hunter (New York: Norton, 1973), pp. 113-14; *The Lyric Potential: Arrangements and Techniques in Poetry*, ed. James E. Miller et al. (Glenview, Ill.: Scott, Foresman, 1974), pp. 256-57; *The Poem as Process*, ed. David Swanger (New York: Harcourt, Brace, Jovanovich, 1974), p. 212-13; Agnes Stein, *The Uses of Poetry* (New York: Holt, Rinehart and Winston, 1975), pp. 240-41; *Modern Poems*, ed. Richard Ellman and Robert O'Clair (New York: Norton, 1976), pp. 259-60; *Dartmouth Alumni Magazine*, 69 (May 1977), 41; *The Treasury of American Poetry*, ed. Nancy Sullivan (Garden City, N.Y.: Doubleday, 1978), pp. 510-11; *News of the Universe: Poems of Twofold Consciousness*, ed. Robert Bly (San Francisco: Sierra Club Books, 1980), pp. 230-31; *Beowulf to Beatles and Beyond*, ed. David R. Pichaske (New York: Macmillan, 1981), pp. 216-17; *Do Not Go Gentle: Poems on Death*, ed. William Packard (New York: St. Martin's, 1981), pp. 97-99; *Poetry: An Introduction*, ed. Ruth Miller and Robert A. Greenberg (New York: St. Martin's, 1981), pp. 417-18; *To Read Literature*, ed. Donald Hall (New York: Holt, Rinehart and Winston, 1981), pp. 641-42; *Literature*, ed. James H. Pickering and Jeffrey D. Hoeper (New York: Macmillan, 1982), pp. 887-88; *Poetry: Sight and Insight*, ed. James W. Kirkland and F. David Sanders (New York: Random House, 1982), p. 375; *Participating in the Poem*, ed. Mary Cunningham et al. (New York: Center for Learning, 1983), p. 219; *The Poem in Question*, ed. Robert E. Bourdette, Jr. and Michael Cohen (New York: Harcourt, Brace, Jovanovich, 1983), pp. 82-83.

Note: The following authorial revision has been identified; page and line numbers refer to the first appearance.

334.9 maggot's] maggots' *Poems of Tomorrow*[+]

C77 "Dissertation by Waxlight." *Listener*, 12 (7 Nov. 1934), 770. Poem. In *RS*, *SP51*. Rept. in *Poems of Tomorrow*, ed. Smith (1935), pp. 40-41.

C78 "1934." *Listener*, 12 (27 Dec, 1934), 1087. Poem. In *RS*, *SP51*, *CP60*, *SP65*, *CP76*. Rept. in *Poems of Tomorrow*, ed. Smith (1935), pp. 42-43; *Twentieth Century American Poetry*, ed. Conrad Aiken (New York: Modern Library), pp. 369-70, and in 2d rev. ed. (1963), pp. 351-52.

C79 "Blue. White. Red. Green." *Bozart-Westminster*, 9 (Spring-Summer 1935), ii. Poem.

C80 "Dissertation by Wax Light (III)." *Bozart-Westminster*, 9 (Spring-Summer 1935), 11. Poem.

C81 "Meditation Two." *Audience*, 8 (1936), 7-9. Poem. In *Qu*, *SP65*, *CP76*, *CP88*; rept. *National Poetry Festival Held in the Library of Congress October 22-24 1962: Proceedings* (Washington, D.C.: Library of Congress, 1964), 202-4.

C82 "To One Returning." *Austin Daily* (29 May 1936), 2. Poem.

C83 "Alphabet Book." *Transition*, no. 24 (June 1936), 11-14. Poem.

C84 "Mais l'amour infini me montera dans l'ame." *Transition*, no. 24 (June 1936), 14-15. Poem. In *CP88*

C85 "If I Could Only Live at the Pitch That Is Near Madness." *New Masses*, 19 Oct. 1937. p. 8. Number 'I' of "Two Poems." In *SI*, *SP51*, *CP60*, *SP65*, *CP76*, *CP88*. Rept. in *Poetry*, 51 (Jan. 1938), 191-92 (as "Poem"); *Mid-Century American Poets*, ed. Ciardi (1950), p. 235; *Modern American and British Poetry*, ed. Untermeyer et al (1955), p. 338; *Perspectives U.S.A.*, no. 10 (Winter 1955), 25; *Fifteen Modern American Poets*, ed. Elliott (1956). p. 24; partially rept. in *Nation's Schools*, 63 (March 1959), p. 68; *Poetry for Pleasure: The Hallmark Book of Poetry* (Garden City, N.Y.: Doubleday, 1960), pp. 379-80; *Word, Meaning, Poem*, ed. Morse Peckham and Seymour Chatham (New York: Crowell, 1961), pp. 647-48; *Literature for Writing: An Anthology of Major British and American Authors*, ed. Martin Steinmann and Gerald Willen, 2d ed. (Belmont, Ca.: Wadsworth, 1962), p. 681; *Adventures in Poetry*, ed. Edwin C. Custer (New York: Harcourt, Brace, 1964), pp. 536-37; *A Quarto of Modern Literature*, ed. Leonard Bacon, 5th ed. (New York: Scribner's, 1964), p. 469; *Today's Poets*, ed. Walsh (1964), p. 39; *The Complete Reader*, ed. Beal and Korg, 2d ed. (1967), p. 594; *A Book of Modern Poetry*, ed. McDermott and Lowery (1970), p. 188; *The Responsible Man*, ed. C. Jeriel Howard and Richard Tracz (San Francisco: Canfield Press, 1970), p. 61; *A Little Treasury of Modern Poetry*, ed. Williams 3d ed. (1970), pp. 433-34; *Literature in America: The Modern Age*, ed. Charles Kaplan (New York: Free Press, 1971), p. 361; *Messages: A Thematic Anthology of Poetry*, ed. X.J. Kennedy (Boston: Little, Brown, 1973); *American Literature: The Makers and the Making*, ed. Brooks et al. (1973), v. 2, pp. 2919-2920, and in shorter ed. (1974), p. 1739; *50 Modern American and British Poets 1920-*

1970, ed. Untermeyer (1973), p. 61; *The Treehouse: An Introduction to Literature*, ed. Linda Stanley and Sheena Gillespie (Cambridge, Mass.: Winthrop, 1974), pp. 186-87; *Structure and Meaning*, ed. Anthony Dubé et al. (Boston: Houghton, Mifflin, 1976), p. 595; *The Penguin Book of American Verse*, ed. Geoffrey Moore (Harmondsworth: Penguin, 1977), pp. 418-19; *Dartmouth Alumni Magazine*, 69 (May 1977), 43; *Literature*, ed. James Burl Hogins, 2d. ed. (Chicago: Science Research Associates, 1977), p. 555. *Communicative Reading*, ed. Elbert R. Brown et al., 4th ed. (New York: Macmillan, 1978), p. 285; *Fine Frenzy: Enduring Themes in Poetry*, ed. Robert Baylor and Brenda Stokes, 2d ed. (New York: McGraw-Hill, 1978), pp. 34-35; *Always Begin Where You Are: Themes in Poetry and Song*, ed. Walter Lamb (New York: McGraw-Hill, 1979), p. 52; *The Art of Interpretation*, ed. Wallace A. Bacon, 3d ed. (New York: Holt, Rinehart, Winston, 1979), pp. 58-59.

Note: The following authorial revision has been identified; page and line numbers refer to the first appearance.

8.15 necessity] Necessity *Poetry*] necessity *SI*[+]

C86 "Now Is The Air Made Of Chiming Balls." *New Masses*, 19 Oct. 1937, p. 8. Number 'II' of "Two Poems." In *SI*, *SP51*, *CP60*, *SP65*, *CP76*, *CP88*. Rept. in *Perspectives U.S.A.*, no. 10 (Winter 1955), 28; *Today's Poets: American and British Poetry Since the 1930's*, ed. Walsh (1964), pp. 36-37.

C87 "From 'Suite in Prison'." *New York Times*, 25 Nov. 1937, p.30. Poem. As Part 'VI' of "Suite in Prison" in *RS*, *SP51*, *CP60*, *CP76*, *CP88*. Rept. in *The New York Times Book of Verse*, ed. Thomas Lask (New York: Macmillan, 1970), p. 107.

C88 "To Come Closer to Thee," *Poetry*, 51 (Jan. 1938), 190. First of "Four Poems." *Note:* "If I Could Only Live at the Pitch That Is Near Madness" (C85) is here reprinted as "Song," the third of "Four Poems."

C89 "Anglo-Saxon Song." *Poetry*, 51 (Jan. 1938), 191. Second of "Four Poems." In *SI*.

C90 "Song for the Death of my Uncle in Illinois." *Poetry*, 51 (Jan. 1938), 192-93. Fourth of "Four Poems." In *SI*. *Note*: The following authorial revision has been identified; page and line numbers refer to the first appearance.

192.7 resolution;] ~:

C91 "I Fear Those Visions." *New York Times*, 8 April 1938, p. 14. Poem.

C92 "The Humanist." *New York Times*, 24 April 1938, p. 8 (E). Poem. In *SI*, *SP51*, *CP60*, *SP65*, *CP76*, *CP88*. Rept. in *The American Tradition in Literature*, ed. Bradley et al., rev. ed. (1961), v. 2, pp. 1542-43, and in 3d ed, (1967), p. 1623.

C93 "Where Is My Ego Flown?" *New York Times*, 6 July 1938, p. 22. Poem.

C94 "John Holmes Introduces a Guest Poetry Critic," *Boston Evening Transcript*, 9 Nov. 1938, p. 7. Essay-review of Frederic Prokosch, *The Carnival*; and Stephen Spender, *Trial of a Judge*.

C95 Untitled statement about T.S. Eliot. *Harvard Advocate*, 125 (Dec. 1938), 18-19.

C96 "Poets and the European Sickness." *Virginia Quarterly Review*, 15 (Winter 1939), 145-49. Review of Robert Francis, *Valhalla and Other Poems*; Ben Belitt, *The Five-Fold Mesh*; Willard Maas, *Concerning the Young*; Kay Boyle, *A Glad Day*.

C97 "Ballad of the Sedative." *Hika* (Kenyon College, Gambier, Ohio, literary magazine), 5 (Feb. 1939), 10. Poem.

C98 "When I Think of Her" (later "When I Think of Her the Power of Poetry Arises"). *Kansas City Journal*, 12 Feb. 1939, p. 22. Poem. In *SI*.

C99 Untitled review of Yvor Winters, *Maule's Curse*. *Harvard Advocate*, 125 (April 1939), 33-34.

C100 "A New Word-Sculpture." *New York Herald Tribune Books*, 30 April 1939, p. 20 (IX). Rev. of *The Antigone of Sophocles*, trans. Dudley Fitts and Robert Fitzgerald.

C101 "Warmth and Ease and Charm and Aptitude." *Poetry*, 54 (June 1939), 160-63. Rev. of Merrill Moore, *M: 1000 Autobiographical Sonnets*.

C102 "I Went To See Irving Babbitt." *Harvard Advocate*, 125 (June 1939), 10. Poem. In *SI, CP60, SP65, CP76, CP88*. Rept. in *The Oxford Book of American Light Verse*, ed. William Harmon (New York: Oxford, 1979), p. 430; *Gladly Learn and Gladly Teach*, ed. Helen Plotz (New York: Greenwillow, 1981), p. 79.

C103 "Poem ['The vision of the world']." *Hika*, 6 (June 1939), 12.

C104 "From 'The Human Being [Fingers are largely filibusters, fictive flukes]'." *Vindex* (St. Mark's School, Southborough, Mass., student literary magazine), 63 (June 1939), 176. Poem. *Note:* An offprint of this poem was prepared; see above, **B10**.

C105 "Rumination ['Already it has happened']." *Seven*, no. 4 (Summer 1939), 32. Poem. In *SI*. *Note*: The following authorial revisions have been identified; page and line numbers refer to the first appearance.

    32.7 eyes] ~,
    32.29 Life's] life's
    32-30 to doubt, to] or doubt, or

C106 "Poem in Construction ['But waves before my eyes']." *Furioso*, 1 (Summer 1939), 14-16. Rept. as pts. 1-3 of "The Inspissation" in *New Directions Seven* (Norfolk, Conn.: New Directions, 1942), pp. 49-53 (**B18**).

C107 "From 'The Human Being'". *Furioso*, 1 (Summer 1939), 16. Poem.

C108 "To a Poet" (later titled "Go To the Shine That's On a Tree"). *New Yorker*, 15 (9 Sept. 1939), 52. Poem. In *Un*, *CP60*, *SP65*, *CP76*, *CP88*. Rept. in *In-between Times* (St. Mark's School, Southborough, Mass., student newspaper), 27 Oct., 1939, p. 2; as "Go To the Shine That's On a Tree" in *Fifteen Modern American Poets*, ed. Elliott (1956), pp. 30-31; *Untune the Sky: Poems of Music and Dance*, ed. Helen Plotz (New York: Crowell, 1957), p. 15; *The American Tradition in Literature*, ed. Bradley et al., rev. ed. (1961), v. 2, p. 1544, and in 3d ed. (1967), pp. 1624-25; *The Achievement of Richard Eberhart*, ed. Engels (1968), p. 4; *Lyric Poems*, ed. Howard (1968), p. 97; *Patterns in Poetry*, ed. Harry M. Brown and John Milstead (Glenview, Ill.: Scott, Foresman, 1968), p. 401; *Dartmouth Alumni Magazine*, 69 (May 1977), 42. *Note*: The original title, "To a Poet," was chosen by *New Yorker* editors but later rejected by RE.

C109 "To Critics." *New Republic*, 100 (18 Oct. 1939), 314. Rept. in *Spectator*, 164 (15 March 1940), 362.

C110 "The Notion of Hell." *Poetry*, 55 (Nov. 1939), 101-3. Rev. of Ronald Bottrall, *The Turning Path*.

C111 "A Meditation." *Furioso*, 1 (Spring 1940), 7-10. Poem. In *SI*, *SP51*, *CP60*, *CP76*, *CP88*. Rept. in *New Poems 1940*, ed. Oscar Williams (New York: Yardstick Press, 1941), pp. 95-100; *A Little Treasury of American Poetry*, ed. Oscar Williams (New York: Scribner's, 1948), pp. 695-98; *Fifteen Modern American Poets*, ed. Elliott (1956), pp. 25-29. *Note*: The following authorial revision has been identified; page and line numbers refer to the first appearance.

     53.24 you] your [*sic*] *SI*] you *SP51*[+]

C112 "The Scarf of June." *Furioso*, 1 (Spring 1940), 11. Poem. In *SI*, *SP51*, *CP60*, *CP76*, *CP88*.

C113 "Metamorphosis." *Harvard Advocate*, 126 (April 1940), 16. Poem.

C114 "12, Canterbury Street." *Hika*, 6 (May 1940), 14. First of four "Early Poems."

C115 "I Seek Tall Trees for Melodies." *Hika*, 6 (May 1940), 14. Second of four "Early Poems."

C116 "To a Girl Suffering from a Leg Injury for Three Years," *Hika*, 6 (May 1940), 14. Third of four "Early Poems."

C117 "Beyond Cambridge." *Hika*, 6 (May 1940), 14. Fourth of four "Early Poems."

C118 "From 'Poem in Construction [I wrote Helen a letter but got no reply]'." *Poetry*, 56 (June 1940), 140-43. Rept. as pt. I of "Ingathering" in *New Directions*, no. 7 (1942), 53-56.

C119 "For John Brooks Wheelwright" (later titled "Sometimes the Longing For Death"). *Modern Quarterly*, 11 (Summer 1940), 110. Poem. As "Sometimes the Longing For Death" in *Un*, *CP60*, *CP76*, *CP88*; rept. as "Poem" in *Accent*, 5 (Spring 1945), 179.

C120 "A Mixed Bag." *Poetry*, 56 (August 1940), 274-77. Rev. of Glyn Jones, *Poems*; Roy Fuller, *Poems*; Henry Treece, *38 Poems*.

C121 "Two Loves." *New Republic*, 103 (2 Sept. 1940), 300. Poem. In *SI*, *SP51*, *CP60*, *SP65*, *CP76*, *CP88*. Rept in *American Signatures*, ed. Rae Beamish (Rochester, N.Y.: Black Faun, 1941), p. 70 (B14); *A Century of Writers (1855-1955)*, ed. Low et al. (1955), p. 571; *Fifteen Modern American Poets*, ed. Elliott (1956), p. 23; *Chief Modern Poets of England and America*, ed. Sanders et al., 4th ed. (1962), v. 2, p. 406, and in 5th ed. (1970), v. 2, p. 363; *Love's Aspects: The World's Great Love Poems*, ed. Jean Garrigue (Garden City, N.Y.: Doubleday, 1975), p. 286. *Note*: In all printings subsequent to the first, all lines are set flush left.

C122 "But To Reach The Archimedean Point." (later titled 'Mysticism Has Not the Patience to Wait For God's Revelation'). *Partisan Review*, 7 (Sept.- Oct., 1940), 357-58. Poem. As 'Mysticism Has Not the Patience to Wait For God's Revelation' in *PNS*, *BO*, *SP51*, *CP60*, *SP65*, *CP76*, *CP88*. Rept. in *Modern Poetry American and British*, ed. Friar and Brinnin (1951), p. 280; *The Norton Anthology of Modern Poetry*, ed. Ellmann and O'Clair (1973), p. 664. *Note*: The following authorial revision has been identified; page and line numbers refer to the first appearance.

    358.11 "The...is,"] ("~...is,")

C123 "Q's Revisions." *Kenyon Review*, 2 (Autumn 1940), 496-99. Rev. of Sir Arthur Thomas Quiller-Couch, *The New Oxford Book of English Verse*.

C124 "The Largess." *Southern Review*, 6 (Autumn 1940), 368-9. Poem. In *SI*, *SP50*, *CP60*, *CP76*, *CP88*. Rept. in *New Poems 1942: An Anthology of British and American Verse*, ed. Oscar Williams (Mt. Vernon, N.Y.: Peter Pauper Press, 1942), pp. 84-5; *Twentieth Century American Poetry*, ed. Conrad Aiken (New York: The Modern Library, 1944), pp. 366-67; *A Little Treasury of American Poetry*, ed. Oscar Williams (New York: Scribner's, 1948), pp. 687-88; *A Little Treasury of Modern Poetry, English & American*, ed. Oscar Williams (New York: Charles Scribner's Sons, 1952), pp. 434-35.

C125 "Those Who Love Struggle." *Vice Versa*, 1 (Nov.-Dec. 1940), 20. Poem. In *SI*. *Note*: The following authorial revisions have been identified; page and line numbers refer to the first appearance.

    20.6 stoical] ~,

    20.11 hidden] ~,

C126 "The Needle of the Eye." *Common Sense*, 9 (Dec. 1940), 25. Poem. In *SI*. *N.B.*: Issued in mid-Nov. 1940.

C127 "Ce pays nous ennuie, O mort! Appareillons!" *Decision*, 1 (January 1941), 22. Poem.

C128 "From 'Poem in Construction [Consider the more intricate and ingenious situations]'." *Decision*, 1 (January 1941), 23. Rept. as pt. III of "The Inspissation" in *New Directions*, no. 7 (1942), 52-53 (**B18**). *Note*: The following authorial revisions have been identified; page and line numbers refer to the first appearance.

23.5 arch-conspirators] ~ ∧ ~
23.17 labourers] laborers
23.21 those] these
23.23 finniky] finicky
23.27 wings] ~;

C129 "Angelic Perspectives." *Poetry*, 57 (Jan. 1941), 276-78. Rev. of Eugene Jolas, *Planets and Angels*.

C130 "From Poem in Construction (X) ['And at Lake Geneva, which is in Wisconsin,']." *Vice Versa*, 1 (Jan.-Feb. 1941), 1-3. Rept. as pt. 'III' of "Ingathering" in *New Directions*, no. 7 (1942), 59-62. Rept. in *A Little Treasury of American Poetry*, ed. Oscar Williams (New York: Scribner's, 1948), pp. 689-91. *Note*: The following authorial revision has been identified; page and line numbers refer to the first appearance.

1.3 summer of 193-] ~,

C131 "A World-View." *Tuftonian* (Tufts College, Medford, Mass.), 1 (May 1941), 16-17. Poem. Published separately, **A4**. Rept. in *New Directions*, no. 7 (1942), 67-72.

C132 "A Human Good." *Poetry*, 58 (June 1941), 146-48. Rev. of Walter de la Mare, *Collected Poems*.

C133 "Three Poets." *Furioso*, 1 (Summer 1941), 62-68. Rev. of Marya Zaturenska, *The Listening Landscape*: Horace Gregory, *Poems 1930-1940*; and John Peale Bishop, *Selected Poems*.

C134 "The Expense of Critical Reason." *Accent* 2 (Autumn 1941), 51-55. Rev. of R.P. Blackmur, *The Expense of Greatness*; John Crowe Ransom, *The New Criticism*; Allen Tate, *Reason in Madness*.

C135 "Poem ['There is an evil in the air']." *Diogenes*, 1 (Autumn 1941), 108. Poem. In *PNS*.

C136 "Poem ['Experience is like a cloud of summer time']." *Diogenes*, 1 (Autumn 1941), 109. Poem.

C137 "From 'Poem in Construction [There is a place in stoical Autumn, a glass]'." *Vice Versa*, 1 (Jan. 1942), 33-36. As "Song" in *PNS* and *BO*. Rept. *New Directions*, no. 7 (1942), pp. 59-62; *A Little Treasury of American Poetry*, ed. Williams (1948), pp. 689-91.

C138 "The Extreme Water." *Southern Review*, 7 (April 1942), 862. Poem. *Note:* The following poems are rept. in this number of *Southern Review*: "I Walked Out to the Graveyard to See the Dead" (from **A3**), p. 861; "In the Night When Destruction Shall Shake the World" (from **A3**), p. 861.

C139 "When Love Has Given the Waylay To Our Powers." *Harvard Advocate*, 128 (April 1942), 31. Number "1" of "Three Poems."

C140 "The Sun-lit Ants Their Shadows Feign, Obsess." *Harvard Advocate*, 128 (April 1942), 31. Number "2" of "Three Poems."

C141 "The Suicide Gassed in the Brooklyn Garret." *Harvard Advocate*, 128 (April 1942), 31. Number "3" of "Three Poems."

C142 "To H.E.B.: August 29, 1941." *Poetry*, 60 (April 1942), 1-3. First of "Seven Poems."

C143 "New Hampshire, February." *Poetry*, 60 (April 1942), 3-4. Second of "Seven Poems." In *BO, SP51, CP60, SP65, CP76, NH, CP88*. Rept. in *Fifteen Modern American Poets*, ed. Elliott (1956), p. 30; *The Modern Poets: An American-British Anthology*, ed. John Malcolm Brinnin and Bill Read (New York: McGraw-Hill, 1963), p. 76, and in rev. ed. (1970), pp. 90-91; *Language, Form and Idea*, ed. T. Benson Strandness et al. (New York: McGraw-Hill, 1963), p. 332; *A Quarto of Modern Literature*, ed. Leonard Bacon, 5th ed. (New York: Scribner's, 1964), p. 469; *Poetry is for People*, ed. Martha McDonough and William C. Doster (Boston: Allyn and Bacon, 1965), p. 213; *The Achievement of Richard Eberhart*, ed. Engel (1968), p. 29; *The Poem: An Anthology*, ed. Stanley B. Greenfield and A. Kingsley Weatherhead, 2d ed. (New York: Appleton-Century-Crofts, 1968), p. 351, and in 2d ed. (1972), p. 425; *A Little Treasury of Modern Poetry English and American*, ed. Williams, 3d ed. (1970), pp. 438-39; *Introduction to Poetry*, ed. William C. Cavanaugh (Dubuque, Iowa: William C. Brown, 1974), pp. 181-82; *Sounds and Silences: Poems for Performing*, ed. Robert W. Boynton and Maynard Mack (New York: Hayden Book Co., 1975); *Dartmouth Alumni Magazine*, 69 (May 1977), 41.

C144 "Of Truth: The Protagonist Speaking." (later titled "Of Truth"). *Poetry*, 60 (April 1942), 4-5. Third of "Seven Poems." As "Of Truth" in *BO*. Rept. in *New Poems 1943: An Anthology of British and American Verse*, ed. Oscar Williams (New York: Howell, Soskin, 1943), p. 83; *The Zephyr Book of American Verse*, ed. Ebba Dalin (Stockholm: Continental, 1945). pp. 267-68.

C145 "Dublin Afternoon." *Poetry*, 60 (April 1942), 6. Fourth of "Seven Poems." Rept. in *American Writing 1943: The Anthology of the American Non-Commercial Magazine*, ed. Allan Swallow (Boston: Bruce Humphries, 1944), p. 106.

C146 "To Evade the Whirlwind." *Poetry*, 60 (April 1942), 6-7. Fifth of "Seven Poems." Rept. *Fantasy*, 10 (no. 26, 1942), 7.

C147 "The Dream." *Poetry*, 60 (April 1942), 7. Sixth of "Seven Poems." In *PNS, BO, SP51, CP60, CP76, CP88*. Rept. *New Poems 1942: An Anthology of British and American Verse*, ed. Oscar Williams (Mount Vernon, N.Y.: Peter Pauper Press, 1942), pp. 81-82; *The Zephyr Book of American Verse*, ed. Ebba Daline (Stockholm: Continental Book Co., 1945), pp. 266-67.

C148 "The Blindness of Poets." *Poetry*, 60 (April 1942), 8. Seventh of "Seven Poems."

C149 "Rumination ('When I can hold a stone within my hand')." *Atlantic Monthly*, 169 (May 1942), 603. In *BO, SP51, CP60, SP65, CP76, CP88*. Rept. in *Atlantic*, 169 (May 1942), 603; *New York Times Book Review*, 28 Dec. 1947; *A Little Treasury of American Poetry*, ed. Williams (1948), p. 694, and in rev. ed. (1952), p. 436, 3rd ed. (1970), p. 433; *The American Tradition in Literature*, ed. Bradley et al., rev. ed. (1961), v. 2, p. 1541, and in 3rd ed. (1967), p. 1622; *53 American Poets Today*, ed. Ruth Witt-Diamant and Rikutaro Fukuda (Tokyo: Kenkyusha, 1962), p. 5; *The Force of Few Words*, ed. Korg (1966), p. 20; *Fifteen Modern American Poets*, ed. Elliott (1967), p. 24-25; *College English: The First Year*, ed. Morris et al., 5th ed. (1968), p. 694, and in 7th ed. (1978), p. 588; *Imaginative Literature*, ed. Morris et al. (1968), p. 334, and in 3d ed. (1978), p. 358; *Lyric Poems*, ed. Coralie Howard (New York: Franklin Watts, 1968), p. 96; *A College Book of Modern Verse*, ed. Main (1970), p. 237; *Contemporary Poetry in America*, ed. Williams (1973), p. 6.

C150 "Big Top." *Poetry*, 60 (June 1942), 165-68. Rev. of *New Directions 6* (1941).

C151 "Band of Usable Monuments." *American Prefaces*, 8 (Autumn 1942), 51-52. Poem.

C152 "Ur-Review." *Accent*, 3 (Winter 1943), 121-22. Rev. of Wallace Stevens, *Notes Toward a Supreme Fiction*.

C153 "The Game." *Chimera*, 1 (Winter 1943), 44. Poem. In *BO*. Rept. in *American Writing 1944: The Anthology and Yearbook of the American Non-Commercial Magazine*, ed. Helen Ferguson Caukin and Alan Swallow (Boston: Bruce Humphries, 1945), p. 175; *New Voices: Atlantic Anthology*, ed. Nicholas Moore and Douglas Newton (London: Fortune Press, 1945), pp. 175-76.

C154 "In a Gunner's Eye." *Common Sense*, 12 (March 1943), 88-89. Unsigned letter.

C155 "Not So Many." *Nation*, 156 (8 May 1943), 681. Letter signed 'Richard Eberhart, Lieut. U.S.N.R., Hollywood, Fla., April 24'.

C156 "Beginning of a Beginning." *New Republic*, 108 (14 June 1943), 803. Rev. of Delmore Schwartz, *Genesis: Book One*.

C157 "The Preacher Sought to Find Out Acceptable Words." *Nation*, 157 (21 Aug. 1943), 214. Poem. In *PNS, BO*. Rept. in *Poetry Q*, 6 (Spring 1944), 4; *The War Poets; an Anthology of the War Poetry of the 20th Century*, ed. Oscar Williams (New York: The John Day Co., 1945), pp. 123-24.

C158 "Heavenly Mindedness." *Poetry*, 62 (Sept. 1943), 347-50. Rev. of John Pick, *Gerard Manley Hopkins: Priest and Poet*.

C159 "Triptych." *Chimera*, 2 (Autumn 1943), 15-25. Verse play. In *PNS, BO, CP60, CVP, CP76, CP88*.

C160 "White Lily and Hail." *Chimera*, 2 (Winter-Spring 1944), 33-34. Poem.

C161 "You Would Think The Fury of Aerial Bombardment" (later titled "The Fury of Aerial Bombardment"). *Kenyon Review*, 6 (Spring 1944), 189. Number 'I' of three poems under collective title "Verse More or Less Topical." As "The Fury of Acrial Bombardment" in *PNS*, *BO*, *SP51*, *CP60*, *SP65*, *CP76*, *CP88*. Rept. as "The Fury of Aerial Bombardment" in *New Poems 1944: An Anthology of American and British Verse, with a Selection of Poems from the Armed Services*, ed. Oscar Williams (New York: Howell, Soskin, 1944), p. 220; *The War Poets: An Anthology of the War Poetry of the 20th Century*, ed. Oscar Williams (New York: John Day, 1945), p. 123; *A Little Treasury of American Poetry*, ed. Williams (1948), p. 693, and in 3d ed. (1970), p. 438; *Mid-Century American Poets*, ed. Ciardi (1950), p. 237; *Perspectives U.S.A.*, no. 4 (Summer 1953), 19-20; *The Penguin Book of Modern American Verse*, ed. Moore (1954), p. 231, and in rev. ed. (1977), p. 418; *The Pocket Book of Modern Verse*, ed. Williams (1954), pp. 458-59; *Exploring Poetry*, ed. Rosenthal and Smith (1955), p. 674; *How Does a Poem Mean?*, ed. John Ciardi (Boston: Houghton, Mifflin, 1959), pp. 998-99; *The Poem: A Critical Anthology*, ed. Josephine Miles (Englewood Cliffs, N.J.: Prentice-Hall, 1959), p. 138; *American Poetry*, ed. Karl Shapiro (New York: Thomas Y. Crowell, 1960), pp. 209-10; *Understanding Poetry*, ed. Cleanth Brooks and Robert Penn Warren, 3d ed. (New York: Holt, Rinehart and Winston, 1960), pp. 503-4, and in 4th ed. (1976), p. 172; *Discovering Modern Poetry*, ed. Elizabeth Drew and George Conner (New York: Holt Rinehart and Winston, 1961), pp. 258-60; *Modern Poetry*, ed. Maynard Mack et al., 2d ed. (Englewood Cliffs, N.J.: Prentice-Hall, 1961), p. 334; *American Literature Survey*, ed. Milton R. Stern and Seymour Gross, (New York: Viking, 1962), v. 4 ("The Twentieth Century"), p. 569, and in rev. and expanded ed. (1968), pp. 595-96; *Chief Modern Poets of England and America*, ed. Sanders et al., 4th ed. (1962), v. 2, p. 407, and in 5th ed. (1970), v. 2, p. 364; *Literature for Writing: An Anthology of Major British and American Writers*, ed. Martin Steinmann and Gerald Willen, 2d ed. (Belmont, Ca.: Wadsworth, 1962), p. 680; *Anthology of Modern Poetry*, ed. John Wain (London: Hutchinson, 1963), p. 157; *Introduction to Literature: Poems*, ed. Lynn Altenbernd and Leslie L. Lewis (New York: Macmillan, 1963), p. 475; *Poetry in English*, ed. Warren Taylor and Donald Hall (New York: Macmillan, 1963), pp. 638-39, and in 2d ed. (1970); *A Selection of Contemporary Religious Poetry*, ed. Samuel Hazo (Glen Rock, N.J.: Den's Books, 1963), p. 42; *Twentieth Century Poetry*, ed. Brinnin and Read (1963), p. 77, and in 2d ed. (1970), pp. 101-2; *A New Directions Reader*, ed. Hayden Carruth and J. Laughlin (Norfolk, Conn.: New Directions, 1964), pp. 59-60; *Today's Poets*, ed. Walsh (1964), pp. 39-40; *Ideas in Poetry*, ed. Oscar H. Fidell (Englewood Cliffs, N.J.: Prentice-

Hall, 1965), pp. 132-33; *Introduction to the Poem*, ed. Boynton and Mack (1965), pp. 190-91; *Poems and Poets*, ed. David Aloian (St. Louis: McGraw-Hill, 1965), pp. 394-95; *The Poetry of War 1939-1945*, ed. Ian Hamilton (London: Alan Ross, 1965), p. 139; *The Faber Book of Modern Verse*, ed. Michael Roberts, 3d ed. (London: Faber, 1966), p. 212; *An Introduction to Poetry*, ed. X.J. Kennedy (Boston: Little, Brown, 1966), pp. 60-61, and in 2d ed. (1971), p. 50, 3d ed. (1974), p. 45, 5th ed. (1982), p. 55; *The Province of Poetry*, ed. Edwin B. Benjamin (New York: American Book Co., 1966), p. 152; *The New Modern Poetry*, ed. M.L. Rosenthal (New York: Macmillan, 1967), p. 55; *The Achievement of Richard Eberhart*, ed. Engel (1968), p. 32; *The Twentieth Century Revised and Expanded*, ed. Milton R. Stern and Seymour L. Gross (New York: Viking, 1968), pp. 595-96; *Poetry of War Resistance from 2300 B.C. to the Present*, ed. Scott Bates (New York: Grossman, 1969), p. 178; *Icarus: An Anthology of Literature*, ed. John H. Bens and Douglas R. Baugh (New York: Macmillan, 1970), p. 409; *The Modern Poets*, ed. Brinnin and Read (1970), pp. 101-2; *The Total Experience of Poetry*, ed. Ruth and Marvin Thompson (New York: Random House, 1970), p. 140-41; *The Voice that is Great Within Us: American Poetry of the Twentieth Century*, ed. Hayden Carruth (New York: Bantam, 1970), pp. 246-47; *Voices of Poetry*, ed. Allen Kirschner (New York: Dell, 1970), p. 74; *Literary Types and Themes* ed. Maurice McNamee at al., 2d ed. (New York: Holt, Rinehart and Winston, 1971), p. 660-61; *The Realities of Literature*, ed. Richard F. Dietrich (Waltham, Mass.: Xerox College Publishing, 1971), p. 176; *Twentieth Century Poetry*, ed. Carol Marshall (Boston: Houghton, Mifflin, 1971); *Themes in American Literature*, ed. Charles Genthe and George Keithley (Lexington, Mass.: Heath, 1972), p. 660; *Words into Flight: An Introduction to Poetry*, ed. Richard Abcarian (Belmont, Ca.: Wadsworth, 1972), p. 93; *American Literature: The Makers and the Making*, ed. Brooks et al. (1973), v. 2, p. 2920, and in shorter ed. (1974), p. 1739; *Contemporary Poetry in America*, ed. Williams (1973), p. 5; *The Norton Anthology of Modern Poetry*, ed. Ellmann and O'Clair (1973), p. 665; *The Norton Introduction to Literature: Poetry*, ed. J. Paul Hunter (New York: Norton, pp. 23-24, and in 2d ed. (1981), p. 423; *An Introduction to Poetry*, ed. Kennedy, 3d ed. (1974); *Introduction to Poetry*, ed. William C. Cavanaugh (Dubuque, Iowa: William C. Brown, 1974), pp. 372-73; *Poetry: Points of Departure*, ed. Henry Taylor (Cambridge, Mass.: Winthrop, 1974), pp. 253-54; *Puddingstone*, 1 (Spring 1974), 4; *An Approach to Literature*, ed. Brooks et al., 5th ed. (1975), p. 382; *The Heath Introduction to Poetry*, ed. Joseph de Roche (Lexington, Mass.: Heath, 1975), p. 353, and in 1984 ed., p. 362; *Poems Since 1900: An Anthology of British and American Verse in the Twentieth Century*, ed. Colin Falck and Ian Hamilton (London: Macdonald and Jane's, 1975); *Introducing Poems*, ed. Linda Wagner and C. David Mead (New York: Harper & Row,

1976); *The Modern Age: Literature*, ed. Leonard Lief and James F. Light, 3d ed. (New York: Holt, Rinehart and Winston, 1976), p. 649; *Modern Poems*, ed. Ellmann and O'Clair (1976), p. 261; *The Norton Introduction to Literature*, ed. Bain et al., 2d ed. (1977), p. 605; *Dartmouth Alumni Magazine*, 69 (May 1977), 42; *Fine Frenzy: Enduring Themes in Poetry*, ed. Robert Baylor and Brenda Stokes (New York: McGraw-Hill, 1978), p. 254; *The Treasury of American Poetry*, ed. Sullivan (1978), pp. 509-10; *The Practical Imagination: Stories, Poems, Plays*, ed. Northrup Frye et al. (New York: Harper & Row, 1980), pp. 818-19; *Poetry: An Introduction*, ed. Ruth Miller and Robert A. Greenberg (New York: St. Martin's, 1982), p. 288; *Literature: An Introduction to Fiction, Poetry and Drama*, ed. X.J. Kennedy, 3d ed. (Boston: Little, Brown, 1983), p. 1947.

Note: The following authorial revision has been identified; page and line numbers refer to the first appearance.

189.10 by the] ~ *PNS*+

C162 "Dam Neck, Virginia." *Kenyon Review*, 6 (Spring 1944), 190. Number 'II' of three poems under collective title "Verse More or Less Topical." In *PNS, BO, SP51, CP60, SP65, CP76, CP88*. Rept. in *New Poems 1944*, ed. Williams (1944), p. 219-20; *The War Poets*, ed. Williams (1945), pp. 122-23; *A Little Treasury of American Poetry*, ed. Williams (1948), pp. 694-95; *The Pocketbook of Modern Verse*, ed. Williams (1954), p. 459; *Modern American and Modern British Poetry*, ed. Louis Untermeyer, with Karl Shapiro and Richard Wilbur, rev. shorter ed. (New York: Harcourt, Brace, 1955), pp. 338-39; *The Achievement of Richard Eberhart*, ed. Engel (1968), pp. 31-32; *Puddingstone*, 1 (Spring 1974), 3. *Note*: "Speech From a Play" (**B17**) is rept. on p. 191 of this issue as number 'III' of three poems under collective title "Verse More or Less Topical."

C163 "Empson's Poetry." *Accent*, 4 (Summer 1944), 195-207. Essay. In *OPP*. Rept. in *Accent Anthology*, ed. Kerker Quinn and Charles Shattuck (New York: Harcourt, Brace, 1946), pp. 571-88.

C164 "The Protagonist." *Humanist*, 4 (Oct. 1944), 117. Poem.

C165 "Recipe for Abstinence." *Osprey* (Naval Air Station, Wildwood, N.J., weekly bulletin), 3 (Jan. 12 1945), p. 4. Unsigned article (authorship confirmed by RE).

C166 "The Drunkard." *Accent*, 5 (Spring 1945), 180. Poem. *Note*: "Poem ['Sometimes the longing for death']." (**C119**) rept. on p. 179.

C167 "On Seeing an Egyptian Mummy in Berlin, 1932." *Quarterly Review of Literature*, 3 (1946), 29. Poem. In *CP76, CP88*. Rept. in *Quarterly Review of Literature*, 19 (no. 1-2, 1974), 50.

C168 "Ode to a Chinese Paper Snake." *Quarterly Review of Literature*, 3 (1946), 29-32. Poem. In *BO, SP51, CP60, CP76, CP88*. Rept. in *The Criterion Book of Modern American Verse*, ed. W.H. Auden (New York: Criterion

Books, 1956), pp. 230-33; *The Achievement of Richard Eberhart* (1968), pp. 60-62; *Quarterly Review of Literature* (30th Anniversary Poetry Retrospective), 29 (nos. 1-2, 1974), 47-50.

C169 "Search for Perfection." *Poetry*, 67 (Jan. 1946), 212-15. Rev. of John Crowe Ransom, *Selected Poems*.

C170 "Nonino Dialectic." *Sewanee Review*, 54 (Spring 1946), 275-78. First of "Three Poems."

C171 "An Allowance." *Sewanee Review*, 54 (Spring 1946), 279. Second of "Three Poems."

C172 "Leave Me My Golden Horn of Hours." *Sewanee Review*, 54 (Spring 1946), 280. Third of "Three Poems."

C173 "The Magical." *Foreground* (Harvard Univ., undergraduate literary magazine), 1 (Spring 1946), 124-25. In *BO*.

C174 "The Wind as an Abstract God." *Poetry*, 68 (July 1946), 202. This poem and the one that follows are collectively titled "From'The Kite'". The entire sequence, "The Kite," is rept. in *Hudson Review*, 9 (Summer 1956), 165-77. In *Qu*, *SP65*. *Note*: The following authorial revisions or textual variants have been identified; page and line numbers refer to the first appearance.

   202.6 élan] elan *Hudson Review*+

   202.11 Maneuverable] manoeuverable *Hudson Review*+

C175 "Aerialism." *Poetry*, 68 (July 1946), 203-5. Poem. In *Qu*, *SP65*. *Note*: The following authorial revisions have been identified; page and line numbers refer to the first appearance.

   203.1 To] A...barefoot. To [175.32-176.10] *Qu*+

   203.6 far out] ~-~ *Qu*+

   203.15-16 *normal leading between lines*] *extra leading Qu*+

   203.16 But] By *Qu*+

C176 "Meditation by an Old Barn in the Heat of Summertime." *Poetry*, 68 (July 1946), 205-7. Poem.

C177 "R.G.E." *Frontier Nursing Service*, Fall 1946, 42. In *SB*, *CP76*, *CP88*; presumably rept. in *New York Times* before 1970, but unlocated; *New York Times Book of Verse*, ed. Thomas Lask (New York: Macmillan, 1970), p. 72.

C178 "An Airman Considers His Power." *Furioso*, 2 (Fall 1946), 53. Poem. In *BO*, *SP51*, *CP60*, *CP76*, *CP88*.

C179 "The Full Weakness of Man." *Poetry Quarterly* (England) 1946-47. In *BO*. Rept. in *American Sampler: A Selection of New Poetry*, ed. Francis Coleman Rosenberger (Iowa City: Prairie Press, 1951), pp. 33-34.

C180 Untitled review of Conrad Aiken, *The Kid*. *Furioso*, 3 (Winter 1947), 68-69.

C181 "At the End of War." *Ark*, (Spring 1947), 16-18. Poem. In *BO*, *CP60*, *CP76*, *CP88*. Rept. in *Now*, 8 (May-June 1947), 28-30.

C182 "A Ceremony by the Sea." *Virginia Quarterly Review*, 23 (Spring 1947), 232-24. Poem. In *BO, CP60, CP76, CP88*. Rept. in *The Poetry of War*, ed. Hamilton (1965), pp. 137-38; *Poems from* The Virginia Quarterly Review, ed. Charlotte Kohler (Charlottesville: Univ. Press of Virginia, 1969), pp. 106-7.

C183 "Four Poets." *Sewanee Review*, 55 (Spring 1947), 324-36. Rev. of Pablo Neruda, *Residence on Earth and Other Poems*; Robert Lowell, *Lord Weary's Castle*; Thomas Merton, *A Man in the Divided Sea*; and Reed Whittemore, *Heroes and Heroines*.

C184 Untitled text of RE's Lecture at Mills College, April 1946. *Pacific*, 2 (April 1947), 18-26. In *OPP* as "The Theory of Poetry."

C185 "Notes to a Class in Adult Education." *Accent*, 7 (Summer 1947), 251-53. Review of Wallace Stevens, *Transport to Summer*.

C186 "Aesthetics after War." *Poetry Q*, 9 (Summer 1947), 82-87. Poem In *Un, CP60, CP88*.

C187 "Death Then the Last, Then the Depth." *Contemporary Poetry*, 7 (Autumn 1947), 4. Poem.

C188 "Pink Elf, O Master Child." *Contemporary Poetry*, 7 (Autumn 1947), 4. Poem.

C189 "God to Man." *Contemporary Poetry*, 7 (Autumn 1947), 4-5. Poem.

C190 "A Word for Modern Poetry." *English Leaflet*, 46 (Dec. 1947), 142-43. Essay.

C191 "Bright Hour of Europe." *Botteghe Oscure*, 2 (1948), 282. Poem.

C192 "Sea Scape with Parable." *Botteghe Oscure*, 2 (1948), 283-84. In *Un*. Rept. in *Hudson Review*, 2 (Spring 1949), 54-5; *Poems of Doubt and Belief: An Anthology of Modern Religious Poetry*, ed. Tom F. Driver and Robert Pack (New York: Macmillan, 1964), pp. 149-50.

C193 "Jewels of Rhythm." *New York Times Book Review*, 11 Jan. 1948, p. 4. Review of Richard Wilbur, *The Beautiful Changes*.

C194 "Eberhart's Grave Piece." *Explicator*, 6 (Feb. 1948), 1, 3. RE's explication of his own poem which is contained on pp. 2, 4; rept. in *Reading Modern Poetry*, ed. Engle and Carrier (1955), pp. 273-74.

C195 "Eberhart's 'The Young Hunter'." *Explicator*, 6 (Feb. 1948), 3,5. RE's explication of his own poem which is rept. on p. 4.

C196 "I Did Not Die Enough." *New York Times Book Review*, 8 Feb. 1948, p. 4. Review of Stephen Spender, *Returning to Vienna 1947*.

C197 "From 'Letter I.' " *Poetry*, 72 (April 1948), 14-16. Poem. In *Un*. Rept. in *Quarterly Review of Literature*, 5 (1950), 243-54 (as part of complete poem).

C198 "Energy, Movement, and Reality." *New York Times*, 20 June 1948, p. 4. Rev. of William Carlos Williams, *Paterson* (Book Two).

C199 "Burned Alive." *Poetry Chapbook,* 7 (Fall 1948), 20. Poem.

C200 "Song of the Nerves." *Poetry,* 73 (Oct. 1948), 43-45. Rev. of John Berryman, *The Dispossessed.*

C201 "Art and Zeitgeist." *Poetry,* 73 (Dec. 1948), 173-76. Rev. of Muriel Rukeyser, *The Green Wave.*

C202 "Chant of the Forked Lightning." *Tiger's Eye,* 1 (Dec. 1948), 68. Poem. In *Un, LR.*

C203 "Poem ['The truth hurt worse than a thought bullet']." *Wind and the Rain,* 5 (Winter 1948-49), 164.

C204 "Pound's New Cantos." *Quarterly Review of Literature,* 5 (no. 2, 1949), 174-91. Essay-review on Ezra Pound, *Pisan Cantos.* In *OPP.*

C205 "A Legend of Viable Women." *Kenyon Review,* 11 (Winter 1949), 83-86. Poem. In *Un, CP60, SP65, CP76, CP88.* Rept. in *Mid-Century American Poets,* ed. Ciardi (1950), pp. 230-33; *New Directions in Prose and Poetry,* no. 12 (1950), 114-17; *Modern Verse in English,* ed. David Cecil and Allen Tate (New York: Macmillan, 1958), pp. 476-79. *Note:* The following authorial revisions have been identified; page and line numbers refer to the first appearance.

> 84.20 thirty three] ~-~ Un^+
>
> 84.24 perceived] percepted Un^+
>
> 85.3 gayety] gaiety Un^+

C206 "Four Poets and Their Work." *Virginia Quarterly Review,* 25 (Winter 1949), 123-28. Review of Robinson Jeffers, *The Double Axe*; *The Collected Poems of John Peale Bishop*; William Carlos Williams, *The Clouds, Aigeltinger, Russia, and Other Verse*; Edith Sitwell, *The Song of the Cold.*

C207 "Fragment of New York, 1929." *Western Review,* 13 (Winter 1949), 79-86. Poem. In *Un, CP60, CP76, CP88.*

C208 Untitled rev. of Oscar Williams, *Selected Poems. Contemporary Poetry,* 8 (Winter 1949), 12.

C209 "The Tobacconist of Eighth Street." *American Letters,* 1 (Feb. 1949), 9. Poem. In *Un, CP60, SP65, CP76, CP88.* Rept. in *Poetry-Ireland,* no. 7 (Oct. 1949), 13; *Mid-Century American Poets,* ed. Ciardi (1950), p. 243; *Perspectives USA,* no. 10 (Winter 1955), 31; *As I Pass, O Manhattan: An Anthology of Life in New York,* ed. Esther Morgan McCullough (North Bennington, Vt.: Coley Taylor, 1956), pp. 736-37; *Today's Poets: American and British Poetry Since the 1930's,* ed. Chad Walsh (New York: Scribner's, 1964), p. 41; *The Achievement of Richard Eberhart,* ed. Edgel (1968), p. 34; *Muse of Fire: Approaches to Poetry,* ed. H. Edward Richardson and Frederick B. Shroyer (New York: Knopf, 1971), pp. 112-13; *Literary Spectrum,* ed. Emil and Sandra Roy (Boston: Allyn and Bacon, 1974), p. 96.

C210 "The Muse—with Yankee Accent." *Saturday Review of Literature*, 32 (19 March 1949), 8-9, 36. Essay.

C211 "The Poet as Tightrope Walker." *Saturday Review of Literature*, 32 (19 March 1949), 30. Poem. Rept. in *New York Herald Tribune*, 10 April 1949, p. 10.

C212 "The Rock." *Virginia Quarterly Review*, 25 (Spring 1949), 226. Poem. Rept. in *Poems from the* Virginia Quarterly Review *1925-1967*, ed. Charlotte Kohler (Charlottesville, Va.: Univ. Press of Virginia, 1969), p. 108.

C213 "God and Man." *Virginia Quarterly Review*, 25 (Spring 1949), 227-28. Poem. In *Un*, *CP60*, *CP76*, *CP88*. Rept. in *Poems from the* Virginia Quarterly Review *1925-1967*, ed. Kohler (1969), pp. 109-10. *Note*: The following authorial revision has been identified; page and line numbers refer to the first appearance.

227.10 receding] recedes *Un*+

C214 "Select Seventy." *Saturday Review of Literature*, 32 (4 June 1949), 20. Rev. of *The New British Poets*, ed. Kenneth Rexroth.

C215 Untitled rev. of Mary Owings Miller, *Wheel of Paper*. *Contemporary Poetry*, 9 (Summer 1949), 12.

C216 "West Coast Verse." *New York Times Book Review*, 10 July 1949, p. 10. Rev. of *Poets of the Pacific: Second Series*, ed. Yvor Winters.

C217 "Reality! Reality! What Is It?" *Wake*, no. 8 (Autumn 1949), 5-6. Poem. In *Un*. Rept in *Fifteen Modern American Poets*, ed. George P. Elliott (New York: Holt, Rinehart and Winston, 1967), pp. 31-33.

C218 "Nefretiti." *Wake*, no. 8 (Autumn 1949), 7. Poem.

C219 "The Visionary Eye." *Wake*, no. 8 (Autumn 1949), 7-8. Poem.

C220 "A Love Poem." *Wake*, no. 8 (Autumn 1949), 8. Poem. In *Un*, *CP60*, *CP76*, *CP88*.

C221 "Choosing a Monument." *Western Review*, 14 (Autumn 1949), 58-62. Verse-drama. In *Un*.

C222 "How Is Your Ditentive 'I'- Persona?" *Tiger's Eye*, 1 (Oct. 1949), 128-32. RE's comments to "To Be or Not: Six Opinions on Dr. Trigant Burrow's *The Neurosis of Man*."

C223 "For Goethe in His Youth." *Glass Hill 2*, (Dec. 1949), 1. Poem.

C224 "8:29." *Glass Hill 2*, (Dec. 1949), 7. Poem.

C225 "What If Remembrance." *Glass Hill 2*, (Dec. 1949), 33. Poem. In *Un*, *SP65*. Rept. in *Fifteen Modern American Poets*, ed. Elliott (1956), p. 31.

C226 "Subdued Poetic Fire." *New York Times Book Review*, 11 Dec. 1949, p. 5. Rev. of Osbert Sitwell, *England Reclaimed*.

C227 "The Verbalist of Summer." *Botteghe Oscure*, 5 (1950), 367-71. Poem. In *Un*, *CP60*, *CP76*, *CP88*. Rept. in *Kenyon Review*, 13 (Summer 1951), 381-84. *Note*: In the original appearance the entire poem is set in italic but American spelling conventions are followed throughout.

C228 "Peep Show." *Hika* (Kenyon College), 15, no. 2 (1950), 8-9. Poem. *Note*: RE's note on the poem appears on p. 9.

C229 "Letter I." *Quarterly Review of Literature*, 5 (1950), 243-54. Poem. Rept. in *New Directions 12* (1950), pp. 105-14. *Note*: A portion of this poem appeared earlier in *Poetry*, 72 (April 1948), 14-16; see above, **C196**.

C230 "A Gauze." *Wake*, no. 9 (1950), 40. Poem.

C231 "The Roc." *Wake*, no. 9 (1950), 41-42. Poem. In *GP*. Rept. in *Chief Modern Poets of England and America*, ed. Sanders et al., 4th ed. (1962), v. 2, pp. 408-10, and in 5th ed. (1970), v. 2, pp. 365-67.

C232 "Middle Way." *Poetry* 75 (January 1950), 239-40, 242. Rev. of Edwin Muir, *The Labyrinth*.

C233 "The Image of Ourselves." *New York Times Book Review*, 12 Feb. 1950, p. 5. Rev. of Vivienne Koch, *William Carlos Williams;* and William Carlos Williams, *Paterson* (Book Three).

C234 Untitled rev. of David Daiches, *A Study of Literature for Readers and Critics;* and William Van O'Connor, *Sense and Sensibility in Modern Poetry. The Journal of Aesthetics & Art Criticism*, 8 (March 1950), 198.

C235 "Indian Summer." *Poetry*, 76 (April 1950), 10. First of "Six Poems." In *Un*.

C236 "Politics." *Poetry*, 76 (April 1950), 11. Second of "Six Poems."

C237 "Talk at Dawn." *Poetry*, 76 (April 1950), 12. Third of "Six Poems."

C238 "Order and Disorder." *Poetry*, 76 (April 1950), 13. Fourth of "Six Poems." In *Un*. Rept. in *Poems of Doubt and Belief*, ed. Driver and Pack (1964), p. 89.

C239 "Forms of the Human." *Poetry*, 76 (April 1950), 14. Fifth of "Six Poems." In *Un, CP60, SP65, CP76, CP88*. Rept. in *Fifteen Modern American Poets*, ed. Elliott (1956), p. 35; *Take Hold!*, comp. Lee Bennett Hopkins (New York: Thomas Nelson, 1974).

C240 "The Forum." *Poetry*, 76 (April 1950), 15. Sixth of "Six Poems."

C241 "Baudelaire." *Nine*, 2 (May 1950), 110. Poem. In *Un*. Rept. in *Sewanee Review*, 59 (Spring 1951), 293.

C242 "Theme from Haydn." *Furioso*, 5 (Summer 1950), 68-69. Poem. In *GP*.

C243 "Speech from a Play." *Saturday Review of Literature*, 33 (1 July 1950), 28. Poem.

C244 "War and Poetry." *Beloit Poetry Journal*, 1 (Fall 1950), 6. Poem. In *Un*. Rept. in *New York Times Book Review*, 17 Dec. 1950, p.2; *Botteghe Oscure*, 7 (1951), 336-37.

C245 "That Final Meeting." *Beloit Poetry Journal*, 1 (Fall 1950), 7. Poem. In *Un*. Rept. in *Poetry Awards 1951* (Philadelphia: Univ. of Pennsylvania Press, 1951), 25.

C246 "Oedipus ['Oedipus should have found exit from his dilemma']." *Inventario*, 3 (Autumn 1950), 68-69. Poem. In *Un*, *CP60*, *CP76*, *CP88*. Rept. in *Prompter* (Brattle Theater, Cambridge, Mass.), 1 (Spring 1951), 12; *Dialogue/Exchange*, 5 (Oct. 1957), 13-15. See below, C .

C247 "The Defense of Poetry." *Poetry*, 77 (Nov. 1950), 89-97. RE's account of the Harvard Poetry Conference, August 1950, with synopses of addresses by John Crowe Ransom, Stephen Spender, Peter Viereck, Marianne Moore, Randall Jarrell, Peter Emmanuel, and Kenneth Burke; see below, **F68**.

C248 "Major Poet and Literary Innovator." *New York Times Book Review*, 17 Dec. 1950, pp. 1, 12. Rev. of William Carlos Williams, *The Collected Later Poems*.

C249 "Phoenixes Again." *Botteghe Oscure*, 7 (1951), 337-39. Poem. In *Un*. *Note:* "War and Poetry" (**C244**) rept. on pp. 336-37. *Note*: The first appearance is set in all italics, whereas reprinted appearances are set in roman. The following authorial revisions have been identified; page and line numbers refer to the first appearance.

    338.27 *fluid*] fluent

    339.11 *aspires*] yearns

    339.24 *Beauty, truth, and rarity*] Order, calm, and luxury

C250 "What the World Is." *Poetry-New York*, no. 4 (1951), 16-17. Poem.

C251 "The Power of Art." *Poetry-New York*, no. 4 (1951), 17. Poem.

C252 "The Poet-Weathervane." *Wake*, no. 10 (1951), 13-14. Poem. In *Un*.

C253 "To Bill Williams." *Wake*, no. 10 (1951), 14. Poem. In *Qu*, *PP*. Rept. in *Nation*, 176 (31 May 1958), 501; *Anthology of Magazine Verse for 1958*, ed. William Stanley Braithwaite (New York: Schulte, 1959), p. 59. *Note*: The following authorial revisions have been identified; page and line numbers refer to the first appearance.

    14.14 architecture] idiom Qu^+

    14.15 form] forms Qu^+

C254 "The Horse Chestnut Tree." *Wake*, no. 10 (1951), 15. Poem. In *Un*, *CP60*, *SP65*, *CP76*, *CP88*. Rept. in *New Poems by American Poets*, ed. Rolfe Humphries (New York: Ballantine, 1953), pp. 55-56; *The Pocket Book of Modern Verse: English and American Poetry of the Last Hundred Years from Walt Whitman to Dylan Thomas*, ed. Oscar Williams (New York: Pocket Books, 1954), p. 461; *Modern American and Modern British Poetry*, ed. Louis Untermeyer, shorter ed. (New York: Harcourt, Brace, 1955), p. 337; *New Pocket Anthology of American Verse from Colonial Days to the Present*, ed. Oscar Williams (New York: World Publishing, 1955), p. 173; *Perspectives USA*, no. 10 (Winter 1955), 30-31; *The Criterion Book of Modern Amer-*

ican Verse, ed. W.H. Auden (New York: Criterion Books, 1956), pp. 233-34; *Fifteen Modern American Poets*, ed. George P. Elliott (1956), p. 33; *The Atlantic Book of British and American Poetry*, ed. Edith Sitwell (Boston: Little, Brown, 1958), pp. 959-60; *The Poem: A Critical Anthology*, ed. Josephine Miles (Englewood Cliffs, N.J.: Prentice-Hall, 1959), pp. 138-39; *St. Louis Post-Dispatch*, 18 Oct. 1959, p. 2 (B); *Poetry for Pleasure: The Hallmark Book of Poetry* (Garden City, N.Y.: Doubleday, 1960), pp. 88-89; *Discovering Modern Poetry*, ed. Elizabeth Drew and George Connon (New York: Holt, Rinehart and Winston, 1961), p. 67; *F.T. Palgrave's The Golden Treasury of the Best Songs and Lyrical Poems* (Centennial Ed.), ed. Oscar Williams (New York: Mentor Books-New American Library, 1961), pp. 538-39; *Poems: Wadsworth Handbook and Anthology*, ed. C.F. Main and Peter J. Seng (San Francisco: Wadsworth, 1961), pp. 150-51, in the 2d ed. (1965), pp. 156-57, and in the 4th ed. (197), pp. 200-1; *Chief Modern Poets of England and America*, ed. Sanders et al., 4th ed., v. 2, pp. 407-8, and in the 5th ed. (1970), v. 2, pp. 364-65; *Modern American Poetry Modern British Poetry*, ed. Louis Untermeyer, new and enl. ed. (New York: Harcourt, Brace, 1962), pp. 578-79; *A Selection of Contemporary Religious Poetry*, ed. Samuel Hazo (Glen Rock, N.J.: Deus Books, 1963), p. 41; *Poems of Doubt and Belief*, ed. Driver and Pack (1964), pp. 148-49; *Today's Poets*, ed. Walsh (1964), pp. 40-41; *The Case for Poetry: A Critical Anthology*, ed. Frederick L. Gwynn at al., 2d ed. (Englewood Cliffs, N.J.: Prentice-Hall, 1965); *Poems and Poets*, ed. David Aloian (St. Louis: McGraw-Hill, 1965), pp. 397-98; *Scholastic Teacher* (Practical English), (7 Oct. 1965), 13; *The Distinctive Voice: Twentieth Century American Poetry*, ed. William J. Martz (Glenview, Ill.: Scott Foresman, 1966), pp. 148-49; *100 American Poems in the Twentieth Century*, ed. Perrine and Reid (1966), pp. 194-95; *The Province of Poetry*, ed. Edwin B. Benjamin (New York: American Book Co., 1966), pp. 270-71; *A College Treasury of Fiction, Drama, Poetry*, ed. Paul Jorgensen and Frederick B. Shroyer, 2d ed. (New York: Scribner's, 1967), pp. 562-63; *The Achievement of Richard Eberhart*, ed. Engel (1968), p. 30; *Amerikanske Stemmer*, ed. Jens Nyholm (Copenhagen: Arne Frost-Hansens Forlag, 1968), p. 148, with Danish trans. on p. 147; *Patterns in Poetry*, ed. Harry M. Brown and John Milstead (Glenview, Ill.: Scott Foresman, 1968), pp. 401-1; *A Book of Modern American Poetry*, ed. Jane McDermott and Thomas V. Lowery (New York: Harcourt, Brace, 1970), pp. 186-87; *A Little Treasury of Modern Poetry English and American*, ed. Williams, 3d ed. (1970), p. 437; *Being Born and Growing Older: Poems and Images*, ed. Bruce Vance (New York: Van Nostrand, Reinhold, 1971); *Muse of Fire: Approaches to Poetry*, ed. H. Edward Richardson and Frederick B, Shroyer (New York: Knopf, 1971), pp. 95-96; *A Reading Apprenticeship*, ed. Norman A. Brittin (New York: Holt, Rinehart, and Winston, 1971), pp. 457-58; *The Realities of Literature*, ed. Richard F.

Dietrich (Waltham, Mass.: Xerox College Publishing, 1971), pp. 173-74; *The Touch of a Poet*, ed. Paul C. Holmes and Harry E. Souza (New York: Harper & Row, 1976), p. 145; *Expansive Light* (New York: The Sacred Fire, 1977), pp. 26-27; *Dartmouth Alumni Magazine*, 69 (May 1977), p. 43; *Adventures in American Literature* (Heritage Edition), ed. Francis Hodgins and Kenneth Silverman (New York: Harcourt, Bracc, Jovanovich, 1980), pp. 694-95; *Poetry: Sight and Insight*, ed. James W. Kirkland and F. David Sanders (New York: Random House, 1982), pp. 375-76.

C255 "To My Son Aged Four." *Wake*, no. 10 (1951), 16. Poem. In *Un*.

C256 "The Look." *Wake*, no. 10 (1951), 16-17. Poem. In *Un*. Rept. in *Wind and the Rain*, 7 (nos. 2-3, 1951), 123. *Note*: The following authorial revision has been identified; page and line numbers refer to the first appearance.

16.8 nothing but] only

C257 "Indian Pipe." *Wake*, 10 (1951), 17. Poem. In *Un*, *CP60*, *SP65*, *CP76*, *CP88*. Rept. in *New York Times Book Review*, 30 Dec. 1951, p. 2; *Poets in Progress*, ed. Edward Hungerford (Evanston, Ill.: Northwestern Univ., 1962), p. 78; *Three Dimensions of Poetry*, ed. Vincent Stewart (New York: Scribner's, 1969), p. 44.

C258 "To One, Who, Dead, Sees His Poems in Print One Hundred Years Later." *Wake*, no. 10 (1951), 17018. Poem. In *Un*. *Note*: RE rewrote the final line of this poem for inclusion in *Un*; page and line numbers refer to the first appearance.

19.12 In...cacophony.] Death...sea.

C259 "On the Fragility of Mind." *Wake*, no. 10 (1951), 18. Poem. In *Un*, *CP60*, *SP65*, *CP76*, *CP88*. Rept. in *Poetry*, 82 (Aug. 1953), 261. *Note*: The following authorial revision has been identified; page and line numbers refer to the first appearance.

18.16 forms] ~, *Un*[+]

C260 "The Apparition," *Poetry*, 77 (March 1951), 311-21. Verse-play. In *CVP*.

C261 "Oddments of History." *Origin*, 1 (Spring 1951), 60. Poem.

C262 "Oedipus ['It seems abrogative to reach for Oedipus']." *Prompter* (Brattle Theatre, Cambridge, Mass.), 1 (Spring 1951), 12. Poem.

C263 "At Night." *University of Kansas City Review*, 17 (Spring 1951), 204. Poem. In *Un*, *CP60*, *SP65*, *CP76*, *CP88*. Rept. in *The Achievement of Richard Eberhart*, ed. Engle (1968), p. 31; *Love's Aspects: The World's Great Love Poems*, ed. Jean Garrigue (Garden City, N.Y.: Doubleday, 1975), p. 274; *Love Hungers to Abound*, ed. Helen Plotz (New York: Greenwillow, 1978), p. 170.

C264 "An Excellent Redaction." *Poetry*, 78 (April 1951), 49-53. Rev. of Theodore Morrison, *The Dream of Alcestis*.

C265 "A Vision Welded to the World." *New York Times Book Review*, 17 June 1951, pp. 5, 18. Rev. of William Carlos Williams, *Paterson*, (Book Four).

C266 "The Mischief." *Beloit Poetry Journal*, 1 (Summer 1951), 16. Poem.

C267 Untitled rev. of Paul Engle, *The Word of Love* and *Poems from the Iowa Poetry Workshop. Furioso*, 6 (Fall 1951), 78-80.

C268 "Deep, Lyrical Feelings." *New York Times Book Review*, 16 Dec. 1951, p. 4. Rev. of Theodore Roethke, *Praise to the End*.

C269 "Five Poets." *Kenyon Review*, 14 (Winter 1952), 168-72. Rev. of *Selected Poems of Horace Gregory*; Randall Jarrell, *The Seven-League Crutches*; Robert Lowell, *The Mills of the Kavanaughs*; Howard Nemerov, *Guide to the Ruins*; and Radcliffe Squires, *Where the Compass Spins*.

C270 "Poem ['I was the carrier of fate']." *Beloit Poetry Journal*, 2 (Spring 1952), 16. Poem.

C271 "Motion as Grace." *Beloit Poetry Journal*, 2 (Spring 1952), 17. Poem. In *Un. Note*: The following authorial revisions have been identified; page and line numbers refer to the first appearance.

   17.1 blue] new
   17.9 Carretto] Caretto

C272 "The Stevens Prose." *Accent*, 12 (Spring 1952), 122-25. Rev. of Wallace Stevens, *The Necessary Angel*.

C273 "It Was Today." *Epoch*, 4 (Spring 1952), 67-68. Poem.

C274 "The Dream of Time." *Epoch*, 4 (Spring 1952), 68. Poem. In *Un*.

C275 "The Seasons." *Kenyon Review*, 14 (Spring 1952), 327-30. Poem in four titled parts: "Winter Man," p. 327; "Spring Man," p. 328; "The Man of Summer," p. 329; and "The Man of Autumn," p. 330. In *CP60, CP88*.

C276 "The Great Stone Face." *Dartmouth Alumni Magazine*, 44 (June 1952), 25. Poem. In *Un*.

C277 "Book of Nature." *Virginia Quarterly Review*, 28 (Summer 1952), 369-70. Poem. In *Un, CP60, SP65, CP76, CP88*. Rept. in *Poems of Doubt and Belief*, ed. Driver and Pack (1964), pp. 38-39; *Poems from the* Virginia Quarterly Review *1925-1967*, ed. Kohler (1969), pp. 111-12.

C278 "New Looks at Yeats." *Virginia Quarterly Review*, 28 (Autumn 1952), 618-21. Rev. of Thomas Parkinson, *W.B.Yeats: Self Critic*; T.R. Henn, *The Lonely Tower*; and Vivienne Koch, *W.B. Yeats: The Tragic Phase*.

C279 "The Skier and the Mountain." *Poetry*, 81 (Oct. 1952), 33-34. Poem. In *Un, CP60, CP76, CP88*. Rept. in *The Achievement of Richard Eberhart*, ed. Engel (1968), pp. 64-65.

C280 "Lines to an Old Man." *Voices,* no. 149 (Sept.-Dec. 1952), 12-13. Poem. In *Un. Note:* The following authorial revision had been identified; page and line numbers refer to the first appearance.

   13.9 Let] Then let

C281 "Things as They Are." *New Republic*, 127 (10 Nov. 1952), 20-21. Rev. of William Carlos Williams, *The Build-Up*.

C282 "The Pattern of MacLeish's Poetry." *New York Times Book Review*, 23 Nov. 1952, pp. 5, 48. Rev. of Archibald MacLeish, *Collected Poems 1917-1952*.

C283 "The Tone is Delicate." *New York Times Book Review*, 18 Jan. 1953, p 21. Rev. of O.V. de Lubicz Milosz, *Fourteen Poems* (trans. Kenneth Rexroth).

C284 "A Voyage of the Spirit." *New York Times Book Review*, (15 Feb. 1953), 25. Review of Kenneth Rexroth, *The Dragon and The Unicorn*.

C285 "Easter Absolutes." *Poetry*, 81 (March 1953), 357. First of "Six Poems."

C286 "Blessed Are the Angels in Heaven." *Poetry*, 81 (March 1953), 357-58. Second of "Six Poems." In *CP60, CP76, CP88*.

C287 "Grape Vine Shoots." *Poetry*, 81 (March 1953), 358-59. Third of "Six Poems." In *Un*.

C288 "The Voyage." *Poetry*, 81 (March 1953), 359-60. Fourth of "Six Poems." In *CP60, CP88*. *Note*: The following authorial revision has been identified; page and line numbers refer to the first appearance.

360.12 rocks'] rock's *CP60*+

C289 "Order Again." *Poetry*, 81 (March 1953), 360-61. Fifth of "Six Poems." In *Un*. *Note*: The following authorial revision has been identified; page and line numbers refer to the first appearance.

360.11 free] ~,

C290 "The Lost Poem." *Poetry*, 81 (March 1953), 361-62. Sixth of "Six Poems." In *Un*.

C291 "On Hearing Bertrand Russell On Mind and Body." *Dartmouth Quarterly*, 8 (Spring 1953), 14. Poem.

C292 "Lyric." *Dartmouth Quarterly*, 8 (Spring 1953), 15. Poem.

C293 "Clear, Precise, Controlled." *New York Times Book Review*, (26 April 1953), 10. Review of John Lehmann, *The Age of the Dragon Poems 1930-1951*.

C294 "To Evan." *Hudson Review*, 6 (Summer 1953), 206-7. Poem. In *GP, CP60, SP65, CP76, CP88*. Rept. in *The Cry of Rachel: An Anthology of Elegies on Children*, ed. Sister Mary Immaculate (New York: Random House, 1966), pp. 28-29.

C295 "The Human Being is a Lonely Creature." *Hudson Review*, 6 (Summer 1953), 207. Poem. In *Un, CP60, SP65, CP76, CP88*. Rept. in *New Poems by American Poets*, ed. Humphries (1953), p. 53; *Fifteen Modern American Poets*, ed. Elliott (1956), pp. 35-36; *Poems: Wadsworth Handbook and Anthology*, ed. C.F. Main and Peter J. Seng, 2d ed. (Belmont, Ca.: Wadsworth, 1965), p. 198, and in 4th ed. (1978), pp. 218-19. *The Achievement of Richard Eberhart*, ed. Engel (1968), p. 36.

C296 "The Dry Rot." *Hudson Review*, 6 (Summer 1953), 208. Poem. In *Un*, *CP60*, *CP76*, *CP88*.

C297 "La Crosse at Ninety Miles an Hour." *Hudson Review*, 6 (Summer 1953), 208-9. Poem. In *Qu*, *SP65*, *CP88*. Rept. in *The Achievement of Richard Eberhart*, ed. Engel (1968), p. 41; *America Forever New: A Book of Poems*, ed. Sara and John E. Brewton (New York: Crowell, 1968), 205-6.

C298 "The Noble Man." *Kenyon Review*, 15 (Summer 1953), 411-12. Poem. In *CP60*, *CP88*. Rept. in *The Pocket Book of Modern Verse*, ed. Williams (1954), pp. 460-61. *Note*: The following authorial revisions have been identified between the first appearance and book publication in *CP60*; page and line numbers refer to the first appearance.

411.13-14 olympianly, Openly.] profoundly, In fervour.

412.8 self-pity] ~∧ ~

C299 "Resources of the World." *Kenyon Review*, 15 (Summer 1953), 412-13. Poem.

C300 "Creators." *Paris Review*, 1 (Summer 1953), 50. Poem.

C301 "Jealousy." *Poetry*, 82 (Aug. 1953) 262. Second of "Three Poems." *Note:* "On the Fragility of the Mind" (C259) is here reprinted as the first of "Three Poems."

C302 "Seeing is Deceiving." *Poetry*, 82 (Aug. 1953), 262-63. Third of "Three Poems." In *GP*, *CP60*, *CP76*, *CP88*.

C303 "A Book About Modern Poetry." *Poetry*, 82 (Aug. 1953), 282-87. Rev. of Babette Deutsch, *Poetry in Our Time*.

C304 "Speaking of Books (later titled "Why I Write Poetry)". *New York Times Book Review*, 23 Aug. 1953, p. 2. In *OPP* as "Why I Write Poetry"; rept. as "Why I Say it in Verse," in *A College Treasury*, ed. Jorgensen and Shroyes, 2d. ed. (1967), pp. 392-93.

C305 "Mediterranean Song." *Experiment*, 7 (no. 1, 1954), 140. Poem. In *CP60*, *CP76*, *CP88*. *Note:* RE was guest editor of this number of *Experiment*. *Note*: The following authorial revisions have been identified; page and line numbers refer to the first appearance.

140.3 Carcassonne.] ~,

140.4 Etna,] ~∧

140.6 sanctions,] ~∧

140.6 jocund,] ~∧

140.7 Mediterranean,] ~∧

C306 "In the Blood." *New Ventures*, 1 (no. 1, 1954), 31-32. Poem.

C307 "Impatience as a Gesture of Divine Will." *New Ventures*, 1 (no. 1, 1954), 32. Poem. In *Qu*. *Note*: The following authorial revisions have been identified; page and line numbers refer to the first appearance.

32.1 *et passim* Impatience] impatience

32.10 Authority] authority

C308 "Preamble II." *Sewanee Review*, 62 (Winter 1954), 84-100. Verse-play, with "Note" by RE, on pp. 99-100. In *CVP*.

C309 "Idols of Imagination." *Trinity Review*, 8 (Spring 1954), 8. Poem. In *GP*. Rept. in *Fifteen Modern American Poets*, ed. Elliott (1956), p. 36.

C310 "The Glance." *Trinity Review*, 8 (Spring 1954), 8. In *GP*.

C311 "Saucy Love of Life." *New York Times Book Review*, 9 May 1954, p. 5. Review of Dylan Thomas, *Under Milk Wood*.

C312 "What Is the Question." *Voices: A Journal of Poetry*, no. 154 (May-Aug. 1954), 34.

C313 "Closing Off the View." *Trinity Review*, 8 (May 1954), 24. Poem. First of "Two Poems" (dedicated to Wallace Stevens).

C314 "The Meaning of Indian Summer." *Trinity Review*, 8 (May 1954), 24. Poem. Second of "Two Poems" (dedicated to Wallace Stevens).

C315 "Common Charms from Deep Sources." *New York Times Book Review*, 30 May 1954, p. 6. Rev. of Louise Bogan, *Collected Poems 1923-53*. Rept. in *Critical Essays on Louise Bogan*, ed. Martha Collins (New York: G.K. Hall, 1984), pp. 67-68.

C316 "Some Men Have It Early." *Chicago Review*, 8 (Summer 1954), 52. Poem. Rept. in *The Chicago Review Anthology*, ed. David Ray (Chicago: Univ. of Chicago Press, 1959), 185.

C317 "Yonder." *Chicago Review*, 8 (Summer 1954), 53. Poem. In *CP60*, *CP88*. Rept. in *The Chicago Review Anthology*, ed. Ray (1959), 184-85; *The Gift Outright*, ed. Helen Plotz (New York: Greenwillow, 1977), p. 178.

C318 "Time and Dylan Thomas." *Virginia Quarterly Review*, 30 (Summer 1954), 475-78. Review of Elder Olson, *The Poetry of Dylan Thomas*.

C319 "'The More I Have Traveled...'" *New York Times Book Review*, 10 Oct. 1954, p. 14. Rev. of Archibald MacLeish, *Songs for Eve*.

C320 "The Giantess." *Poetry*, 85 (Nov. 1954), 94-95. First of "Three Poems." In *GP*, *CP60*, *CP76*, *CP88*.

C321 "World's Havoc." *Poetry*, 85 (Nov. 1954), 97. Second of "Three Poems."

C322 "The Project." *Poetry*, 85 (Nov. 1954), 97. Third of "Three Poems." In *Qu*, *CP88*. Rept. in *The Achievement of Richard Eberhart*, ed. Engel (1968), 49-50.

C323 "Some Memories of Dylan Thomas." *Yale Literary Magazine*, 122 (Nov. 1954), 5-6. Memoir. Rept. in *Dylan Thomas: The Legend and the Poet*, ed. E.W. Tedlock (London: Heinemann, 1960), pp. 55-57.

C324 "Prose, Poetry and the Love of Life." *Saturday Review of Literature*, 37 (20 Nov. 1954), 20, 38. Rev. of *Selected Essays of William Carlos Williams*.

C325 "On a Squirrel Crossing the Road in Autumn, in New England." *London Magazine*, 1 (Dec. 1954), 50. Poem. In *GP*, *CP60*, *SP65*, *CP76*,

CP88. Rept. in *The New Pocket Anthology of American Verse*, ed. Oscar Williams (The Pocket Library, 1955), p. 169; *Poet's Choice*, ed. Paul Engle and Joseph Langland (New York: Dial, 1962), p. 60, with RE's explanation of why he chose this poem on p. 61; *Adventures in American Literature*, ed. Edmund Fuller and B. Jo Kinnick (New York: Harcourt, Brace, and World, 1963), v. 2, p. 231; *Poems: The Wadsworth Handbook and Anthology*, ed. C.F. Main and Peter J. Seng (Belmont, Ca.: Wadsworth, 1965), pp. 137-38; *Modern Poets: British and American* (Dayton, Ohio: George A. Pflaum, 1966), p. 21; *100 American Poems of the Twentieth Century*, ed. Perrine and Reid (1966), p. 196, with RE's rept. comments on the poem on pp. 196-97; *Art and Craft in Poetry*, ed. James T. Lape and Elizabeth Lape (Boston: Ginn and Co., 1967), pp. 278-79; *Scholastic Teacher*, 44 (14 March 1968), 12; *The Achievement of Richard Eberhart*, ed. Engel (1968), p. 38; *American Literature*, ed. Schorer et al. (1968), p. 705; *Currents in Poetry*, ed. Richard Corbin, rev. ed. (New York: Macmillan, 1968), p. 158; *53 Poets of Today*, ed. Ruth Witt-Diamant and Rikutaro Fukuda (Tokyo: Kenkyusha, 1968), p. 4-5; *A Little Treasury of Modern Poetry*, ed. Williams, 3d ed. (1970), pp. 439-40; *Voices of Poetry*, ed. Allen Kirschner (New York: Dell, 1970), pp. 27-28; *The Realities of Literature*, ed. Richard F. Dietrich (Waltham, Mass.: Xerox College Publ., 1971), p. 63; *The Logic of Poetry*, ed. Richard Monaco and John Briggs (New York: McGraw-Hill, 1974), p. 183; *Take Hold! An Anthology of Pulitzer Prize Winning Poems*, ed. Lee Bennett Hopkins (New York: Thomas Nelson, 1974); *The Heath Introduction to Poetry*, ed. Joseph de Roche (Lexington, Mass.: Heath, 1975), pp. 353-54, and in 2d ed. (1984), pp. 362-63; *Contemporary English: Explorations*, ed. Barbara Pannwitt et al. (Morristown, N.J.: Silver Burdett, 1976), p. 63; *The Record* (Wheaton College), 21 May 1976, p. 7; *The Crystal Image: A Poetry Anthology*, ed. Paul Janeczko (New York: Dell, 1977), pp. 36-37; *Expansive Light* (New York: The Sacred Fire, 1977), pp. 32-33; *Dartmouth Alumni Magazine*, 69 (May 1977), 43; *Communicative Writing*, ed. Elbert R. Bowen et al, 4th ed. (New York: Macmillan, 1978), p. 367; *Ocarina Annual*, 9 (1978-79), 75; *Adventures in American Literature* (Heritage Edition), ed. Francis Hodgins and Kenneth Silverman (New York: Harcourt, Brace, Jovanovich, 1980), p. 696; *Roadkills* (Easthampton, Mass.: Cheloniidae Press, 1981), p. 29; *Literature: The Human Experience*, ed. Richard Abcarian and Marvin Klotz, 3d ed. (New York: St. Martin's, 1982), p. 1050; *Poetspeak: In Their Work, About Their Work*, ed. Paul Janeczko (Scarsdale, N.Y.: Bradbury Press, 1983), pp. 164-65.

C326 "Soul." *Botteghe Oscure*, 15 (1955), 203-5. Poem. In *GP*, *CP60*, *CP76*, *CP88*. *Note*: The original appearance is set in italic, but each subsequent setting is in roman. The following authorial revision has been identified; page and line numbers refer to the first appearance.

203.5 *for keeps*] at neap *GP+*

C327 "The Day-Bed." *Botteghe Oscure*, 15 (1955), 205-8. Poem. In *GP*, *CP60*, *SP65*, *CP76*, *CP88*. Rept. in *Fifteen Modern American Poets*, ed. Elliott (1956), pp. 38-41; *Botteghe Oscure Reader*, ed. George Garrett (Middletown, Conn.: Wesleyan Univ. Press, 1974), pp. 86-89. *Note*: The original appearance is set in italic, but each subsequent setting is in roman. The following authorial revisions have been identified; page and line numbers refer to the first appearance.

    205.3 *twenty seven*] ~-~ *GP*+
    207.2 *Apparelling*] Appareling *GP*+

C328 "Sunday in October." *Poetry*, 85 (Feb. 1955), 273. First of "Two Poems." In *GP*, *CP60*, *CP76*, *CP88*. Rept. in *Rushlight* (Wheaton College), 101 (April 1955), 11; *The Achievement of Richard Eberhart*, ed. Engel (1968), pp. 66-67.

C329 "A Young Greek, Killed in the Wars." *Poetry*, 85 (Feb. 1955), 274. Second of "Two Poems." In *CP60*, *CP76*, *CP88*. Rept. in *Anthology of Modern Poetry*, ed. John Wain (London: Hutchinson, 1963), p. 143. *Note*: The following authorial revision has been identified; page and line numbers refer to the first appearance.

    274.1-8 The...precision] *deleted in CP60*+

C330 "Words." *Encounter*, 4 (Feb. 1955), 20. Poem. In *GP*, *CP60*, *SB*, *LR*, *CP88*. Rept. in *The New Pocket Anthology of American Verse*, ed. Williams (1955), p. 172; *The Achievement of Richard Eberhart*, ed. Engel (1968), p. 66; *Expansive Light* (New York: The Sacred Fire, 1977), p. 31.

C331 "The Wisdom of Insecurity." *Hudson Review*, 8 (Spring 1955), 82-83. Poem. In *GP*, *CP60*, *SP65*, *CP76*, *CP88*. Rept. in *The New Pocket Anthology of American Verse*, ed. Williams (1955), pp. 171-72; *The Achievement of Richard Eberhart*, ed. Engel (1968), pp. 39-40.

C332 "The Forgotten Rock." *Hudson Review*, 8 (Spring 1955), 84. Poem. In *CP60*, *SP65*, *CP76*, *CP88*. Rept. in *London Magazine*, 2 (April 1955), 48-49; *The New Pocket Anthology of American Verse*, ed. Williams (1955), p. 170.

C333 "Cousin Florence." *Hudson Review*, 8 (Spring 1955), 85. Poem. In *GP*, *CP60*, *SP65*, *CP76*, *CP88*. Rept. in *Today's Poets*, ed. Walsh (1964), pp. 42-43.

C334 "Four Exposures." *Beloit Poetry Journal*, 5 (Spring 1955), 16-19. Poem. In *Qu*, *CP76*, *CP88*.

C335 "Cold Fall." *Poet*, no. 11 (Spring 1955). Poem. In *GP*.

C336 "Going to Class Under Greek Statues." *Rushlight* (Wheaton College, Norton, Mass.), 101 (April 1955), 10. In *GP*. Rept. in *Voices*, (Sept.-Dec. 1955), 32. *Note*: The following authorial revision has been identified between the reprinted appearance in *Voices* and book publication in *GP*; page and line numbers refer to the earlier appearance.

    10.23 Mastering the] ~

C337 "Using the Meditative Means." *Kenyon Review*, 17 (Summer 1955), 447-48. Poem.

C338 "With Images of Actuality." *New York Times Book Review*, 17 July 1955, p. 4. Rev. of Elizabeth Bishop, *Poems*.

C339 "Salem." *Yankee*, 20 (Sept. 1955), 34. Poem. In *GP*, *CP88*. Rept. in *Themes in American Literature*, ed. Charles Genthe and George Keithly (Lexington, Mass.: D.C. Heath, 1972), p. 552.

C340 "The Visionary Farms: Scene 15." *Quarterly Review of Literature*, 8 (no. 3, 1955), 169-75. Complete version in *CVP*.

C341 "Silver and Gold." *Poetry*, 87 (Oct. 1955), 48-50. Rev. of *The Collected Poems of Edith Sitwell*.

C342 "To the Heart's Depths." *New York Times Book Review*, 18 Dec. 1955, p. 4. Rev. of Ruthven Todd, *A Mantelpiece of Shells*; and Ben Belitt, *Wilderness Stair*.

C343 Untitled comments to a symposium on Ezra Pound's poetry, in *Nuova Corrente*, nos. 5-6 (1956), 212-13, with an Italian translation on 214-15.

C344 "Summer Landscape." *Folder 4* (1956), 57. In *GP*, *CP60*, *CP76*, *CP88*. Rept. in *A New Folder*, ed. Daisy Aldan (New York: Folder Editions, 1959), p. 84.

C345 "The Fig That Floats." *Poetry London-New York*, 1 (Winter 1956), 29-30. Poem. In *LR*.

C346 "The Whole View." *Poetry London-New York*, 1 (Winter 1956), 30-31. Poem. In *GP*, *LR*.

C347 "American Passion." *Saturday Review of Literature*, 39 (18 Feb. 1956), 49. Rev. of William Carlos Williams, *Journey to Love*.

C348 "Sea-Ruck." *Poetry London-New York*, 1 (March-April 1956), 10. Poem. In *Qu*, *CP76*, *CP88*. Rept. in *Moods of the Sea: Masterworks of Sea Poetry*, ed. George C. Solley and Eric Steinbaugh (Annapolis, Md.: Naval Inst. Press, 1981), p. 267.

C349 "What Gives." *Poetry London-New York*, 1 (March-April 1956), 10-11. Poem. In *CP60*, *CP76*, *CP88*.

C350 "Autumnal." *Departure*, 3 (Spring 1956), 3. Poem. In *CP60*, *CP76*, *CP88*.

C351 "To Helen, with a Playbill." *Nation*, 182 (7 April 1956), 283. Poem. In *GP*.

C352 "The Other Side of the Mind." *Nation*, 182 (14 April 1956), 309, 312. Rev. of Aldous Huxley, *Heaven and Hell*.

C353 "Futures." *Nation*, 182 (21 April 1956), 343, Poem.

C354 "Anima." *New Republic*, 124 (30 April 1956), 17. Poem. In *CP60*, *SP65*, *CP76*, *CP88*.

C355 "Strong, Sensitive and Balanced." *New York Times Book Review*, 24 June 1956, p. 5. Rev. of Richard Wilbur, *Things of This World*.

C356 "The Sacrifice." *Beloit Poetry Journal*, 6 (Summer 1956), 29. Poem. In *CP60*, *CP76*, *CP88*.

C357 "Sermon on the Amount of Love." *Kenyon Review*, 18 (Summer 1956), 365 67. Poem.

C358a "The Kite." *Hudson Review*, 9 (Summer 1956), 165-77. Poem. In *Qu*, *SP65*. *Note*: The following authorial revisions and textual variants have been identified; page and line numbers refer to the first appearance.

165.1-167.37 I *Putting the Thing Together. It is Going to be Five Feet Tall* It... metropolitan.] *deleted in Qu*+

    168.1 II] I Qu+
    168.10 III] II *Qu*+
    170.14 IV] III *Qu*+
    170.21 screweyes] screw eyes *Qu*+
    172.27 V] IV *Qu*+
    173.15 VI] V *Qu*+
    175.30 VII] VI *Qu*+

C358b Untitled review of Brewster Ghiselin, *The Nets*. *Western Humanities Review*, 10 (Summer 1956), 293. Rept. in *The Water of Light*, ed. Henry Taylor (Salt Lake City: Univ. of Utah Press, 1976), p. 91.

C359 "Attitudes." *Poetry*, 88 (Aug. 1956), 318. Poem in two titled parts: "Irish Catholic" and "New England Protestant." In *CP60*, *SP65*, *CP76*, *CP88*. Rept. in *Today's Poets*, ed. Walsh (1964), p. 44. Part two, "New England Protestants" rept. separately in *Take Hold! An Anthology of Pulitzer Prize Winning Poems*, ed. Lee Bennett Hopkins (New York: Thomas Nelson, 1974); *Life Hungers to Abound*, ed. Helen Plotz (New York: Greenwillow, 1978), p. 111.

C360 "Only in the Dream." *Poetry*, 88 (Aug. 1956), 319. In *GP*, *CP60*, *SP65*, *CP76*, *CP88*.

C361 "Thrush Song at Dawn." *Poetry*, 88 (Aug. 1956), 320. In *GP*, *CP60*, *CP76*, *CP88*. Rept. in *Best Poems of 1956* (Palo Alto, Ca.: Stanford Univ. Press, 1957), p. 31; *Poets in Progress*, ed. Hungerford (1962), pp. 83-84. *Note*: The following authorial revision has been identified; page and line numbers refer to the first appearance.

    320.18 Richness] richness *GP*+

C362 "Vast Light." *Nation*, 183 (4 Aug. 1956), 104. Poem. In *GP*. Rept. in *The New Modern Poetry*, ed. M.L. Rosenthal (New York: Macmillan, 1967), pp. 55-56; *Chief Modern Poets of England and America*, ed. Sanders et al., 4th ed. (1962), pt. 2, p. 410, and in 5th ed. (1970), pt. 2, p. 367. *Note*: The following authorial revision has been identified; page and line numbers refer to the first appearance.

    104.3 flows] lets,

C363 "West Coast Rhythms." *New York Times Book Review*, 2 Sept. 1956, pp. 7, 18. Essay-review of new work by the San Francisco "Beats," including Allen Ginsberg, Michael McClure, Lawrence Ferlinghetti, Gary Snyder, and Phillip Whalen. In *OPP*; rept. in *To Eberhart from Ginsberg* (Lincoln, Mass.: Penmaen, 1976), pp. 41-45; *On the Poetry of Allen Ginsberg*, ed. Lewis Hyde (Ann Arbor: Univ. of Michigan, 1984), pp. 24-25.

C364 "Sportive Accolade." *Nation*, 183 (8 Sept. 1956), 206. Poem.

C365 "The Mother Part." *Sewanee Review*, 64 (Autumn 1956), 600-2. Poem. In *Qu.*

C366 "Love Among the Ruins." *Nation*, 183 (13 Oct. 1956), 310. Poem. In *CP60*, *CP76*, *CP88*.

C367 "Gusto, Verve and Flair." *New York Times Book Review*, 21 Oct. 1956, p. 59. Rev. of Roy Campbell, *Talking Bronco*.

C368 "The Poet as Teacher." *Dartmouth Alumni Magazine*, 49 (Nov. 1956), 20-23. Essay. In *OPP*.

C369 "Lines to the Dead in an Old New Hampshire Graveyard." *Dartmouth Alumni Magazine*, 48 (Nov. 1956), 22. Poem. *Note*: This poem, here first published, was written in 1926, during RE's senior year at Dartmouth.

C370 "Song of Remembrance." *New Republic*, 135 (19 Nov. 1956), 19. Poem.

C371 "The Supreme Authority of the Imagination." *Prairie Schooner*, 30 (Dec. 1956), 352. Poem. In *CP60*, *CP76*, *CP88*. Rept. in *The Achievement of Richard Eberhart*, ed. Engel (1968), p. 70.

C372 "The Record." *Prairie Schooner*, 30 (Dec. 1956), 353. Poem. In *Qu.* Rept. in *The Distinctive Voice: Twentieth-Century American Poetry*, ed. William J. Martz (Glenview, Ill.: Scott, Foresman, 1966), pp. 150-51.

C373 "By the Stream." *Colorado Review*, 1 (Winter 1956-57), 31. Poem. In *CP60*, *CP76*, *CP88*.

C374 "Clocks." *ArkII/Moby 1* (1957), 40. Poem. In *Qu.*

C375 "Snow." *Ark II/Moby 1* (1957), 40. Poem.

C376 "Half Round." *Nimrod*, 1 (Winter 1957), 28. Poem.

C377 "Villanelle." *Spectrum*, 1 (Winter 1957), 37. Poem. In *CP60*, *CP76*, *CP88*. Rept. in *The Achievement of Richard Eberhart*, ed. Engel (1968), p. 68; *The Realities of Literature*, ed. Richard F. Dietrich (Waltham, Mass.: Xerox College Publishing, 1971), pp. 175-76.

C378 "The Oak." *Dartmouth* (Dartmouth College, Hanover, N.H., student newspaper), 21 January 1957, p. 2. Poem. In *CP60*, *SP65*, *CP76*, *CP88*; also published separately (see above, **A15**). Rept. in *New Yorker*, 34 (29 Nov. 1958), 47.

C379 "Poetry and Religion." *Dartmouth*, 21 Jan. 1957, p. 2. Text of a discussion presented by RE to the Dartmouth Christian Union, 20 Jan. 1957.

C380 "A Spell of Time." *Voices*, no. 162 (Jan. -April, 1957), 18. Poem.

C381 "Like a Broad River Flowing." *New York Times Book Review*, 13 Jan. 1957, p. 6. Rev. of W.S. Merwin, *Green with Beasts.*

C382 "Religious Consciousness and Poetry." *Dartmouth*, 21 Jan. 1957, p. 2. Article.

C383 "The Form is New." *New York Times Book Review*, 24 Feb. 1957, p. 37. Rev. of Irving Layton, *The Improved Binoculars.*

C384 "To Auden on His Fiftieth." *Times Literary Supplement*, 15 March 1957, p. 162. Poem. In *Qu*, *PP*, *CP76*, *CP88*. Rept. in *Harvard Advocate*, 108 (no. 2-3, 1974), 23; *Gladly Learn and Gladly Teach*, ed. Helen Plotz (New York: Greenwillow, 1981), pp. 64-65.

C385 "True North." *Nation*, 184 (16 March 1857), 238. Poem.

C386 "A Note on Poetry." *Trinity Review* (Trinity College, Hartford, Conn., undergraduate literary mag.), 11 (Spring-Summer 1957), 26.

C387 "What is Art?" *Trinity Review*, 11 (Spring-Summer 1957), 26. Brief note.

C388 "A Commitment." *Trinity Review*, 11 (Spring-Summer 1957), 26. Poem. In *CP60*, *SP65*, *CP76*, *CP88*.

C389 "The Return." *Encounter*, 8 (April 1957), 21. Poem. In *GP*, *CP60*, *SP65*, *CP76*, *CP88*. Rept. in *Encounters: An Anthology from the First Ten Years of* Encounter *Magazine*, ed. Stephen Spender (New York: Basic Books, 1963), p. 535.

C390 "Fables of the Moon." *Encounter*, 8 (April 1957), 53. Poem. In *GP*, *CP60*, *CP76*, *CP88*.

C391 "Willkie's Life and His World in This Many-Sided Medley." *New York Herald Tribune Book Review*, 28 April 1957, p. 4. Rev. of Muriel Rukeyser, *One Life.*

C392 "Protagonists." *Audience*, 1 (May 1957), 54. Poem. In *CP60*, *CP76*, *CP88*. Rept. in *The Achievement of Richard Eberhart*, ed. Engel (1968), p. 67. *Note*: The following authorial revision has been identified; page and line numbers refer to the original appearance.

54.20 Believed: Do] ~∧ do

C393 "Memory of Meeting Yeats, AE, Gogarty, James Stephens." *Literary Review*, 1 (Autumn 1957), 51-56. Essay. In *OPP*. Rept. as "Memory of Meeting Yeats," in *W.B. Yeats: Interviews and Recollections*, ed. E.H. Mikhail (London: Macmillan, 1977), pp. 193-95.

C394 "Apple Buds." *Literary Review*, 1 (Autumn 1957), 56. Poem. In *CP60*, *SP65*, *CP76*, *CP88*. *Note*: This poem was written by RE when he was 17.

C395 "Dialogue: The Poet and the Professor." *Dialogue/Exchange*, 5 (Oct. 1957), 13-16. Includes excpts. from RE's letters to Richard J. Sontesifer, concerning his poem "Oedipus."

C396 "Hoot Owls." *Nation*, 175 (7 Dec. 1957), 437. Poem. In *CP60*, *CP76*, *CP88*.

C397 "Poem ['The tears of the ancients']." *Botteghe Oscure*, no. 22 (1958), 255. Poem; rept. in *New York Times*, 24 May 1971, p. 30.

C398 "Request." *Botteghe Oscure*, no. 22 (1958), 255-56. Poem. In *CP60*, *PP*, *CP76*, *CP88*. *Note*: The original appearance is set in italic, but subsequent printings are in roman. The dedication of this poem, *"For Dame Edith Sitwell,"* appears in *CP60⁺*.

C399 "Ospreys in Cry." *Botteghe Oscure*, no. 22 (1958), 256-57. Poem. In *CP60*, *SP65*, *CP76*, *CP88*. Rept. in *New Poems 1960*, ed. Anthony Cronin et al. (London: Hutchinson, 1960), p. 49.

C400 "The Visitor." *Mutiny*, 1 (Winterspring 1958), 93. First poem of "Summer Revisited: Three Poems."

C401 "At the Canoe Club." *Mutiny*, 1 (Winterspring 1958), 93. Second poem of "Summer Revisited: Three Poems." In *CP60*, *PP*, *CP76*, *CP88*.

C402 "Tonal Depth." *Mutiny*, 1 (Winterspring 1958), 94. Third poem of "Summer Revisited: Three Poems."

C403 "The Parker River." *Kenyon Review*, 20 (Winter 1958), 20-24. Poem, In *CP60*, *CP76*, *CP88*. *Note*: The following authorial revision has been identified; page and line numbers refer to the first appearance.

21.32 faithless glimmed] ~- glimmed *CP60⁺*

C404 "Hölderlin, Leopardi, and H.D." *Poetry*, 91 (Jan. 1958), 260-65. Rev. of *Selected Poems of Hölderlin*, ed. J.B. Leishman; *Poems from Giacomo Leopardi*, trans. J.F.A. Heath-Stubbs; and H.D., *Selected Poems*.

C405 "The Garden God." *Nation*, 186 (22 Feb. 1958), 160. Poem. In *CP60*, *CP76*, *CP88*. Rept. in *Anthology of Magazine Verse for 1958*, ed. William Stanley Braithwaite (New York: Schulte Publ. Co., 1958), pp. 56-57. *Note*: Stanza 7 is deleted in *CP60⁺*.

C406 "Austere Poem." *Grecourt Review*, 1 (March 1958), 7. In *CP60*, *CP76*, *CP88*. *Note*: An offprint of this poem and the one following was prepared for distribution by the poet; see A17.

C407 "Light Verse." *Grecourt Review*, 1 (March 1958), 8-9.

C408 "Night and Day." *Vox* (Dartmouth College student literary magazine), 1 (Spring 1958), 13. Poem.

C409 "Eberhart's 'Ur Burial'." *Explicator*, 16 (May 1958), 7. RE's explication of his own poem, which is rept. on p. 6.

C410 "Perception as a Guided Missile." *Voices*, no. 166 (May-Aug. 1958), 13-16. Poem. In *CP60*, *CP76*, *CP88*. *Note*: The following authorial revisions have been identified; page and line numbers refer to the first appearance.

15.2 absolutes!] ~?! *CP60⁺*
15.23 inmost] captive *CP60⁺*

C411 "Tree Swallows." *London Magazine*, 5 (June 1958), 15-17. Poem. In *CP60, CP76, CP88*.
C412 "Fortune's Mist." *Nation*, 186 (June 1958), 518. Poem. In *CP60, CP76, CP88*. Rept. in *Anthology of Magazine Verse for 1958*, ed. Braithwaite (1959), pp. 58-59.
C413 "Half-Bent Man." *New Yorker*, 34 (7 June 1958), 38. Poem. In *CP60, CP76, CP88*. Rept. in *Anthology of Magazine Verse for 1958*, ed. Braithwaite (1959), p. 60; *The Achievement of Richard Eberhart*, ed. Engel (1968), pp. 73-74; *The New Yorker Book of Poems* (New York: Viking, 1969), p. 290; *Communicative Performance of Literature*, ed. Carolyn A. Gilbert (New York: Macmillan, 1977), p. 138. *Note*: The following authorial revision has been identified; page and line numbers refer to the first appearance.
38.18 dark, own] own, dark *CP60*+
C414 "Some from the Top of the Head, Others from the Heart." *New York Times Book Review*, 22 June 1958, p. 4. Rev. of R.G. Everson, *Three Dozen Poems*; Denise Levertov, *Overland to the Islands*; Kenneth Patchen, *Poemscapes*.
C415 "The Clam Diggers and Diggers of Sea Worms." *Ladies' Home Journal*, 75 (July 1958), 126. Poem. In *CP60, CP76, CP88*. Rept. in *Anthology of Magazine Verse for 1958*, ed. Braithwaite (1959), p. 61; *Maine Lines: 101 Contemporary Poems about Maine*, ed. Richard Aldridge (Philadelphia: Lippincott, 1970), pp. 79-80. *Note*: The following authorial revisions have been identified; page and line numbers refer to the first appearance.
Title CLAM DIGGERS] THE CLAM DIGGERS AND DIGGERS OF SEA WORMS *CP60*+
126.20 maneuvering] manoeuvering *CP60*+
126.26 maybe] may be *CP60*+
126.47 And love deep as time] Time-deepened love *CP60*+
C416 "Central Violence." *Saturday Review of Literature*, 4 (12 July 1958), 30-32. Rev. of Kenneth Patchen, *Selected Poems*.
C417 "A Ship Burning and a Comet all in One Day." *New Yorker*, 34 (23 Aug. 1958), 77. Poem. In *CP60, SP65, CP76, CP88*. Rept. in *Today's Poets: American and British Poetry Since the 1930's*, ed. Chad Walsh (New York: Scribner's, 1964), pp. 44-45; *The New Yorker Book of Poems* (1969), p. 628; *Maine Lines*, ed. Aldridge (1970), pp. 87-88.
C418 "The Place." *New Statesman*, 56 (6 Sept. 1958), 292. Poem. In *Qu, SP65, LR, CP88*. Rept. in *The Distinctive Voice: Twentieth-Century American Poetry*, ed. William J. Martz (Glenview, Ill.: Scott, Foresman, 1966), 149-50; *The Achievement of Richard Eberhart*, ed. Engel (1968) pp. 42-43; *Cafe at St. Marks: The Apalachee Poets*, ed. Van K. Brock (Tallahassee, Fla.: Anhinga Press, 1975), pp. 45-46.

C419 "A Vision of Life and Man that Drives the Poet On." *New York Times Book Review*, 14 Sept. 1958, p. 4. Rev. of William Carlos Williams, *Paterson* (Book Five).

C420 "Escape to Discovery." *New York Times Book Review,* 28 Sept. 1958, p. 26. Rev. of Harry Roskolenko, *Poet on a Scooter.*

C421 "Outer and Inner Verse Drama." *Virginia Quarterly Review*, 34 (Autumn 1958), 618-23. Review of Archibald MacLeish, *J.B.*

C422 Untitled rev. of Reginald L. Cook, *The Dimensions of Robert Frost. Vermont History*, 26 (Oct. 1958), 314-15.

C423 "A Soldier Rejects His Times Addressing His Contemporaries." *Nation*, 187 (1 Nov. 1958), 315. Poem. In *CP60, CP76, CP88*.

C424 "Creative Splendor." *New York Times Book Review*, 9 Nov. 1958, p. 34. Rev. of Theodore Roethke, *Words for the Wind.*

C425 "In After Time." *Nation*, 187 (27 Dec. 1958), 500. Poem. In *CP60, SP65, CP76, CP88*.

C426 "Notes on Poetry." *Nieuw*, no. 2 (1959), 1-3. Expt. from RE's notebook.

C427 "High Afternoon." *Inscape*, no. 2 (1959), 2. Poem.

C428 "The Hard Structure of the World." *Nation*, 188 (25 April 1959), 368. Poem. In *CP60, CP76, CP88*. Rept. in *The Acheivement of Richard Eberhart*, ed. Engel (1968), pp. 72-73; *Maine Lines*, ed. Aldridge (1970), pp. 81-82.

C429 "A Poet's People." *New York Times Book Review*, 3 May 1959, pp. 4, 27. Rev. of Robert Lowell, *Life Studies.*

C430 "Matador." *Poetry Northwest*, 1 (June 1959), 12. First of "Two Poems." In *Qu, CP76, CP88*. Rept. in *The Achievement of Richard Eberhart*, ed. Engel (1968), p. 50; *The Norton Anthology of Poetry*, ed. Arthur M. Eastman (New York: Norton, 1970), p. 1069.

C431 "Nexus." *Poetry Northwest*, 1 (June 1959), 12-13. Second of "Two Poems." In *Qu, SP65, CP76, CP88*.

C432 "Spring Mountain Climb." *American Scholar*, 28 (Summer 1959), 354-55. Poem. In *CP60, CP76, CP88*. Rept. in *The Golden Year: The Poetry Society of America Anthology 1910-1960*, ed. Melville Cain et al. (New York: Fine Editions Press, 1960), pp. 84-85; *Quartet from the Golden Year* (Washington, D.C.: Univ. Press of Washington, D.C., 1961), pp. 1-2.

C433 "Ernest Chenaur (1937-1958)." *Vox* (Dartmouth College, Hanover, N.H., literary mag.), 2 (Summer 1959), 3. Poem. Rept. in *Nieuw*, no. 4 (1959-60), 9; *TriQuarterly*, 2 (Winter 1960), 25.

C434 "Light from Above." *Poetry*, 95 (Oct. 1959), 1-2. Poem. In *CP60, SP65, CP76, CP88*. Rept. in *The Guiness Book of Poetry 1960/61* (London: Putnam, 1962), p. 54.

C435 "The Blue Grains." *Poetry*, 95 (Oct. 1959), 2. Poem.

C436 "The Spider." *Poetry*, 95 (Oct. 1959), 3-4. Poem. In *Qu, CP76, CP88*. Rept. in *Today's Poets*, ed. Walsh (1964), pp. 47-48. *The Achievement of Richard Eberhart*, ed. Engel (1968), pp. 48-49; *The Poetry Anthology*, ed. Daryl Hine and Joseph Pariri (Houghton Mifflin, 1978), pp. 362-63.

C437 "A Testament." *Poetry*, 95 (Oct. 1959), 4-5. Poem. In *CP60, CP76, CP88*. *Note*: The following authorial revision has been identified; page and line numbers refer to the first appearance.

    4.17 arise...the] sing...and *CP60*[+]

C438 "Late Summer." *Poetry*, 95 (Oct. 1959), 5-6. Poem.

C439 "Riches." *Poetry*, 95 (Oct. 1959), 6-7. Poem.

C440 "The Still Spirit." *Ladies' Home Journal*, 76 (Nov. 1959), 152. Poem.

C441 Untitled article about meeting the Russian poet Sholokov. *Liberation*, 4 (Nov. 1959), 9.

C442 "Equivalence of Gnats and Mice." *Times Literary Supplement*, 6 Nov. 1959, p. xxiv (in special supplement titled "The American Imagination"). Poem. In *CP60, CP76, CP88*. Rept. in *The Guiness Book of Poetry 1959/60* (London: Putnam, 1961), 55.

C443 "Birth and Death." *Times Literary Supplement*, 6 Nov. 1959, p. xxxii (in special supplement titled "The American Imagination"). Poem. In *CP60, SP65, CP76, CP88*.

C444 Untitled excerpt from letter to the editor, *Austin Daily*, 15 Dec. 1959, p. 3 (A).

C445 "The Passage." *Virginia Quarterly Review*, 36 (Winter 1960), 63-67. Poem. In *CP60, CP76, CP88*. Rept. in *Poems from the* Virginia Quarterly Review, ed. Kohler (1969), pp. 113-16.

C446 "Divarication." *TriQuarterly*, 2 (Winter 1960), 25. Poem. *Note*: "Ernest Chenaur (1937-1958)" is rept. on p. 25.

C447 "Loss (To V.R. Lang)." *Massachusetts Review*, 1 (Feb. 1960), 297. Poem. In *Qu, CP76, CP88*.

C448 "Ives." *Chelsea*, 7 (May 1960), 75. Poem. In *CP88*. Rept. in *Fragments*, 14 (no. 1, 1973), 3; *Chelsea*, no. 42-43 (1983), 56.

C449 "Throwing the Apple." *Carolina Quarterly*, 7 (Summer 1960), 16. Poem. In *CP60, CP76, CP88*. See below, **C450**.

C450 "On 'Throwing the Apple'." *Carolina Quarterly*, 7 (Summer 1960), 17-19. RE's essay on his own poem "Throwing the Apple".

C451 "A New England Bachelor." *Transatlantic Review*, no. 4 (Summer 1960), 92. Poem. In *Qu, SP65, CP76, CP88*. Rept. in *Modern American Poetry Modern British Poetry*, ed. Louis Untermeyer, new and enl. ed. (New York: Harcourt, Brace and World, 1962), pp. 580-81; *The Achievement of Richard Eberhart*, ed. Engel (1968), p. 45; *The Norton Anthology of Modern Poetry*, ed. Richard Ellmann and Robert O'Clair (New York: Norton, 1973),

p. 667. *Note*: The *Transatlantic Review* text is set in italic, whereas all subsequent reprintings are in roman. The following authorial revision has been identified; page and line numbers refer to the first appearance.

92.2 Mass.] Massachusetts

C452 "The Gods of Washington D.C." *Transatlantic Review*, no. 4 (Summer 1960), 93. Poem. In *CP60*, *CP76*, *CP88*. Rept. in *Washington and the Poet*, ed. Francis Coleman Rosenberger (Charlottesville, Va.: Univ. Press of Virginia, 1977), p. 12. *Note*: The *Transatlantic Review* text is set in italic, whereas subsequent reprintings are in roman.

C453 "The Craft of the Lyric Line." *Saturday Review of Literature*, 42 (2 July 1960), 23, 32. Rev. of Ramon Guthrie, *Graffiti*; Reed Whittemore, *The Self-Made Man*; Hayden Carruth, *The Crow and the Heart*; and David Galler, *Walls and Distances*.

C454 "A Moment of Equilibrium Among the Islands" (later titled "Moment of Equilibrium Among the Islands"). *New Yorker*, 36 (16 July 1960), 64. Poem. In *Qu*, *SP65*, *CP76*, *CP88*. Rept. in *The Achievement of Richard Eberhart*, ed. Engel (1968), p. 46.

C455 "The Elegance of Stately Measures." *Nieuw*, no. 6 (Sept. 1960) 19. Poem. Rept in *New Yorker*, 36 (4 Feb. 1961), 34.

C456 "Dream and Reality." *Chelsea*, no. 8 (Oct. 1960), 18. Poem.

C457 "Rainscapes, Hydrangeas, Roses, and Singing Birds." *London Magazine*, 7 (Oct. 1960), 11-12. Poem. In *Qu*, *SP65*. Rept. in *Audience*, 2 (Spring 1961), 23-24; *Modern American Poetry Modern British Poetry*, ed. Untermeyer, new and enl. ed. (1962), p. 581; *National Poetry Festival Held in the Library of Congress, October 22-24, 1962: Proceedings* (Washington, D.C.: Library of Congress, 1964), pp. 199-200; *Expansive Light* (New York: The Sacred Fire, 1977), p. 29.

C458 "A Maine Roustabout." *London Magazine*, 7 (Oct. 1960), 12. Poem. In *Qu*, *SP65*, *CP76*, *CP88*. Rept. in *To Play Man Number One: Poems of Modern Man*, ed. Sara Hannum and John Terry Chase (New York: Atheneum, 1969), pp. 45-46; *Maine Lines*, ed. Aldridge (1970), p. 77; *Brooksville* [Maine] *Annual Report : 1987*, p. 4.

C459 "The Incomparable Light." *Nation*, 191 (15 Oct. 1960), 250. Poem. In *CP60*, *SP65*, *CP76*, *CP88*. Rept. in *Modern Religious Poems: A Contemporary Anthology*, ed. Jacob Trapp (New York: Harper & Row, 1964), pp. 245-46; *Ski*, 35 (Oct. 1970), 86. *Note*: The following authorial revision has been identified; page and line numbers refer to the first appearance.

250.4 growing] ~ up *CP60*+

C460 "Rationalists and Naturalists." *Poetry Dial*, 1 (Winter 1961), 2. Poem.

C461 "The Golden Road." *Plume & Sword* (Univ. of Virginia, Charlottesville, student lit. mag.), March 1961, 2. Poem.

C462 "Spirit." *Prairie Schooner*, 35 (Spring 1961), 60-61. Poem.

C463 "Divorce." *Shenandoah*, 12 (Spring 1961), 43. Poem. In *Qu*. Rept. in *Shenandoah*, 35 (nos. 2-3, 1984), 122.

C464 "Mirror of MacLeish." *Nation*, 192 (8 April 1961), 108-9. Rev. of Archibald MacLeish, *Poetry and Experience*.

C465 "Extremity." *Voices*, no. 176 (Sept.-Dec. 1961), 16. Poem. In *SB*, *CP88*.

C466 "The Inward Rock." *Nation*, 193 (7 Oct. 1961), 232. Poem. In *Qu*, *SP65*. *Note*: The following authorial revision has been identified; page and line numbers refer to the first appearance.

      232.11 great] grave,

C467 "Encounters and Letters." *Dartmouth College Library Bulletin*, 4 (Dec. 1961), 57-60. Memoir of Wallace Stevens, pp. 57-58, with expts. from Stevens' letters to RE on pp. 58-60.

C468 "The Lament of a New England Mother." *Quarterly Review of Literature*, 12 (1962), 3-5. Poem. In *Qu*, *CP76*, *CP88*.

C469 Untitled statement on the poetry of Philip Booth, Isabella Gardner, Donald Hall, Daniel Hoffman, and Ned O'Gorman, in *Wilson Library Bulletin*, 36 (Jan. 1962), 367-68.

C470 "Father and Daughter." *Pennsylvania Literary Review*, 12 (no. 2, 1962), 7. Poem. In *Qu*.

C471 "A Central Spirit." *Dasein*, 1 (no. 1-2, 1962), 84. Poem.

C472 "A New England View: My Report." *Greensleeves* (Dartmouth College, Hanover, N.H., undergraduate lit. mag.), 4 (Feb. 1962), 22. Poem. In *Qu*, *SP65*. Rept. in *Kenyon Review*, 25 (Spring 1963), 294; *National Poetry Festival Held in the Library of Congress, October 22-24, 1962: Proceedings* (1964), p. 199; *Greensleeves*, 4 (no. 1, 1974), 22.

C473 "Poetry in Contemporary America." *Dartmouth*, 15 Feb. 1962, p. 2. Article.

C474 "Tragedy as Limitation: Comedy as Control and Resolution." *Tulane Drama Review*, 6 (June 1962), 3-14. Essay.

C475 "Devils and Angels." *Tulane Drama Review*, 6 (June 1962), 15-32. Drama. In *CVP*.

C476 "The Mad Musician." *Tulane Drama Review*, 6 (June 1962), 33-53. Drama. In *CVP*.

C477 "Sea Burial from the Cruiser *Reve*." *New Yorker*, 38 (25 Aug. 1962), 107. Poem. In *Qu*, *SP65*, *CP76*, *CP88*. Rept. in *The Achievement of Richard Eberhart*, ed. Engel (1968), p. 44; *The New Yorker Book of Poems* (1969), p. 625-26; *Maine Lines*, ed. Aldridge (1970), p. 84. *Note*: The following authorial revision or textual variant has been identified; page and line numbers refer to the first appearance.

      107.3 "Reve"] *Reve Qu*+

C478 "Celebrations for Mankind." *New York Times Book Review*, 9 Sept. 1962, p. 4. Rev. of Muriel Rukeyser, *Waterlily Fire: Poems 1935-1962*.

C479 "The Struggle." *Poetry*, 101 (Oct.-Nov. 1962), 34. Poem. In *Qu*, *SP65*.

C480 "Dream Journey of the Head and Heart." *Poetry*, 101 (Oct.-Nov. 1962), 35-36. Poem. In *Qu*, *SP65*, *CP76*, *CP88*. Rept. in *National Poetry Festival Held in the Library of Congress, October 22-24, 1962: Proceedings* (1964), pp. 200-1.

C481 "Hark Back." *Poetry*, 101 (Oct.-Nov. 1962), 36. Poem. In *Qu*, *SP65*. Rept. in *The New Orlando Poetry Anthology 2*, ed. Anca Vrbovska et al. (New York: New Orlando Publications, 1963), pp. 26-27; *National Poetry Festival Held in the Library of Congress, October 22-24, 1962: Proceedings* (1964), pp. 198-99; *Today's Poets*, ed. Walsh (1964), p. 46; *The Distinctive Voice*, ed. Martz (1966), pp. 151-52.

C482 "Winter Kill." *Poetry*, 101 (Oct.-Nov. 1962), 37. Poem. In *Qu*, *SP65*, *CP76*, *NH*, *CP88*.

C483 "Meditation One." *Sewanee Review*, 71 (Winter 1963), 82-84. Poem. In *Qu*, *SP65*.

C484 "Ultimate Song." *New England Galaxy*, 4 (Winter 1963), 46-47. Poem. In *Qu*, *CP76*, *CP88*. Rept. *Yorkshire Post*, (2 Feb. 1967), 7.

C485 "For the Wedding of Dave and Eloise." *Lynx*, no. 3 (Jan. 1963), 13. Poem.

C486 "Meditation Two." *Audience*, 8 (1 Feb. 1963), 7-9. Poem. In *Qu*, *SP65*, *CP76*, *CP88*. Rept. in *Dartmouth Alumni Magazine*, 49 (March 1963), 9-12; *National Poetry Festival Held in the Library of Congress, October 22-24, 1962: Proceedings* (Washington: Library of Congress, 1964), 202-4.

C487 "Am I My Neighbor's Keeper?" *Saturday Review of Literature*, 46 (2 Feb. 1963), 37. Poem. In *Qu*, *SP65*, *CP76*, *CP88*. Rept. in *The Contemporary Poet as Artist and Critic*, ed. Anthony Ostroff (Boston: Little Brown, 1964), p. 142; *Today's Poets*, ed. Walsh (1964), pp. 45-46; *The Poem: An Anthology*, ed. Stanley B. Greenfield (New York: Appleton-Century-Crofts, 1968), p. 351, and 2d ed. (1972), p. 426.

C488 "Poetry at Dartmouth." *Dartmouth Alumni Magazine*, 55 (March 1963), 25-32, 92. Article.

C489 "To a Poet Who Has Had a Heart Attack." *Shenandoah*, 14 (Spring 1963), 15. Poem. In *Qu*.

C490 "Later or Sooner." *Shenandoah*, 14 (Spring 1963), 16. Poem. In *Qu*, *CP76*, *CP88*.

C491 "The Seal." *Green World*, 1 (Spring 1963), 21. Poem. In *Qu*. *Note*: The lines in the last Stanza were reordered for inclusion in *Qu*.

C492 "The World Situation." *Encounter*, 20 (April 1963), 16. Poem. In *Qu*.

C493 "Poetry as Individualism." *Response* (Princeton Univ.), April 1963, 10-11. Essay.

C494 "The Music of Values." *New York Times Book Review*, 5 May 1963, p. 4. Rev. of Conrad Aiken, *The Morning Song of Lord Zero.*

C495 "Evtushenko in Washington." *Massachusetts Review*, 4 (Summer 1963), 785-89. Article.

C496 Untitled comments on creativity, in *Arts in Society*, 2 (no. 3, 1963), 31.

C497 "Ruby Daggett." *Greensleeves*, 6 (Fall 1963), 21. Poem. In *Qu, SP65, CP76, NH, CP88.* Rept. in *Nation*, 198 (20 April 1964), 398.

C498 "Death by Drowning." *Greensleeves*, 6 (Fall 1963), 22. Poem. In *Qu.* Rept. in *Saturday Review of Literature*, 47 (8 Feb. 1964), 35.

C499 "The Gesture." *Greensleeves*, 6 (Fall 1963), 22. Poem. In *Qu, SP65, CP76, CP88.* Rept. in *National Poetry Festival Held in the Library of Congress, October 22-24 1962: Proceedings* (1964), p. 201.

C500 "Kaire." *Greensleeves*, 6 (no. 1, 1963), 23. Poem. In *Qu, SP65, CP76, CP88.* Rept. in *Whetstone*, 4 (no. 3, 1964), 96-97; *Yorkshire Post*, (16 Nov. 1967), 9; *The Norton Anthology of Modern Poetry*, ed. Ellmann and O'Clair (1973), p. 666.

C501 "Hardening into Print." *Greensleeves*, 6 (no. 1, 1963), 24. Poem. In *Qu, SP65, CP76, NH, CP88.* Rept. in *The Norton Anthology of Poetry*, ed. Eastman (1970), p. 1069.

C502 "Emerson and Wallace Stevens." *Literary Review*, 7 (Autumn 1963), 51-71. Essay. In *OPP.*

C503 "Vision ['Two hummingbirds as evanescent as']". *New Yorker*, 39 (5 Oct. 1963), 54. Poem. In *Qu, CP76, CP88.* Rept. in *The Achievement of Richard Eberhart*, ed. Engel (1968), pp. 53-55; *The New Yorker Book of Poems* (1969), pp. 768-69.

C504 "Flux." *New York Review of Books*, 1 (31 Oct. 1963), 21. Poem. In *Qu, SP65, CP76, CP88.* Rept. in *Maine Lines*, ed. Aldridge (1970), pp. 85-86; *The Voice that is Great Within Us*, ed. Carruth (1970), pp. 247-48; *Contemporary Poetry in America*, ed. Miller Williams (New York: Random House, 1973), p. 6; *The Human Condition: Literature Written in the English Language*, ed. James F. Miller, Jr. et al. (Glenview, Ill.: Scott, Foresman, 1974), p. 495; *Poetspeak*, ed. Janeczko (1983), p. 99. *Note*: In all collected appearances stanzas 4-6 "The...Head," have been transposed as the first through third stanzas. No further authorial revisions have been identified.

C505 "What Holds Us Here?" *New York Times Book Review*, 10 Nov. 1963, p. 18. Rev. of Evan S. Connell, Jr., *Notes from a Bottle Found on the Beach at Carmel.*

C506 "Memory, Confrontation, Desire." *Key Reporter* (mag. of Phi Beta Kappa), 29 (Winter 1963-64), 1. Poem. *Note*: First read by RE at the Swarthmore College commencement, 9 June 1963. "Desire," pt. 3 of this poem, rept. in *New York Times Book Review*, 23 Feb. 1964, p. 2.

C507 "The Wagner Poets: Comments on the Wagner Poets." *Wagner Literary Magazine*, no. 4 (1963-64), 81-83. Essay.

C508 "The Lost." *Whetstone*, n.s. 1 (no. 1, 1964), 93-94. Poem. In *Qu*, *SP65*, *CP76*, *CP88*.

C509 "Eagles." *Whetstone*, n.s. 1 (no. 1, 1964), 95. Poem. In *Qu*, *SP65*, *PP*, *LR*. Rept. in *Times Literary Supplement*, (13 Dec. 1974), 1414.

C510 "Off Pemaquid." *Times Literary Supplement*, 63 (16 Jan. 1964), p. 51. Poem. In *SP65*. Rept. in *Greensleeves*, 6 (no. 2, 1964), 37; *The Achievement of Richard Eberhart*, ed. Engel (1968), p. 48.

C511 "Again." *Poetry Review* (Tampa, Fla.), no. 2 (Feb. 1964), np.

C512 Untitled review of James M. Reid et al., *Poetry: A Closer Look* and *Steps to Reading Literature*. *Dartmouth Alumni Magazine*, 56 (Feb. 1964), 5.

C513 "Father and Son." *Pennsylvania Literary Review*, 12 (no. 2, 1964), 4-6. Poem. In *Qu*.

C514 "The Master's Image." (later titled "The Master Image"). *Now*, 4 (Spring 1964), 7. Poem. As "The Master Image" in *Qu*.

C515 "Gestures Rich in Purpose." *Shenandoah*, 15 (Summer 1964), 5. Poem. In *SB*.

C516 "From the Manuscript of Eberhart's 'The Driver'." *Shenandoah*, 15 (Summer 1964), 6. Poem.

C517 "Cold White Death." *Atlantic*, 214 (Sept. 1964), 73. Poem.

C518 "The Ascent." *Sewanee Review*, 72 (Autumn 1964), 620-23. Poem. In *SB*. *Note*: The following authorial revisions have been identified between the first appearance and book publication in *SB*; page and line numbers refer to the first appearance.

    622.8 Which...south,] Luminescent,...drouth,

    622.26 is,] ~∧

    623.14 be:] ~;

C519 "Ordeal." *Hollins Critic*, 1 (Oct. 1964), 9. Poem. In *SP65*. *Note*: "The Assassin" is rept. on p. 11.

C520 "On Gretchen's 13th Birthday." *Poetry Review* (University of Tampa, Fla.), no. 5 (1965), np. Poem.

C521 "Tones of Evening." *Encounter*, 24 (March 1965), 41. Poem.

C522 "Fishing for Snakes." *Encounter*, 24 (March 1965), 41. Poem. In *SP65*. *Note*: Also publ. separately as a broadside; see above, **A22**.

C523 "The Immortal Type." *Southern Review*, n.s. 1 (Spring 1965), 428-29. Poem. In *SB*. *Note*: The following authorial revision has been identified; page and line numbers refer to the first appearance.

    429.1 the] this

C524 "The Eclipse." *Southern Review*, n.s. 1 (Spring 1965), 429. Poem. Rept. in *Harvard Advocate*, 99 (April 1965); *The Rider Book of Mystical Verse*, ed. J.M. Cohen (London: Rider, 1983), p. 53.

C525 "Action and Poetry." *Greensleeves*, 8 (Spring 1965), 31. Poem. In *SP65*. Rept. in *East Side Review*, 1 (Jan. 1966), 55; *Brogue*, 1 (Summer 1968), 10. *Note*: "Tones of Evening" is rept. on pp. 32-33.

C526 "The Echoing Rocks." *Greensleeves*, 8 (Spring 1965), 32-33. Poem. In *SP65*. *Note*: The following authorial revision has been identified; page and line numbers refer to the first appearance.

    32.14 feelings] feeling,

C527 "The Birth of the Spirit." *Harvard Advocate*, 99 (April 1965), 10. Poem. In *SB*, *CP88*. *Note*: "The Eclipse" (C524) is rept. on p. 10. The dedication in the original appearance, "For Theodore Roethke (1908-1963)," is omitted in *SB*.

C528 "Roberts Rules of Order." *Harvard Advocate*, 99 (April 1965), 10. Poem. Published separately as A23; rept. in *Penny Paper*, 2 (May 1965), 17; *Tower* (Dartmouth College, Hanover, N.H., student lit. mag.), 1 (Winter 1978), 21.

C529 "The Matin Pandemoniums." *New Yorker*, 41 (10 April 1965), 42. Poem. In *SP65*. Rept. in *The New Yorker Book of Poems* (1965), p. 422. *Note*: The following authorial revisions have been identified between first appearance and book publication in *SP65*; page and line numbers refer to first appearance.

    42.2 echoes;] ~,
    42.5 calls. The] ~; the

C530 "A Quiet Tone from a Rich Interior." *New York Times Book Review*, 20 June 1965, p. 5. Rev. of *The Complete Poems of Frederick Goddard Tuckerman*.

C531 "On Theodore Roethke's Poetry." *Southern Review*, n.s. 1 (Summer 1965), 612-20. Essay. *Note*: First delivered as a lecture at San Francisco College, 27 October 1964.

C532 "Hill Dream of Youth, Thirty Years Later." *Atlantic*, 216 (July 1965), 63. Poem. In *SB*, *CP76*, *CP88*. Rept. in *The Achievement of Richard Eberhart*, ed. Engel (1968), p. 81. *Note*: The following authorial revisions have been identified between the first appearance and book publication in *SP65*; page and line numbers refer to the first appearance.

    63.4 lmagination [sic]] imagination
    63.24 From the] ~

C533 "Echoes of Keats and Shakespeare." *New York Times Book Review*, 18 July 1965, p. 5. rev. of John Masefield, *Old Raiger and Other Verse*.

C534 "At McSorley's Bar." *East Side Review*, 1 (Jan. 1966), 54. Poem. In *SP65*. "Action and Poetry" (C525) is rept. on p. 55. *Note*: The following authorial revision has been identified; page and line numbers refer to the first appearance.

    54.12 well.] ~,

C535 "The Illusion of Eternity." *East Side Review*, 1 (Jan. 1966), 55. Poem. In *SP65*, *CP76*, *CP88*. *Note*: The following authorial revisions have been identified; page and line numbers refer to the first appearance.

    55.2 gold] ~,

    55.5-6 eternity. A] ~. As...eternity. A [108.5-11]

    55.10-11 *normal leading*] *stanza break*

C536 "Vicente Huidobro (1893-1948)." *East Side Review*, 1 (Jan. 1966), 66-71. RE's reading of Huidobro's poem "The Art of Poetry." *Note*: Originally read on "The Image Chile Program," at Georgetown Univ., 27 Sept. 1963.

C537 "Speaking Plain and Fancy." *New York Times Book Review*, 23 Jan. 1966, p. 35. Rev. of *The Selected Poems of John Holmes*; Louis Zukovsky, *All: The Collected Short Poems 1923-58*.

C538 "The Vastness and Indifference of the World." *Saturday Review of Literature*, 49 (12 Feb. 1966), 46. Poem. in *SB*, *CP76*, *CP88*. Rept. in *Golden Horn 1965* (American Literary Annual, Istanbul, Turkey, 1965), pp. 37-38; *The Achievement of Richard Eberhart*, ed. Engel (1968), p. 84. *Note*: The following authorial revision has been identified; page and line numbers refer to the first appearance.

    46.11 slaughter,] ~; *SB*+

C539 "Criticism of a Poem About Criticism." *Christian Science Monitor*, (18 Aug. 1966), 8. Essay with criticism of RE's own poem "The Critic with His Pained Eye."

C540 "Looking Head On." *Harvard Advocate* (Centennial Issue), 100 (Fall 1966), 13. Poem. In *SB*, *CP76*, *CP88*.

C541 "Colleoni of the Word." *Transatlantic Review*, no. 22 (Autumn 1966), 61-63. Poem.

C542 "Robert Frost: His Personality" *Southern Review*, n.s. 2 (Oct. 1966), 762-88. Essay. In *OPP*.

C543 "Shock or Shut Up." *New York Times Book Review*, 13 Nov. 1966, p. 6. Review of Andrew Glaze, *Damned Ugly Children*.

C544 "New Love." *Saturday Evening Post*, 239 (31 Dec. 1966), 43. Poem. In *SB*.

C545 "The Tomb by the Sea with Cars Going By." *Mundus Artium*, 1 (Winter 1967), 34. Poem. In *SB*; rept. in *Chicago Tribune Magazine*, (19 Nov. 1967), 64.

C546 "Cliff." *Mundus Artium*, 1 (Winter 1967), 35. Poem. In *SB*.

C547 "II ['What shall I call that other one but a fool']." *Massachusetts Review*, 8 (Winter 1967), 94. First of "Seven Sonnets." In *31S*. *Note*: These sonnets, part of a group of 31, were written between 11 May and 11 June 1932.

C548 "VI ['How shall I quell the rains of male abuse']." *Massachusetts Review*, 8 (Winter 1967), 95. Second of "Seven Sonnets." In *31S*.

C549 "XV ['When dead the winter snows in crystals shine']." *Massachusetts Review*, 8 (Winter 1967), 5. Third of "Seven Sonnets." In *31S*. Rept. in *The Uses of Poetry*, ed. Agnes Stein (New York: Holt, Rinehart and Winston, 1975), p. 195.

C550 "XVI ['Now time, the armed master of our wills']." *Massachusetts Review*, 8 (Winter 1967), 96. Fourth of "Seven Sonnets." In *31S*.

C551 "XXII ['And law displaced by gangster's childishness']." *Massachusetts Review*, 8 (Winter 1967), 96. Fifth of "Seven Sonnets." In *31S*.

C552 "XXIV ['This is your marriage night, and I with you']." *Massachusetts Review*, 8 (Winter 1967), 97. Sixth of "Seven Sonnets." In *31s*.

C553 "XXVI ['O fair vibrations of clear reaching day!']." *Massachusetts Review*, 8 (Winter 1967), 97. Seventh of "Seven Sonnets." In *31S*.

C554 "The Mastery." *Southern Review*, n.s. 3 (Jan. 1967), 117. Poem. In *SB*. Rept. in *The Achievement of Richard Eberhart*, ed. Engel (1968), p. 76. *Note*: "Marrakech" (**B82**) rept. on pp. 115-16.

C555 "The Ides Of March." *Southern Review*, n.s. 3 (Jan. 1967), 118-19. Poem. In *SB*, *CP76*, *CP88*; also published separately as **A25**. Rept. in *The Achievement of Richard Eberhart*, ed. Engel (1968), p. 77; *This is My Best in the Third Quarter of the Twentieth Century*, ed. Burnett (1970), pp. 91-92. *Note*: The following authorial revision has been identified; page and line numbers refer to the first appearance.

118.19 Spring] Springtide *SB*+

C556 "The Explorer on Main Street." *Southern Review*, n.s. 3 (Jan. 1967), 119-20. Poem. In *SB*, *CP76*, *NH*, *CP88*. Rept. in *The Achievement of Richard Eberhart*, ed. Engel (1968), 79-80.

C557 "A Wedding on Cape Rosier." *Southern Review*, n.s. 3 (Jan. 1967), 121. Poem. In *SB*, *CP76*, *CP88*. Rept. in *The Achievement of Richard Eberhart*, ed. Engel (1968), p. 82.

C558 "On Returning to a Lake in Spring." *Southern Review*, n.s. 3 (Jan. 1967), 122. Poem. In *SB*, *CP76*, *NH*, *CP88*. Rept. in *The Achievement of Richard Eberhart*, ed. Engel (1968), p. 79.

C559 "The Winds." *Nation*, 204 (13 Feb. 1967), 218. Poem. In *SB*. Rept. in *The New Orlando Poetry Anthology 2*, ed. Anca Vrbovska et al., v. 3 (New York: New Orlando Publications, 1968), p. 49.

C560 "Haystack." *Nation*, 204 (13 March 1967), 346. Poem. In *SB*. *Note*: The text of the original appearance is set in all italic, whereas it is set in roman in *SB*. The following authorial revision has been identified; page and line numbers refer to the first appearance.

346.2 *eyes*] eyes,

C561 "To My Student, Killed in a Car Crash." *Pantisocarcy* (Frostburg State College, Maryland), 6 (Spring 1967), 5. Poem. In *SB*.

C562 "Lions Copulating." *Nation*, 204 (24 April 1967), 520. Poem. In *SB, CP76, CP88*.

C563 "To Marianne Moore on Her 80th Birthday." *PSA Bulletin*, 57 (May 1967), 16. Poem. *Note*: RE's quoted comments on the occasion are found on pp. 15-16.

C564 "Lear." *Yorkshire Post*, (25 May 1967), 9. Poem.

C565 "Music Over Words." *Nation*, 204 (19 June 1967), 791. Poem. Rept. in *The New Orlando Poetry Anthology*, ed. Vrbovska et al., v. 3 (1968), pp. 46-47.

C566 Untitled response to "Questions on Censorship." *Arts in Society* (Univ. of Wisconsin, Madison), 4 (Summer 1967), 285-86.

C567 "To the Field Mice." *Quest*, 2 (Summer 1967), 122. Poem. In *SB, CP76, CP88*. Rept. in *Golden Horn 1967* (New York: Poetry Society of America, 1967), p. 45; *A Book of Animal Poems*, ed. William Cole (New York: Viking, 1973).

C568 "Archibald MacLeish's 'Herakles'." *Virginia Quarterly Review*, 43 (Summer 1967), 499-503. Rev. of Archibald MacLeish, *Heracles*.

C569 "Sanders Theater (The Phi Beta Kappa Poem, 1967)." *Harvard Alumni Bulletin*, 8 July 1967, 15. In *SB, CP76, CP88*.

C570 "Mexico Phantasmagoria: The Pretenatural Wilderness of the Subliminal Spirit." (later titled "Mexico Phantasmogoria") *Poetry*, 110 (Sept. 1967), 400-5. Poem. In *SB* as "Mexico Phantasmagoria." *Note*: The following authorial revisions have been identified; page and line numbers refer to the first appearance.

404.7 Our] our
404.8 child like] childlike

C571 "Ball Game." *New American Review*, no. 1 (Sept. 1967), 284. In *SB, CP88*. Rept. in *Mindscapes*, ed. Richard Peck (New York: Delacorte, 1971); *Scholastic Voice*, 56 (18 April 1974), 5; *Shadowbox*, ed. Kathryn D. McMillan and Joanne Kish Dean (New York: Harcourt, Brace, Jovanovich, 1975), p. 120; *Expansive Light* (New York: Sacred Fire, 1977), p. 26.

C572 "To the Mad Poets." *New American Review*, no. 1 (Sept. 1967), 285. In *SB, LR, CP88*.

C573 Untitled letter to the editor, in *Shenandoah*, 19 (Autumn 1967), 68-69. Letter concerning "Not with a Bang," William Heyen's review of T.S. Eliot, *Poems Written in Early Youth*, which also appears in this issue, pp. 81-84.

C574 "Old Question." *Poem* (Huntsville, Ala.), 1 (Nov. 1967), 3. Poem. In *FG, CP88*.

C575 "The Enigma." *New Yorker*, 43 (18 Nov. 1967), 64. Poem. In *CP88*. Rept. in *The Achievement of Richard Eberhart*, ed. Engel (1968), p.

78; *The New Yorker Book of Poems* (1969), p. 196; *Poetry in English*, ed. Warren Taylor and Donald Hall, 2d ed. (New York: Macmillan, 1970).

C576 "In Favor of Froth" (later titled "Froth"). *Genesis : Grasp*, 1 (no. 1, 1968), 36. Poem. As "Froth" in *FG, CP76, CP88*. Rept. in *Expansive Light* (New York: Sacred Fire, 1977), 28; *Poet*, 22 (Aug. 1981), 60. *Note*: The following authorial revisions have been identified; page and line numbers refer to the first appearance.

   36.6 up, for] ~. For *FG*+
   36.7 Cliffs] Small cliffs *FG*+
   36.7 in a] form and *FG*+
   36.8 reaching,] *deleted FG*+
   36.9 very like] like *FG*+

C577 "Cutting Back." *Mundus Artium*, 2 (Winter 1968), 88. Poem.

C578 "Half Way Measure." *Mundus Artium*, 2 (Winter 1968), 88. Poem.

C579 "Swiss New Year." *Saturday Review of Literature*, 51 (10 Feb. 1968), 46. Poem. In *SB*. Rept. in *The New Orlando Poetry Anthology 2*, ed. Vrbovska (1968), pp. 50-51. *Note*: The following authorial revision has been identified; page and line numbers refer to the first appearance.

   46.59 jubilate] jubilant *SB*+

C580 "White Night of the Soul." *Mundus Artium*, 2 (Spring 1968), 41. Poem. In *SB*.

C581 "Thumbsucking." *Nation*, 206 (1 April 1968), 453-54. Rev. of Conrad Aiken, *Thee: A Poem*.

C582 "Poems of a Japanese Sojourn." *Nation*, 206 (22 April 1968), 548-49. Rev. of Kenneth Rexroth, *The Heart's Garden / The Garden's Heart*.

C583 "Trying to Read Through My Writing." *Chelsea*, no. 22-23 (June 1968), 51. Poem. In *SB*.

C584 "Personal Statement." *New York Times Book Review*, 23 June 1968, pp. 24, 26. Rev. of Muriel Rukeyser, *The Speed of Darkness*.

C585 "The Swallows Return." *Quest*, 3 (Summer-Fall, 1968), 37. Poem. In *FG, CP76, CP88*. Rept. in *Poet* (Madras, India), 22 (March 1981), 15.

C586 "The Bower." *Quest*, 3 (Summer-Fall 1968), 38-39. Poem. In *FG, CP76, CP88*.

C587 "The Poet on His Work." *Christian Science Monitor*, 18 Aug. 1968, p. 8. Essay.

C588 "The Wedding." *Chicago Tribune Magazine*, 10 Nov. 1968, p. 90. Poem. In *FG, CP76, CP88*. *Note*: The following authorial revision has been identified; page and line numbers refer to the first appearance.

   90.13 hover] ~,

C589 "Warr." *Poetry New York*, 1 (no. 1, 1969), 3. Poem. Rept. in *University Review*, 2 (15 Oct. 1969), p. 2.

C590 "Logos." *Poetry New York*, 1 (no. 1, 1969), 4. Poem.

C591 "Envoi." *Poetry New York*, 1 (no. 1, 1969), 4. Poem.

C592 Untitled statement on contemporary poetry in *Occident*, 3 (Spring-Summer 1969), 105-6.

C593 "John Ledyard." *Times Literary Supplement*, 22 May 1969, p. 552. Poem. In *FG, CP76, CP88*. Rept. in *Poet*, 27 (October 1986), 16.

C594 "The Art of William Carlos Williams." *Kenyon Review*, 31 (Summer 1969), 415-19. Rev. of James Guimond, *A Discovery and Possession of America*.

C595 "Inability to Depict an Eagle." *New American Review*, no. 7 (Aug. 1969), 159. In *FG*. Rept. in *The Gift Outright: America to Her Poets*, ed. Helen Plotz (New York: Greenwillow, 1977), p. 15.

C596 "Track." *New Yorker*, 45 (13 Sept. 1969), 105. Poem. In *FG, CP76, CP88*.

C597 "The Incredible Splendor of the Magnificent Scene." *Chicago Tribune Magazine*, 23 Nov. 1969, p. 67. Poem. In *FG*.

C598 "Two Poets: Donald Hall, Ruth Pitter." *Boston Sunday Globe Book Review* (Christmas Edition), 7 Dec. 1969, p. 8. Rev. of Donald Hall, *The Alligator Bride*; and Ruth Pitter, *Collected Poems*.

C599 "Stealth and Subtleties of Growth." *Southern Review*, n.s. 6 (Winter 1970), 155-56. Poem. In *FG, CP88*.

C600 "The Secret Heart." *South Florida Poetry Journal*, no. 4-5 (1970), 106. First of "Two Poems." In *FG, CP76, CP88*. Rept. in *Poet*, 27 (Feb. 1986), 76.

C601 "A Man Who Was Blown Down by the Wind." *South Florida Poetry Journal*, no. 4-5 (1970), 107. Second of "Two Poems." In *CP88*.

C602 "For the Dartmouth Poetry Symposium, January 1970." *South Florida Poetry Journal*, no. 4-5 (1970), 122-23. RE's random thoughts on poetry; see **B104** and **F53**.

C603 Untitled rev. of John Masefield, *Grace Before Plowing: Fragments of an. Autobiography. South Florida Poetry Journal*, no. 4-5 (1970), 124-29.

C604 "The Soul." *Quarterly Review of Literature*, no. 1-2 (1970), 64. Poem. In *FG*.

C605 "Lorca." *Quarterly Review of Literature*, 17 no. 1-2 (1970), 65. Poem. In *PP, LR, CP88*.

C606 "Outgoing, In Coming." *Quarterly Review of Literature*, 17 (no. 1-2, 1970), 66. Poem. In *FG*. Rept. in *Poet*, 24 (Feb. 1983), 19. *Note*: The following authorial variant has been identified; page and line numbers refer to the first appearance.

66.2 air.] ~,

C607 "Gulled." *New River*, no. 2 (1970), 19-20. Poem. In *CP88*.

C608 "Autumn." *New York Quarterly*, no. 1 (Winter 1970), 24-25. Poem. In *WL*.

C609 "Emily Dickinson." *Southern Review*, n.s. 6 (Winter 1970), 156-58. Poem. In *FG, CP76, PP, CP88*. Rept. in *Poet*, 23 (Feb. 1982). 72-3.

C610 "Man's Fate." *Southern Review*, n.s. 6 (Winter 1970), 158-59. Poem.

C611 "Fracture Within." *Southern Review*, n.s. 6 (Winter 1970), 159-60. Poem.

C612 "Hardy Perennial." *Southern Review*, n.s. 6 (Winter 1970), 160-61. Poem. In *FG, CP76, CP88*. Rept. in *Poet*, 25 (Feb. 1984), 72.

C613 "Here and Now." *Southern Review*, n.s. 6 (Winter 1970), 161-62. Poem.

C614 "A Dirty Hand." *Poetry*, 115 (Feb. 1970), 345-46. Rev. of *A Dirty Hand: The Literary Notebooks of Winfield Townley Scott.*

C615 "Despair." *New Yorker*, 45 (14 Feb. 1970), 35. Poem. In *FG, CP76, CP88*. Rept. in *Poetry Is for People*, ed. Westerbrook and Gooch (1973), p. 70; *The Uses of Poetry*, ed. Stein (1975), p. 25; *Pancontinental Premier Poets*, ed. Bohumila Falkowski et al. (Madras, India: World Poetry Society Intercontinental, 1982), p. 3.

C616 "Love On." *Jeopardy*, 6 (March 1970), 62. Poem.

C617 "Suicide Note." *New Yorker* 46 (March 28 1970), 36. Poem. In *FG, CP76, CP88*.

C618 "Will." *Saturday Review of Literature*, 53 (28 March 1970), 73. Poem. Rept. in *This is My Best in the Third Quarter of the Twentieth Century*, ed. Burnett (1970), pp. 97-98.

C619 "The Anxiety I Felt in Guanajuato." *Shenandoah*, 21 (Spring 1970), 76. Poem. In *FG, CP76, CP88*.

C620 "Vision ['I came into the street...']." *Virginia Quarterly Review*, 46 (Spring 1970), 240. Poem.

C621 "To Kenya Tribesmen, The Turkana." *Virginia Quarterly Review*, 46 (Spring 1970), 241. Poem. In *FG, CP88*. Rept. on back cover of *The Poetry Society of America Bulletin*, 62 (Nov. 1972), 7.

C622 "Adam Cast Forth" (Jorge Luis Borges). *Poetry*, 116 (Aug.-Sept. 1970), 299. Trans. by RE. In *CP76, CP88*.

C623 "One Morning in 1649" (Jorge Luis Borges). *Poetry*, 116 (Aug.-Sept. 1970), 300. Trans. by RE.

C624 "A Rose for Milton" (Jorge Luis Borges). *Poetry*, 116 (Aug.-Sept. 1970), 301. Trans By RE.

C625 Untitled review of Samuel French Morse, *Wallace Stevens*. *Boston Globe*, 13 Sept. 1970, p. 68.

C626 "The Breathless." *Chicago Tribune Magazine*, 27 Sept. 1970, p. 6. Poem. In *FG, CP76, CP88*.

C627 "The Loosening." *Antioch Review*, 30 (Fall-Winter 1970-71), 328. Poem. In *FG*. Rept. in *Speaking of ... Interpretation*, ed. Charlotte Lee (Glen-

view, Ill: Scott Foresman, 1975), p. 150. *Note*: The following authorial revisions have identified; page and line numbers refer to the first appearance.
    first 10 lines ordered as couplets] first 10 lines are separated from each other by extra leading
    328.14 death,] ~.

C628 "United 555." *Poetry*, 117 (Oct. 1970), 39. Poem. In *CP76, CP88*. Rept. in *Poetry: An Introduction and Anthology*, ed. Edward Proffitt (Boston: Houghton Mifflin, 1981), p. 219. *Note*: The following authorial revision has been identified; page and line numbers refer to the first appearance.
    39.1 Saint] St.

C629 "Time Passes." *Poetry*, 117 (Oct. 1970), 40. Poem. in *FG, CP76, CP88*. Rept. in *Premier Poets The Ninth Biennial Anthology*, ed. Krishna Srinivas (Madras, India/Campbell, Cal.: World Poetry Society, 1986), 3.

C630 "As If You Had Never Been." *New Yorker*, 46 (3 Oct. 1970), 38. Poem. In *FG, CP76, CP88*. Rept. in *Eye's Delight: Poems of Art and Architecture*, ed. Helen Plotz (New York: Greenwillow, 1983), p. 26.

C631 "Homage to the North." *New Yorker*, 46 (12 Dec. 1970), 54. Poem. In *FG, CP76, CP88*. Rept. in *Expansive Light* (1977), pp. 30-31; *Poet*, 24 (Oct. 1983), 1; *Poet*, 26 (Oct. 1985), 3.

C632 "Playing Ball with the Dead." *Decal Poetry Review*, no. 1 (1971), 60. Poem.

C633 "The Icicle." *The New England Galaxy*, 12 (Winter 1971), 56. Poem. As "Icicle" in *FG*.

C634 "The Other Gerard." *New York Quarterly*, no. 5 (Winter 1971), 43-44. Poem.

C635 "Emerging." *Charles Street Journal*, 1 (Feb.-March 1971), 44. Poem. In *FG*.

C636 "Death in the Mines." *Virginia Quarterly Review*, 47 (Spring 1971), 229. Poem. In *CP76, CP88*. Rept. in *Best Poems of 1971: Borestone Mountain Poetry Awards 1972*, (Palo Alto, Ca.: Pacific Books, 1972), p. 30.

C637 "Reading Room, The New York Public Library." *Virginia Quarterly Review*, 47 (Spring 1971), 230. Poem. In *FG, CP76, CP88*. Rept. in *A Geography of Poets*, ed. Edward Field (New York: Bantam, 1979), p. 379; *New York: Poems*, ed. Howard Moss (New York: Avon, 1980), p. 66.

C638 "Balance." *Jeopardy*, 7 (Spring 1971), 60. Poem.

C639 "Absolute Silence." *Granite*, 1 (Spring 1971), 21. Poem. In *FG*.

C640 "Los Arcos" (La Paz). *Friends of the Smith College Library Newsletter* (Northampton, Mass.), April 1971, 1. Trans by RE. In *WL*.

C641 Untitled excerpt from a letter to the editor, *Austin Daily*, 24 May 1971, p. 3(A).

C642 "Idleness." *Antaeus*, no. 3 (Fall 1971), 72-73. Poem. In *FG*. *Note*: The following authorial revision has been identified; page and line numbers refer to the first appearance.

72.6 siluacra] simulacra

C643 "Redemption." *Antaeus*, no. 3 (Fall 1971), 74. Poem. In *CP76*, *CP88*.

C644 "Fisher Cat." *New Yorker*, 47 (23 Oct. 1971), 146. Poem. As "The Fisher Cat" in *FG, CP76, NH, LR, CP88*. Rept. in *A Green Place*, ed. William Jay Smith (New York: Delacorte, 1982), pp. 152-53.

C645 "Hatred of the Old River." *Chicago Tribune Magazine*, 24 Oct. 1971, p. 9. Poem. In *CP76, CP88*.

C646 "Man and Nature." *Saturday Review*, 54 (13 Nov. 1971), 40. Poem. In *CP76, LR, CP88*. Rept. in *50 Modern American and British Poets, 1920-1970*, ed. Louis Untermeyer (1973), p. 62; *Poetry Now*, vol. 6, no. 5, issue 35 (1982), 3.

C647 "Insomnia." *Counter Measures*, no. 1 (1972), 17. Poem.

C648 "On Encountering the Great-Great-Grandson of William Wordsworth." *Counter Measures*, no. 1 (1972), 18. Poem.

C649 "Long Term Suffering." *Mill Mountain Review*, 2 (no. 2, 1972), 80. Poem. In *FG, CP76, CP88*. Rept. in *A Geography of Poets*, ed. Field (1979), p. 378; *Gladly Learn and Gladly Teach*, ed. Plotz (1981), p. 93.

C650 "Differences." *Mill Mountain Review*, 2 (no. 2, 1972), 81. Poem.

C651 "Lenses." *Virginia Quarterly Review*, 48 (Spring 1972), 214-16. Poem. In *FG*.

C652 "On the Suicide of F.O. Matthiessen." *Hellcoal Annual Two* (Brown Univ., Providence, R.I.), April 1972, 12. Poem.

C653 Untitled review of John Gill, (ed.) *New American and Canadian Poetry, Boston Sunday Globe Book Review*, 14 May 1972, 69.

C654 "The Young and the Old." *Nation*, 214 (19 June 1972), 793. Poem. In *FG, CP76, PP, CP88*. *Note*: The text is set in italic in the original version but in roman in subsequent printings. The following authorial revision has been identified; page and line numbers refer to the first appearance.

Dedication] *(For W.B. Yeats) FG*+

C655 "Love Sequence with Variations." *Harvard Advocate*, 106 (Summer 1972), 36-37. Poem. In *WL*. *Note*: The following authorial revisions have been identified; page and line numbers refer to the first appearance.

36.38-39 *no stanza break*] *stanza break*
36.80-81 *no stanza break*] *stanza break*
36.108-109 *no stanza break*] *stanza break*
37.12-13 *no stanza break*] *stanza break*

"Making Love to a Page"

37 *[section* IV *untitled]*] *Making Love to a Page*

37.50 England] Langland

37.52-53 *no stanza break*] *stanza break*

C656 "You Think They Are Permanent But They Pass." *New Republic*, 167 (1 July 1972), 22. Poem. In *FG*, *CP76*, *CP88*.

C657 "Gnat on My Paper." *Times Literary Supplement*, 28 July 1972, p. 860. Poem. In *FG*, *CP76*, *CP88*.

C658 "Broken Wing." *Atlantic*, 230 (August 1972), 73. Poem. As "Broken Wing Theory" in *FG*, *CP76*, *CP88*; rept. in *Poet*, 22 (Oct. 1981), 75.

C659 Untitled review of B.C. Heezen and C.D. Hollister, *The Face of the Deep*, *Limnology and Oceanography*, 17 (Sept. 1972), 801-2.

C660 "Placation of Reality." *Stone Drum*, 1 (Fall 1972), 50-51. Poem. In *CP88*.

C661 "Order." *Concerning Poetry* (Western Washington State College, Bellingham), 5 (Fall 1972), 9-10. Poem. In *LR*. *Note*: The following authorial revision has been identified; page and line numbers refer to the first appearance.

9.7 got] was

C662 "Evening Bird Song." *Concerning Poetry*, 5 (Fall 1972), 10. In *FG*, *CP76*, *CP88*. Rept. in program for "A Reading by Richard Eberhart, 8 May 1975" (SUNY, Brockport), p. 3.

C663 "Meaningless Poem." *Concerning Poetry*, 5 (Fall 1972), 11. Poem. In *FG*, *CP76*, *CP88*.

C664 "Fish Dinner 1972." *Pulse* (Lamar Univ., Beaumont, Texas), 15 (Fall 1972), 15. Poem.

C665 "Vermont Idyll." *Poetry*, 121 (Nov. 1972), 79. Poem. In *CP76*, *CP88*.

C666 "Plain Song Talk." *Poetry*, 121 (Nov. 1972), 80. Poem.

C667 "Worldly Failure." *Quadrant* (Australia), 16 (Nov.-Dec. 1972), 22. Poem. In *CP76*, *PP*, *CP88*. Rept. in *Miscellany Two* (Occasional Paper No. 13), ed. Reginald L. Cook (Montpelier, Vt.: Vermont Academy of Arts and Sciences, 1974), p. 12.

C668 "Emblem." *New Yorker*, 48 (9 Dec. 1972), 47. Poem. In *CP76*, *CP88*.

C669 "A Haphazard Poetry Collecting." *Chicago Review*, 24 (Spring 1973), 57-70. Essay. In *OPP*.

C670 "The Scouring." *Widening Circle*, 1 (Spring 1973), 17. Poem. In *CP76*, *CP88*.

C671 "General Points." *Agenda*, 2 (Spring-Summer 1973), 41-44. RE's answers to *Agenda's* "American Rhythm Questionnaire." Excerpt rept. in *From the Hills*, ed. William Plumley and Shirley Young Campbell (Charleston, W. Va.: MHC Publications, 1974), p. 23.

C672 "Wild Life and Tamed Life." *Agenda*, 2 (Spring-Summer 1973), 68. Poem. In *CP88*.

C673 "Angels and Man." *New York Quarterly*, no. 14 (Spring 1973), 78-80. Poem. In *WL*. *Note*: Three significant typographical errors are contained in the first printing of this poem. These errors, with the corrected reading, appear below. Page and line number refer to the appearance in *New York Quarterly*.

    79.2 neon] noon

    79.23 us] as

    79.39-40 *stanza break*] *no stanza break*

C674 "Light, Time, Dark." *Pulse*, 15 (Spring 1973), 9. Poem. In *CP76*, *CP88*.

C675 "Goners." *Pulse*, 15 (Spring 1973), 16. Poem.

C676 "The Hop-Toad." *Pulse*, 15 (Spring 1973), 16. Poem. In *CP76*, *CP88*. Rept. in *Sou'Wester*, 2 (Fall 1973), 25, with RE's brief introductory note preceeding the poem; *Poetry London / Apple Magazine*, no. 2 (1982), 16.

C677 "Going to Maine." *Pulse*, 15 (Spring 1973), 16. Poem. In *LR*, *CP88*. Rept. in *Shaman*, no. 1 (Autumn 1973), 45; *Bangor* (Maine) *Daily News*, 15 August 1974, p. 6. *Note*: The following authorial revisions have been identified; page and line numbers refer to the first appearance.

    16.16 when] When

    16.24 there ~!

C678 "Portrait of Rilke." *Chicago Tribune Magazine*, 1 April 1973, p.6. Poem. In *PP*, *CP76*, *CP88*.

C679 "Eberhart." *Center Stage* (Dartmouth College Players Program, Hanover, N.H.) 3 (14 May 1973), 4-5. RE's comment's on his verse plays.

C680 "No News is Good Muse." *Guardian* (London), 29 June 1973. As "Poetry and Politics" in *OPP*. *N.B.*: Not examined.

C681 "Poetry." *Nation*, 217 (2 July 1973), 28. Poem.

C682 "Three Kids." *Times Literary Supplement*, 6 July 1973, p. 768. Poem. In *CP76*, *CP88*.

C683 "Literary Death." *Granite*, no. 6 (Autumn 1973), 152-54. Essay. In *OPP*.

C684 "Big Rock." *Prairie Schooner*, 47 (Fall 1973), 230. Poem. In *CP76*, *CP88*.

C685 Untitled letter to John L. Sweeney (containing the complete text of 'If I Could Only Live at the Pitch That Is Near Madness'). *Dartmouth College Library Bulletin*, 14 (Nov. 1973), 3.

C686 "W.H. Auden: A Memoir by Richard Eberhart." *Dartmouth*, 28 Nov. 1973, p. 2.

C687 "Trying to Hold it All Together." *Dartmouth*, 28 Nov. 1973, p. 2. Poem. In *CP76*, *PP*, *CP88*. Rept. in *PSA Bulletin*, 63 (Dec. 1973), 16; *Harvard Advocate*, 108 (no. 2-3, 1974), 61.

C688 Untitled tribute to W.H. Auden, in *PSA Bulletin*, 63 (Dec. 1973), 13-15.

C689 "How Do I Further Spend My Glory?" *Chicago Tribune Magazine*, 2 Dec. 1973, p. 20. Poem. In *LR*.

C690 "Winter Squirrels in Pine Trees." *Chicago Tribune Magazine*, 2 Dec. 1973, p. 20. Poem. In *WL*.

C691 "Vision Through Timothy." *Dart*, 3 (no. 1, 1974), 24. Poem. In *CP76, CP88*.

C692 "Usurper." *Fragments* (Seattle Univ., Wash.), 15 (no. 1, 1974), 11. Poem. In *CP76, CP88*.

C693 "A Tribute to W.H. Auden." *Harvard Advocate*, 108 (no. 2-3, 1974), 30-31. Essay. In *OPP*.

C694 "Old Tree by the Penobscot." *Falling Fountains*, 1 (Jan. 1974), 14. Poem. In *CP76, CP88*.

C695 "Inchiquin Lake, Penobscot Bay." *Times Literary Supplement*, 25 Jan. 1974, p. 78. In *CP76, CP88. Note*: The collected appearance contains a dedication to Jack and Moira Sweeney and corrects an error in line 19, mature] nature.

C696 "A Telling." *Paintbrush*, 1 (Spring 1974), 3. Acrostic. In *LR. Note*: The following authorial revision has been identified; page and line numbers refer to the first appearance.

    3.14 grow] know

C697 "Once More, O Ye . . ." *Florida Quarterly*, 6 (Spring 1974), 59. Poem. In *CP76, CP88*. Rept. in *American Poetry Review*, 4 (July-Aug, 1975), 45.

C698 "Island Message." *Florida Quarterly*, 6 (Spring 1974), 60-61. Poem. In *LR. Note*: The following authorial revision has been identified; page and line numbers refer to the first appearance.

    60.24 youthful-pent] flesh-pent

C699 "Eberhart's 'Experience Evoked'." *Explicator*, 32 (May 1974), 17. RE's explication of his own poem, which is rept. on p. 16.

C700 "Introduction." *Poesis*, no. 1 (June 1974), 3-5. Introduction-essay.

C701 "Far Out." *Chicago Tribune Magazine*, 9 June 1974, p.40. Poem. In *LR*.

C702 "Slow Boat Ride." *New Yorker*, 50 (15 July 1974), 34. Poem. In *CP76, CP88*.

C703 Untitled remarks from Jean Garrigue's memorial service, St. Luke's Chapel, New York, N.Y., 3 Feb. 1973. *Poetry Pilot* (Oct. 1974), 10. *Note*: RE was poetry editor of this issue, and his remarks are contained in an uncredited article titled "Poetry Editor" (pp. 9-10).

C704 "Harsh Rocks." *Chicago Tribune Magazine*, 29 Dec. 1974, sec. 9, p. 16. Poem.

C705 "The Visionary." *Poetry Now*, 1 (no. 6, 1974), 4. Poem. In *LR*.

C706 "Life and Death / Jean Garrigue (1914-1972)." *Quarterly Review of Literature* (30th Anniv. Poetry Retrospective), 19 (no. 1-2, 1974), 556.

Poem. In *CP76, PP*. Rept. in *Twentieth Century Literature*, 29 (Spring 1983), 34. *Note*: RE listed incorrectly the year of Jean Garrigue's birth in the title of the original appearance; 1914 has been changed to 1913 in subsequent appearances.

C707 "Celebration of Late August." *Song*, no. 1 (1975), 25. Poem.

C708 "Unknown Poet." *Mississippi Review*, 4 (no. 1, 1975), 11. Poem.

C709 "Mother Swallow." *Poetry Now*, vol. 2, no. 6, issue 11 (1975), 6. In *LR*. .

C710 "A Certain Distance." (later titled "A Certain Distance from Man") *Poetry Now*, vol. 2, no. 6, issue 12 (1975), 4. As "A Certain Distance from Man" in *LR*.

C711 "The Melancholy Fit." *Poetry Now*, vol. 2, no. 6, issue 12 (1975), 4. In *LR*.

C712 Untitled statement about poetry, in *Poet* 16 (Jan. 1975), p. [verso of front wrapper].

C713 Letter to Dr. Krishna Srinivas, in *Poet*, 16 (Jan. 1975), p. 3.

C714 "On Anthologies Including the New Norton Anthology of Modern Poetry." *American Poetry Review*, 4 (Jan.-Feb. 1975), 35-37. Essay-review.

C715 "A Way Out." *Times Literary Supplement*, 17 Jan. 1975, p. 56. Poem. In *CP76, CP88*. Rept. in *Best Poems of 1975: Borestone Mountain Poetry Awards 1976* (Palo Alto, Ca.: Pacific Books, 1976), pp. 28-28. *Note*: The text of the original appearance is set in all italic but in roman in subsequent publications. The following textual variants have been identified; page and line numbers refer to the first appearance.

> 56.45 binding] blinding
> 56.50 skis] skiis
> 374.11 away,] ~∧

C716 "Inner Voyage." *Paintbrush*, no. 3 (Spring 1975), 5. Poem.

C717 "New York Prospect." *Paintbrush*, no. 3 (Spring 1975), 6. Poem. In *LR*.

C718 "Undercliff Evening." *Paintbrush*, no. 3 (Spring 1975), 7. Poem. In *CP76, CP88*.

C719 "Word Plays." *Crucible* (Univ. of South Carolina, Columbia), Spring 1975, 3. Poem.

C720 "Letter to Andrew Foster." *Paris Review*, 16 (Spring 1975), 71-74. Poem. *Note*: "A Note on *Letter to Andrew Foster*," signed 'R.E.' follows the poem, on p. 74.

C721 "Incidence of Flight." *Virginia Quarterly Review*, 51 (Spring 1975), 243. Poem. In *CP76, FP, LR, CP88*.

C722 "In the Air." *Southern Review*, n.s. 11 (April 1975), 373-74. Poem. In *WL*.

C723 "Razzle-Dazzle." *Southern Review*, n.s. 11 (April 1975), 374-75. Poem.

C724 "Mind and Nature." *Southern Review*, n.s. 11 (April 1975), 375-76. Poem. In *CP76*, *CP88*. *Note*: The following authorial revisions have been identified; page and line numbers refer to the first appearance.

    376.9 magnificent] harsh

    376.11 my duration on earth] earth duration

    376.14 earth is grand] ~, fixed,

C725 "Coast of Maine." *New Yorker*, 51 (7 April 1975), 38. Poem. In *CP76*, *CP88*. Rept. in *Best Poems of 1975* (1976), p. 30.

C726 "Mistaken Identity." *Nation*, 220 (26 April 1975), 505. Poem. In *LR*, *CP88*.

C727 "Face, Ocean." *Chicago Review*, 27 (Summer 1975), 123. Poem. In *CP76*, *PP*, *CP88*. *Note*: The following authorial revision has been identified; page and line numbers refer to the first appearance.

    123.6 Shape] Eminence

C728 "Fat Spider." *Chicago Review*, 27 (Summer 1975), 124. Poem. In *WL*.

C729 "What You Keep on Your Mantlepiece." *American Poetry Review*, 4 (July 1975), 45. Poem. In *WL*. "Once More O Ye . . ." rept. on p. 45. *Note*: The following authorial revision has been identified; page and line numbers refer to the first appearance.

    45.2 mutifaricity] multifariousness

C730 "Sagacity." *Poetic Horizons 76* (Gainesville, Fla. Poetic Association), p. 11. Poem. In *WL*, *CP88*. Rept. in *Poetry Now*, vol. 3, no. 1, issue 13 (1976), 5.

C731 "Jeffers." *Poetry Now*, vol. 3, nos. 4-6, (1976), 34. Poem.

C732 "The Flag." *Poetry Now*, vol. 3, nos. 4-6, (1976), 34. In *LR*, *CP88*.

C733 "Good Place." *Forum* (Univ. of Houston, Tex.), 13 (Winter 1976), 15. Poem. In *LR*.

C734 "Snowfall." *Atlantic*, 237 (Feb. 1976), 95. Poem. As "A Snowfall" in *WL*, *CP88*. Rept. in *Fifty Contemporary Poets: The Creative Process*, ed. Alberta T. Turner (New York: David McKay, 1977), pp. 85-86.

C735 "Address to God." *Times Literary Supplement*, 12 March 1976, p. 278. Poem.

C736 "Delicacy." *Paintbrush*, 3 (Spring 1976), 5. Poem.

C737 "The Lovers." *A Galaxy of Verse* (Fort Worth, Tex.), 2 (Spring-Summer 1976), 72. Poem.

C738 "Passage." *New Letters*, 42 (Summer 1976), 37. Poem. In *LR*. Rept. in *From A to Z: 200 Contemporary American Poets*, ed. David Ray (Chicago: Swallow Books, 1981), p. 47.

C739 "A Dance for Vance." *Tower* (Dartmouth College, Hanover, N.H., literary magazine.), 1 (Summer-Fall 1976), 30-31. Poem.

C740 "The Fort and the Gate." *Times Literary Supplement*, 10 Sept. 1976, p. 1114. Poem. In *WL*; also published separately as **A40**.

C741 "Alcaic." *California State Poetry Quarterly*, 4 (Fall 1976), 37. Poem.

C742 "Sapphic." *California State Poetry Quarterly*, 4 (Fall 1976), 37. Poem.

C743 "The Bones of Coleridge." *Times Literary Supplement*, 24 Dec. 1976, p. 1602. Poem. In *WL*, *CP88*.

C744 "Statement" (on freedom and form in poetry). *Mississippi Review*, 6 (no. 1, 1977), 28. Rept. in part in *New York Quarterly*, no. 20 (1978), 28.

C745 "Waiting for Something to Happen." *Mississippi Review*, 6 (no. 1, 1977), 29-30. Poem. In *LR*. Rept. in *Touchstone*, 21 (Fall 1984), 9.

C746 "Address to Time." *Vanderbilt Poetry Review*, 2 (no. 3-4, 1977), 20-21. Poem. In *LR*.

C747 "Waiting." *Poets On: Roots*, 1 (Spring 1977), 34. Poem. In *LR*.

C748 "How to Make Something of the Rocks." *Bellingham Review*, 1 (Spring 1977), 25. Poem. In *LR*.

C749 "From 'Vignettes'." *Wallace Stevens Journal*, 1 (Spring 1977), 36. Expt. from longer poem (see below C755). Rept. in *New York Quarterly*, no. 20 (1978), 29-33.

C750 "Lilac Feeling." *New Letters*, 43 (Summer 1977), 39. Poem. In *LR*.

C751 "Cooperation Is No Competition." *Forum*, 15 (Summer-Fall 1977), 12. Poem. In *LR*.

C752 "Reflections on Wallace Stevens." *Southern Review*, n.s. 13 (July 1977), 417-18. Article. In *OPP*.

C753 "Great Principles are Thrown Down by Time." *New York Times* (31 Dec. 1977), 17. Poem. In *LR*, *CP88*. Rept. in *Mickle Street Review* (1980), 28-29.

C754 "Hour." *Poetry Now*, vol. 4, no. 1, issue 19 (1978), 5. Poem. In *LR*.

C755 "Vignettes." *New York Quarterly*, no. 20 (1978), 29-33. Poem. In *LR*. *Note*: Minor textual variants have been noted between first appearance and book publication, but no authorial revisions are present.

C756 "A Loon Call." *New England Review*, 1 (Winter 1978), 140. Poem. In *WL*, *CP88*.

C757 "The Swinging Bridge." *Berkeley Poetry Review*, no. 6-7 (Spring 1978), 110. Poem. In *WL*, *FP*, *LR*, *CP88*.

C758 "How It Is." *Times Literary Supplement*, 28 April 1978, p. 461. Poem. In *LR*, *CP88*.

C759 "Presentation to Robert Lowell of the National Medal for Literature." *Proceedings of the American Academy and Institute of Arts and Letters*, no. 28 (1978), 33. Text of RE's presentation.

C760 Untitled acceptance speech for the 1977 National Book Award in Poetry, in *Proceedings of the American Academy and Institute of Arts and Letters*, no. 28 (1978), 46-48.

C761 "Classification." *Devil's Millhopper*, May 1978, 12. Poem. In *FP*, *LR*. *Note*: The following authorial revisions have been identified; page and line numbers refer to the first appearance.

12.7 or] Or
12.8 of] Of
12.10 What] what

C762 "The Poem." *Tamarisk*, 2 (Summer 1978), 5. Poem. In *LR*.

C763 "Touch and Go." *High Country News*, 10 (2 June 1978), 2. Poem. In *LR*.

C764 "Rifkin Movement." *Times Literary Supplement*, 7 July 1978, p. 759. Poem. In *WL*, *CP88*.

C765 "In Situ." *Atlantic*, 242 (Sept. 1978), 62. Poem. In *WL*. *Note*: The following authorial revisions have been identified; page and line numbers refer to the first appearance.

62.3-4 They caw, you] *no line break*
62.11 Likewise.] ~,

C766 "Death in a Taxi." *American Poetry Review*, 7 (Sept.-Oct. 1978), 34. Poem. In *WL*.

C767 "A Rich Kiss." *American Poetry Review*, 7 (Sept.-Oct. 1978), 34. Poem. In *LR*.

C768 "Introduction." *Annex 21* (Univ. of Nebraska, Omaha), no. 2 (1979), 72. Statement of introduction to Frederick Zydek, "Lights Along the Missouri," on pp. 73-107 of this number.

C769 "A Token." *College of Charleston* (West Virginia) *Miscellany*, Spring 1979, 1. Poem. In *LR*.

C770 "Ben Franklin." *Devil's Millhopper*, May 1979, 11-12. Poem. In *LR*. *Note*: The following authorial revisions have been identified; page and line numbers refer to the first appearance.

11.22 I, too,] ~^~^
11.24 answer] ~.
12.10 (violence)] *deleted*

C771 "Accolades." *Harpoon*, 1 (Summer-Fall 1979), 20-21. Poem.

C772 "Ceremonial." *Forum*, 17 (Summer-Fall 1979), 26. Poem. In *CP88*.

C773 "Offering to the Body." *Poetry*, 134 (Sept. 1979), 342-43. Poem. In *WL*.

C774 "Speculative Nature Note." *Poetry*, 134 (Sept, 1979), 343. Poem. In *WL*.

C775 "Fog." *New Republic*, 181 (15 Sept. 1979), 28. Poem. In *LR*.

C776 "A Whack at Empson." *Poetry London / Apple Magazine*, 1 (Autumn 1979), 24-25. Poem. In *LR*. *Note*: A postscript from a letter by RE to the editor is contained on p. 25.

C777 "Consultant's Choice." *Quarterly Journal of the Library of Congress*, 36 (Fall 1979), 381-82. RE's choice of James Merrill's book of poems, *Mirabell*, and his reasons for the choosing this title.

C778 "Harvard Stadium." *Wallace Stevens Journal*, 3 (Fall 1979), 99. Poem. In *LR*, *CP88*.

C779 "Comments." *West Hills Review*, 1 (Fall 1979), 20. Prose statement about Walt Whitman. *Note*: "Centennial for Whitman" is rept. on pp. 16-19.

C780 "Throwing Yourself Away." *Poet* (Madras, India), 20 (Oct. 1979), 1. Poem. In *LR*, *CP88*. Rept. in *Stand*, 25 (Autumn 1984), 4.

C781 "How the Spirit Descends in the Man." *Practices of the Wind*, no. 1 (1980), 25. Poem. As "Spirit Descends in Man" in *WL*. *Note*: The following authorial revisions and textual variants have been identified; page and line numbers refer to the first appearance.

    title How the Spirit Descends in the Man] Spirit Descends in Man

    25.1 The man] Man

    25.4 axe] ax

    25.6 was the] ~

    25.11-14 The...revealed.] *deleted*

C782 "Feat." *Pteranodon*, no. 4 (1980), 5. Poem. In *LR*.

C783 "Time's Clickings." *Virginia Quarterly Review*, 56 (Winter 1980), 66-67. Poem. In *Su*, *WL*.

C784 "Dark Memories." *Prosery*, 1 (Winter 1980), 2. Poem. In *LR*. *Note*: The following authorial revisions have been identified; page and line numbers refer to the first appearance.

    2.9 it.] ~,

    2.10 gull.] ~,

C785 "Sea Storm." *American Poetry Review*, 9 (March-April 1980), 7-8. Poem. In *LR*, *CP88*.

C786 "Storm and Quiet." *Kentucky Poetry Review*, 16 (Summer-Fall 1980), 9. Poem. In *NH*, *LR*.

C787 "A Line of Verse of Yeats." *Kentucky Poetry Review*, 16 (Summer-Fall 1980), 10. Poem. In *LR*, *CP88*.

C788 "Hysteria of Communication." *Paintbrush*, 7-8 (no. 13-16, 1980-81), 14. Poem. in *LR*.

C789 "Emerson's Concord." *Paintbrush*, 7-8 (no. 13-16, 1980-81), 15. Poem. In *LR*, *CP88*.

C790 "Target." *Ploughshares*, 7 (no. 1, 1981), 40-41. Poem. In *LR*.

C791 "Homage to James Laughlin." *Conjunctions*, no. 1 (1981), 141.

Prose statement. *Note*: Issued in card cover as well as cloth boards with dust jacket.

C792 "Testimony." *Conjunctions*, no. 1 (1981), 141-42. Poem. In *LR*, *CP88*.

C793 "Isabella Gardner's Poems." *Reaper*, 1 (1981), 28-29. Rev. of Isabella Gardner, *New and Selected Poems*.

C794 "Slant Angle." *Cumberland Poetry Review*, 1 (Winter 1981), 8. Poem. In *LR*. *Note*: The following authorial revision has been identified; page and line numbers refer to the first appearance.

    15.4-5 *no stanza break*] *stanza break*

C795 "Understanding the Impossible." *Cumberland Poetry Review*, 1 (Winter 1981), 9. Poem. In *LR*. *Note*: The following authorial revision has been identified; page and line numbers refer to the first appearance.

    191.23 nonbeing] non-being

C796 "Dusty Answer." *Times Literary Supplement*, 20 March 1981, p. 307. Poem. In *LR*.

C797 "Frank Stanford." *Ironwood*, 9 (Spring 1981), 137-38. Essay.

C798 "Louise." *Times Literary Supplement*, 22 May 1981, p. 562. Poem. In *LR*.

C799 "Old Memory." *PN Review 24*, 8 (Autumn 1981), 21. Poem. In *LR*.

C800 "Grandson." *Poetry London / Apple Magazine*, no. 2 (1982), 16. Poem. In *LR*. "The Hop-Toad" (**C676**) is rept. on p. 16. *Note*: RE deleted the second stanza, "Born...time?", for inclusion in *LR*.

C801 "As We Go." *Poetry Now*, vol. 6, no. 5, issue 35 (1982), 2. Poem. In *LR*.

C802 "Old Dichotomy: Choosing Sides." *Times Literary Supplement*, 1 Jan. 1982, p. 3. Poem. In *LR*, *CP88*. Rept. in *Literary Review*, 25 (Summer 1982), 525.

C803 "Fog 1 ['Fog may be total or partial or light']." *Negative Capability*, 2 (Spring 1982), 9. Poem. In *LR*. *Note*: The following authorial revisions and textual variants have been identified; page and line numbers refer to the first appearance.

    9.9 eyelight] eyesight
    9.12 propellor] propeller
    9.13 knife between the teeth] without a knife
    9.14 Then] They

C804 "Fog 2 ['The implications of fog are enormous']" *Negative Capability*, 2 (Spring 1982), 10. Poem. In *LR*.

C805 "Author's Note." *Literary Review*, 25 (Summer 1982), 521. Statement on poetry.

C806 "The Ideal and the Real." *Literary Review*, 25 (Summer 1982), 523. Poem. In *LR*, *CP88*.

C807 "Shiftings." *Literary Review*, 25 (Summer 1982), 524. Poem. In *LR*. Rept. in *Poetry Now*, vol. 6, no. 5, issue 35 (1982), 3. *Note*: The following authorial revision has been identified; page and line numbers refer to the first appearance.

> 524.12 life] ~,

C808 "New Marriage." *Literary Review*, 25 (Summer 1982), 526. Poem.

C809 "Somewhere Else." *Literary Review*, 25 (Summer 1982), 527. In *LR*, *CP88*.

C810 "Dead Skunk." *Times Literary Supplement*, 9 July 1982, p. 736. Poem. In *CP88*. Rept. in *The Bread Loaf Anthology of Contemporary American Poetry*, ed. Robert Pack, Sydney Lea, and Jay Parini (Hanover: University Press of New England, 1985), 70-71.

C811 "Edna Millay." *Tamarack*, 2 (Winter 1982-83), 2-4. Essay.

C812 "Question Mark." *Poetry Review*, 1 (no. 1, 1983), 79-80. Poem. In *CP88*.

C813 "The Humanist." *Prophetic Voices*, 1 (no. 1, 1983), 64. Poem.

C814 "Commas in Wintertime." *American Poetry Review*, 12 (March-April 1983), 41. Poem. In *LR*, *CP88*. Rept. in *Touchstone* (publication of the Poetry Society of New Hampshire), 21 (Fall 1984), 9.

C815 Untitled contribution to "Jean Garrigue: A Symposium," in *Twentieth Century Literature*, 29 (Spring 1983), 32-34. *Note:* RE's poem "Life and Death" (C706) is rept. on p. 34.

C816 "The Real and the Unreal." *Negative Capability*, 3 (Summer 1983), 14-16. Essay. Rept. in *Negative Capability*, 6 (Spring-Summer 1986), 138-140.

C817 "Going Backward Going Forward." *Denver Quarterly*, 18 (Autumn 1983), 78. Poem. In *CP88*.

C818 "River Water Music." *Denver Quarterly*, 18 (Autumn 1983), 79. Poem. In *CP88*. Rept. in *The Bread Loaf Anthology of Contemporary American Poetry*, ed. Robert Pack, Sydney Lea, and Jay Parini (Hanover: University Press of New England, 1985), 69.

C819 "Making Poetry a Continuum: Selected Correspondence [of Richard Eberhart and William Carlos Williams], with an Introduction by Stephen Corey." *Georgia Review*, 37 (Fall 1983), 533-64. RE's letters are found on pp. 540, 542-44, 546-47, 548-50, 553-55, 556-59, 560-61, 563-64. Rept. in *The Pushcart Prizes IX: Best of the Small Presses*, ed. Bill Henderson (Wainscott, N.Y.: Pushcart Press, 1984), pp. 170-202.

C820 "Mystery of the Abstract." *West Hills Review*, 4 (1983-84), 48. Poem. In *CP88*.

C821 "Babette Deutsch 1895-1982." *Proceedings of the American Academy and Institute of Arts and Letters*, 2d. ser., no. 34 (1983, i.e. 1984), 67-68. Tribute to Babette Deutsch.

C822 "Key West." *Quill* (Univ. of Tampa, Fla., literary journal), 7 (1984), 68. Poem. In *FP, LR, CP88*.

C823 "The Killer." *Southern Review*, n.s. 20 (Jan. 1984), 116-23. Poem. In *LR, CP88*. *Note*: The following authorial revisions and textual variants have been identified; page and line numbers refer to the first appearance.

116.18 Titanic.] ~,
117.23 Corso,] ~∧
118.8 Day-Lewis] ~∧~
118.24 Steffanson] Stefansson
120.20 unknowing.] ~,

C824 "Poetry Commentary." *Touchstone*, 21 (Feb. 1985), 10-11. Text of speech given in honor of Donald Hall, 20 Oct. 1984.

C825 "Listing." *Atlantic*, 253 (March 1984), 82. Poem. In *CP88*.

C826 "A Clerihew for Allan Gaylord." *Bennington Review*, no. 17 (Spring 1985), 63. Poem. In *CP88*.

C827 Untitled statement for special anniversary issue of *New York Quarterly*, 26 (Spring 1985), 119. *Note*: An excerpt from RE's craft interview (E60) is found on pp. 34, 36 of this issue.

C828 "Boat Race Speculation." *Open Places*, no. 38-39 (Spring 1985), 216. Poem.

C829 "21st Century Man." *New England Review / Breadloaf Quarterly*, 7 (Spring 1985), 298. Poem. In *CP88*. Rept. in *Consultants' Reunion 1987: A Keepsake Anthology of the Fiftieth Anniversary Celebration of the Consultantship in Poetry* (Washington, D.C.: Library of Congress, 1987), 17-18.

C830 "To the Harps." *Verse*, no. 2 (April 1985), 9. Poem.

C831 "The Hand." *Michagan Quarterly Review*, 24 (Summer 1985), 390. Poem. In *CP88*.

C832 "On the 100th Birthday of Scott Nearing." *New York Quarterly*, no. 27 (Summer 1985), 40. Poem.

C833 "The Angels." *Negative Capability*, 5 (Fall 1985), 81-2. Poem. In *CP88*. Rept. in *The Bread Loaf Anthology of Contemporary American Poetry*, ed. Robert Pack, et al. (1985), pp. 72-3.

C834 "White Pines, Felled 1984." *Negative Capability*, 5 (Fall 1985), 83-4. Poem. Rept. in *The Bread Loaf Anthology of Contemporary American Poetry*, ed. Robert Pack, et al (985), pp. 71-2.

C835 "Velvet Rocks." *Albatross*, no. 1 (1986), 27. Poem. In *CP88*.

C836 "Deep Fishing." *Kenyon Review*, n.s. 8 (Spring 1986), 24-25. Poem. In *CP88*.

C837 "Slow Fading." *South Coast Poetry Journal*, 1 (Spring 1986), 12. Poem.

C838 "Unique." *South Coast Poetry Journal*, 1 (Spring 1986), 12. Poem.

C839 "Letter to Ruth Herschberger." *Negative Capability*, 6 (Spring-Summer 1986), 115-117. Letter. *Note*: A facsimile of the original holograph letter appears on pp. 112-114. *Note*: This is a Special Richard Eberhart issue of *Negative Capability*.

C840 "Laocoon." *Negative Capability* 6 (Spring-Summer 1986), 118. Poem. In *CP88*.

C841 "Moment That Stays but Passes." *Negative Capability*, 6 (Spring-Summer, 1986), 119-20. Poem.

C842 "Achievement, Ninth Symphony." *Negative Capability*, 6 (Spring-Summer 1986), 121. Poem.

C843 "Growing Up: The Jungle, The Orchard, The River." *Negative Capability*, 6 (Spring-Summer 1986), 122-24. Poem.

C844 "Summer Incident." *Negative Capability*, 6 (Spring-Summer 1986), 125-26. Poem.

C845 "Care and Love." *Negative Capability*, 6 (Spring-Summer 1986), 127. Poem.

C846 "Poetry as World Value." *Negative Capability*, 6 (Spring-Summer 1986), 129-30. Address delivered to the Fifth World Congress of Poets, March 1981.

C847 "The Library of Congress." *Negative Capability*, 6 (Spring-Summer 1986), 131-4. Essay.

C848 "Speech Given in Honor of Donald Hall at the Poet Laureate of New Hampshire Testimonial Banquet in Concord, NH on October 10, 1984." *Negative Capability*, 6 (Spring-Summer 1986), 135-7.

C849 "Homage to a Teacher." *Negative Capability*, 6 (Spring-Summer 1986), 141-2. Essay.

C850 "Hornets by the Sill." *Michigan Quarterly Review*, 25 (Summer 1986), 540. Poem. In *CP88*.

C851 "Going." *Dartmouth Alumni Magazine*, 79 (Nov. 1986), 15. Poem. In *CP88*.

C852 "All of Us." *Sewanee Review*, 95 (Winter 1987), 1. Poem.

C853 "How I Became a Royal White Elephant, Third Class." *American Heritage*, 38 (Feb.-March 1987), 44-47. Autobiographical essay. *N.B.*: Also contains a brief interview; see E73.

C854 "Death of a Friend." *New York Quarterly*, no. 32 (Spring 1987), 49. Poem.

C855 "Academic Responsibility." *New York Quarterly*, no. 33 (Summer 1987), 65. Poem.

C856 "Stone Fence." *Partisan Review*, 54 (Summer 1987), 423. Poem.

C857 "Singular, Desolate, Out of It." *Poetry*, 151 (Oct.-Nov. 1987), 49. Poem.

C858 "Speech of Acceptance." *Poetry*, 151 (Oct.-Nov. 1987), 49. Poem.

C859 "Dog Days." *Worcester Review*, 9, no. 2 (c. Nov. 1987), 10. Poem.

D
Blurbs

D1 Isabella Gardner, *Birthdays from the Ocean* (Boston: Houghton, Mifflin, 1955). RE's blurb on back of dust jacket.

D2 Winfield Townley Scott, *The Dark Sister* (New York: New York Univ. Press, 1958). RE's blurb on back of dust jacket.

D3 Jean Garrigue, *A Water Walk by the Villa d'Este* (New York: St. Martin's Press, 1959). RE's blurb on front flap of dust jacket.

D4 Melvin Walker LaFollette, *The Clever Body* (San Francisco: Spenserian Press, 1959). RE's blurb on back of card cover.

D5 George Abbe, *Collected Poems 1932-1961* (Peterborough, N.H.: Richard R. Smith Co., 1961). RE's blurb on back of dust jacket.

D6 Isabella Gardner, *The Looking Glass* (Chicago: Univ. of Chicago Press, 1961). RE's blurb on back of card cover.

D7 Dilys Laing, *Poems from a Cage* (New York: Macmillan, 1961). RE's blurb on back of card cover.

D8 Mary Oliver, *No Voyage and Other Poems* (Boston: Houghton, Mifflin, 1965). RE's blurb on back flap of dust jacket (cloth issue) and back of card cover (Paperback issue).

D9 Robert Dawson, *Six Mile Corner* (Boston: Houghton, Mifflin, 1966). RE's blurb on back of dust jacket.

D10 Civille Handy, *Earth House* (Wenatchee, Wash.: Creative Aids for Education, 1968). RE's blurb on back of card cover.

D11 *The Shivurrus Plant of Mopant*, comp. by Gerald Hausman (Santa Fe, N.M.: Giligia Press, 1968). RE's blurb on front flap of dust jacket.

D12 Richard Moore, *A Question of Survival* (Athens: Univ. of Georgia, 1971). RE's blurb on printed yellow card laid in at back of clear glassine dust jacket.

D13 Muriel Rukeyser, *The Seed of Darkness* (New York: Vintage Books, 1971). RE's blurb on back of card cover.

D14 Scott Donaldson, *Poet in America: Winfield Townley Scott* (Austin: Univ. of Texas, 1972). RE's blurb on back of dust jacket.

D15 *Straw for the Fire: From the Notebooks of Theodore Roethke 1943-1963*, ed. David Wagoner (Garden City, N.Y.: Anchor Books, 1972). RE's blurb on back of card cover.

D16 Carlos Baker, *The Gay Head Conspiracy* (New York: Scribner's, 1973). RE's blurb on front flap of dust jacket.

D17 Jean Garrigue, *Studies for an Actress* (New York: Macmillan, 1973). RE's blurb on back of dust jacket.

D18 Muriel Rukeyser, *Breaking Open* (New York: Random House, 1973). RE's blurb on back of dust jacket.

D19 Mahmoud Darweesh, *Splinters of Bone* (trans. by B.M. Bennani) (Greenfield Center, N.Y.: Greenfield Review Press, 1974). RE's blurb on back of card cover.

D20 Andrew Glaze, *A Masque of Surgery* (London: Menard Press, 1974). RE's blurb (excpt. from *NYTBR*) on back of card cover.

D21 Leo Connellan, *Another Poet in New York* (New York: Living Poets Press, 1975). RE's blurb on back of dust jacket (cloth issue) and back of card cover (paperback issue).

D22 Anne Marx, *Hear of Israel* (Francestown, N.H.: Quill Press, 1975). RE's blurb on back of dust jacket.

D23 Ralph J. Mills, Jr., *Cry of the Human: Essays on Contemporary American Poetry* (Urbana: Univ. of Illinois, 1975). RE's blurb on front flap of dust jacket.

D24 Philip Booth, *Available Light* (New York: Viking, 1976). RE's blurb on back of dust jacket.

D25 Leo Connellan, *First Selected Poems* (Pittsburgh, Pa.: Univ. of Pittsburgh, 1976). RE's blurb on front flap of dust jacket (cloth issue) and on back of card cover (paperback issue).

D26 Hans Juergensen, *Journey Toward the Roots* (Petersburg, Fla.: Valkyrie Press, 1976). RE's blurb on front flap of dust jacket (cloth issue) and on back of card cover (paperback issue).

D27 David Posner, *The Sandpipers: Selected Poems (1965-1975)* (Gainesville: Univ. Presses of Florida, 1976). RE's blurb on back of dust jacket.

D28 Leon Stokesbury, *Often in Different Landscapes* (Austin: Univ. of Texas, 1976). RE's blurb on back of dust jacket (cloth issue) and on back of card cover (paperback issue).

D29 Eve Triem, *The Process: Poems 1960-1975* (Seattle, Wash.: Querencia, 1976). RE's blurb on back of dust jacket.

D30 Donald E. Axinn, *Sliding Down the Wind* (Chicago: Swallow Press, 1977). RE's blurb on back of dust jacket.

D31 Robert Huff, *The Ventriloquist: New and Selected Poems* (Charlottesville: Univ. Press of Virginia, 1977). RE's blurb on back flap of dust jacket.

D32 Douglas Lawder, *Trolling* (Boston: Little, Brown, 1977). RE's blurb on back flap of dust jacket.

D33 Sallie Nixon, *Second Grace* (Durham, N.C.: Moore Publishing, 1977). RE's blurb on back of card cover.

D34 Anthony Ostroff, *A Fall in Mexico* (Garden City, N.Y.: Doubleday, 1977). RE's blurb on back of card cover.

D35 William Packard, *First Selected Poems* (New York: Pylon Press, 1977). RE's blurb on back of card cover.

D36 Nicholas Rinaldi, *The Resurrection of the Snails and Other Poems* (Winston-Salem, N.C.: John F. Blair, 1977). RE's blurb on back of dust jacket (cloth issue) and on back of card cover (paperback issue).

D37 Edmund Skellings, *Face Value* (Orlando, Fla.: Univ. Presses of Florida, 1977). RE's blurb on back of dust jacket.

D38 Leo Connellan, *Death in Lobster Land* (Fort Kent, Maine: Great Raven Press, 1978). RE's blurb on back of card cover.

D39 Nixeon Civille Handy, *Earth House* (Wenatchee, Wash.: Creative Arts for Education, 1978). RE's blurb on back of dust jacket.

D40 Edmund Pennant, *Dream's Navel* (Roanoke, Va.: Lintel, 1979). RE's blurb on back of card cover.

D41 Timothy Steele, *Uncertainties and Rest* (Baton Rouge: Louisiana State University Press, 1979). RE's blurb on front flap of dust jacket.

D42 Theodore Weiss, *Views and Spectacles: New and Selected Shorter Poems* (New York: Macmillan, 1979). RE's blurb on back of card cover.

D43 Douglas Worth, *Triptych* (Cambridge, Mass.: Apple-Wood Press, 1979). RE's blurb on back of dust jacket (cloth issue) and on back of card cover (paperback issue).

D44 Janet Burroway, *Material Goods* (Orlando: Univ. Presses of Florida, 1980). RE's blurb on back of paper boards.

D45 Lola Haskins, *Planting the Children* (Orlando: Univ. Presses of Florida, 1980). RE's blurb on back of paper boards.

D46 Anne Marx, *Face Lifts for All Seasons* (Francestown, N.H.: Golden Quill Press, 1980). RE's blurb on back of dust jacket.

D47 Raymond Roseliep, *Listen to Light* (Ithaca, N.Y.: Alembric Press, 1980). RE's blurb on back of dust jacket.

D48 Robert Siegel, *In a Pig's Eye* (Orlando: Univ. Presses of Florida, 1980). RE's blurb on back of paper boards.

D49 Leo Connellan, *Massachusetts Poems* (Chester, Mass.: Hollow Spring Press, 1981). RE's blurb on back of card cover.

D50 Stephen Corey, *The Last Magician* (Huntington, N.Y.: Water Mark Press, 1981). RE's blurb on back of card cover.

D51 Andrew Glaze, *I Am the Jefferson County Courthouse and Other Poems* (Birmingham, Ala.: Thunder City Press, 1981). RE's blurb (excpt. from *NYTRB*) on back of card cover.

D52 *Of Solitude and Silence: Writings on Robert Bly*, ed. Richard Jones and Kate Daniels (Boston: Beacon Press, 1981). RE's blurb on back of dust jacket.

D53 Raymond McCarty, *Trumpet in the Twilight of Time* (Memphis, Tenn.: Volunteer Publications, 1981). RE's blurb on back of dust jacket.

D54 Richard Meade, *Swimming the Channel* (Chicago: Storm Press, 1981). RE's blurb on back of dust jacket (Cloth issue) and on back of card cover (paperback issue).

D55 Richard Moore, *Empires* (Princeton, N.J.: Ontario Review Press, 1981). Re's blurb on back of dust jacket.

D56 Dean Pumphrey, *Sheltered at the Edge* (Atascadero, Ca.: Solo Press, 1981). RE's blurb on back of card cover.

D57 Robert Siegel, *Whalesong* (Westchester, Ill.: Crossway Books, 1981). RE's blurb on back flap of dust jacket.

D58 Larry Brenner, *Drinking in the Spirit* (Cambridge, Mass.: Sin Press, 1982). RE's blurb on back of card cover.

D59 Hans Juergensen, *The Record of a Green Planet* (Baltimore: Linden Press, 1982). RE's blurb on back of card cover.

D60 Sydney Lea, *The Floating Candles* (Urbana: Univ. of Illinois, 1982). RE's blurb on back of dust jacket (cloth issue) and on back of card cover (paperback issue).

D61 Julia Older, *Oonts and Others* (Greensboro, N.C.: Unicorn, 1982). RE's blurb on back of card cover.

D62 Jay Parini, *Anthracite Country* (New York: Random House, 1982). RE's blurb on back of dust jacket (cloth issue) and back of card cover (paperback issue).

D63 Nicholas Rinaldi, *We Have Lost Our Fathers* (Orlando: Univ. Presses of Florida, 1982). RE's blurb on back of paper boards.

D64 Vivian Shipley, *Jack Tales* (Greenfield Center, N.Y.: Greenfield Review Press, 1982). RE's blurb on back of card cover.

D65 Leo Connellan, *Shatterhouse* (Chester, Mass.: Hollow Spring Press, 1983). RE's blurb on back of card cover.

D66 Lyn Lifshin, *Madonna Who Shifts for Herself* (Long Beach, Ca.: Applebaza Press, 1983). RE's blurb on back of card cover.

D67 Cedric Williams, *Chocorua and Other Poems* (Dublin, N.H.: Willaim L. Bauhan, 1983). RE's blurb on back of dust jacket.

D68 Norman Friedman, *The Magic Badge: Poems 1953-1984* (Austin, Tex.: Slough Press, 1984). RE's blurb on back of card cover.

D69 J.W. von Goethe, *Faust I and II*, trans. Stuart Atkins (Boston: Suharkamp/Insel, 1984). RE's blurb on back of dust jacket.

D70 Robert A. Brooks. *Roman Epistle* (Dublin, N.H.: William L. Bauhan, 1984). RE's blurb on back of card cover.

D71 Sandra M. Gilbert, *Emily's Bread* (New York: Norton, 1984). RE's blurb on back of dust jacket (cloth issue) and on back of card cover (paperback issue).

D72 Lola Haskins, *Castings* (Woodstock, Vt.: Countryman Press, 1984). RE's blurb on back of card cover.

D73 Marc Kaminsky, *The Road From Hiroshima* (New York: Simon and Schuster, 1984). RE's blurb on back of dust jacket.

D74 Bink Noll, *The House* (Baton Rouge: Louisiana State Univ. Press, 1984). RE's blurb on back of card cover.

D75 Edmund Pennant, *Misapprehensions* (Roanoke, Va.: Lintel, 1984). RE's blurb on back of card cover.

D76 Rosanna Warren, *Each Leaf Shines Separate* (New York: Norton, 1984). RE's blurb on back of dust jacket. *Note:* RE's blurb first appeared on a flyer accompanying Rosanna Warren's *Snow Day* (Winston-Salem, N.C.: Palaemon, 1981).

D77 Leo Connellan, *The Clear Blue Lobster-Water Country* (New York: Harcourt, Brace, Jovanovich, 1985). RE's blurb on back of dust jacket (cloth issue) and on back of card cover (paperback issue).

D78 Ralph Harper, *The Sleeping Beauty* (New York: Cowley, 1985). RE's blurb on back of card cover.

D79 Robert Huff, *Shore Guide to Flocking Names* (Bellingham, Waash.: Fanferon Press, 1985). RE's blurb on back of card cover.

D80 Anne Marx, *A Further Semester* (Dublin, N.H.: William L. Bauhan, 1985). RE's blurb on back of dust jacket.

D81 William Packard, *Saturday Night at San Marcos* (New York: Thunder's Mouth Press, 1985). RE's blurb on back of dust jacket.

D82 Thelma Parker, *The Sacred Round* (Anacortes, Wash.: Island Publishers, 1985). RE's blurb on back of card cover.

D83 Nicholas Rinaldi, *Bridge Fall Down* (New York: St. Martin's, 1985). RE's blurb on back of dust jacket.

D84 Nicholas Rinaldi, *The Luftwaffe in Chaos* (Mobile, Ala.: Negative Capability Press, 1985). RE's blurb on front flap of dust jacket.

D85 Edmund Skellings, *Living Proof* (Miami: Florida International Univ. Press, 1985). RE's blurb on back of dust jacket.

D86 Dave Smith, *Local Assays* (Urbana: Univ. of Illinois, 1985). Re's blurb on front flap of dust jacket.

D87 "The Twentieth Annual Poetry Awards" (Long Island Univ., N.Y., C.W. Post Campus, 16 April 1986). RE's blurbs contained on front and back card cover.

D88 Liesel Mueller, *Second Language* (Baton Rouge: Louisiana State Univ. Press, 1986). RE's blurb on back of dust jacket.

D89 Harry Crews, *All We Need of Hell* (New York: Harper & Row, 1987). RE's blurb on back flap of dust jacket.

D90 Kate Kelly, *Barking at Sunspots* (New York: Justin Books, 1987). RE's blurb on back of card cover.

D91 Natalie Safir, *To Face the Inscription* (La Jolla, Ca.: La Jolla Poets Press, 1987). RE's blurb on back of card cover.

D92 Caitlin Thomas, with George Tremlett, *Caitlin: Life With Dylan Thomas* (New York: Henry Holt, 1987). RE's blurb on back of dust jacket.

E
Interviews and Published Comments

E1 "On Campus." *Wheaton Alumnae Quarterly*, January 1955, 22-23. Article about RE, which includes his comments on being at Wheaton as poet-in-residence, and on poetry in general.

E2 "Eberhart Reads Poetry, Traces Literary Career." *Dartmouth* (Dartmouth College, Hanover, N.H., student newspaper), 12 Oct. 1956, p. 1. Article that includes RE's quoted comments on poetry in general, as well as his statement, "As a mobile is suspended from the ceiling, poetry is suspended from the soul."

E3 "The December 27th Meeting." *PSA Bulletin* (The Poetry Society of America), 47 (January 1957). Includes quoted or paraphrased comments by RE, pp. 4-6.

E4 Robert Sussman, "Studying with Richard Eberhart." *Dartmouth*, 21 Feb. 1957, p. 2. Article that includes RE's quoted comments on the subjective nature of poetry; how poetry "defines" him; and teaching poetry.

E5 W. Thomas Hyuck, "Dame Edith Sitwell." *Dartmouth*, 30 April 1957, p. 2. Article that includes a brief quoted comment by RE on Dame Edith Sitwell.

E6 "Birth of a Poem." *Nation's Schools*, 63 (March 1959), 68. Article that includes RE's brief quoted comments on how art "should be universal" and on the dichotomy between the serious and not-so-serious poets in America.

E7 "Should Teach Poetry Early, Eberhart Advises Teachers." *Washington* (D.C.) *Post*, 25 Oct. 1959, p. 18 (A). Unsigned article that includes RE's comments on the teaching of poetry.

E8 Untitled comments by RE on his work, in *Current Biography*, 22 (Jan. 1961), 22-24.

E9 Mark A. Roseman, "Professor Richard Eberhart Honored; Poet Wins Bollingen Prize from Yale." *The Dartmouth*, 9 Jan. 1962, p. 1. Article that includes RE's quoted comments on receiving the Bollingen Prize, as well as his brief reminiscences on his student years at Dartmouth.

E10 David H. Bowman, "Richard Eberhart: Two Plays." *The Dartmouth*, 4 April 1962, p. 2. Article that includes RE's brief paraphrased comments on his verse-plays, "The Mad Musician" and "Devils and Angels."

E11 Bourne Ruthrauff, "Poet Eberhart Discusses Tragedy; Cites Modern Audience Inadequacy—Informally Analyzes Own Poems." *Daily Pennsylvanian* (Univ. of Pennsylvania), 5 April 1962, p. 1. Article based on an interview that includes RE's quoted comments on tragedy, with *Hamlet* as example, and on his own poems and the transcendental nature of many of them.

E12 M.B.A, "Nor of Mind." *Daily Pennsylvanian*, 9 April 1962, p. 3. Article based on an interview that includes RE's quoted comments on the birth of a poem as a "miracle"; the Beats, especially Allen Ginsberg; poets and academia; and the current situation of poetry in the U.S.

E13 "Philo Speakers Dispute U.S. Attitude on Poetry." *Daily Pennsylvanian*, 11 April 1962, p. 1. Article that includes a brief quoted statement from RE on contemporary American poetry, which he sees in a "vigorous state."

E14 Tom Jones, "Eberhart Compares Trancendentalist Emerson with Modern Poet Stevens." *Trinity Tripod* (Trinity College, Hartford, Conn.), 23 April 1963, pp. 1, 2. Article based on an interview, containing lengthy quoted comments on Ralph Waldo Emerson and Wallace Stevens.

E15 "Eberhart Edits Undergraduate Poems." *Dartmouth*, 1 Nov. 1963, pp. 1, 2. Article that includes RE's brief quoted comments on *Thirty-Five Dartmouth Poems*.

E16 Fanny Butcher, "Mencken Has the Last laugh." *Chicago Tribune Magazine of Books*, 17 Nov. 1963, p. 4. Article based on an interview that includes RE's paraphrased comments on H.L. Mencken.

E17 Jeffrey Marshall, "An Interview with Richard Eberhart." *William and Mary Review*, 2 (Winter 1964), 1-14. In *OPP*. Topics include relativism and absolutism in poetry; Tennyson and other early influences on RE's poetry; poets RE admires, including Wallace Stevens, William Carlos Williams, W.H. Auden, Stephen Spender, C. Day-Lewis, and Louis MacNeice; RE's problems with modern poetry; why today's students "fear" poetry; RE's verse plays; organizational and institutional promotion of poetry; "The Groundhog" and other early poems.

E18 "Eberhart's Adaptation of de Vega Verse Drama Appears as *The Bride from Mantua*." *Dartmouth*, 2 April 1964, p. 2. Article that includes RE's quoted comments on his adaptation of Lope de Vega's *El Castigo sin Veranza*.

E19 Denis Donoghue, "An Interview with Richard Eberhart." *Shenandoah*, 15 (Summer 1964), 6-29. In *OPP*. Topics include place and time in poetry; RE as a poet of "large themes"; Wallace Stevens and William Carlos Williams; RE's poem "On the Fragility of the Mind"; Wordsworth as influence; RE's World War II poems; T.S. Eliot and Christian poets; and RE's Maine poems.

E20 "Speaker Explains Role of Poet." *Syracuse* (N.Y.) *Herald Journal*, 9 April 1965, p. 2. Article based on an interview that includes RE's quoted comments on poetry and science.

E21 Larry Steinman, "Richard Eberhart Awarded Pulitzer Prize for Recent Publication of Selected Poems." *Dartmouth*, 3 May 1966, p. 1. Article based on an interview that includes RE's quoted comments on receiving the Pulitzer Prize for his *Selected Poems*.

E22 William J. Cardoso, "Pulitzer Prize for Poetry Goes to Richard Eberhart." *Valley News* (Lebanon, N.H.), 3 May 1966, p. 1. Article based on an interview that includes RE's quoted comments on receiving the Pulitzer Prize, as well as on his poetry in general.

E23 Fergus Hoffman, "Pulitzer Prize Poem Born Here." *Seattle Post-Intelligencer*, 4 May 1966, p. 4(A). Article based on an interview that includes RE's quoted comments on his visit to Seattle in 1956, and his poem "The Noble Man."

E24 John Dorsey, "Richard Eberhart Reads, Talks at Goucher." *Baltimore Sun Magazine*, 18 Dec. 1966, pp. 9, 11. Article based on an interview that includes RE's quoted comments on "The Groundhog"; poetic influences; an earlier visit to Baltimore (with Robert Lowell and John Holmes); teaching; "The Cancer Cells"; the interpretation of poetry; and "The Sacrifice."

E25 Michael Drapkin, "Poet-Prof Rhymes Delightful Paradox." *Pittsburgh Press*, 16 Feb. 1967, p. 1 (B). Article based on an interview that includes RE's quoted comments on his belief in "inspiration"; work habits; and his poem "Marrakech".

E26 Fergus Hoffman, "A Pulitzer Prize Poet Faces Life, Rain." *Seattle Post-Intelligencer*, 29 March 1967, p. 13. Article based on an interview that includes RE's quoted comments on his cross-country drive to Washington; the "waning" of the Beat movement, but how Allen Ginsberg's work has sustaining power; and himself and other poets (Dylan Thomas, Theodore Roethke, and Allen Ginsberg) as "celebrationists" (RE's term): "They do not shrink from life; they face it to the full."

E27 Sue Lockett, "Prof. Sees Spiritualism as True Poetic Concern." *University of Washington Daily* (Seattle), 30 March 1967, p. 4. Article based on an interview that includes RE's paraphrased comments on how the experiences of life result in poetry; teaching; and poetry as an inspired process, with remarks on his contemporaries in general.

E28 Julie Emery, "Visiting Poet Performs 'Aerial Wizardry'." *Seattle* (Wash.) *Times*, 7 May 1967, p. 7(A), with photograph of RE on p. 3(A). Article based on an interview that includes RE's quoted comments on kite-flying; his inability to write occasional poems; and his desire through poetry "to make the world anew."

E29 Untitled comments by RE on Marianne Moore, in *PSA Bulletin* (Poetry Society of America), 57 (May 1967), 15-16. RE's poem, "To Marianne Moore on Her 80th Birthday" is contained on p. 16.

E30 Untitled comments on living in Princeton, N.J., in *Princeton University Library Chronicle*, 29 (Autumn 1967), 70-71.

E31 Chuck Thegze, "Poetess Discusses Poetry." *Dartmouth*, 23 Oct. 1967, p. 2. Article about Carolyn Kizer that includes RE's quoted comments on Kizer.

E32 Elizabeth P. Nadas, "Richard Eberhart." *Harvard Crimson*, 5 March 1968, p. 2. Article based on an interview that includes RE's quoted comments on poetry and the Vietnam War; his Christian beliefs; and his particular belief in "ultimate mysteries."

E33 William Durrett, "An Interview with Richard Eberhart." *Brogue* (Belhaven College, Jackson, Miss., student literary magazine), 1 (Summer 1968), 12-20. Topics include politics and poetry; "moral" poetry; Robert Penn Warren; writing poetry as a "mysterious" act; changes in his recent poems *(Shifts of Being)*; the revision process; T.S. Eliot and William Carlos Williams; writing habits; and the public reaction to his poetry.

E34 Jay Farness, "Poet Eberhart's Reality Harbors Man in Nature." *Manotou Messenger*, (St. Olaf College, Northfield, Minn.), 11 Oct. 1968, p. 8. Article based on an interview. Topics include living in New England; poetic influences; and reading his poems in public.

E35 "Poets, Society, and Religion." *Lutheran Witness*, 87 (Nov. 1968), 20-22. Includes RE's quoted comments to a symposium, "Poets, Society, and Religion," on pp. 20, 22.

E36 Carol Neef, "Poet Says Verse Reveals an Age." *Tampa* (Fla.) *Tribune*, 16 April 1969, p. 2 (B). Article based on an interview that includes RE's comments on how poetry expresses the times; the "generalizing power" of poetry; place of poetry in the world; and "cold and hot" poetry.

E37 William G. Jasperjohn, "Eberhart to Give Poetry Readings." *Dartmouth*, 23 May 1969, p. 1. Article that includes RE's quoted comments on his "compulsion" to say what he has to say in poetry.

E38 "The Function of Poetry." *MLA Newsletter*, 1 (Nov. 1969), p. 1. Article that includes excerpts from RE's remarks (prepared and informal) on the purpose of poetry to members attending a session of the 1968 Modern Language Association meeting at Chicago.

E39 David K. Aylward, "New Anthology Includes Eberhart." *Dartmouth*, 26 Oct. 1970, p. 2. Article based on an interview that includes RE's quoted comments on his inclusion in Whit Burnett's *This Is My Best* (**B100**).

E40 David Nix, "Is Poetry Dead? Not to Eberhart." (Tucson) *Arizona Daily Star*, 3 March 1971, p. 6(C). Article based on an interview that includes RE's quoted comments on student writing; the "vigorous state" of contemporary poetry; William Carlos Williams and Wallace Stevens; viewing himself as "metaphysical and contemplative'; and his recent "political" poems.

E41 "Poetry Readings." *Sophian* (Smith College, Northhampton, Mass., student newspaper), 22 April 1971, p. 5. Brief article that includes RE's quoted comments on his "poetry collection," based on his informal address to the Smith College Friends of the Library.

E42 Rosalie Seltz, "Early Austin Years Are Recalled by Fames Poet." *Austin* (Minn.) *Daily Herald*, 22 may 1971, p. 1. Article based on an interview that includes RE's quoted comments on his childhood in Austin.

E43 Rosalie Seltz, "Eberhart Voices Meaning of Life at AHS Graduation." *Austin Daily Herald*, 4 June 1971, p. 1. Article that contains excerpts from RE's commencement address as well as quoted and paraphrased comments on the war in Vietnam.

E44 Joel Foley, "Poet Richard Eberhart Captivates Wachusett." *Reflections* (Waschusett Regional High School, Holden, Mass., student magazine), Dec. 1971, p. 1. Interview. Topics include RE's beginnings as a poet; writing habits; and early influences on his poetry.

E45 John Kaminski, "Richard Eberhart Hits Zenith of U.S. Poetry." *Valley News* (Lebanon, N.H.), 11 Jan. 1973, pp. 1, 3. Article based on an interview. Includes RE's quoted comments on the importance of poetry; his dislike of "elitism" in poetry; Yevtushenko; and teaching poetry.

E46 Michael Cannito et al., "An Interview with Richard Eberhart." *Pulse* (Lamar University, Beaumont, Tex.), (Spring 1973), 10-15. In *OPP*. Rept. in *Rectangle* (publication of Sigma Tau Delta), 50 (Spring 1975), 4-17. Topics include RE's writing habits and the creative act; "The Groundhog"; the "endless possibilities of poetry"; poems he admires, especially William Carlos Williams, Wallace Stevens, and Robert Frost; "New Hampshire, February"; Gerard Manley Hopkins; D.H. Lawrence; the role of the poet; the dialectic between humanism and mysticism in RE's poetry; and his advice to young poets.

E47 Dee Roe, "Poet Relates Experiences." *The Review* (University of Delaware, Newark, student newspaper), 10 April 1973, pp. 11, 13. Article based on an interview. Includes RE's quoted comments on the spiritual nature of poetry; how his poem "Evil" is a personal response to the war in Vietnam; and his experience in World War II.

E48 Untitled remarks on Jean Garrigue, rept. from his eulogy, delivered 3 Feb. 1973, at St. Luke's Chapel, New York City, in *Poetry Pilot*, October 1974, p. 10. *Note*: RE was guest editor of this issue.

E49 David Dodd, "Eberhart Brings His Poetry to the Cow Town." *California Aggie* (Univ. of California, Davis), 3 Nov. 1975, p. 7. Interview. Topics include the purpose of poetry; RE's poems "The Cancer Cells" and "For a Lamb"; and the varied interpretations of some of his poems.

E50 Del McColm, "Vivid Poet, Rare Teacher." *Davis* (Cal.) *Enterprise*, 28 Nov. 1975, p. 6. Article based on an interview. Includes RE's quoted comments on the state on contemporary American poetry; teaching poetry; Bob Dylan and "popular" poetry; and his career as a poet.

E51 Jane Bonin, "Richard Eberhart: Some Thoughts on Verse Drama." *Southwestern Review* (Univ. of Southwestern Louisiana, Lafayette), Spring 1976, 14-17. Topics include the Poet's Theatre and "The Visionary Farms."

E52 Donnel Nunes, "With a Touch of the Poet." *Washington Post*, 18 July 1976, pp. 1, 2(E). Article based on an interview. Includes RE's quoted comments on poetry and truth; the "changing nature of things"; and Maine. *Note*: This article was rept. under different titles as "Trying to Be a Truth-Sayer" *(Newsday)*; "No Poet Gets the Success He'd Wanted" (Wilmington, Del., *Evening Journal*); "The Poet Laureate Wore Bermuda Shorts" *(Milwaukee Journal)*; and "Prize-Winning Poet Still Searching for Truth at 72" (New Orleans, La., *Times-Picayune*).

E53 David Bianculli, "A Poet Talks About His Craft." *Gainesville* (Fla.) *Sun*, 7 Nov. 1976, pp. 4-6. Interview. Topics include growing up in Austin, Minn.; influence of Tennyson on his work; teaching at Dartmouth; the "spiritual basis" of poetry; student years at Cambridge; RE's life as a poet; and the continuing influence of Wordsworth, Blake, and Hopkins.

E54 Reed Sparling, "Eberhart: 50 Years of Poetry." *Dartmouth*, 19 Nov. 1976, pp. 1, 10. Article based on an interview. Includes RE's quoted comments on poetry as a "way of discovering the depths of life"; his efforts as "obsessive and dynamic"; poetry as a "social act"; his pleasure at the waning of the New Criticism; and "time as the great examiner" of all poetry.

E55 John Simsen, "73-Year-Old Poet Driven by 'Psychic Energy'." *Alligator* (Univ. of Florida, Gainesville, student newspaper), 20 April 1977, p. 16. Article based on an interview. Includes RE's quoted comments on his own work and how he is getting "stronger all the time."

E56 Lisanne Renner, "Prize-Winning Poet Nurtures Student Work." *Alligator* ("Entertainment supplement), 20 April 1977, p. 6. Article based on an interview. Includes RE's quoted comments on his early poetry; the influence of Tennyson on his work; the purpose of poetry; World War II; the poet's interaction with the "real world"; teaching poetry; and the universality of poetry.

E57 Irv Broughton, "An Interview with Richard Eberhart." *American Poetry Review*, 6 (May-June 1977), 30-36. In *OPP*. Topics include RE's definition of "major poet"; suicide and death as themes in poetry; Blake and Borges; the "desert island trick" of evaluating poetry; A.E. Housman; hero worship; democracy and poetry; love as a topic in RE's poetry; imagination and poetry; why RE could not be a "hermit" poet; I.A. Richards; D.H. Lawrence; criticism of RE's publishing too much; the poet's obligation to poetry; Robert Lowell; responding to criticism; Rebert Frost; risks the writer takes; religious poets; Graves and Yeats; music and poetry; and the Poets' Theatre.

E58 David Bianculli, "Eberhart Is Ambivalent' About Book Award." *Gainesville Sun* ("Sunday" supplement), 1 May 1977, p. 13. Article that includes RE's quoted comments on receiving the 1977 National Book Award for poetry.

E59 William Packard, "Visit with Eberhart." *New York Times Book Review*, 1 Jan. 1978, pp. 10, 20-21. Interview. Topics include poetry as a career; criticism; "The Groundhog"; "The Bells of a Chinese Temple"; and democratic institutions. *Note*: An unknown number of offprints of this interview, on pale yellow wove paper, were prepared for distribution by RE and Packard; one leaf printed on both sides.

E60 "Craft Interview with Richard Eberhart." *New York Quarterly*, no. 20 (1978), 16-26. In *OPP*. Topics include RE's writing habits; his poem "Hardening into Print"; revision of his work; poetry workshops; his feelings about the writer's isolation; contemporary poetic style and form; and choosing models for one's work.

E61 Ruth Dean, "The State of Poetry in America." *Washington Star*, 6 March 1978, pp. 1(A), 4(D). Article based on an interview that includes RE's quoted comments on the contemporary poetry scene, on p. 1(A) only.

E62 Michael Kernan, "13 Bards, and Prose in Praise of Poetry." *Washington Post*, 7 March 1978, pp. 1, 11(C). Article based on an interview that includes RE's quoted comments on verse drama, on p. 11(C) only.

E63 Charles G. Bolte, "Poet at Full Ahead." *Dartmouth Alumni Magazine*, 71 (Sept. 1978), 36-38. Article that includes RE's quoted comments on Dartmouth and spending his summers in Maine.

E64 Margaret Thomson Shonbrun, "Richard Eberhart Is Singing Because He's a Poet." *Gainesville Sun*, 5 April 1979, p. 1 (B). Rev. on *Of Poetry and Poets* that includes RE's quoted comments from a conversation on his poetry specifically, and on poetry in general.

E65 Stephanie Henkel, "A Heart Still Wonder-Welling." *Concord* (N.H.) *Monitor*, 21 Sept. 1979, pp. 1, 14. Article based on an interview that includes RE's quoted comments on Allen Ginsberg's *Howl*; his Christian beliefs; Wordsworth, Blake and Hopkins as his primary influences; poems as "spells against death"; and his work habits.

E66 C.A. Bustard, "Poet Eberhart Feels Tug of Senses." *Richmond* (Va.) *Times-Dispatch*, 19 Nov. 1979, p. 1 (C). Article based on an interview that includes RE's quoted comments on his recent work; Robert Frost; kinds of poetic language; and his contemporaries in general.

E67 Sue Walker, "Interview with Richard Eberhart." *Negative Capability*, 2 (Summer 1982), 16-28. Topics include the "creation" of poems; "The Groundhog"; teaching poetry; free verse; negative capability as a means of dealing with the will to create; T.S. Eliot, especially "Prufrock" and "The Wasteland"; RE's advice to young poets; Anne Sexton; vanity publishing; and his changing attitudes towards writing.

.

E68 Nancy Robertson, "Newport Honors the State's Poet." *Valley News*, 27 Aug. 1982, pp. 1, 10. Article based on an interview that includes RE's quoted comments on the profession of poetry; reaching an audience through poetry; Eliot and Pound; "A Maine Roustabout"; and recent work.

E69 Alan Mark, "Themes of Recurrence and Unity in the Vision of an American Poet. An Interview with Richard Eberhart." *The Student* (Wake Forest Univ., Winston-Salem, N.C., undergraduate literary magazine), Fall 1982, 32-38. Topics include RE's poems about death; the Beat poets; Pound; Dante; RE's writing habits; how many readers miss the "meaning" in his poems; Robert Frost; RE's verse plays; how his vision of the Greek spirit colors his poetry; his technique and the process of revision. *Note*: "For a Lamb" is rept. on p. 38, and "The Cancer Cells" on p. 39.

E70 "People" (column), *Vox* (Dartmouth College alumni newspaper), 6-26 June 1983, p. 6. Article that includes RE's quoted comments on the purpose of the American Academy of Arts and Letters.

E71 Jay Parini, "Richard Eberhart at Eighty: The Long Reach of Talent." *Dartmouth Alumni Magazine*, 77 (Sept. 1984), 45-48. Article that includes brief quoted comments from RE.

E72 Sue Walker, "Interview with Richard Eberhart." *Negative Capability* (special RE number), 6 (Spring-Summer, 1986), 97-111. Topics include "The Groundhog" and "The Soul Longs to Return Whence It Came"; I.A. Richards and R.P. Blackmur as friends and influences; critics; teaching poetry; Auden and St. Mark's School; Ruth Hershberger; influences on his poetry, especially Tennyson; his mother's early death and how it influenced his work; his relationship with his English publishers; writing habits; and work-in-progress.

E73 Nardi Reeder Campion, "The Poet at 82." *American Heritage*, 38 (Feb.-March 1987), pp. 46-47. Brief article based on an interview that includes RE's quoted comments on St. Mark's School; his service in World War II; and writing poetry. *N.B.*: This article accompanies **C853**.

F
Material Duplicated from Typescript

The items in this section were originally reproduced by spirit duplication process from RE's typescript original, on rectos only, unless noted otherwise. Yellowish white duplicator paper measures 11 x 8 1/2 in. Watermarks are described as following: Paper A is watermarked with an orb traversed by parallel rules between which is '*Standard*' and '*DUPLICATOR I COPY PAPER I MADE IN U.S.A*'; Paper B is watermarked '[in open face] S M M CO I DUPLICATOR I [in roman] MADE IN U.S.A.'; Paper C: '[in script] Nekoosa I [in roman] DUPLICATOR I MADE IN U.S.A.'; Paper D: '[open face script] NEKOOSA I [in roman] DUPLICATOR'; Paper E is watermarked 'GOLD LABEL I [rule] I A.B. DICK I [rule] I MIMEOGRAPH'; Paper F: row of 9 verticle single-rule frames with '[in open face] NEKOOSA I DUPLICATOR'; Paper G 'BOND I [open face script] Nekoosa'; Paper H 'INTERNATIONAL I [within an oblong oval] BUSINESS PAPER'; Paper I '[open face, 'E' within a sheild] I DUPLICATOR'.

> **F1** "Absolute Silence." Paper D. See **C639**.
> **F2** "Action and Poetry." Paper C. See **C525**.
> **F3** "Adam Cast Forth" (after Borges). Paper D. See **C622**.
> **F4** "Againt [sic] the Wood Thrush." Paper C. See **A27**.
> **F5** "Am I My Neighbor's Keeper?" Paper C. See **C487**.
> **F6** "American Hackluyt [sic]." Paper D. See **A39**.
> **F7** "And Today We Have the Playing of Names." Paper D.
> **F8** "Angles and Man." 3 unnumbered leaves. Paper D. See **C675**.
> **F9** "The Ascent." 2 leaves. Paper C. See **C518**.
> **F10** "As If You Had never Been." Paper D. See **C630**.
> **F11** "As It Is." Paper D.
> **F12** "The Assassin." Paper C. See **C519**.
> **F13** "At McSorley's Bar." Paper C. See **C534**.
> **F14** "Autumn." Paper C. See **C608**.
> **F15** "Ball Game." Paper C. See **C571**.
> **F16** "Balm of Iliad" (later titled "When I Think of Her the Power of Poetry Arises"). Paper A. See **C98**.
> **F17** "Ben Bellitt [sic] Reads His Poetry." Paper C. Announcement for reading, headed 'Professor Eberhart I 202 Sanborn I October 9, 1966'.
> **F18** "Big Rock." Paper D. See **C684**.
> **F19** "Boston." 3 leaves; [1] 2-3. Paper C. Dated '1/6/67' at top. See **B85**.

F20 "The Bower." Paper C. See **C586**.

F21 "The Breathless." Paper D. See **C626**.

F22 "The Bride from Mantua I by I Lope De Vega Carpio. I Put into verse form by Richard Eberhart.'. 68 numbered leaves. Hectographed from RE's typescript original, on rectos only; spiral bound in unprinted, pale yellow wrappers. *Note*: One copy in the compiler's collection is rubberstamped in green ink on the front wrapper in the author's holograph, 'Corrected copy I 11/15/63'. The play was produced by the Dartmouth Players, Hanover, N.H., on 5-9 May 1964.

F23 "Broken Wing Theory." Paper D. See **C658**.

F24 "Carolyn Kizer, noted poet..." 2 leaves, [1]-2. Paper C. Prose statement by RE for circulation among members of the Dartmouth College English Dept.

F25 "C. Day Lewis Lectures On I Thomas Hardy's Poetry." Paper C. Prose statement by RE for circulation among members of the Dartmouth College English Dept.

F26 "Charge to the Initiates of Phi Beta Kappa I Richard Eberhart April 25, 1985 The University of Florida, Gainesville." 3 leaves, [1] 2-3; unwatermarked paper. Reproduced from RE's typescript original by xerox process, for distribution to Phi Beta Kappa initiates, University of Florida, Gainesville.

F27 "Chocorua." (1964). 5 leaves, [1] 2-5. Paper C. First leaf contains RE's home address, the date 15 June 1964, and 'Trial Run'. *Note*: One copy in the compiler's collection contains RE's holograph note, "reworked Nov. 1 '69', with his revisions. See below **F28**.

F28 "Chocorua." (1969). 5 leaves, 1-5. Paper D. Revised version of F27. See **A53**. *Note*: The revised version also carries RE's home address on the first leaf, but differs in the dates listed at the conclusion of the poem (1964, 1969)'.

F29 "The Clam Diggers and Diggers of Sea Worms." Paper C. See above **C415**.

F30. "Cold White Death." Paper C. See above **C517**.

F31 "Colleoni of the Word." 2 unnumbered leaves. Paper C. See **C541**.

F32 "Creators." Unwatermarked Paper. See **C300**.

F33 "A Dance for Vance." Paper D. See **C739**.

F34 "Death in the Mines." Paper D. See **C636**.

F35 "Depths." Paper F. See **A58**.

F36 "Despair." Paper C. See **C615**.

F37 "Devils and Angels." First version. 29 leaves; one unnumbered leaf with title and list of characters, 1954, and Wheaton College, Norton, Mass., [1-28]. Unwatermarked paper. See **F38**.

F38 "Devils and Angels." Revised version. 26 leaves, numbered 1-26. Grayish white, unwatermarked paper. Hectographed from RE's typescript original, on rectos only. See **F37** and **C475**.

F39 "The Echoing Rocks." Paper C. See **C526**.

F40 "The Elegance of Stately Measures." Paper C. See **C455**.

F41 "The Enigma." Paper C. See **C575**.

F42 "Epitaph." Paper D.

F43 "Evil." Paper C. See **B100**.

F44 "Experience Is Like a Cloud of Summertime." Paper A.

F45 "The Explorer on Main Street." Unwatermarked paper. See **C556**.

F46 "The Extreme Water." Paper A. See **C138**.

F47 "The Face, The Axe, and Time." Paper C. See **A24**.

F48 "Face, Ocean." Paper D. See **C728**.

F49 "Far Out." Paper D. See **C701**.

F50 "The Fisher Cat." Unwatermarked paper. See **C644**.

F51 "Fishing for Snakes." Paper C. See **C522**.

F52 "Flow of Thought." Paper D. See **A39**.

F53 "For the Dartmouth Poetry Symposium January 1970." 2 unnumbered leaves. Paper D.

F54 "The Fort and the Gate." Unwatermarked paper; '(1975)' typed at base. See **C740**.

F55 "For What Can Warr, But Endless Warr Still Breed." Paper C.

F56 "[From 'Poem in Construction']. 4 unnumbered leaves. Unwatermarked paper. Contains "Compulsion in Hid in the Blood: Conflicts" (**B17**), "Analysis of a Turn of the Hand, or the Storm"; "This Hunger for Death is the Strangest Thing" (**F189**), and "The Incorruptibility of Nature."

F57 "From Poem in Construction ['And at lake Geneva, which is in Wisconsin,']." 2 leaves; [1]-2. Unwatermarked paper. See **C130**. *Note*: This section is identified by RE as '(x'.

F58 "From Poem in Construction ['Consider the more intricate and ingenius situations']." Unwatermarked paper. See **C128**. *Note:* Identified by RE as section 'c iii'.

F59 "From Sighting forthcoming from Chatto and Windus 1946." 4 leaves, each of which measures 15 x 8 1/2 in. Grayish white, unwatermarked paper. Hectographed from RE's typescript original, on rectos only, Contains "Ode to the Chinese Paper Snake" (**C168**), "For a Lamb" (**C64**), "The Fury of Aerial Bombardment" (**C161**), "Dam Neck, Virginia" (**C162**), and "The Helldiver Gunner" (**B26**).

F60 "The Full of Joy Do not Know; They Need Not." Paper B. See **A3**. *Note*: Original title at top of poem X-ed out by RE before making copies.

F61 "The Garden God." Paper C. See **C405**.

F62 "Gestures Rich in Purpose." Paper C. See **C515**.

F63 "Going to Class Under Greek Statues." Unwatermarked paper. Dated '11/54 2/55' at top. See **C336**.

F64 "Goners." Paper C. See **C675**.

F65 "Gulled." Paper C. See **C606**.

F66 "Hand-View." 2 unnumbered leaves. Unwatermarked paper. See **B17**.

F67 "Hardy Perennial." Paper C. See **C612**.

F68 "Harvard Summer School I Conference on I The Defense of Poetry I August 14-17 1950 I [Harvard emblem] I Harvard University I Cambridge 38, Massachusetts'. 166 leaves. Hectographed from typescript original on rectos only. Contains RE's contribution to the symposium, "Poets and Their Problems," on p. 140. See **C247**.

F69 "The Haystack." Paper C. See **C560**.

F70 "Here and Now." Paper C. See **C613**.

F71 "Hill Dream of Youth, Thirty Years Later." Paper C. See **C532**.

F72 "Homage to the North." Paper D. See **C631**.

F73 "Hoot Owls." Paper C. See **C396**.

F74 "The Hop-Toad." Paper D. See **C676**.

F75 "How Do I Further Spend My Glory?" Paper D. See **C689**.

F76 "How I Write Poetry." 23 leaves, [1] 2-23. Paper G. Hectographed from typescript original, on rectos only. See **B81** and **C304**. *Note*: At top of first (unnumbered) leaf, RE has typed 'VOICE OF AMERICA I CENTRAL SERVICES PROGRAM DIVISION I FORUM BRANCH', and at conclusion of final leaf, his address and 'Completed 12/27/63 1/14/64'.

F77 "The Icycle." Paper D. See **C633**.

F78 "The Ides of March." Paper C. See **C555**.

F79 "Idleness." Paper D. See **C642**.

F80 "The Illusion of Eternity." Paper C. See **C535**.

F81 "Inability to Depict an Eagle." Paper C. See **C595**.

F82 "The Incredible Splendor of the Magnificent Scene." Paper D. See **C597**.

F83 "Inchiquin Lake, Penobscot Bay." Paper D. See **C695**.

F84 "Insomnia." Paper D. See **C647**.

F85 "The Intractable Nature of Reality." Paper C.

F86 "I Saw a Horde of Ph.Ds [sic]." Unwatermarked paper.

F87 "Ives." Paper D. See **C448**.

F88 "John Ledyard." Paper C. See **C593**.

F89 "The Killer: On the Assassination of President Kennedy." Paper C. See **B74**.

F90 "Kinaesthesia." Paper C. See **B97**.

F91 "Life and Death: Jean Garrigue (1914-1972). Paper D. See **C706**.

F92 "Ladies and Gentlemen..." Paper C. 5 leaves, [1] 2-5. Address presented to the Modern Language Association, 27 December 1968. At top of first (unnumbered) leaf, 'Yaddo Dec. 19 1968'.

F93 "Life Words." Paper C.

F94 "Light, Time, Dark." 2 leaves, [1]-2. Paper C. See **C674**.

F95 "Lilting." Paper C.

F96 "Lions Copulating." Paper C. See **C562**.

F97 "Literary Death." 5 leaves, [1] 2-5. Paper D. See **C683**.

F98 "A Little While." Paper D.

F99 "Lofty Principle." Paper F.

F100 "Logos c. 1930." Paper D. See **C590**.

F101 "The Loosening." Unwatermarked paper. See **C627**.

F102 "Lorca." Paper D. See **C605**.

F103 "Love On." Paper D. See **C616**.

F104 "Love Sequence with Variations." 6 leaves, [1] 2-6. Unwatermarked paper. See **C655**.

F105 "The Mad Musicain." 39 leaves, [1] 2-39. Unwatermarked paper. Hectographed from RE's typescript original, on rectos only. See **C476**.

F106 "Man and Nature." Unwatermarked paper. See **C646**.

F107 "A Man of the Forties." Paper A. Dated 'September 1940' at base.

F108 "Man's Fate." Paper D. See **C610**.

F109 "A Man Who Was Blown Down by the Wind." Paper D. See **C601**.

F110 "Marrakech." Paper C. See **B90**.

F111 "The Mastery." Paper D. See **C554**.

F112 "The Matin Pandemoniums." Paper C. See **C529**.

F113 "Meaning Death." Unwatermarked paper.

F114 "Meaningless Poem." Paper D. See **C663**.

F115 "A Meditation." 31 leaves, [1] 2-31. Paper A. Dated 'September 1938' at top of first leaf.

F116 "Members of the English Department:" Paper C. Memo dated 'October 10, 1966', concerning a reading by Ben Belitt.

F117 "Mexico Phantasmagoria." 3 leaves, numbered 1-3. Paper C. See **C570**.

F118 "Mind and Nature." Unwatermarked paper. See **C725**.

F119 "Mistaken Identity." Paper F. See **C727**.

F120 "A Moment of Equilibrium Among the Islands." Unwatermarked paper. Hectographed from RE's typescript original, on recto only. See **C454**.

F121 "Music Over Words." Paper C. See **C565**.

F122 "Mysticism Has Not the Patience to Wait for God's Revelation." Paper A. Dated 'March 1940' at base. See **C122**.

F123 "New Love." Paper C. See **C544**.

F124 "New Vows." Paper D.

F125 "Nexus." Paper C. See **C431**.

F126 "Night Song." Paper C. See **B102**.

F127 "The Noble Man." Unwatermarked paper. See **C298**.

F128 "Notes on Poetry." 3 leaves, [1] 2-3. Paper C. Dated at top of first (unnumbered) leaf, '1/1966'. See **B84**.

F129 "Notes on Poetry." 5 leaves, [1] 2-5. Paper C. Dated at top of first (unnumbered) leaf, 'February 1968'.

F130 "Notes on Poetry I by Richard Eberhart I Conference on the Future of the Humanities I Sponsored by Daedalus I The Journal of the American Academy of Arts and Sciences I Boston, Massachusetts I Unedited Draft I Not for Release." 6 leaves, [1] 2-6. Paper D. Text hectographed from prepared typescript, on rectos only; wire-stitched in light grayish green wrappers.

F131 "Notes on Poetry." 2 unnumbered leaves. Unwatermarked paper. Dated at top of first (unnumbered) leaf, 'Seattle January 1972'.

F132 "Off Pemaquid." Paper C. See **C510**.

F133 "Old Question." Paper C. See **C574**.

F134 "Old Tree by the Penobscot." Paper D. See **C694**.

F135 "On Encountering the Great-Great-Grandson of William Wordsworth." Paper D. See **C648**.

F136 "On Returning to a Lake in Spring." Unwatermarked paper. See **C558**.

F137 "On the Suicide of F.O. Matthiessen." Unwatermarked paper. See **C652**.

F138 "Once More, O Ye..." Paper F. See **C697**.

F139 "One Morning in 1649" (after Borges). Paper D. See **C623**.

F140 "An Open Gate." Paper C. See **A27**.

F141 "Opulence." Paper C. See **B75**.

F142 "Ordeal." Paper C. See **C519**.

F143 "Ospreys in Cry." Paper C. See **C399**.

F144 "Outgoing, Incoming." Paper C. See **C607**.

F145 "The Parker River." 3 leaves, [1] 2-3. Paper C. Dated '(1956)' at bottom of third leaf. See **C403**.

F146 "Partial List of Works Published by Richard Eberhart." 3 leaves, [1] 2 [3]. Paper A. *Note*: This vita was prepared by RE when his job at St. Mark's School, Southborough, Mass., was terminated in 1940.

F147 "The Passage." 3 leaves, [1] 2-3. Paper C. Dated '1/58' at conclusion of poem. See **C445**.

F148 "The Phi Beta Kappa Poem I Swarthmore College, June 9, 1963 I *Memory, Confrontation, Desire*. 3 leaves, numbered 1-3. Unwatermarked paper. Hectographed from RE's typescript original, on rectos only. See **C506**.

F149 "Pierrot an Aesthetic Distance." Paper F.

F150 "Placation of Reality." Paper D. See **C660**.

F151 "Plain Song Talk." Paper D. See **C666**.

F152 "Playing Ball with the Dead." Paper C. See **C632**.

F153 "Poem ['The tears of the ancients']." Paper C. See **C397**.

F154 "Poem ['The vision of the world']." Paper B. See **C103**.

F155 "Poem in Construction." 4 leaves, [1] 2-4. Unwatermarked paper. Dated '11-17-39' at top of first (unnumbered) leaf, with RE's holograph signature contained at base of final leaf. Contains "I Wrote Helen a Letter But Got No Reply" (**C118**), "And the Chinese Bells of the Temple Tolled" (**A1**), "There is a Place in Stoical Autumn, a Glass." (**C137**).

F156 "Poems by Richard Eberhart." 3 unnumbered leaves. Paper H. Contains "Seals, Terns, Time" (**B42**), "The Place" (**C418**), "The Supreme Authority of the Imagination" (**C371**), "Half-Bent Man" (**C413**).

F157 "Poems I Selected by Richard Eberhart I for Discussion at I The Capitol Page School I October 20, 1956." Unnumbered title leaf and 9 numbered leaves. Unwatermarked paper. Hectographed from prepared typescript, on rectos only. Contains "The Horse Chestnut Tree" (**C254**), "Seals, Terns, Time" (**B42**), "The Cancer Cells" (**B27**), "The Fury of Aerial Bombardment" (**C161**), as well as poems by Dylan Thomas, William Empson, Gerard Manley Hopkins, and W.B. Yeats.

F158 "The Poet." Unwatermarked paper. See **A39**.

F159 "Poetry." Paper D. See **C681**.

F160 "Poetry and Games." Paper F. See **A58**.

F161 "Prospectus." Paper C.

F162 "Quarrel with a Cloud." Paper D. See **A33**.

F163 "Razzle-Dazzle." Paper D. See **C724**.

F164 "The Reading Room in the New York Public Library." Unwatermarked paper. See **C637**.

F165 "Request." Paper C. See **C398**. *Note*: The dedication to Dame Edith Sitwell does not appear in this version.

F166 "Richard Eberhart I Acceptance Speech for the I National Book Award in I Poetry for I Collected Poems: 1930-1976..." 3 leaves, [1] 2-3. Light bluish green unwatermarked paper. Hectographed from prepared typescript, on rectos only. In *OPP*.

F167 "Richard Eberhart: Poetry Topics to think about. Possibly for Papers." Paper C. *Note*: A classroom assignment of unknown date.

F168 "The Rolling Eye." Paper C. See **A27**.

F169 "A Rose and Milton" (after Borges). Paper D. See **C624**. [Borges, Sel Poems, ed. Giovanni, 1971].

F170 "Sailing Away." Paper C.

F171 "Santa Claus in Oaxaca." Paper C. See B87.

F172 "The Secret Heart." Paper D. See C600.

F173 "Sestina." Unwatermarked paper. See B26.

F174 "A Ship Burning and a Comet All in One Day." Paper C. See C417.

F175 "Sociogramaphonology." Paper C.

F176 "Some Memories of Dylan Thomas." 3 leaves, [1] 2-3. Unwatermarked paper. See C323.

F177 "Song ['Better have your say;']." Paper B.

F178 "Sonnets." 8 leaves, [1-4] 5-8. Paper B. Contains 26 sonnets numbered I-XXVI; all in *31S*.

F179 "The Soul." Paper D. See C604.

F180 "Soul Struggle." Paper C.

F181 "The Spell of Time." Paper C. See C380.

F182 "Sphinx." Unwatermarked paper. See A39.

F183 "The Still Spirit." Paper C. Dated '11/58'. See C440.

F184 "Suicide Note." Paper C. See C617.

F185 "The Supreme Authority of the Imagination." Paper C. See C371.

F186 "Swiss New Year." 2 leaves, numbered 1-2. Paper C. See C579.

F187 "A Testament." Paper C. See C437.

F188 "There Is an Evil in the Air." Paper A. See C135.

F189 "This Hunger for Death is the Strangest Thing." Paper A. See F56.

F190 "Thoor Ballylee." Unwatermarked paper. See A27.

F191 "Three Kids." Unwatermarked paper. See C682.

F192 [Three Poems.] 2 unnumbered leaves. Unwatermarked paper. Contains "Easter 1960" (later titled "Easter"), "Loss" (C447), "Dream and Reality" (C456).

F193 "Time." Paper D. See B117.

F194 "Time Passes." Unwatermarked paper. See C629.

F195 "To Evan." Paper I. See C294 and F196.

F196 "[To Evan] second Version (For Charles and Agnes Butcher)." Unwatermarked paper. Revised version of F195.

F197 "To Evade the Whirlwind..." Paper B. See C146.

F198 "To Harriet Monroe." Paper C. See B75.

F199 "To Kenya Tribesmen, The Turkana." Paper C. See C621.

F200 "To: Members of the Department." Paper C. Memo concerning a reading by Thomas Kinsella, dated October 9, 1967.

F201 "To: The Department." Paper C. Memo concerning a reading by Charles Tomlinson, dated November 13, 1967.

F202 "To the Field Mice." Paper C. See C567.

F203 "To the Mad Poets." Paper C. See C572.

F204 "To Whom It May Concern." Paper C. Statement concerning the poetry of Robert Frost, beginning "I share the wide-spread, common agreement of the centrality to poetry of Robert Frost's imagination." Dated '2/14/55', See **F205**.

F205 "To Whom It May Concern." Paper C. Statement concerning Robert Frost, beginning "Robert Frost sits squarely in the center of life as it is lived beneath its false shows and glitter." Dated 'March 1, 1959.' See **F204**.

F206 "To William Empson" (later titled "A Whack at Empson"). 2 unnumbered leaves. Paper F. See **C776**.

F207 "Tones of Evening." Paper C. See **C521**.

F208 "Track." Paper C. See **C596**.

F209 "Tree Swallows." Paper C. See **C411**.

F210 "Trying to Hold It All Together." Unwatermarked paper. See **C687**.

F211 "Two Poems." Unwatermarked paper. Hectographed from RE's typescript original, on rectos only. Includes "Late Summer" (**C438**) and "Riches" (**C439**).

F212 "United 555." Paper D. See **C628**.

F213 "Usurper." Unwatermarked paper. See **C692**.

F214 "The Vastness and Indifference of the World." Unwatermarked paper. See **C538**.

F215 "Vermont Idyll." Paper D. See **C665**.

F216 "Version Temporary." Unwatermarked paper.

F217 "Vision." Paper D. Version 1, with three stanzas; See **F218**.

F218 "Vision." Paper D. Version 2, with four stanzas. See **C503** and **F217**.

F219 "The Visionary Farms [Scenes I-XIV]." 37 leaves, one unnumbered contents leaf, [1] 2-36. See **A19** and **F220**.

F220 "The Visionary Farms (Scen XV)." 8 leaves, one unnumbered leaf, [1] 2-7. Unwatermarked paper. Hectographed from RE's typescript original, on rectos only. See **C340** and **F219**. *Note*: The first (unnumbered) leaf is signed 'Princeton University | October, 1955', and contains RE's explanation for the addition of this scene to his play.

F221 "The Way It Is." Paper C.

F222 "A Way Out." 2 unnumbered leaves. Paper F. See **C715**.

F223 "The Wedding." Paper C. See **C588**.

F224 "A Wedding on Cape Rosier." Unwatermarked paper. See **C557**.

F225 "When I Think of Her, the Power of Poetry Arises." Paper A. RE's holograph signature reproduced at base, with date in typescript, 'December 1938'. See **C98**.

F226 "Wild Life and Tamed Life." Paper D. See **C672**.

F227 "The Wild Swans of Inverance." Unwatermarked paper. See **A62**.

F228 "Will." Unwatermarked paper. See **C618**.

F229 "The Winds." Unwatermarked paper. See **C559**.

F230 "Winter Squirrels in Pine Trees." Paper D. See **C690**.

F231 "Words." Unwatermarked Paper. See **C330**.

F232 "The World Applauds." Unwatermarked paper.

F233 "Wounds, Wounds, Wounds, Wounds." Unwatermarked paper.

F234 "Yeats." Paper C. reproduced from RE's holograph original.

Note: "Yeats" is a study aid for students studying "The Gyre and Its Images."

G
Recordings

G1 "Poems of Richard Eberhart, Read by the Poet, Himself." [Np: World Wide Broadcasting Foundation, 1938]. 2-12, 78. Privately recorded 9 December 1938.

Contains on Record 1, side A, "The Groundhog," "Maze," "In a Hard Intellectual Light"; side B, "In the Evening Stark and Bare," "The Transfer"; record 2, side A, "Serenely Down Wide Water..."; side B, blank.

G2 *Richard Eberhart Reading His Own Poems.* Cambridge, Mass.: Harvard Vocarium Records, 1941. P1034-1037. 2-12, 78. Harvard Film Service H.F.S. 1487-1490.

Contains on P1034 (side A), "Maze," "For a Lamb," "Where Are Those High and Haunting Skies"; "The Return of Odysseus"; p1035 (side B), "In a Hard Intellectual Light," "The Groundhog"; P1036 (side A), "The Scarf of June," "Two Loves," "Burden," "Now Is the Air Made of Chiming Balls"; P1037 (side B), "Man's Greed and Envy Are So Great," "If I Could Only Live at the Pitch That is Near Madness," "I Walked Out to the Graveyard to See the Dead," "Those Who Love Struggle."

G3 *Lt. Comdr. Richard Eberhart Reading Poetry.* Washington, D.C.: Library of Congress, 1944. Order No. 630. 6-12, 78. Recorded 2 December 1944. *Note*: For original tape, See **G17**.

Contains on Side 1, "World War," "The Preacher Sought to Find Out Acceptable Words," "Dam Neck, Virginia"; Side 2, "The Fury of Aerial Bombardment," "Two Loves," "In Prisons of Established Craze," "The Largess,"; Side 3, "The Young Hunter," "Now is the Air Made of Chiming Balls," "The Child," "I Went to See Irving Babbitt," "Recollection of Childhood"; Side 4, "A Meditation"; Side 5, "A Meditation" (concluded); Side 6, "I Walked Out to the Graveyard to See the Dead," "There is an Evil in the Air," "Sometimes the Longing for Death"; Side 7, "In the Night When Destruction Shall Shake the World," "Four Lakes' Days"; Side 8, "Four Lakes' Days" (concluded); Side 9, "Maze," "Request for Offering," "The Groundhog"; Side 10, "Man's Greed and Envy are So Great," "The Goal of Intellectual Man," "Death Is Indescribably Much on Me"; Side 11, "In a Hard Intellectual Light," "My Bones Flew Apart," "Song ['There is a place in stoical autumn']"; Side 12, "Retrospective Forelook," "The Lyric Absolute."

G4 "Richard Eberhart." Cambridge, Mass.: Harvard Film Service, 1947. Privately produced for the poet. H.F.S. 3078, 3082, 3088. 3-12, 78. Recorded 1 March 1947.

Contains on Record H.F.S. 3078, side A, "The Orchard," "The Pasture," "The Cemetary"; side B, "Retrospective Forelook," "Rumination," "Cover Me Over, Clover"; H.F.S. 3082, side A, "At the End of War"; side B, "An Airman Considers His Power," "A Ceremony by the Sea"; H.F.S. 3088, side A, "Ode to the Chinese Paper Snake"; side B, "The Preacher Sought to Find Out Acceptable Words"; "Dam Neck, Virginia," "The Fury of Aerial Bombardment."

G5 *Twentieth Century Poetry in English.* Washington, D.C.: Library of Congress, 1949. Album P1. 5-12, 78.

Record P4 contains on side A (LC 1670), "Now Is the Air Made of Chiming Balls," "Dam Neck, Virginia," "The Fury of Aerial Bombardment"; and on side B (LC 1671), "The Groundhog." Printed text of poems loosely inserted in album.

G6 *Poet's Gold: Verses of Today*, sel. Whit Burnett. New York: RCA, 1955. LM-1883. 1-12, LP.

Contains on side 2, RE's poems "If I Could Live at the Pitch..." and "The Human Being is a Lonely Creature," read by Norman Rice.

G7 *Richard Eberhart Reading His Poems.* Boston: Fassett Recording Studio, 1958. 3-12, LP. Private pressing for the poet, 1 November 1958.

Contains on record 1, side 1, "For a Lamb," "In a Hard Intellectual Light," "Now is the Air Made of Chiming Balls," "If I Could Only Live at the Pitch...," "New Hampshire, February," "Dam Neck, Virginia," "The Fury of Aerial Bombardment," "Go to the Shine That's on a Tree," "The Tobacconist of Eighth Street," "Seals, Terns, Time"; side 2, "The Human Being is a Lonely Creature," "Cousin Florence," "Sea-Hawk," "To Evan," "Words"; record 2, side 1, repeats record 1, side 2; record 2, side 2, "Four Exposures," "Attitudes," "To a Young Greek Killed in the Wars," "A Soldier Rejects His Time...," "Protagonists," "Blessed Are the Angels in Heaven," "Villanelle," "Life as Visionary Spirit," "Patience as a Gesture of Divine Will," "In the Blood," "Yonder," "Some Men Have It Early," "The Project," "The Sacrifice"; record 3, side 1, "Anima," "The Canoe Club," "To Bill Williams," "To Auden on His Fiftieth," "What Gives," "By the Stream," "The Oak," "In the Garden," "The Lost Children," "A Stone," "The Visitor," "The Garden God"; record 3, side 2, "Half-Bent Man," "The Diggers of Clams...," "A Ship Burning and a Comet...," "In After Time."

G8 *Twentieth Century Poetry in English: An Album of Modern Poetry*, ed. Oscar Williams. Washington, D.C.: Library of Congress, 1959. 3-12, LP. PL 20-22.

Record PL 21, side A, contains RE reading "The Horse Chestnut Tree," and "The Groundhog." A brochure containing the text accompanies this set.

G9 *Anthology of Contemporary American Poetry*, sel. and ed. by George Abbe. New York: Folkways Records, 1961. FL 9735. 1-12, LP.

Contains on side 1 RE's poem "The Horse Chestnut Tree," read by George Abbe. *Note*: The text is rept. in a booklet that accompanies the album.

G10 *Yale Series of Recorded Poets: Richard Eberhart*. New Haven, Conn.: Carillon Records, 1961. YP 314. 1-12, LP. Audio Cardalog 61001.

Contains "This Fevers Me," "Go to the Shine That's on a Tree," "Now is the Air Made of Chiming Balls," "On a Squirrel Crossing the Road...," "Sea-Hawk," "Seals, Terns, Time," "New Hampshire, February," "The Hard Structure of the World," "Indian Pipe," "The Cancer Cells," "The Book of Nature," "If I Could only Live at the Pitch that is Near Madness," "For a Lamb," "The Horse Chestnut Tree," "The Soul Longs to Return...," "I Walked Out to the Graveyard to See the Dead," "The Tobacconist of Eighth Street," "Cousin Florence," "Dam Neck, Virginia," "The Fury of Aerial Bombardment," "War and Poetry," "The Dry Rot," "Words," "The Verbalist of Summer," "Half-Bent Man," "A Ship Burning and a Comet...," "Nothing but Change," "The Wisdom of Insecurity," "Only in the Dream," "Great Praises."

G11 *A Little Treasury of 20th Century American Poetry*, ed. Oscar Williams. New York: Colpix Records, 1963. PS 1001 (v. 2 of 2). 2-12, LP. P5RM-3277.

Side 2 contains RE reading "If I Could only Live...," "The Fury of Aerial Bombardment," "On a Squirrel Crossing the Road..." *Note*: texts are rept. on the inner sleeve of the album.

G12 *Many Voices* (to accompany *Adventures in American Literature*). New York: Harcourt, Brace and World, 1963. 2-12, LP (v. 2 of 2).

Contains on record 1, side 2 RE reading "On a Squirrel Crossing the Road..." *Note*: On the same disc RE reads Richard Wilbur's poem "Year's End."

G13 *An Album of Modern Poetry: British, American*, ed. Oscar Williams. New York: Gryphon Records, 1963. GR 902/3/4. 3-12, LP.

Contains on record 2, side 1 RE reading his poems "The Horse Chestnut Tree" and "The Groundhog." *Note*: A booklet containing the texts accompanies the album.

G14 *Richard Eberhart Reads from His Own Works*. New York: Decca Records, 1965. DL 9145.

Contains on side 1, "This Fevers Me," "Go to the Shine That's on a Tree," "Now Is the Air made of Chiming Balls," "On a Squirrel Crossing the Road...," "Sea-Hawk," "Seals, Terns, Time," "New Hampshire, February," "The Hard Structure of the World," "Indian Pipe," "The Cancer Cells," "The Book of Nature," "If I Could Only Live at the Pitch...," "For a Lamb," "The Horse Chestnut Tree," "The Soul Longs to Return...," "I Walked Out to the

Graveyard...," "The Tobacconist of Eighth Street"; side 2, "Cousin Florence," "Dam Neck, Virginia," "The Fury of Aerial Bombardment," "Warr and Poetry," "The Dry Rot," "Words," "The Verbalist of Summer," "Half-Bent Man," "A Ship Burning and a Comet All in One Day," "Nothing But Change," "The Wisdom of Insecurity," "Only in the Dream," "Great Praises."

Note: This is a reissue of **G10**.

G15 *Richard Eberhart Reading His Poetry*. New York: Caedmon Records, 1968. TC 1243. 1-12, LP. L.C. R68-2656.

Contains "The Fury of Aerial Bombardment," "Seals, Terns, Time," "For a Lamb," "The Groundhog," "If I Could Only Live at the Pitch...," "New Hampshire, February," "The Horse Chestnut Tree," "The Cancer Cells," "On A Squirrel Crossing the Road...," "A Meditation," "Go to the Shine that's on a Tree," "Rumination," "I Walked out to the Graveyard to See the Dead," "Sea-Hawk," "Nothing but Change," "The Incomparable Light," "La Crosse at Ninety Miles an Hour," "The Place," "Sea Burial from the Cruiser *Reve*," "A Maine Roustabout," "Am I My Neighbour's Keeper?" "Hardening into Print," "A New England Bachelor," "The Illusion of Eternity," "The Mastery," "Marrakech," "The Ides of March," "The Explorer on Main Street," "A Wedding on Cape Rosier," "On Returning to a Lake in Spring."

G16 *The Spoken Arts Treasury of 100 Modern American Poets*. New York: Spoken Arts, 1969. SA-P-18. 18-12, LP. L.C. 78-750876.

Record 8 (SA 1047), side B contains RE reading "For a Lamb," "Seals, Terns Time," "The Human Being is a Lonely Creature," "The Oak," "A Ship Burning and a Comet...," "Spring Mountain Climb," "Equivalence of Gnats and Mice."

TAPES

G17 "Richard Eberhart Reading His Poems in the Recording Laboratory, 2 December 1944." Washington, D.C.: Library of Congress, 1944. T 2689-3.

Contains "World War," "The Preacher Sought to Find Out Acceptable Words," "Dam Neck, Virginia," "The Fury of Aerial Bombardment," "In Prisons of Established Craze," "The Largess," "The Young Hunter," "The Child," "I Went to See Irving Babbitt," "Recollection of Childhood," "Man's Greed and Envy Are So Great," "The Goal of Intellectual Man," "Death is Indescribably Much on Me," "In a Hard Intellectual Light," "My Bones Flew Apart," "Song," "Retrospective Forelook," "The Lyric Absolute," "Now is the Air Made of Chiming Balls," "The Groundhog." *Note*: See **G3**.

G18 "Richard Eberhart Reading His Poems at His Home in Cambridge, Massachusetts, 13 May 1951." Washington, D.C.: Library of Congress, 1951. T 1830-1.

Contains "If I Could Only Live at the Pitch...," "I Walked Out to the Graveyard...," "An Airman Considers His Power," "New Hampshire, February," "Sea Scape with Parable," "The Verbalist of Summer" (pts. I-III), "The Tobacconist of Eighth Street," "That Final Meeting," "War and Poetry," "Theme from Haydn," "A Gauze," "The Roc," "The Mischief," "Reality! Reality! What Is It?" "The Visionary Eye," "A Love Poem," "Odd Events of History," "Concord Cats," "What the World Is," "Indian Summer," "Politics," "Talk at Dawn," "Order and Disorder," "A Legend of Viable Women," "Forms of the Human," "The Forum," "An Herb Basket."

G19 "Richard Eberhart Reading His Poems at a Recording Studio in Storrs, Connecticut, in 1953." Washington, D.C.: Library of Congress, 1953. T 2195.

Contains "Fragments of New York, 1929," "Indian Pipe," "The Cancer Cells," "A Legend of Viable Women," "Motion as Grace," "The Great Stone Face," "The Dry Rot," "The Book of Nature," "To My Son, Aged Four," "Aesthetics After War," "Go to the Shine That's on a Tree," "Sea Scape with Parable," "The Tobacconist of Eighth Street," "Pleasures of the Morning," "Great Praises," "The Lost Poem," "To Evan," "La Crosse at Ninety Miles an Hour," "Creators," "The Noble Man," "Resources of the World," "What If Remembrance?" "Sometimes the Longing for Death," "At Night," "A Love Poem," "Widsdom," "The Horse Chestnut Tree," "Seals, Terns, Time," "The Look," "Indian Summer," "Forms of the Human," "That Final Meeting," "Concord Cats," "An Herb Basket," "To One Who, Dead, Sees His Poems in Print One Hundred Years Later," "The Skier and the Mountain," "Imagination," "The Human Being is a Lonely Creature," "Phoenixes Again."

G20 "Richard Eberhart Reading His Poems in the Coolidge Auditorium, 12 March 1956." Washington, D.C: Library of Congress, 1956. T 2426.

Contains: "If I Could Only Live at the Pitch that is Near Madness," "The Groundhog," "New Hampshire, February," *Devils and Angels* (a verse play), "Seals, Terns, Time," "The Horse Chestnut Tree," "Cousin Florence," "What Gives," "Thrush Song at Dawn," "To Helen, With a Playbill."

G21 "Richard Eberhart Reading His Poems With Comment in the Coolidge Auditorium, 28 September 1959." Washington, D.C.: Library of Congress, 1959. T 2908.

Contains "The Oak," "For a Lamb," "If I Could only Live at the Pitch...," "New Hampshire, February," "The Fury of Aerial Bombardment," "The Cancer Cells," "Seals, Terns, Time," "The Horse Chestnut Tree," "Cousin Florence," "Sea-Hawk," "Salem," "Attitudes," "A Young Greek,

Killed in the Wars," "Villanelle," "The Scarifice," "Lucubration," "Love Among the Ruins," "At the Canoe Club," "What Gives," "Throwing the Apple," "Half-Bent Man," "The Clam Diggers...," "A Ship Burning and a Comet...," "Light from Above," "Equivalence of Gnats and Mice," "On A Squirrel Crossing the Road..."

G22 "Seminar at the Library of Congress with Students and Faculty Members from George Washington University, Washington, D.C., 14 October 1959." Washington, D.C.: Library of Congress, 1959. T 2970. RE conducts a seminar on poetry.

G23 "Seminar at the Library of Congress with Students and Faculty Members from American University, Washington, D.C., 28 October 1959." Washington, D.C.: Library of Congress, 1959. T 2969. RE conducts a seminar on poetry.

G24 "Seminar at the Library of Congress with Students and Faculty Members from the University of Maryland, College Park, Maryland, 24 November 1959." Washington, D.C.: Library of Congress, 1959. T 3035. RE conducts a seminar on poetry.

G25 "Seminar at the Library of Congress with Students and Faculty Members from Catholic University of America, Washington, D.C., 1 December 1959. Washington, D.C.: Library of Congress, 1959. T 3036. In addition to RE's seminar on poetry, Ned O'Gorman reads from his work.

G26 "Seminar at the Library of Congress with Students and Faculty Members from Howard University, Washington, D.C., 24 February 1960." Washington, D.C.: Library of Congress, 1960. T 3055. RE conducts a seminar on poetry.

G27 "Richard Eberhart Reading His Poems with Comment in the Coolidge Auditorium, 24 October 1960." Washington, D.C.: Library of Congress, 1960. T 3185.

Contains *The Apparition* (a verse play), "The Rape of the Cataract," "I Went to See Irving Babbitt," "The Groundhog," "The Goal of Intellectual Man," "The Lyric Absolute," "Dam Neck, Virginia," "The Fury of Aerial Bombardment," "Brotherhood of Men," "The Cancer Cells," "The Horse Chestnut Tree," "Forms of the Human," "The Oak," "The Book of Nature," "To Evan," "The Wisdom of Insecurity," "The Voyage," "A Ship Burning and a Comet...," "On a Squirrel Crossing the Road...," "Equivalence of Gnats and Mice," "The Imcomparable Light," "A New England Bachelor," "A Maine Roustabout," "Spirit," "Easter 1960."

G28 "Seminars at the Library of Congress with Students and Teachers from Coolidge and Roosevelt High Schools, 8 November 1960, and with Students from Dunbar High School, 15 November 1960." Washington, D.C.: Library of Congress, 1960. T 3206. RE's seminars on poetry.

G29 "Richard Eberhart Reading His Poems with Comment in the Coolidge Auditorium, 15 May 1961." Washington, D.C.: Library of Congress, 1961. T 3339.

Contains "For a Lamb," "Where are Those High and Haunting Skies," "The Groundhog," "1934," "Now Is the Air Made of Chiming Balls," "Recollection of Childhood," "Man's Greed and Envy are So Great," "The Goal of Intellectual Man," "If I Could Only Live at the Pitch...," "I Walked Out to the Graveyard...," "The Fury of Aerial Bombardment," "Indian Pipe," "Go to the Shine That's on a Tree," "The Cancer Cells," "Seals, Terns, Time," "The Horse Chestnut Tree," "Oedipus," "Cousin Florence," "Sea-Hawk," "The Voyage," "Autumnal," "The Lost Children," "The Hard Structure of the World," "Ospreys in Cry," "Half-Bent Man," "Spring Mountain Climb," "A New England Bachelor," "A Maine Roustabout," "Sea Burial from the Cruiser *Reve*," "Rainscapes, Hydrangeas, Roses and Singing Birds," "Easter 1960," "The Inward Rock," "On a Squirrel Crossing the Road..."

H
Musical Settings

H1 "Cover Me Over." Set to music by Edward Cone. One leaf reprod. from composer's original manuscript; dated 3 May 1956. Unpublished.

H2 "Burden." Set to music by John C. Worley. Five leaves reprod. on nine sides from composer's original manuscript; dated July 1966. Unpublished.

H3 "Evil." Set to music by Elie Siegmeister. Eight leaves reprod. on eight sides from composer's orig. manuscrpipt, dated 6 Dec. 1967; glued in thick light blue paper wrapper with cover label. Unpublished.

H4 "Four Songs." Set to music by Elie Siegmeister, Ten leaves reprod. on seventeen sides from composer's orig. manuscript, dated 31 Dec. 1967, and 2 Jan. 1868; glued in thick light blue paper wrapper with cover label. Unpublished. Includes "Ways and Means," "Later or Sooner," "When Doris Danced," and "To Catch the Meaning."

H5 "In the Silence of Contemplation," Set to music by Annette LeSiege. 28 leaves reprod. on 55 sides from composer's original manuscript, dated 1982; spiral-bound in unprinted tan paper covers. Unpublished, Contains settings of five poems by RE: "If I Could Only Live at the Pitch That Is Near Madness," "A Love Poem," "Only in the Dream," "The Illusion of Eternity," and "In After Time."

I
Translations

ARABIC

I1 Sayegh, Tawfig, ed. [*Fifty Poems from Contemporary American Poetry*]. Beirut: Dar El-Yaqza, 1963.

Contains translations af "A Legend of Viable Women" and "The Fury of Aerial Bombardment."

DANISH

I2 Nyholm, Jens. *Amerikanske Stemmer*. Copenhagen: Arene-Forst-Hansens Forlag, 1968.

Contains translations of "If I Could Only Live at the Pitch That Is Near Madness," "The Horse Chestnut Tree," and "The Groundhog."

FRENCH

I3 Bosquet, Alain. *Anthologie de la Poesie Americaine des Origines à Nos Jours*. Paris: Librairie Stock, 1956.

Contains a translation of: "The Tobacconist of Eighth Street."

I4 Lowenfels, Walter, with Nan Braymer. 89 *Poètes Américains Contre la Guerre au Vietnam*. Paris: Éditions Albin Michel, 1967.

Contains a translation of "World War."

GERMAN

I5 Steinbrinker, Günther, with Rudolf Hartung. *Panorama Moderner Lyrik*. Berlin: Sigbert Mohn Verlag, nd.

Contains translations of "The Tobacconist of Eighth Street" and "Burden."

ITALIAN

I6 Rosati, Salvatore, et al. *Poeti Inglesi e Americani*. Rome: Botteghe Oscure, 1958.

Contains translations of "Bright Hour of Europe" and "Sea-Scape with Parable."

I7 Izzo, Carlo. *Poesia Americana del '900*. Parma: Ugo Guando Editore, 1963.

Contains translations of "Imagining How It Would Be to Be Dead," "The Dream," and "The Groundhog."

J
Odds and Ends

J1 "The Poems of Gene Derwood." New Rochelle, N.Y.: Spoken Arts Records, 1955. Phono-disc. RE reads Derwood's poems "In Common" and "Porism" on side 2.

J2 "The Dartmouth College Museum Presents the Class of 1926 Reunion Show, June 1962, 'Avocations'." Nine stapled leaves reprod. from typescript original. Leaf 3 contains "Invocation to Avocation 1926," a poem by RE.

J3 "The Poetry of Robinson Jeffers Read by Judith Anderson." New York: Caedmon Records, 1970. Phonodisc. Back of sleeve contains a long statement by RE about Jeffer's poetry.

J4 *Self-Portrait: Book People Picture Themselves*, ed. Burt Britton (New York: Random House, 1976). Contains a reprod. of RE's self-portrait on p. 94. *N.B.*: Issued in cloth with dust jacket and card cover.

J5 Brief untitled comment on front wrapper of a brochure, "Twentieth Annual Poetry Awards" (Long Island Univ., New York) 16 April 1986.

Index

Abbe, George, D5, G9

"Absolute Silence," A33, C639, F1

"Academic Responsibility," C855

Accent, C134, C152, C163, C165-66, C185, C272

Accent Anthology, ed. Quinn and Shattuck (1946), B24, C163

"Accommodating Oneself to September," A58

Account of childhood reading (RE), B109

"Achievement, Ninth Symphony," C842

The Achievment of Richard Eberhart, ed. Engel (1968), A2a, A3a, A7a, A13a, A18a, A20a, A25, B18, B25, B45, B70, B82, B87, B90, C31, C52, C76, C108, C143, C161-2, C168, C209, C254, C263, C279, C295, C297, C322, C325, C328, C330-31, C372, C377, C392, C413, C418, C428, C436, C451, C454, C477, C503, C510, C532, C538, C554-55, C557-58

"Accolades," C771

Acknowledgement in *Nineteen Dartmouth Poems* (RE), B91

"Action in Poetry," A24, C525, F2

"Adam Cast Forth" (after Borges), A39, A62, C622, F3

Adams & Lowell (printers), A22

"Address to God," A58, C735

"Address to Time," A58, C746

"The Advantage of the Outside," A16, B39

Adventures in American Literature, ed. Fuller and Kinnick (1963), C325

Adventures in American Literature, ed. Hodgins and Silverman (1980), C254, C325

Adventures in Poetry, ed. Custer (1964), C85

"Aerialism," A20, A24, C175

"Aesthetics After War," A13, A18, A39, A62, C186, G19

After this Exile (Viray), B79

"Again," C511

"Against the Wood Thrush," A27, F4

Agenda, B117, C671-2

The Age of the Dragon . . . (Lehmann), rev. by RE, C293

Aiken, Conrad, A11a, A18b, A24, A39c, C180, C494, C581

"An Airman Considers His Power," A7, A11, A18, A39, A62, C178, G4, G18

"The Airy Vent," A58

Albatross, C835

An Album of Modern Poetry: British, American, G13

"Alcaic," C741

Allen, Don Cameron, B60

"Allen Ginsberg: A Man of Spirit," B156

Alligator, E55-56

The Alligator Bride (Hall), rev. by RE, C598

"All of Us," C852

"An Allowance," C171

All: The Collected Short Poems 1923-58 (Zukofsky), C537

All We Need of Hell (Crews), D89

"Alphabet Book," C83

Alpha-Pavia, A57, B157

"Altars," C22

Alvarez, A., A33a

Always Begin Where You Are . . ., ed. Lamb (1979), C85

America Forever New . . ., ed. Brewton (1968), C297

American Academy of Arts and Letters, A62, C759, E70

"American Academy Introduction," A62

American Christmas, ed. Schott and Myers, 2d ed. (1967), B87

The American Experience in Literature, ed. Bradley et al., A3a

The American Genius, ed. Sitwell (1951), C76

"American Hackluyt [sic]," F6

"American Hakluyt," A39, A62

American Heritage, C853, E73

American Literature, ed. Schorer et al. (1968), C76, C325

American Literature: A Brief Anthology, ed. Bonslog and Korn (1949), B25

American Literature: The Makers and the Making, ed. Brooks et al., B8, B76, C85, C161

American Literature: Readings and Critiques, ed. Stallman (1961), C76

American Literature Survey, ed. Stern and Gross (1968), C76, C161

American Lyric Poems . . ., ed. Olson (1964), C76

"American Passion," C347

American Poetry, ed. Shapiro, A3a, C76, C161

American Poetry Review, C714, C729, C766-67, C785, C814

American Prefaces, C151

American Sampler . . ., ed. Rosenberger (1951), C179

American Scholar, C432

American Signatures, ed. Beamish (1941), B15, C121

The American Tradition in Literature, ed. Bradley et al. (1961), A13a, B8, C64, C92, C108, C149

American Writing 1943, ed. Swallow, B20, C145

American Writing 1944, ed. Caukin and Swallow, B22, C153

Amerikanske Stemmer, ed. Nyholm (1968), C254, I2

"Am I My Neighbor's Keeper?" A20, A24, A34, A62, B73, B76, B81, C487, F5, G15

Ammons, A.R., A47n

"Analogue of Unity in Multeity," A16, A18, A24, A39, A62, B36

"Analysis of a Turn of the Hand, or the Storm," F56

"And All Shall Fade Away," B3

"And at Lake Geneva, Which Is in Wisconsin," A11, B17, C130, F57

"And the Chinese Bells of the Temple Tolled," F155

"And Today We Have the Playing of Names," F7

"Angelic Perspectives," C129

"The Angels," A62, B154, C833

"Angels and Man," A48, C673, F8

"Anglo-Saxon Song," A3, C89

Anhinga Press," B122

"Anima," A18, A24, A36, A39, A62, C354, G7

Annex 21, C768

"Another Change in Chapel," C15

Another Poet in New York (Connellan), D21

Antaeus, C642-43

Anthologie de la Poèsie Americaine... (Bosquet), I3

An Anthology Introducing Poetry, ed. Coleman and Theobald (1964), C76

An Anthology of American Poetry, ed. Kreymborg (1941), B5

Anthology of Contemporary American Poetry, G9

An Anthology of Famous English and American Poetry, ed. Benét and Aiken (1945), C76

Anthology of Magazine Verse for 1958 . . ., ed. Braithwaite (1959), B50, C253, C405, C412-13, C415

Anthology of Modern Poetry, ed. Wain (1963), A18a, B27, C161, C329

Anthracite Country (Parini), D62

The Antigone of Sophocles, trans. Fitts and Fitzgerald, rev. by RE, C100

Antioch Review, C627

"The Anxiety I Felt in Guanajuato," A33, A39, A62, C619

"The Apparition," A19, C260, G27

"Apple Buds," A18, A24, A39, A62, C394

Appleseeds and Beercans . . ., ed. Wells et al. (1974), A18a, B25

An Approach to Literature, ed. Brooks et al. (1975), B8, C161

Aralia Press, A37

Arizona Daily Star, E40

Arizona Trade Bindery, B66

Ark, B140, C181

Ark II / Moby I, C374-75

Armitage, Merle, B94

Art and Craft in Poetry, ed. Lape (1967), C325

"Art and Zeitgeist," C201

The Art of Interpretation, ed. Bacon (1979), C85

"The Art of William Carlos Williams," C594

The Arts (Dartmouth College), B3, B5

Arts In Society, C496

The Arts Anthology, B3, C5, C48

The Ascent," A27, C518, F9

Ashbery, John, A60n

"As If You Had Never Been," A33, A39, A62, C630, F10

As I Pass, O Manhattan . . ., ed. McCullough (1956), C209

"As It Is," F11

"Tha Assassin," A39, A62, C519, F12

Astor, Susan, A57n

"As We Go," A58, C801

"At Archie Peisch's Funeral," B161

Atheneum (publ.), B98

Atkins, Stuart, D69

"At Lake Geneva," B25

The Atlantic Book of British American Poetry, ed. Sitwell, C254

Atlantic Brief Lives, ed. Kronenberger (1971), B108

Atlantic Monthly, C149, C517, C532, C658, C734, C765, C825

"At McSorley's Bar," A24, C534, F13

"At Night," A13, A18, A24, A62, B90, C263, G19

Attacks of Taste, ed. Byrne and Penzler (1971), B109

"At the Canoe Club," A18, A38-39, A62, C401, G21

"At the End of the War," A7, A18, A39, A62, C181, G4

"The Attic," B90

"Attitudes," A18, A24, A39, A62, B47, B76, C359, G7, G21

"Attitudes (Irish Catholic)," A36

Auden, W.H., A3a, B10, B12, C686, C688, C693

Audience, C81, C392, C486
"Austere Poem," A17-18, A39, A62, C406
Austere Poem and Light Verse, A17
"Author's Note," C805
Austin Daily, C7, C82, C444, C641, E42-43
Austinian, B1
Author, B56
Authors Take Sides on Vietnam, ed. Woolf and Bagguley (1967), B86
"Autumn," A48, C608, F14
"Autumnal," A18, A39, A62, C350, G29
Available Light (Booth), D24
Axinn, Donald E., D30
Aylward, David K., E39

"Babbette Deutsch 1895-1982," C821
Bagguley, John, B86
Baker, Carlos, D16
Baker Library Press (Dartmouth College), B14
"Balance," C638
"Ballad of the Sedative, C97
Ballantine Books, B32, B45
"Ball Game," A27, A39, A62, F15
"Balm of Iliad," F16
Baltimore Sun Magazine, E24
"Band of Usable Monuments," C151
Bangor Daily News, C677
Banyan Press, A9
Barking at Sunspots (Kelly), D90
"Barriers," C6
Basic Books, B74, B81
"Bats," A58
"Baudelaire," A13, C241
The Beasts & The Elders (Siegel), B114
Beat movement, E12, E26, E69
The Beautiful Changes (Wilbur), rev. by RE, C193

Beck, Dorothy, A30, B111
Beck, Emily Morrison, B108
Beecham, Audrey, A3b
The Beginning (RE), A36
"Beginning of a Beginning," C156
Being Born and Growing Older, ed. Vance (1971), C254
Belhaven College, E33
Belitt, Ben, C96, C342
"Belief," A58
Bellingham Review, C748
"The Bells of a Chinese Temple," A1, A18, A24, A39, A62, E59
"Ben Bellitt [sic] Reads His Poetry," F17
Beloit Poetry Journal, B37, B44, C244-45, C266, C270-71, C334, C356
Beloit Poetry Journal Chapbook Number Five (1957), B44
Beloit Poetry Journal Chapbooks Number Three, B37
"Beneath Rich Stars," C4
"Ben Franklin," A58, C770
Bennanni, Badreddine, B89, D19
Bennanni, Ben, B145
Bennington Review, C286
Beowulf to Beatles and Beyond, ed. Pichaske (1981), C76
Berger, Sid, A44
Bergonzi, Bernard, A39c
Berkeley Poetry Review, C757
Berryman, John, C200
Best Minds, ed. Morgan and Rosenthal (1986), B156
Best Poems of 1956 (1957), B46, C361
Best Poems of 1971, B113, C636
Best Poems of 1975 (1976), B130, C715, C725
"Better Management," A49, A51, A58

Better Management (RE), A49
"Beyond Cambridge," C117
"Beyond San Rapiña," A2
Bianculli, David, E53, E58
"Big Rock," A39, A62, C684, F18
"Big Top," C150
"Birth and Death," A18, A24, A39, A62, C443
Birthdays from the Ocean (Gardner), D1
"Birth of a Poem," E6
"The Birth of the Spirit," A27, A39, A62
Bishop, Elizabeth, C338
Bishop, John Peale, C133, C206
Bixler, Michael, B125
Black Faun Press, B15
Blackburn, Thomas, B47
Blackmur, R.P., A3b, C134, E72
Blake, William, E53, E57, E65
"Blessed Are the Angels in Heaven," A18, A39, A62, C286, G7
"The Blindness of Poets," A3a*n*, C148
"The Block," A58
"The Blue Grains," C435
"Blue Spring," A46, A48, A55
"Blue. White. Red. Green." C79
Bly, Robert, D52
BOA Editions, A46
"Boat Race Speculation," C828
Bogan, Louise, C135
Bolte, Charles G., E63
Bond Wheelwright Co., B78
"The Bones of Coleridge," A48, A62, C743
Bonin, Jane, E51
A Book of Animal Poems, ed. Cole (1973), A16a
"A Book About Modern Poetry," rev. by RE, C303

A Book of Modern American Poetry, ed. McDermott and Lowery (1970), C76, C85, C254
A Book of Modern Verse (1939), C76
"The Book of Nature," A13, A18, A24, A39, A62, C277, G10, G14, G19, G27
Booth, Philip, A60n, C469, D24
Bosquet, Alain, I3
"Boston," A27, B85, F19
Boston Evening Transcript, C94
Boston Globe, C625
Boston Sunday Globe Book Review, C598, C653
Botteghe Oscure, C191-92, C227, C244, C249, C326-27, C397-99, I6
Botteghe Oscure Reader, ed. Garrett (1974), C327
Bott, Michael, A2a
Bottrall, Ronald, C110
"Boulder," C62
Boullata, Kamal, B145
Bourjaily, Vance, B40
"The Bower," A33, A39, A62, C586, F20
Bower, Ruth, B12
Bowman, David H., E10
Boyers, Robert, B105
Boyle, Kay, C96
Bozart-Westminster, C79-80
Bradbury Press, B146
Brandeis University Bulletin, A3a
Braithewaite, Willaim Stanley, B50
A Bravery of Earth (RE), A1
Braybrooke, Neville, B60
Braymer, Nan, I4
Bread, Hashish and Moon, ed. Bennanni (1982), B145
The Bread Loaf Anthology of Contemporary American Poetry, ed. Pack et al. (1985), B154, C810, C833-34

Breaking Open (Rukeyser), D18
"The Breathless," A33, A39, A62,
   C626, F21
Brenner, Larry, D58
"The Bride from Mantua," E18, F22
Bridge Fall Down (Packard), D83
"Brief Candle," B161
"Bright Hour of Europe," C191, I6
Brilliant, Alan, B145
Britton, Burt, J4
Brogue, C525, E33
"The Broken Pen," A62
"Broken Wing," C658; see "Broken
   Wing Theory"
"Broken Wing Theory," A33, A39,
   A62, C658, F23
Bronk, William, B14*n*
Brook, J.M., B159
Brooks, Robert A., D70
Brotherhood of Men (RE), A9
"Brotherhood of Men," A9, A11,
   A18, A39, A62, G27
Broughton, Irv, B57
Brower, Reuben, A35, B75
Brown, Francis, B34
Brown, Harry, A3b
Bruccoli Clark Laymen Book, B159
Bruce Humphries (publ.), B20, B22
"Bruges," C30
Bryant, William Cullen, B157
The Build-Up (W.C. Williams), rev.
   by RE, C281
Bullock, Marie, A60
Bulletin (PSA), E3, E29
"Burden," A3, A3*n*, A11, A18, A24,
   A39, A62, G2, H2, I5
"Burned Alive," C199
Burnett, Whit, B100, E39, G6
Burr, Michael R., B70
Burr Oaks (RE), A7
"Burr Oaks," A7, A11, A18, A39,
   A62

Burroway, Janet, D44
Bustard, C.A., E66
Butcher, Charles II, A8
Butcher, Fanny, E16
Butler and Tanner Ltd, A1b
"But to Reach the Archimedean
   Point," A3a*n*, C122
Byrne, Evelyn B., B109
"By the Physical Act of Lying By a
   Stream," B17
"By the Stream," A18, A39, A62,
   C373, G7

Caedmon Records, G15, J1, J3
*Café at St. Marks: The Apalachee
   Poets*, ed. Brock et al. (1975),
   B122, C418
"The Cage," A39, A62
Caitlin: Life With Dylan Thomas
   (Thomas), D92
Calder, Alexander, B16
California Aggie, E49
California State Poetry Quarterly,
   C741-42
"Calligraphy," A13
Cambridge Poetry, 1929, B5
Cambridge Review, C54-55, C59-61
Campbell, Neil, C1
Campbell, Roy, C367
Campbell, Shirley Young, B117
"The Cancer Cells," A13, A18, A24,
   A39, A62, B27, B54, B76, B81,
   E24, E49, E69, F157, G10, G14-
   15, G19, G21, G27, G29
Cannito, Michael, E46
"The Canoe Club," G7
Cape, Jonathan, A1a
"Caravan of Silence," A2, A11, A18,
   A39, A62, B5
Cardoso, Willaim J., E22
"Care and Love," C845
Carillon Records, G10

The Carnival (Prokosch), rev. by RE, C94

Carolina Quarterly, C449-50

"Carolyn Kizer, Noted Poet . . .," F24

Carpenter, Margaret Haley, B50,

Carrier, Constance, A57*n*

Carrier, Warren, B38

Carrousel Press, A30

Carruth, Hayden, C453

The Case for Poetry, ed. Gwynn et al., A3a, C254

Casper, Leonard, B79

Castings (Haskins), D72

"The Cathedral at Palma," B15

Caukin, Helen Ferguson, B22

"The Cauldron," (col.), C12-13

"C. Day Lewis Lectures . . .," F25

CEA Chap Book (1963), B68

CEA Critic, B68

A Celebration of Poets, ed. Allen (1967), B60

"Celebration of Late August," C707

A Celebration of Teachers (1984), B155

"Celebrations for Mankind," rev. by RE, C478

"Cellar," B6

"The Cemetary," G4

"Centennial for Whitman," A16, A18, A39, A62, B37, C779

Center Stage, C679

"A Central Spirit," C471

"Central Violence," rev. by RE, C416

A Century for American Writers 1855-1955, ed. Low et al. (1955), C121

A Century of Winter, A3a

"Ce Pays Nous Ennuie, O Mort!" C127

"Ceremonial," A62, C772

"A Ceremony by the Sea," A7, A18, C182, G4

"A Certain Distance," C710; see "A Certain Distance from Man"

"A Certain Distance from Man," A58, C710

"The Challenge of the Air," A58

"Chant of the Forked Lightening," A13, A58, C202

Chappell, Fred, A47*n*

"Charge to the Initiates of Phi Beta Kappa . . .," F26

Charles Street Journal, C635

Chatto & Windus, A2a, A3a, A7a, A11a, A13a, A16a, A18a, A20b, A27b, A33a, A39c, B7

Chelsea, C448, C456, C583

"Chialism," A13

Chicago Review, C316-17, C669, C727-28

The Chicago Review Anthology, ed. Ray (1959), B52, C316-17

Chicago Tribune, B97

Chicago Tribune Magazine, A27a, B26, C545, C588, C597, C626, C645, C678, C689, C701, C704, E16

Chief Modern Poets of England and America, ed. Sanders et al. A2a, A3a, C76, C115, C161, C231, C254, C362

"The Child," A3, A3a*n*, A11, A18, A39, A62, G3, G17

Childhood's Journey (Eaton), B118

Chimera, C153, C159-60

Chocorua (RE), A53

"Chocorua," A53, A58, F27-28

Chocorua and Other Poems (Williams), D67

"Choosing a Monument," A13, C221

Christian Science Monitor, C539, C587

"Christmas Night," A3
"Christmas Tree," A20, A39, A62
Ciardi, John, B27
"Circe," C28
"The Clam Diggers and the Diggers of Sea Worms," A18, A39, A62, B50, C415, F29, G21
Clark, Eleanor, B8
Clark, LaVerne H., A33a-b, B123
"Classification," A55, A58, C761
"Class Ode," C46
The Clear Blue Lobster-Water Country (Connellan), D77
"Clear, Precise, Controlled," rev. by RE, C293
Clemente, Vince, A57n, B158
"A Clerihew for Alan Gaylord," A62, C826
The Clever Body (La Follette), D4
"Cliff," A27, C546
"Clocks," A20, C374
"Closing Off the View," C313
The Clouds . . . (W.C. Williams), rev. by RE, C206
"Coast of Maine," A39, A62, B130, C725
Colby, Vineta, B41
"Cold Fall," A16, B42, C335
"Cold White Death," C517, F30
Collected Later Poems (W.C. Williams), rev. by RE, C248
Collected Poems (de la Mare), rev. by RE, C132
Collected Poems (H.D.), rev. by RE, C24
Collected Poems 1917-1952 (MacLeish), rev. by RE, C282
Collected Poems 1923-53 (Bogan), rev. by RE, C315
Collected Poems 1932-1961 (Abbe), D5
Collected Poems 1930-1960 (RE), A18

Collected Poems 1930-1976 (RE), A39
Collected Poems 1930–1986 (RE), A62
The Collected Poems of Edith Sitwell, rev. by RE, C341
The Collected Poems of John Peale Bishop, rev. by RE, C206
Collected Poems (Pitter), rev. by RE, C598
Collected Verse Plays (RE), A19
The College Book of British and American Verse, ed. Hiatt and Park (1964), C76
A College Book of Modern Verse, ed. Main (1970), A13a, C76, C149
College English Association, B68
College English: The First Year, ed. Morris et al. (1968), C76, C149
College of Charleston Miscellany, C769
A College Treasury . . , ed. Jorgensen and Shroyer (1967), B27, C76, C254, C304
"Colleoni of the Word," C541, F31
Collins, Martha, B150, C315
"Coloma," A48
Colorado Review, C373
The Colour of Saying . . ., ed. Maud and Davies (1963), C76
Colpix Records, G11
"The Come-On," A27
"Commas in Wintertime," A58, A62, C814
Commencement Address (Holderness School), B72
Commentary on "On a Squirrel Crossing the Road . . .," " B64, B146
"Comments," C779
Comments on "Am I My Neighbor's Keeper?" B73
"A Commitment," A18, A24, A39, A62, C388

"Common Charms from Deep
  Sources," rev. by RE, B150,
  C3315
Common Sense, C126
*Communicative Performance of
  Literature*, ed. Gilbert (1977),
  C413
Communicative Writing, ed. Bowen
  et al. (1978), C85, C325
"The Community Dog Show," C12
A Complete College Reader, ed.
  Holmes and Towle (1950), C76
*The Complete Poems of Frederick
  Goddard Tuckerman*, rev. by RE,
  C530
The Complete Reader, ed. Beal and
  Korg (1967), C85
*A Comprehensive Anthology of
  American Poetry*, ed. Aiken
  (1944), C76
"Compulsion is Hid in the Blood:
  Conflicts," B17, F56
Concerning Poetry, C661-63
Concerning the Young (Maas), rev.
  by RE, C96
"Concord Cats," A13, A18, A39,
  A62, B90, G18-19
Concord Monitor, E65
Cone, Edward, H1
"Configuration," A62
Conjunctions, C791-92
Connellan, Leo, B128, D21, D25,
  D38, D49, D65, D77
Connell, Evan S., Jr., C505
"Consider the More Intricate and
  Ingenious Situations," C128, F58
Constable, T. and A., A2a, A3a,
  A3a*n*
"Consultant's Choice," C777
Consultant's Reunion 1987 . . , C829
"Contemplation," A20
*Contemporary English:
  Explorations*, ed. Pannwitt et al.
  (1976), C325
*Contemporary New England Poetry:
  A Sampler*, ed. Ruffin, B161
*The Contemporary Poet as Artist
  and Critic*, ed. Ostroff, B73, C487
Contemporary Poetry, C187-89,
  C208, C215
Contemporary Poetry, ed. Miller
  (1954), B36
Contemporary Poetry in America,
  ed. Williams (1973), C31, C76,
  C149, C161, C504
Cook, Albert, B66
Cook, Reginald, B115, C422
"Cooperation Is No Competition,"
  A58, C751
Corey, Stephen, C819, D50
Cott, Jonathan, B142
Counter Measures, C647-48
"Cousin Florence," A16, A18, A24,
  A39, A59, A62, B54, B76, B81,
  C333, G7, G10, G14, G20-21,
  G29
"Cover Me Over," A7, A11, A18,
  A24, A36, A39, A62, B42, B90,
  G4, H1
Coxe, Louis O., A60*n*
Cox, Sidney, B14
"Craft Interview with Richard
  Eberhart," A45, E60
"The Craft of the Lyric Line," rev.
  by RE, C453
"Creative Splendor," C424
"Creators," F32, G19
"Creatures," C300
Crews, Harry, D89
*The Criterion Book of Modern
  American Verse*, ed. Auden
  (1956), C168, C254
Critical Essays on Louise Bogan, ed.
  Collins (1984), B150, C315
"Criticism of a Poem about
  Criticism," C539

"The Critic With His Pained Eye," A3, A18, A24, A36, A39, A62, C539

Cronin, Anthony, B55

Crossing America (Connellan), B128

The Crow and the Heart (Carruth), rev. by RE, C453

Crucible, C719

The Cry of Rachel, ed. Sister Mary Immaculate (1966), B45, C294

Cry of the Human (Mills), B119, D23

The Crystal Image . . ., ed. Janeczko (1977), C325

Cumberland Poetry Review, C794-95

Cummington School of the Arts, A10

Cunningham, J.V., A60*n*

Current Biography, E8

Currents in Poetry, ed. Corbin (1968), C325

"Cutting Back," C577

"Cynic Song," A2, B6

Daily Pennsylvanian, E11-13

"Dame Edith Sitwell," E5

"Dam Neck, Virginia," A6-7, A11, A18, A24, A39, A59, A62, B21, B25, B33, B90, C162, F59, G3-5, G7, G10, G14, G17, G27

Damned Ugly Children (Glaze), C543

"A Dance for Vance," C739, F33

Daniels, Kate, D52

"Dark Memories," A55, A58, C784

The Dark Sister (Scott), D2

Dart, C691

Dartmouth, C378-79, C382, C473, C686-87, E2, E4-5, E9-10, E15, E18, E21, E31, E37, E39, E54

Dartmouth Alumni Magazine, A3a, A13a, B27, C36, C64, C76, C85, C108, C143, C161, C254, C276, C325, C368-69, C512, C851, E63, E71

Dartmouth Bema, C4, C9, C20-21, C46

Dartmouth College Library Bulletin, C467, C685

"The Dartmouth College Museum Presents the Class of 1926 Reunion Show," J2

Dartmouth Publications, B62, B67, B77, B80, B84, B91, B95, B99, B104

Dartmouth Quarterly, C291-92

Dartmouth Verse 1922-1932, B5, C52

Darweesh, Mahmond, D19

Dasein, C471

Davenport, John, A39c, B5

David Lewis (publ.), B105

David McKay Co. (publ.), B135

Davis Enterprise, E50

Dawson, Robert, D9

"The Day," (Bouchet), trans. RE, B101

"The Day-Bed," A16, A18, A24, A39, A62, B42, C327

Day-Lewis, Cecil, B47, E17

"Day Song," C44

"Dead Skunk," A62, B154, C810

Dean, Ruth, E61

"Dear Me: —," B1

"Dear Whit," B100

"Death by Drowning," A20, C498

"Death in a Taxi," A48, C766

Death in Lobster Land (Connellan), D38

"Death in the Mines," A39, A62, B113, C636, F34

"Death Is Indescribably Much on Me," A2, G3, G17

"Death of a Friend," C854

"Death, Then the Last, Then the Depth," C187

Decal Poetry Review, C632

Decca Records, G14

Decision, C127-28

"Deep Fishing," A62, C836

"Deep, Lyrical Feelings," C268

"The Defense of Poetry," C247

de la Mare, Walter, C132

"Delicacy," C736

Dell (publ.), B64n

Delora Memorial Fund for World Brotherhood, B139

Denison, T.S. (publ.), B49

Denney, Reuel, B14n

Denver Quarterly, C817-18

Departure, C350

De Pol, John, A57n, B157

"Depths," A58, F35

Derwood, Jean, J1

"Desire," C506n

Desire: Erotic Poetry Through the Ages, ed. Packard (1980), B141

"Despair," C8

"Despair ['O the snows last so long']," A33, A39, A62, C615, F36

Deutsch, Babette, C303, C821

"Devils and Angels," A19, C475, E10, F37-38, G20

Devil's Millhopper, C761, C770

Devin-Adair (publ.), B23

"A Dialogue," B40

Dialogue/Exchange, C246, C395

A Dialogue of Modern Poetry, ed. Bailey (1939), C76

Dial Press, B4, B64

"Dialogue: The Poet and the Professor," C395

The Diamond Anthology, ed. Angoff et al., A27a

Dickey, James, A45, A47n

Dickson, William, B48

Dictionary of Literary Biography Yearbook: 1986, ed. Brook, B159

"Difference," C650

"The Difficulty of Ideas," A62

"The Diggers of Clams and Diggers of Sea Worms," G7

The Dimensions of Robert Frost (Cook), C422

Diogenes, C135-36

"A Dirty Hand," C614

A Dirty Hand (Scott), B94, C614

"Discovery," A58

A Discovery and Possession of America, ed. Guimond, C594

Discovering Modern Poetry, ed. Drew and Conner (1961), C76, C161, C254

Discovery No. 6, ed. Bourjaily (1955), B40

Discovery and Response . . ., ed. Banta and Satterwhite (1970), C76

The Dispossessed (Berryman), rev. by RE, C200

"Dissertation by Wax Light," A2, A11, B7, C77

"Dissertation by Waxlight (III)," C80

The Distinctive Voice, ed. Martz, A1a, A3a, A20a, C64, C256, C372, C418, C481

"Divarication," C446

"The Diver," A20

"Division," A58

"Divorce," A20, C463

Dodd, David, E49

"Dog Days," C859

Dolin, Arnold, B40

Donaldson, Scott, D14

Donoghue, Denis, E19

Do Not Go Gentle: Poems on Death, ed. Packard, B143, C76

Doors Into Poetry, ed. Walsh (1970), B85

Dorn, Alfred, B69, B92

Dorsey, John, E24

The Double Axe (Jeffers), rev. by RE, C206

Doubleday & Co. (publ.) B96, B100

The Dragon and the Unicorn (Rexroth), rev. by RE, C284

Drapkin, Michael, E25

"A Dream," A51, A58, A62

"The Dream," A6-7, A11, A18, A39, A62, B17, C147, I7

"Dream and Reality," C456, F192

"Dream Journey of the Head and Heart," A20, A24, A39, A62, C480

The Dream of Alcestis (Morrison), rev. by RE, C264

"The Dream of Time," C274

Dream's Navel (Pennant), D40

Drinking in the Spirit (Brenner), D58

"The Drunkard," C166

"The Dry Rot," A13, A18, A39, A62, C296, G10, G14, G19

"Dublin Afternoon," B20, C145

Duncan, Harry, A10

The Duodecim Annual 1923, B2

Durrett, William, E33

"Dusty Answer," A58, C796

Dylan, Bob, E50

Dylan Thomas's Choice . . ., ed. Maud and Davies (1964), C76

Dylan Thomas: The Legend and the Poet, ed. Tedlock (1960), B58, C323

Each Leaf Shines Separate (Warren), D76

Eagle, C56, C70

"Eagles," A20, A24, A38, A58, C509

Eakins Press, A26

"Early Austin Years Are Recalled by Famed Poet," E42

"Early Poems," (sec. title), C114-17

Earth House (Handy), D10

The Earth Is the Lord's . . ., ed. Plotz (1965), A13a, A16a

"Earth Sanctions Old Men," A3, A3a*n*

"Easter," F192, G27; See "Easter 1960"

"Easter Absolutes," C285

"Easter 1960 (later "Easter")," G192, G27, G29

East Side Review, C525, C534-36

Eaton, Richard, B118

"Eberhart," C679

Eberhart, Alpha LaRue, A2

Eberhart, Dryden, C1

Eberhart, Elizabeth (RE's sister), A3

Eberhart, Elizabeth B. (Mrs. RE), A7, A11, A16, A18, A20, A27, A33, A48

Eberhart, Gretchen, A13, A18, A20, A27, A33, A45, A48

Eberhart, Mrs. Alpha (RE's mother), A1

Eberhart, Richard Butcher ("Dikkon"), A11, A18, A20, A27, A33, A48

Eberhart, Stephanie, A33

"Eberhart Brings His Poetry to the Cow Town," E49

"Eberhart Compares Transcendentalist Emerson with Modern Poet Stevens," E14

"Eberhart Edits Undergraduate
   Poems," E15
"Eberhart: 50 Years of Poetry," E54
"Eberhart Is 'Ambivalent' About
   Book Award," E58
"Eberhart Reads Poetry, Traces
   Literary Career," E2
"Eberhart's Adaptation of de Vega
   Verse Drama . . ," E18
"Eberhart's 'Experience Evoked',"
   C699
"Eberhart's 'Grave Piece'," B38,
   C194
"Eberhart's 'Seals, Terns, Time,'"
   B110
"Eberhart's 'The Young Hunter',"
   C195
"Eberhart's 'Ur Burial'," C409
"Eberhart to Give Poetry Readings,"
   E37
"Eberhart Voices Meaning of Life at
   Austin High School Graduation,"
   E43
Echoes of Keats and Shakespeare,"
   rev. by RE, C533
"The Echoing Rocks," A24, C526,
   F39
Eckert, Gene, A46
"The Eclipse," C524
"Edgar Lee Masters," A58, A62
"Edna Millay," C811
"8:29," C224
84th Commencement, Holderness
   School (1966), B72
89 Poètes Américains . . .
   (Lowenfels), I4
El Castigo sin Veranza (Lope de
   Vega), E18
"The Elegance of Stately Measures,"
   C455, F40
Eliot, T.S., C95, E19, E33, E67, E68
Elliott, George P., B42

"Elusive Concretions," A13
"Emblem," A39, A62, C668
"Emerging," A33
"Emerson and Wallace Stevens,"
   A45, C502
Emerson, Ralph W., C502, E14
"Emerson's Concord," A58, A62,
   C789
Emery, Julie, E28
"Emily Dickinson," A33, A38-39,
   A62, B103, C609
Emily Dickinson: Letters from the
   World, ed. Harris (1970), B103
Emily's Bread (Gilbert), D71
Empires (Moore), D55
"Empson's Poetry," A45, B24, C163
Encounter, C330, C389-90, C492,
   C521-22
Encounters . . ., ed. Spender (1963),
   C389
"Encounters and Letters," C467
"Energy, Movement, and Reality,"
   C198
Engel, Bernard F., B90
England Reclaimed (O. Sitwell), rev.
   by RE, C226
Engle, Paul, B38, B64, C267
English Leaflet, C190
"The Enigma," A27, A39, A62, B90,
   C575, F41
"Envoi," C591
"Episode," A58
"Epitaph," F42
Epoch, C273-74
"Equivalence of Gnats and Mice,"
   A18, A39, A62, B59, C442, G16,
   G21, G27
"Ernest Chenaur (1937-1958)," C433
Erotic Poetry, ed. Cole, A3a
"Escape to Discovery," rev. by RE,
   C420
"An Evaluation," C42

"An Evaluation Under a Pine Tree, Lying on Pine Needles," A20, A39, A62, B61

Evans, Robert, B67

"Evening Bird Song," A33, A39, A62, C662

Evening Journal, E52

Everson, R.G., C414

"Evil," A27, A39, A62, B100, E47, F43, H3

"Evtushenko in Washington," C495

"Examination of the Psyche: Thoughts of Home," A20, A39, A62

"An Excellent Redaction," rev. by RE, C264

Expansive Light, A20a, C254, C325, C330, C457, C631

"The Expense of Critical Reason," C134

The Expense of Greatness (Blackmur), rev. by RE, C134

"Experience Evoked," A3, A3*an*, A11, A18, A24, A39, A62, C699

"Experience Is Like a Cloud of Summertime," F44

Experiment, C305

Experiment (Cambridge), C52, C55, C57-58, C64, C72, C74

Explicator, A3a, B9, C194, C409, C699

"The Explorer on Main Street," A27, A39, A52, A62, B90, C556, F45

Exploring Poetry, ed. Rosenthal, A3a, C76, C161

"The Extreme Water," C138, F46

"Extremity," A27, A39, A62, C465

Eye's Delight, ed. Plotz (1983), C630

Ezra Pound: The Critical Heritage, ed. Homberger, B112

The Faber Book of Modern Verse, ed. Roberts (1936, 1951, 1966), C76, C161

"Fables of the Moon," A16, A18, A39, A62, C390

"Face in the Clouds Larger than Life Size," A58

Face Lifts for All Seasons (Marx), D46

"Face, Ocean," A38-39, A62, C727, F48

The Face of Poetry, ed. Clarke, B123

"The Face, the Axe, and Time," A24, F47

Face Value (Skellings), D37

Falling Fountains, C694

A Fall in Mexico (Ostroff), D34

The Family Album of Favorite Poems, ed. Ernest (1959), C76

Fantasy, C146

"Fantasy of a Small Idea," A58, A62, B144

"Fantasy of the Impersonal," A58, A62

Farness, Jay, E34

"Far Out," A58, C701, F49

Fassett Recording Studio, G7

"Fate's Election," A58

"Father and Daughter," A20, C470

"Father and Son," A20, C513

"Fat Spider," A48, C728

Faust I and II (Goethe), D69

"Fear of Death by Water," A58

Feather Merchant (pseud. of W.H. Auden), B10

"Feat," A58, C782

Ferguson Press, A21

Ferguson, William, A28

Festschrift for Marianne Moore's Seventy Seventh Birthday, ed. Tambimuttu (1964), B75

Fields of Grace (RE), A33

Fifteen Modern American Poets, ed. Elliott (1956), A1a, A2a, A3a, A13a, B42, C31, C64, C76, C85, C108, C118, C121, C143, C149, C217, C225, C239, C254, C310, C327

"XV ['When dead the winter snows...']," A26, C549

Fifth World Congress (1981), B144

Fifty Contemporary Poets: The Creative Process, ed. Hunter (1977), B135, C734

Fifty Dartmouth Poems, sel. RE (1969), B95

Fifty Modern American and British Poets 1920-1970, ed. Untermeyer (1973), C76, C85, C646

Fifty Poems From Contemporary America, ed. Sayegh, I1

Fifty Six Dartmouth Poems, sel. RE (1972), B110

53 American Poets Today, ed. Witt-Diament and Fukuda (1962), C149

"Fifty Years of American Poetry: A Tribute to Marie Bullock," A60

"The Fight Against the Inert," A58

"The Fig that Floats," A58, C345

Fine Frenzy . . ., ed. Baylor and Stokes (1978), C85, C161

"The Fine Reaches of Enthusiasm," B68

Fire-Tested (Juergensen), B147

First Selected Poems (Connellan), D25

First Selected Poems (Packard), D35

"Fish Dinner 1972," C664

"The Fisher Cat," A33, A39, A52, A58, A62, C644, F50

Fishing for Snakes (RE), A22

"Fishing for Snakes," A22, A24, C522, F51

Fitts, Dudley, C100

Fitzgerald, Robert, A20n, C100

The Five-Fold Mesh (Belitt), rev. by RE, C96

"Five Poems," rev. by RE, C269

"Five Poets," B105, C269

"The Flag," A58, A62, C732

The Floating Candles (Lea), D60

Florida Poems (RE), A55

Florida Quarterly, C697-98

"Flow of Thought," A39, A62, F52

"Flux," A20, A24, A39, A62, B146, C504

"Fog I," A58, C775

"Fog 1 ['Fog may be total . . .']," A58, C803

"Fog II," A58

"Fog 2 ['The implications of fog...']," A58, C804

Folder 4, C344

Foley, Joel, E44

Folger Broadsides, A41, A43

Folger Shakespeare Library, A41, A43

Folkway Records, G9

"For a Lamb," A2, A11, A18, A24, A36, A39, A59, A62, B27, B42, B54, B81, C64, E49, E69, F59, G1, G7, G10, G14-16, G21, G29

"For Blake," A3

The Force of a Few Words, ed. Korg (1966), C76

Fordham Univ. Press, B157

Foreground, C173

Foreword by RE to *The Beasts & The Elders* (Siegel), B114

Foreword by RE to *Cry of the Human* (Mills), B119

Foreword by RE to *Desire: Erotic Poetry through the Ages*, ed. Packard (1980), B141

Foreword by RE to *Do Not Go Gentle: Poems on Death*, ed. Packard (1980), B143

Foreword by RE to *The Face of Poetry* (Clark), B123

Foreword by RE to *Her Beauty Likes Me Well* (Francia and Friedman), B137

Foreword by RE to *Moving Out* (Walker), B127

Foreword by RE to *Paul Sample Retrospective*, B65

Foreword by RE to *The Sandpipers* (Posner), B129

Foreword by RE to *Sixty Dartmouth Poems* (1969), B99

Foreword by RE to *Thirteen Dartmouth Poems* (1958), B48

Foreword by RE to *Thirty Dartmouth Poems* (1959), B53

Foreword by RE to *Thirty Dartmouth Poems* (1965), B80

Foreword by RE to *The Ventriloquist* (Huff), B134

"For Goethe in His Youth," C223

"The Forgotten Rock," A18, A24, A39, A62, C332

"For John Brooks Wheelwright" (later titled "Sometimes the Longing for Death"), C119

"Formative Mastership," A16, A18, A24, A39, A62

"The Form Is New," C383

"Forms of the Human," A13, A18, A24, A36, A39, A62, B42, C239, G18- 19, G27

For Rexroth: The Ark 14, ed. Gardner (1980), B140

"For Rupert Brooke," C35

The Fort and the Gate (RE), A40

"The Fort and the Gate," A40, A48, C740, F54

"For the Dartmouth Poetry Symposium, January 1970," B104, C602, F53

"Fortune's Mist," A18, A39, A62, B50, C412

Forty Dartmouth Poems, sel. RE (1962), B62

XLI Poems (Cummings), rev. by RE, C18

Forum, C733, C751, C772

"The Forum," C240, G18

"For What Can Warr, But Endless Warr Still Breed," F55

"Foundation," B11

Four Dartmouth Poems, B14

"Four Exposures," A20, A39, A62, C334, G7

"Four Lakes' Days," A2, A11, A18, A39, A62, B27, G3

Four Poems (RE), A51

"Four Poets," rev. by RE, C183

"Four Poets and Their Work," rev. by RE, C206

"Four Songs" (Siegmeister), H4

Fourteen Poems (Milosz), rev. by RE, C283

"Four War Poems," sec. in A6

"Fracture Within," C611

"Fragment of New York, 1929," A13, A18, A39, A62, C207, G19

Fragments, C692

"Fragments," A2, B6, C57

Francia, Luis, B137

Francis, Robert, C96

"Frank Stanford," C797

Fredericks, Matthew, A9

Free Gunners Handbook (RE), A5

Freeman, James Oliver, B160

"A Freshman Orientation Course," C17

Friedman, David B137

Friedman, Norman, B68

A Friendly Visit: Poems for Robert Frost, B44

Friends of Smith College Library Newsletter, C640

From A to Z: 200 Contemporary Poets, ed. Ray (1981), C738

"From 'Letter I'," C197

From Love Sequence with Variations (RE), A32

"From 'Poem in Construction'," F56-58

"From Poem in Construction (x) ['And at Lake Geneva . . .']," B18, C130

"From 'Poem in Construction [Consider the more intricate...]'," B18, C128

"From 'Poem in Construction [I Wrote Helen a letter . . .]'," B17, C118

"From 'Poem in Construction [There is a place in stoical autumn, a glass]'," C137

"From Sighting forthcoming from Chatto & Windus 1946," F59

"From 'Suite in Prison'," C87

From the Hills, ed. Plumley (1974), B117, C671

"From 'The Human Being'," C107

"From 'The Human Being [Fingers are largely filibusters . .]'," B10, C104

"From 'The Kite'," C174-75

"From the Manuscript of Eberhart's 'The Driver'," C516

"From 'Vignettes'," C749

Frontier Nursing Service, C177

First in April (Whitaker), A1b

Frost, Robert, B2, C422, E46, E57, E66, E69

"Froth," A33, A39, A62

F.T. Palgrave's The Golden Treasury . . . (Centennial Edition), ed. Williams, B25, C76, C254

Fuller, John, A33a

"The Full of Joy Do Not Know; They Need Not," A3, A3*an*, A11, A18, A39, A62, F60

"The Full Weakness of Man," A7, A179

"The Function of Poetry," E38

Furioso, A3b, B8, C106-7, C111-12, C133, C178, C180, C242, C267

Furnival, John, B131

A Further Semester (Marx), D80

"Furtive Marks on Paper," A13

Furst, J.H., Co., B36

"The Fury of Aerial Bombardment," A6-7, A11, A18, A24, A39, A59, A62, B21, B25, B27, B33, B76, B81, B90, C161, F59, F157, G3-5, G7, G10-11, G14-15, G17, G21, G27, G29, I1

"Futures," C353

"Gainesville Sun," A55, A58

Gainesville Sun, E53, E58, E64

A Galaxy of Verse, C737

Gale Research Company, B159

Galler, David, C453

Gallimaufry (publ.), B123

"The Game," A7, B22, C153

"The Garden God," A18, A39, A62, B50, C405, F61, G7

Gardner, Geoffrey, B140

Gardner, Isabella, C469, C793, D1, D6

Garrett, George, A47*n*, B161

Garrigue, Jean, B101, C815, D3, D17, E48

"A Gauze," C230, G18

The Gay Head Conspiracy (Baker), D16

Gelfand, M.A., A57, B157

"General Points," C671

Genesis: Book One (Schwatrz), rev. by RE, C156

A Geography of Poets, ed. Field, C637, C649

Georgia Review, C819

"Gerard Manley Hopkins," B108

Gerard Manley Hopkins: Priest and Poet (Pick), rev. by RE, C158

"The Gesture," A20, A24, A39, A62, C499

"Gestures Rich in Puropose," A27, C515, F62

Ghiselin, Brewster, B124, C358b

Ghormley, R.E. , pseud. of RE, B12, C26-27, C32

"Ghost—Chaste and White," C23

"The Giantess," A16, A39, A62, C320

The Gift Outright . . ., ed. Plotz (1977), C317, C595

Gilbert, Sandra, B138, D71

Gimdel, Mary, B142

Ginsberg, Allen, B125, B156, E12, E26, E65

G.K. Hall (publ.), B150

A Glad Day (Boyle), rev. by RE, C96

Gladly Learn and Gladly Teach . . ., ed. Plotz (1981), C102, C384, C649

"The Glance," A16, C310

Glass Hill, C223-25

Glaze, Andrew, C543, D20, D51

Glikes, Erwin A., B74

"Gnat on My Paper," A33, A39, A62, C657

"Gnats," A44, A48

"The Goal of Intellectual Man," A3, A11, A18, A24, A39, A62, G3, G17, G27, G29

"God and Man," A13, A18, A39, A62, C213

Godine, David, B80

"The Gods of Washington, D.C.," A18, A39, A41, A62, C452

"God to Man," C189

Goethe, J.W. von, D69

"Going," C851

"Going Backward, Going Forward," A62, C817

"Going to Class Under Greek Statues," A16, C336, F63

"Going to Maine," A58, A62, C677

Golden Horn 1965, C538

Golden Horn 1967, B88

"The Golden Road," C461

"The Gold Standard," B105

The Golden Year . . ., ed. Cain et al. (1960), C432

"Goners," C675, F64

"Good Place," A58, C733

Gotham Book Mart, B12

Gotham Bookmart Press, B16, B109

Go to the Shine That's On a Tree (RE), A29

"Go to the Shine That's on a Tree," A3*an*, A13, A18, A29, A39, A62, B42, B90, C108, G7, G14-15, G19, G29

"Go Your Own Way," C1

Grace Before Plowing (Masefield), C603

Graffiti (Guthrie), C453

"Grandson," A58, C800

Granite, C639, C683

Granite Publications, B111

"Grape Vine Shoots," A13, C287

"Grave Piece," A3, A18, A39, A62, B9, C38, C194

Graves, Robert, E57

"The Great Adventure," C37

The Great Adventure (Banning), rev. by RE, C37

Great Praises (RE), A16

"Great Praises," A13, A18, A24, A39, A59, A62, G10, G14, G19

"Great Principles Are Thrown Down By Time," A58, A62, C753

"The Great Stone Face," A13, C276, G18

"The Great Trees," A55, A58

Grecourt Review, A17, C406-7

"A Greek Returns," C24

A Green Place, ed. Smith (1982), C644

Greensleeves, C472, C497-501, C510, C525-26

The Green Wave (Rukeyser), rev. by RE, C201

Green With Beasts (Merwin), rev. by RE, C381

Greenwood, Douglas McCreary, B149

Green World, C491

Gregory, Horace, B8, C133, C269

"Grip of Cold," A58

"Grotesque-handed Engine, Fool-faced, Servitor," B8

"The Groundhog," A2, A6, A11, A24, A39, A59, A62, B7, B25, B27, B76, B81, B90, B116, B143, C76, E17, E24, E46, E59, E67, E72, G1-3, G5, G8, G10, G13, G15, G17, G20, G27, G29, I2, I7

The Groundhog Revisiting (RE), A34

"The Groundhog Revisiting," A34, A39, A62

Grove, Lieut. W. Berry, A5b-A5c

"Growing Up: The Jungle, The Orchard, The River," C843

Gryphon Records, G13

Guardian (London), C680

Guide to the Ruins (Nemerov), rev. by RE, C269

Guimond, James, C594

The Guinness Book of Poetry 1957/ 58 (1959), B51

The Guinness Book of Poetry 1958/ 59 (1960), B56

The Guinness Book of Poetry 1959/ 60 (1961), B59, C442

The Guinness Book of Poetry 1960/ 61 (1962), C434

"Gulled," A62, F65

"Gusto, Verve and Flair," rev. by RE, C367

Guthrie, Ramon, C453

Halcyon Press, A29

"Half-Bent Man," A18, A39, A62, B50, B90, C413, F156, G7, G10, G14, G21, G29

"Half Round," C376

"Half Way Measure," C578

Hall, Donald, C469, C598, C824, C848

Hallmark Cards (publ.), B87

Hamlet (Shakespeare), E11

"The Hamlet Father," A20, A39, A62

Hammer, Earl, B117

"The Hand," A62, C831

"The Hand and the Shadow," A16, A18, A39, A62, B36

"Hand-View," B17, F66

Handy, Nixeon Civille, D10, D39

"A Haphazard Poetry Collecting," A45, C669

Harcourt, Brace (publ.), B24, B63

"Hardening Into Print," A20, A24, A39, A52, A62, C501, E60, G15

"The Hard Structure of the World," A18, A39, A62, B90, C428, G10, G14, G29

Hardy Perennial (RE), A30

"Hardy Perennial," A30, A33, A39, A62, C612, F67

"Hark Back," A20, A24, B69, B76, C481
"Harmony," A58
The Harper Anthology of Poetry, ed. Nims (1981), B27
Harper, Ralph, D78
Harpoon, C771
Harris, Marguerite, B103
"Harsh Rocks," C704
Hartung, Rudolph, I5
Harvard Advocate, A32, C95, C99, C102, C113, C139-41, C834, C524, C527-28, C540, C655, C687, C693
Harvard Crimson, E32
Harvard Film Service, G4
"Harvard Stadium," A58, A62, C778
"Harvard Summer School Conference on the Defense of Poetry," C247, F68
Harvard Vocarium Records, G2
Haskins, Lola, D45, D72
"Hatred of the Old River," A39, A62, C645
Hauser, Robert, B125, B128
Hausman, Gerald, D11
Hawthorn House, A6
Hayden, Robert, B116
"The Haystack," A27, A39, A62, C560, F69
Hear of Israel (Marx), D22
The Heart's Garden / The Garden's Heart (Rexroth), rev. by RE, C582
"A Heart Still Wonder-Welling," E65
The Heath Introduction to Poetry, ed. de Roche (1975), C161, C325
Heaven and Hell (Huxley), rev. by RE, C352
"Heavenly Mindedness," C158
Hecht, Anthony, A60n

Heezen, B.C., C659
Heidelberg Graphics, B123
"The Height of Man," A20, A39, A62, B90
Heinemann (publ.), B58
Hellcoal Annual Two, C652
"The Helldiver Gunner," B26, F59
Henderson, Bill, B151
Henkel, Stephanie, E65
Henn, T.R., C278
An Herb Basket (RE), A10
"An Herb Basket," A10, A13, G18-19
Her Beauty Likes Me Well (Francia and Friedman), B137
Herbert, James A., B53
"Here and Now," C613, F70
Heroes and Heroines (Whittemore), rev. by RE, C183
Hershberger, Ruth, C839, E72
Heyen, William, A57n
"Hierarchy," C36
"High Afternoon," C427
High Country News, C763
Highlights of Modern Literature, ed. Brown (1954), B34
"High Tide" (Bouchet), trans. by RE, B101
Hika, C97, C114-17, C228
"Hill Climber," C63
"Hill Dream of Youth, Thirty Years Later," A27, A39, A62, B90, C532, F71
Hine, Daryl, B136
"His Own Poetry," B54, C444
Hoffman, Daniel, A33b, A60n
Hoffman, Fergus, E23, E26
Hogarth Press, B5-6
"Hölderlin, Leopardi, and H.D.," rev. by RE, C404
Hollander, John, A35, A47n, A60n
Hollins Critic, C519

Hollister, C.D., C659
Holm, Ernest, B48
Holmes, John, B57, C537, E24
"Homage to a Teacher," C849
"Homage to the North," A33, A39, A62, C631, F72
"Homage to James Laughlin," C791
"Homo Sapiens aetat 21," C25
"Hoot Owls," A18, A39, A62, C396,
"Hopelessness of Achieving the Past," A58
Hopkins Center (Jaffe-Friede Gallery), B65
Hopkins, Gerard Manley, C158, E46, E53
"The Hop-Toad," A39, A62, C676, F74
"Hornets by the Sill," C850
"The Horse Chestnut Tree," A13, A18, A24, A39, A59, A62, B32-33, B42, B54, B63, B76, B81, B90, C254, F157, G8-10, G13-15, G19-21, G27, G29, I2
Houghton, Mifflin (publ.), B136
"Hour," A44, A58, C754
Hour:::Gnats (RE), A44
The House (Noll), D74
Housman, A.E., E57
How Does a Poem Mean? (Ciardi), B27, C161
"How Do I Further Spend My Glory," A58, C689, F75
"How Do I Write Poetry?," F76
Howell, Soskin (publ.), B19, B21
"How I Became a Royal White Elephant, Third Class," C853
"How Is Your Ditentive 'I'-Persona?," C222
"How It Is," A58, A62, C758
"How I Write Poetry," A45, C304
"How I Write Poetry," A45, B81

"How the Spirit Descends in the Man," C781; see "Spirit Descends in Man"
Howl (Ginsberg), B125, E65
"How to Make Something of the Rocks," A58, C748
Hudson Review, A14, C174, C192, C294-97, C331-33, C358a
Huff, Robert, B134, D31, D79
"The Human Being Is a Lonely Creature," A3a*n*, A13, A18, A24, A36, A39, A62, B32, B42, B90, C295, G6-7, G16, G19
The Human Condition . . ., ed. Miller, Jr., et al. (1974), C504
Humanist, C164
"The Humanist," A3, A11, A18, A24, A39, A62, C92, C813
"A Human Good," C132
Humphries, Rolphe, B32, B45
Hunter, Alberta T., B135
Hutchinson (publ.), B55
Huxley, Aldous, C352
Huyck, W. Thomas, E5
"Hyancinths and the Jonquil," C16
"Hysteria of Communication," A58, C788

I Am the Jefferson County Courthouse (Glaze), D51
I.A. Richards: Essays in his Honor, ed. Brower et al., A35, B75
Icarus: An Anthology of Literature, ed. Bens and Baugh (1970), C76, C161
"Ichetucknee," A48, A55, A58, A62
"Icicle," A33, C633, F77
"The Ideal and the Real," A58, A62, C806
Ideas in Poetry, ed. Fidell (1965), C161
The Ides of March (RE), A25

"The Ides of March," A25, A27,
A39, A62, B90, B100, C555, F78
"I Did Not Die Enough," C196
"Idols of Imagination," A16, B42,
C309
"Idleness," A33, C642, F79
"I Fear Those Visions," C91
"If I Could Only Live at the Pitch
That Is Near Madness," A3, A6,
A11, A18, A24, A39, A62, B27,
B42, B54, B76, B81, C85, C88,
C685, G2, G6-7, G10, G14-15,
G18, G20-21, G29, H5, I2
"If This Be Love," A2
"Ilaria del Caretto," C43
"I Like a Pump, That Dirty Water
Draws," B8
"The Illusion of Eternity," A24, A39,
A62, C535, F80, G15, H5
"The Image of Ourselves," C233
"Imagination," A13, G19
Imaginative Literatue . . ., ed. Morris
et al. (1968), C76, C149
"Imagining How It Would Be to Be
Dead," A7, A11, A18, A24, A39,
A62, B25, B42, I7
"The Immortal Type," A27, C523
"Impatience As a Gesture of Divine
Will," A20, C307
"The Impersonal," A46, A58
"Impression," C3
The Improved Binoculars (Layton),
C383
"Inability to Depict an Eagle," A33,
C595, F81
"In After Time," A18, A24, A39,
A62, C425, G7, H5
"In a Hard Intellectual Light," A2,
A11, A18, A24, A39, A62, B42,
G1-3, G7, G17
In a Pig's Eye (Siegel), D48
*The Inauguration of James Oliver
Freeman . . .*, B160

In-between Times, C108
"Inchiquin Lake, Penobscot Bay,"
A39, A62, C695, F83
"Incidence of Flight," A39, A55,
A58, A62, C721
"The Incomparable Light," A18,
A24, A39, A62, C459, G15, G27
"The Incorruptibility of Nature," F56
"The Incredible Splendor of the
Magnificent Scene," A33, C597,
F82
"Independence and Resolution," A16
Indian Earth (Bynner), C73
"The Inevitable," C2
"Indian Pipe," A13, A18, A24, A39,
A62, B81, C257, G10, G14, G19,
G29
"Indian Summer," A13, C235, G18,
G19
"The Ineffable," A7, A11, A18, A39,
A62
"Inexplicable," A58
"Ingathering," B18
"Inner Voyage," C716
"In Prisons of Established Craze,"
A3, A3an, A11, A18, A24, A39,
A62, G3, G17
Inscape, C427
"In Situ," A48, C765
"Insomnia," C647, F84
"The Inspissation," B18
"In Sun," C61
Inter Collegiate Press, B145
Interim, B26
"Interior Events," A13
"Interior Winter Sequence," A48
"The Interrogator," A58
"An Interview" (*American Poetry
Review*), A45, E57
"An Interview" (*New York
Quarterly*), A45, E60
"An Interview" (*Pulse*), A45, E46

"An Interview" (*Shenandoah*), A45, E19

"An Interview" (*William and Mary Quarterly*), A45, E17

"An Interview with Richard Eberhart" (Broughton), A45, E57

"An Interview with Richard Eberhart" (Cannito et al.), A45, E46

"An Interview With Richard Eberhart" (Donoghue), A45, E19

"An Interview with Richard Eberhart" (Durrett), E33

"An Interview with Richard Eberhart" (Jeffrey Marshall), A45, E17

"Interview with Richard Eberhart" (Walker, 1982), E67

"Interview with Richard Eberhart" (Walker, 1986), E67

"In the Air," A48, C722

"In the Blood," C306, G7

"In the Evening Stark and Bare," A2, G1

"In the Garden," A18, A39, A62, B45, G7

In the Fourth World (Gilbert), B138

"In the Night When Destruction Shall Shake the World," A3, C138, G3

"In the Silence of Contemplation," H5

Into the Round Air, ed. Roseliep (1977), B133

"The Intractable Nature of Reality," F85

Introducing Poems, ed. Wagner and Mead (1976), C161

Introducing Poetry, ed. Coleman and Theobald (1964), C76

Introduction by RE to *Bread, Hashish and Moon*, ed. Bennanni (1982), B145

Introduction by RE to *Fifty Dartmouth Poems* (1969), B95

Introduction by RE to *Forty Dartmouth Poems* (1962), B62

Introduction by RE to *In the Fourth World* (Gilbert), B138

Introduction by RE to *John Milton* (1969), B96

Introduction by RE to *Para-Desa* (Stevens), B120

Introduction by RE to *A Poet to His Beloved* (1985), B153

Introduction by RE to *Settling in in Hanover* (Greenwood), B149

Introduction by RE to *To Eberhart from Ginsberg*, B125

"Introduction of Sir Herbert Read," B71

Introduction to Literature, ed. Altenbernd and Lewis (1963), C76, C161

An Introduction to Literature, ed. Singleton and Millet (1966), C76

Introduction to *Poesis*, C700

Introduction to Poetry, ed. Cavanaugh (1974), C143, C161

An Introduction to Poetry, ed. Kennedy (1971, 1974), C161

Introduction to the Poem, ed. Boynton and Mack (1965), C161

Introduction to Zydek, C768

"Invective with Suggestions," A58

Inventario, C246

"The Invitation of the Evening," A58

"Invocation to Avocation 1926," J2

"The Inward Rock," A20, A24, C466, G29

Ironwood, C797

"Isabella Gardner's Poems," C793

"I Saw a Horde of Ph.D's," F86

"I Seek Tall Trees for Melodies," C115

"Island Message," A58, C698

"I Slept Upon a Green Hill in
Spring," C59
"Is Poetry Dead? Not to Eberhart,"
E40
"It Was Today," C273
"Ives," A62, C448, F87
"I Walked Out to the Graveyard to
See the Dead," A3, A3an, A6-7,
A11, A18, A24, A36, A39, A62,
B8, B27, C138, G2-3, G10, G14-
15, G29
"I Walked Over the Grave of Henry
James," A7, A11, A18, A24, A39,
A62
"I Went to See Irving Babbitt," A3,
A3an, A18, A39, A62, C102, G3,
G17, G27
"I Will Not Dare to Ask One
Question," A7, A11, A18, A39,
A62
"I Wrote Helen a Letter But Got No
Reply," B17, C118, F155
Izzo, Carlo, I7

Jack Tales (Shipley), D64
Janeczko, Paul B., B146
Janschka, Fritz, A30
Jargon Society, B131
Jarrell, Randall, C269
Jaspersohn, William G., E37
J.B. (MacLeish), C421
"Jealousy," C301
Jeffares, A. Norman, B132
"Jeffers," C731
Jeffers, Robinson, C206, J3
Jeopardy, C616, C638
"Jerusalem Artichokes," B121
"Jewels of Rhythm," C193
"Job," A2
John Ciardi: Measure of the Man,
ed. Clemente (1987), B158
John Crowe Ransom, ed. Long and
Burr (1964), B70

John Finley (RE), A50
"John Finley," A50, A51, A58, A62
"John Holmes Introduces a Guest
Poetry Critic," C94
John Keats's Porridge, ed. McCabe,
B121
"John Ledyard," A33, A39, A62,
B100, C593, F88
John Milton (1969), B96
"Johnny Dare: The Helldiver
Gunner," B26
Johns Hopkins University Press, B60
Jolas, Eugene, B16, B129
Jonathan Cape (publ.) A1a
Jonathan Cape and Harrison Smith
(publ.), A1b
Jones, Richard, D52
Jones, Tom, A45, E14
Jordan, David, B122
Journal of Aesthetics & Art
Criticism, C234
Journey to Love (W.C. Williams),
rev. by RE, C347
Journey Toward the Roots
(Juergensen), D26
Juergensen, Hans, B147, D26, D59

"Kafka's America," B17
"Kaire," A20, A24, A39, A62, C500
Kaminski, John, E45
Kaminski, Marc, D73
Kanes, Lee, A30
Kansas City Journal, C98
Kaplan, Anne Bernays, B40
Kaplan, Jerome, B125
Keith, Christopher, B110
Kelly, Kate, D90
Kennedy, X.J., B161
Kentucky Poetry Review, C786-87
Kenyon Collegian, B70
Kenyon Review, B19, C123, C161-
62, C205, C227, C269, C275,
C299, C337, C357, C403, C594,
C536

Kernan, Michael, E62
Key Reporter, C506
"Key West," A55, A58, A62, C822
The Kid (Aiken), rev. by RE, C180
"The Killer," A58, A62, C823
"The Killer: On the Assassination of President Kennedy," A24, B74, F89
"Kinaesthesia," A33, A39, A62, B97, F90
Kinsella, Thomas, F200
Kinsey, Carolyn Huff, B66
"The Kiss of Stillness," C67
The Kite (RE), A14
"The Kite," A14, A20, A24, C358a
Kizer, Carolyn, E31
Klopp, Karyl, A25, A34
Koch, Vivienne, C278
Kosofsky, Scott-Martin, B128
Kotlowitz, Robert, B40
Krapf, Norbert, A57n, B157
Kronenberger, Louis, B98, B108
Kuhn, Anne W., A30
Kuhn, James, A30
Kunitz, Stanley, A60n, B41
Kuykendall, Karen, A55

The Labyrinth (Muir), rev. by RE, C232
"La Crosse at Ninety Miles an Hour," A20, A24, A39, A62, B90, C297, G15, G19
"Ladies and Gentleman . . .," F92
Ladies' Home Journal, C415, C440
"The Lady Styx," C7
La Follette, Melvin Walker, D4
Laing, Dilys, D7
Lamar University, E46
"The Lament of a New England Mother," A20, A39, A62, C468
Langland, Joseph, B64
Language, Form and Idea, ed. Strandness et al. (1963), C143

"Laocoon," A62, C840
"L'aprés-midi d'un faune," C66
"The Largess," A3, A3an, A11, A18, A39, A62, B17, B25, C124, G3, G17
The Last Magician (Corey), D50
"Later or Sooner," A20, A39, A62, C490, H4
"Late Summer," C438, F211
Lattimore, Richmond, A30
Laughlin, James, C791
Lawder, Douglas, D32
Lawrence, D.H., E46, E57
Layton, Irving, C383
Lea, Sydney, B154, D60
"Learning from Nature," A46, A48, A62, B139
"Leave Me My Golden Horn of Hours," C172
Lee, Marshall, B98
Lee, Terry, B77
"A Legend of Viable Women," A13, A18, A24, A39, A62, B27-28, C205, G18-19, I1
"Lenses," A33, C651
LeSiege, Annette, H5
"Letter I," A13, B28, C229
"Letter to Andrew Foster," C720
Letter to Dr. Krishna Srinivas, C713
"Letter to Ruth Hershberger," C839
"Let the Tight Lizard on the Wall," A3, A18, A39, A62
Levertov, Denise, C414
Lewis, R.W.B., A18c, A27a
Liberation, C441
Library Associates (Univ. of California, Davis), A44
Library of Congress, B71, B159, G3, G5, G8, G22-29
"The Library of Congress," C847
Library of Congress recording laboratory, G17-21
Licht, Sydney, B128

"Life and Death: Jean Garrigue (1914-1972)," A38-39, A62, C706, C815, F91
Life and Letters Today, A3b
"Life as Visionary Spirit," A18, A39, A62, B90, G7
"Life Necessity," C45
"Life Words," F93
Lifshin, Lyn, D66
"Light, Free Movements," A28
"Light From Above," A18, A24, A39, A62, C434, G21
"Light, Time, Dark," A39, A62, C674, F94
"Light Verse," A17, C407
"Like a Broad River Flowing," C381
"Lilac Feeling," A58, C750
"Lilting," F95
Limnology and Oceanography, C659
"A Line of Verse from Yeats," A58, A62, C787
"Lines to an Old Man," A13, C280
"Lines to the Dead in an Old New Hampshire Graveyard," C369
"Lions Copulating," A27, A39, A62, B141, F96
Listener, C76-78
The Listening Landscape (Zaturenska), rev. by RE, C133
Listen to the Light (Roseliep), D47
"Listing," A62, C825
"Literary Death," A45, C683, F97
Literary Review, C393-94, C502, C802, C805-9
Literary Spectrum, ed. Roy (1974), C209
Literary Types and Themes, ed. McNamee (1971), C161
Literature, ed. Hogins (1977), C85
Literature, ed. Pickering and Hoeper (1982), C76

Literature: The Human Experience, ed. Abcarian and Klotz (1982), C325
Literature: An Introduction . . ., ed. Kennedy (1983), C161
Literature for Understanding, ed. Cohen (1966), B25, C76
Literature for Writing . . ., ed. Steinmann and Willen (1962), C76, C85, C161
Literature in America: The Modern Age, ed. Kaplan (1971), C76, C85
Little, Brown (publ.), B73, B108
A Little Treasury of American Poetry, ed. Williams (1948), A7a, B25, C76, C111, C124, C130, C137, C149, C161-62
A Little Treasury of Great Poetry, English and American, ed. Williams, (1947) C76
A Little Treasury of Love Poems . . ., ed. Holmes, A2a
A Little Treasury of Modern Poetry, English and American, ed. Williams (1948, 1952, 1970), A2a, A3a, A13a, B27, C64, C76, C82, C85, C124, C143, C254, C325
A Little Treasury of 20th Century American Poetry, G11
"A Little While," F98
Liveright Publishing, B13
Living Proof (Skellings), D85
Local Assays (Smith), D86
Lockett, Sue, E27
"Lofty Principle," F99
The Logic of Poetry, ed. Monaco and Briggs (1974), C325
"Logos c. 1930," C590, F100
London Magazine, B37, C332, C411, C457-58
London Mercury, C62-63

London, Michael, B105
The Lonely Tower (Henn), rev. by RE, C278
Long, D. David, B70
The Long Reach (RE), A58
"The Long Swing," A55, A62
"Long Term Suffering," A33, A39, A62, C649
"The Look," A13, C256, G19
"Looking at the Stars," A20, A39, A62
"Looking Down," C49
The Looking Glass (Gardner), D6
"Looking Head On," A27, A39, A62, C540
"A Loon Call," A48, A62, C756
"The Loosening," A33, C627, F101
"Lorca," A38, A58, A62, C605, F102
Lords Weary's Castle (Lowell), rev. by RE, C183
"Los Arcos" (La Paz), A48, C640
Lospecchio Press, B156
"Loss (to V.R. Lang)," A20, A39, A62, C447, F192
"The Lost," A20, A24, A39, A62, C508
"The Lost Children," A18, A39, A62, B45, B90, G7, G29
"The Lost Poem," A13, C290, G19
"Louise," A58, C797
"Love Among the Ruins," A18, A39, A62, C366, G21
Love Hungers to Abound, ed. Plotz (1978), C263, C359
"Love on," C616, F103
"Love Pieces," A27
"A Love Poem," A13, A18, A39, A62, C220, G18-19, H5
"Love Poetry," A58
"The Lovers," C737
Love Aspects . . ., ed. Garrigue (1975), C121, C263

"Love Sequence With Variations," A48, C655, F104
"The Love Song of J. Alfred Prufrock" (Eliot), E67
Lowell House Printers, A25
Lowell, Robert, A18a, A18b, A27a, A27b, A33a, A39c, C183, C269, C759, E24, E57
Lowenfels, Walter, I4
"The Low Swing," A58
"Lt. Comdr. Richard Eberhart Reading Poetry," G3
"Lucubration," A18, A39, A62, B47, G21
The Lüftwaffe in Chaos (Rinaldi), D84
Lundgren, Robert, B69, B92
Lutheran Witness, E35
"Lying Still," A58
Lynx, C485
"Lyric," C292
"The Lyric Absolute," A6-7, A18, A39, A62, G3, G17, G27
Lyric Poems, ed. Howard (1968), A13a, C108, C149
The Lyric Potential, ed. Miller, Jr., A1a, B116, C76
The Lyric Psalter, ed. Mayer (1940), B13

Maas, Willard, C96
MacArthur, Mary, B123
McCabe, Vintoria, B121
McCarty, Raymond, D53
McColm, Del, E50
McCorison, Marcus, A15
McCurdy, Deborah, B125
McCurdy, Michael, A29, A38a, B125, B128
McKeon, Edith, A26
MacLeish, Archibald, B109, C282, C319, C421, C464
Macmillan (publ.), B132

MacNeice, Louis, E17
Madeira & Toasts for Basil Bunting's 75th Birthday, ed. Williams (1977), B131
"The Mad Musician," A19, C476, E10, F105
Madonna Who Shifts For Herself (Lifshin), D66
"The Magical," A7, C173
The Magic Badge (Friedman), D68
Maia, see Padelford, Louise Hawkes; A3a, A3a*n*, A26*n*, C54-55
Maine Lines . . ., ed. Aldridge (1970), A16a, A18a, C415, C417, C428, C458, C477, C504
"A Maine Roustabout," A20, A24, A36, A39, A62, C458, E68, G15, G27, G29
"Maine Summer High Color Luuncheon," A46, A58
"Mais l'Amour Infini Me Montera dans L'Ame," A39, A62, C84
"Major Poet and Literary Innovator," C248
"Making Poetry a Continuum . . ," B151, C819
"Man and His Fellows," C39
Man and His Fellows (Hopkins), rev. by RE, C39
"Man and Nature," A39, A58, A62, C646, F106
Mandala: Literature for Critical Analysis, ed. Guerin et al. (1970), C76
A Man in the Divided Sea (Merton), rev. by RE, C183
"Man Is God's Nature," A16
"The Man of Autumn," C275
"A Man of Sense," A13, A58
"The Man of Summer," C275
"A Man of the Forties," F107
A Mantlepiece of Shells (Todd), rev. by RE, C342

Manotou Messenger, E34
"Man's Fate," C610, F108
"Man's Greed and Envy Are So Great," A3, A18, A39, A62, G2-3, G17, G29
"Man's Type," A33, A39, A62
"A Man Who Was Blown Down by the Wind," A39, A62, C601, F109
"The Man With the Green Glasses," B2
Many Voices, G12
Mark, Alan, E69
"Marrakech," A27, A39, A62, B82, B90, B100, C554, E25, F110, G15
Marshall, Jeffrey, E17
Marx, Anne, D22, D46, D80
Masefield, John, C533, C603
A Masque of Surgery (Glaze), D20
Massachusetts Poems (Connellan), D49
Massachusetts Review, C447, C495, C547-53
"The Master Image," A20, C514
Master Poems of the English Language, ed. Williams (1966), B83, C76
"The Mastery," A27, B90, C554, F111, G115
"Matador," A20, A39, A62, B90, C430
Material Goods (Burroway), D44
"The Matin Pandemoniums," A24, C529, F112
Maule's Curse (Winters), C99
"Maya and the Hunter," A2, C54
M.B.A., E12
Mayer, Harry H., B13
"May Evening," A20, A24, A39, A62, B70, B90
May, James Boyer, B69, B92
"Maze," A2, A6, A11, A18, A24, A39, A62, B5, G1-3

"M.D.," C32
Meade, Richard, D54
"Meaning Death," F113
"Meaningless Poem," A33, A39,
    A62, C663, F114
"The Meaning of Indian Summer,"
    C314
"A Meditation," A3, A3an, A11,
    A18, A39, A62, B25, B42, C111,
    F115, G3, G15
"Meditation by an Old Barn in the
    Heart of Summertime," C176
"Meditation of God," A33
"Meditation One," A20, A24, C483
"Meditation on the Sun," A2
Meditations on a Great Man Gone
    (Slobodkin), B78
"Meditation Two," A20, A24, A39,
    A62, B71, C81
"Meditation II" (Audience), C81
"Meditation Two ['Style is the per-
    fection of a point of view'],"
    C486
"Mediterranean Song," A16, A18,
    A39, A62, C305
"The Melancholy Fit," A58, C711
"Members of the English
    Department," F116
"Memoir," B44
"A Memoir," poem by RE, A62
"A Memoir" (RE), B75
"Memory," A27, A39, A62
"Memory and Desire," A58, B69
"Memory, Confrontation, Desire,"
    C506, F148
"Memory of Learning 'Thanatopsis'
    in Youth," B157
"Memory of Meeting Yeats, AE,
    Gogarty, James Stephens," A45,
    B132, C393
"Mencken Has the Last Laugh," E16
Mencken, H.L., E16

Mentor Books, B34
Meredith, William, A47n
Merrill, James, A60n
Merton, Thomas, C183
Merwin, W.S., A60n, C301
Messages . . ., ed. Kennedy (1973),
    C85
"Metamorphosis," C113
"Mexico Phantasmagoria," A27,
    F117
MHC Publications, B102, B107,
    B117
Michael Joseph (publ.), B47
Michigan Quarterly Review, C831,
    C850
Midwestern University, A23
Mickle Street Review, C753
Mid-Century American Poets, ed.
    Ciardi, A2a, B8, B27, C64, C76,
    C85, C161-62, C205, C209
"Middle Way," C232
"Midwinter," A58
Mikhail, E.H., B132, C393
Millay, Edna, C811
"Millennia," B161
Miller, Dorothy Munns, B139
Miller, James E., Jr., B116
Miller, Mary Owings, B34, C215
Miller, Orville Crowder, B139
Mill Mountain Review, C649-50
The Mills of the Kavanaughs
    (Lowell), rev. by RE, C269
Mills, Ralph J., Jr., B119, D23
Milwaukee Journal, E52
"Mind," A58
"Mind and Nature," A39, A62,
    C724, F118
The Mind of John Keats (Thorpe),
    rev. by RE, C40
"Mirror of MacLeish," C464
Mirrors: An Introduction to Poetry
    1925, ed. Knott and Reaske
    (1975), A16a

Misapprehensions (Pennant), D75
A Miscellany of American Poetry
  1925, rev. by RE, C34
Miscellany Two, ed. Reginald Cook
  (B115), C667
"The Mischief," C266, G18
Mississippi Review, C708, C744-45
"Mistaken Identity," A55, A58, A62,
  C726, F119
"A Mixed Bag," C120
Miya, Frank, B62
MLA Newsletter, E38
The Modern Age, ed. Lief and Light,
  B25, C161
Modern American and British
  Poetry, ed. Untermeyer (1955),
  A7a, A13a, C76, C85, C162,
  C254, C451, C457
Modern American Poetry: New and
  Enlarged Edition, ed. Untermeyer
  (1962), C76
Modern Poems, ed. Ellman and
  O'Clair (1976), C76, C161
Modern Poetry, ed. Mack et al.
  (1961), C161
The Modern Poets . . ., ed. Brinnin
  and Read (1963), C143, C161
Modern Poetry American and
  British, ed. Friar and Brinnin,
  A3a, B8, C76, C122
Modern Poetry: British and
  American (1966), C325
Modern Quarterly, C119
Modern Religious Poems, ed. Trapp,
  A1a, A6, A16a, B18, C459
Modern Verse in English 1900-1950,
  ed. Cecil and Tate (1958), C76,
  C205
"A Moment of Equilibrium Among
  the Islands," A20, A24, A39,
  A62, B90, C454, F120
The Moment of Poetry, ed. Allen
  (1962), B60

"The Moment of Vision," A6-7,
  A11, A18, A39, A62
"Moment That Stays But Passess,"
  C841
M: 1000 Autobiographical Sonnets
  (Moore), C101
Monkey, C1n
Moods of the Sea . . ., ed. Solley and
  Steinbaugh (1981), C348
Moore, Marianne, B43, B75, E29
Moore, Merrill, C101
Moore, Richard, D12, D55
"Moosilauke Phantasy," B3
"'The More I Have Traveled . . .',"
  rev. by RE, C319
Morgan, Bill, B156
The Morning Song of Lord Zero
  (Aiken), C494
Morrill, David, B122
Morris Harvey College, B102, B107
Morse, Samuel French, B14n, C625
Mosher Press, B3
"The Mother Part," A20, C365
"Mother Swallow," A58, C709
"Motion as Grace," A13, C271, G19
The Motive for Metaphor
  (Blessington and Rotella), A56
Mountain State Press, A61
Moving Out (Walker), B127
Mueller, Lisel, D88
Muir, Edwin, A18a, A18b, A27a,
  A27b, A33a, C232
Mundus Artium, C546, C577-78,
  C580
Muse of Fire . . ., ed. Richardson and
  Shroyer (1971), C209, C254
"The Muse—With Yankee Accent,"
  C210
Music and Fire, ed. Richardson and
  Shroyer, A3a
"The Music of Values," rev. by RE,
  C494

"Music Over Words," B92, C565, F121

Mutiny, C400-2

"My Bones Flew Apart," A2, A11, A18, A39, A62, G3, G17

"My Brains Are Slipping in the Fields of Eros," A27, A39, A62

"My Desire to Write Poetry," B9

Myers, Robert J., B87

"My Golden and My Fierce Assays," A16, A18, A39, A62

"Mystery of the Abstract," A62, C280

"Mysticism Has Not the Patience to Wait for God's Revelation," A6-7, A11, A18, A24, A39, A62, C122, F122

"The Mystical Beast in the Shadows," A62, B154

"My Temples Quake While Fires Exhale," A7

Nadas, Elizabeth P., E29, E32

Nadja (publ.), A53

"Nannette," B5

Nation, C155, C157, C253, C351-53, C362, C364, C366, C385, C396, C405, C412, C423, C425, C428, C459, C464, C466, C559-60, C581- 82, C654, C681, C726

"National Book Award Acceptance Speech," A45

National Book Award for Poetry (1977), A45, E54, E58

National Council of Teachers of English, B155

National Endowment for the Arts, A42

National Poetry Festival . . . (1964), B71, C457, C480-81, C486, C499

Nation's Schools, C85, E6

Naval Air Station (Wildwood, N.J.), C165

The Necessary Angel (Stevens), rev. by RE, C272

"Necessity," A2, A11, A18, A39, A62, B6, C72

"The Needle of the Eye," A3, C126

Neef, Carol, E36

"Nefretiti," C218

Negative Capability, C803, C816, C833-34, C839-49, E62, E67, E72

Nemerov, Howard, A60n, B81, C269

"The Nets by Brewster Ghiselin," B124, C358b

Neruda, Pablo, C183

The Neurosis of Man (Burrow), C222

New American and Canadian Poetry (ed. Gill), rev. by RE, C653

New American Library, B30-31, B34

New American Review, C595

New and Selected Poems (Gardner), C793

"New Anthology Includes Eberhart," E39

The New British Poets, ed. Rexroth (1949), C214

"New Criticism," E54

The New Criticism (Ransom), C134

New Directions (publ.), A6, A24, A57, B9, B11, B18, B26, B28

New Directions in Prose & Poetry 1937, B9

New Directions in Prose & Poetry 1939, B11

New Directions Number Seven 1942, B18, C106, C128, C130-31, C137

New Directions 10 (1948), B26

New Directions in Prose and Poetry 12 (1950), B28, C205, C229

A New Directions Reader, ed. Carruth and Laughlin (1964), C161

New Directions 6 (1941), rev. by RE, C150

"A New England Bachelor," A20, A24, A39, A62, B63, B90, G451, G15, G27, G29

New England Galaxy, C484, C633

New England Review, A51, C756, C829

"A New England View: My Report," A20, A24, C472

"New Entrpreneurial Man," A62

A New Folder, ed. Aldan (1959), C344

"New Hampshire, February," A7, A11, A18, A24, A39, A52, A62, B42, B54, B81, B90, C143, E43, E46, G7, G10, G14-15, G20-21

New Hampshire: Nine Poems (RE), A52

New Letters, C738, C750

New Letters in America, ed. Gregory and Clark (1937), B8

"New Looks at Yeats," rev. by RE, C278

"New Love," A27, C544, F123

"New Marriage," C808

New Masses, C85-86

The New Modern Poetry, ed. Rosenthal (1967), C161, C362

The New Oxford Book of English Verse, ed. Quiller-Couch, rev. by RE, C123

The New Pocket Anthology of American Verse, ed. Williams (1955), B39, C76, C325, C330-32

New Orlando Poetry Anthology, ed. Vrbovska et al. (1963), B69; 1968, B82, B92, C481, C559, C579

New Orlando Publications, B69, B92

New Poems by American Poets, ed. Humphries (1953), B32, C254, C295

New Poems by American Poets #2, ed. Humphries (1957), B45

New Poems 1940, ed. Williams (1941), C76, C111

New Poems 1942, ed. Williams, B17, C124, C147

New Poems 1943, ed. Williams, B19, C144

New Poems 1944, ed. Williams, B21, C161-62

New Poems 1957, ed. Nott et al., B47

New Poems 1960, ed. Cronin et al. (1960), B55, C399

"Newport Honors the State's Poets," E68

New Republic, A3a, C71, C73, C109, C121, C156, C281, C354, C370, C656, C775

New River, C607

"News," A62

Newsday, E52

News of the Universe . . ., ed. Bly (1980), C76

New Signatures: Poems by Several Hands, B6, C52, C57, C72

"News of the World," A58

New Statesman, C418

New Student, C31

New Ventures, C306-7

New Voices . . ., ed. Moore and Newton (1945), C153

"New Vows," F124

"A New Word-Sculpture," C100

New World Writing: Second Mentor Selection (1952), B30

New World Writing: Third Mentor Selection (1953), B31

New World Writing: Fifth Mentor Selection (1954), B35

New Yorker, C108, C378, C413, C417, C454-55, C477, C503, C529, C596, C615, C617, C630-31, C644, C668, C702, C725

The New Yorker Book of Poems
   (1969), C413, C417, C477, C503,
   C529
New York Herald Tribune, A3b,
   C100, C211
*New York Herald Tribune Book
   Review*, C391
New York: Poems, ed. Moss, C637
"New York Prospect," A58, C717
New York Quarterly, B152, C608,
   C634, C673, C755, C827, C832,
   C854-55, E60
The New York Quarterly
   ("Reflections and Developments,"
   1984), B152
New York Review of Books, C504
"New Year's Eve," A2
New York Times, A3b, A27a, C87,
   C91-93, C177, C198, C753
The New York Times Book of Verse,
   ed. Lask (1970), C87, C177
New York Times Book Review, A2a,
   A3a, C149, C193, C196, C216,
   C226, C233, C244, C248, C257,
   C265, C268, C282-84, C293,
   C304, C311, C315, C319, C338,
   C342, C355, C363, C367, C381,
   C383, C397, C414, C419-20,
   C424, C429, C478, C494, C505-
   6, C530, C533, C537, C543,
   C584, E59
"Nexus," A20, A24, A39, A62,
   C431, F125
Nieuw, C424, C433, C455
"Night and Day," C408
"Night Song," B102, F126
"Night Thoughts," A48
"Nightwatch on the Pacific," C68
Nimrod, C376
Nims, John F., A60*n*
Nine, C241
Nineteen Dartmouth Poems (1968),
   sel. by RE, B91

"Nirvana" (later titled "Cover Me
   Over"), B4, C31, C48; see "Cover
   Me Over"
"1934," A2, A11, A18, A24, A39,
   A62, B7, C78, G29
Nix, David, E37, E40
Nixon, Sallie, D33
"The Noble Man," A18, A39, A62,
   B33, C298, E23, F127, G19
"No Control," A58
Noll, Bink, D74
"No News Is Good Muse," A45,
   C680
"Nonino Dialectic," C170
"No Poet Gets the Success He'd
   Wanted," E52
"Nor of Mind," E12
Northern Lights, ed. Beck (1972),
   B111
Northwest Review, B148
*The Norton Anthology of Modern
   Poetry*, ed. Ellmann and O'Clair
   (1973), C122, C161, C451, C500
The Norton Anthology of Poetry, ed.
   Eastman (1970), A16a, B5, B36,
   C64, C501
*The Norton Introduction to
   Literature*, ed. Bain et al. (1970,
   1977 1981), C76, C161
*The Norton Introduction to
   Literature: Poetry*, ed. Hunter
   (1973), C76
"Nostalgia for Edith Sitwell," A46,
   A48
"A Note," B103
"A Note on Poetry," C386
"Note on *Protest*," B110
*Notes from a Bottle Found on the
   Beach at Carmel* (Connell, Jr.),
   C505
"Notes on Poetry" (1950), B27
"Notes on Poetry" (1959), C426

"Notes on Poetry" (1966), A45, B84, F128
"Notes on Poetry" (1968), F129
"Notes on Poetry . . . (May 16-18, 1968)," F130
"Notes on Poetry (January 1972)," F131
"Notes to a Class in Adult Education," C185
Notes Toward a Supreme Fiction (Stevens), C152
"Nothing But Change," A16, A18, A24, A39, A62, B54, G10, G14-15
"The Notion of Hell," C110
"Not So Many," C155
Nott, Kathleen, B47
No Voyage and Other Poems (Oliver), D8
Now, C181, C514
"Now Is the Air Made of Chiming Balls," A3, A11, A8, A24, A39, A62, B54, B76, C86, G2-3, G5, G7, G10, G14, G17, G29
Nunes, Donnel, E52
Nuova Corrente, C343
Nyholm, Jens, I2

The Oak (RE), A15
"The Oak," A15, A18, A24, A39, A62, C378, G7, G16, G21, G27
Oates, Joyce Carol, A57*n*
Observer (London), B56
Ocarina Annual, C325
Occident, C592
"Ocean View Hotel," C70
"Odd Events of History," G18
"Oddments of History," C261
"Ode" (W.H. Auden), B10
"Ode to Silence," A2, A18, A39, A62

"Ode to the Chinese Paper Snake," A7, A11, A18, A39, A62, B90, C168, F59, G4
"Oedipus," A13, A18, A39, A62, C246, C395, G29
"Oedipus [It seems abrogative . . .']," C262
"Offering to the Body," A48, C773
"Off Pemaquid," A24, B90, C510, F132
"Off Spectacle Isle," A18, A39, A62, B76
Of Poetry and Poets (RE), A45
Of Poetry and Power, ed. Glikes and Schwaber, B74
Of Solitude and Silence, ed. Jones and Daniels, D52
Often in Different Landscapes (Stokesbury), D28
"Of Truth," A7, A58, C144
"Of Truth" (1980), A47
"Of Truth: The Protagonist Speaking," B19, C144
O'Gorman, Ned, C469
Ohio University Press, B101
Older, Julie, D61
"An Old Fashioned American Business Man," A18, A39, A62
"Old Dichotomy: Choosing Sides," A58, A62, C802
"Old Memory," A58, C799
"Old Question," A33, A39, A62, F133
Old Raiger and Other Verse (Masefield), C533
"Old Tom," A20, A39, A62, B56, B90
"Old Tree by the Penobscot," A39, A62, C694, F134
Oliver, Mary, D8
Olson, Elder, C318

"On Anthologies Including the Norton Anthology of Modern Poetry," C714

"On A Squirrel Crossing the Road in Autumn, in New England," A16, A18, A24, A39, A59, A62, B39, B64, B81, B90, B146, C325, G10-12, G14-15, G21, G27, G29

"On Campus," E1

"Once More, O Ye . . .," A39, A62, C697, F138

O'Neal, Robert, B116

"On Encountering the Great-Great Grandson of William Wordsworth," C648, F135

100 Modern Poems, ed. Rodman (1949), A9, C76, C254, C325

One Life (Rukeyser), C391

"On Gretchen's 13th Birthday," C520

"On Hearing Bertrand Russell On Mind and Body," C291

"One Morning in 1649 (after Borges)," C623, F139

"One Way Dialogue," A13

"On First Hearing Beethoven's Opus 127, at 23 Fitzroy Square," A2

"On Getting Used to the World," A16

"Only in the Dream," A16, A18, A24, A36, A62, C360, G10, G14, H5

"Only Perhaps Mine," A62

"On Returning to a Lake in Spring," A27, A39, A52, A62, B90, C558, F136, G15

"On Seeing an Egyptian Mummy in Berlin, 1932," A39, A62, C167

"On Shooting Particles Beyond the World," A13, A18, A24, A39, A62, B25, B90

"On the Fragility of the Mind," A13, A18, A24, A36, A39, A62, C259, C301, E19

"On Theodore Roethke's Poetry," A45, C531

"On the 100th Birthday of Scott Nearing," C832

"On the Subtle Man," A62

"On the Suicide of F.O. Matthiessen," C652, F137

"On 'Throwing the Apple'," C450

Oonts and Others (Older), D61

"An Open Gate," A27, F140

Open Places, C828

"Opportunity," A3*an*

"Opportunity, Tired Cup of Tin," A3

"Opposition," A48, A55, A58, A62

Opulence (RE), A42

"Opulence," A27, A39, A42, A62, B75, F141

"Orchard," A3, A18, A24, A39, A62, B90, G4

"Ordeal," A24, C519, F142

"Order," A58, C661

"Order Again," A13, C289

"Order and Disorder," A13, C238, G18

Origin, C261

Osprey, C165

"Ospreys in Cry," A18, A24, A39, A62, B55, C399, F143, G29

Ostroff, Anthony, B73, D34

"The Other Gerard," C634

"The Other Side of the Mind," rev. by RE, C352

"Outer and Inner Verse Drama," C421

"Outgoing, Incoming," A33, C606, F144

"Out of Sorts Letter Foundery," A57, B157

"Outwitting the Trees," A27, B100
Over the Islands (Levertov), C414
The Oxford Book of Light Verse, ed.
    Harmon, C102
Oxford University Press, A2b, A3b,
    A7a, A11b, A13b, A16b, A18b,
    A18c, A19bn, A20a, A27a, A33a,
    A39a, A48, A62, B106
"O Wild Chaos!," A1, A18, A39,
    A62

Pacific, C184
Pacific Books, B113, B130
Pack, Robert, B40, B154
Packard, William, A52, B140, B143,
    B154, D35, D81, E59
Padelford, Louise Hawkes, A3, A3n,
    A26n, C54n
Paintbrush, C696, C716-18, C736,
    C788-89
Palaemon Press, A47, A60
Palmer, Thelma, D81
Pancontinental Premier Poets, C615
Panorama Moderner Lyrik
    (Steinbrinker), I5
Para-Desa (Stevens), B120
Parini, Jay, D62, E71
Parisi, Foseph, B136
Paris Review, C300, C720
"The Parker River," A18, A39, A62,
    C403, F145
Parkinson, Thomas, B93, C278
Parsons, Raymond, A2a
Parsons, Trekkie, A11a
"Partial List of Works Published by
    Richard Eberhart," F146
Participating in the Poem, ed.
    Cunningham et al. (1983), C76
Partisan Review, A3b, C122, C856
"Passage," A58, C738
"The Passage," A18, A39, A62,
    C445, F147

"The Pasture," G4
Patchen, Kenneth, C414, C416
Paterson (Book Five), rev. by RE,
    C420
Paterson (Book Four), rev. by RE,
    C265
Paterson (Book Three), rev. by RE,
    C233
Paterson (Book Two), rev. by RE,
    C198
"Patience as a Gesture of Divine
    Will," G7
The Pattern of Poetry, ed. Seymour
    and Smith, A1a
Patterns in Poetry, ed. Brown and
    Milstead (1968), A13a, C108,
    C254
"The Pattern of MacLeish's Poetry,"
    rev. by RE, C282
Paul Sample Retrospective (1963),
    B65
Pearlstein, Philip, A42
"Peep Show," C228
"The Peer," A7
Peich, M.A., A37
The Penguin Book of Modern Verse,
    ed. Moore (1954), C76, C85,
    C161- 62
Penmaen Press, A38, B125, B128
Pennant, Edmund, D40, D75
Pennsylvania Council on the Arts,
    A42
Pennsylvania Literary Review, C470,
    C513
Penny Paper, C528
Penny Poems (series), A23
Penzler, Otto M., B108
"People" (col.), E70
"Perception as a Guided Missile,"
    A18, A39, A62, C410
"Personal Statement," rev. by RE,
    C584

Perceptives U.S.A., A2a, A7a, B8, C76, C85-86, C161-62, C209, C254
Peter Owen (publ.), B86
"The Perturbation," B18
Peter Pauper Press, B17
Peterson, Lynn, B157
"The Phi Beta Kappa Poem, Swarthmore College, . . .," see "Memory, Confrontation, Desire," C506, F148
Philips, Jayne Anne, B151
"Philo Speakers Dispute U.S. Attitude on Poetry," E13
"Phoenixes Again," A13, C249, G19
Phoenix Publishing House, B79
"Pierrot on Aesthetic Distance," F149
"Pink Elf, O Master Child," C188
Pisan Cantos (Pound), rev. by RE, C204
"Pitch of Grief," A58
Pitter, Ruth, C598
Pittsburgh Press, E25
"Placation of Reality," A39, A62, C660, F150
"The Place," A20, A24, A58, A62, B122, C418, F156, G15
"Plain Song Talk," C666, F151
Planets and Angels (Jolas), rev. by RE, C129
Planting the Children (Haskins), D45
The Play (RE), A43
"The Play," A43, A48, A62
"Playing Ball With the Dead," C632, F152
The Pleasure of Poetry, ed. Hall (1971), C76
"Pleasures of the Morning," A13, B30, G19
Ploughshares, C790

Plume & Sword, C461
Plumley, William, B102, B107, B117
Plunkett, Edward, B129
PN Review, C799
The Pocket Anthology of Modern Verse, ed. Williams, A3a
The Pocket Book of Modern Verse, ed. Williams (1954), B33, C76, C161-62, C254, C298
Pocket Books, B33, B40
Pocket Library, B39
"The Poem," A58, C762
The Poem: A Critical Anthology, ed. Miles (1959), C161, C254
The Poem: Anthology, ed. Greenfield and Weatherhead (1968, 1972), C143, C487
The Poem as Process, ed. Swanger (1974), C76
"The Poem as Trajectory," A39, A62
"Poem ['Experience is like a cloud...']," C136
"Poem in Construction ['But waves before my eyes']," B18, C106
"Poem in Construction (11-17-39)," B8, F155
The Poem in Question, ed. Bourdette, Jr. and Cohen (1983), C76
"Poem ['I was the carrier of fate']," C270
"Poem of the Least," A58
Poems and Poets, ed. Aloian (1965), C161, C254
"Poems by Richard Eberhart," F156
Poemscapes (Patchen), C414
Poems (E. Bishop), rev. by RE, C338
Poem from a Cage (Laing), D7
Poems from Giacomo Leopardi, trans. Heath-Stubbs, C404

Poems from the Hills, ed. Plumley (1970), B102, *1971*, B107; *1974*, B117

Poems from the Iowa Workshop (ed. Engle), rev. by RE, C267

Poems from The Virginia Quarterly Review, ed. Kohler, C182, C212-13, C277

Poems (Glyn Jones), rev. by RE, C120

"Poems in Construction," poem seq., B18

Poems New and Selected (RE), A6

Poems 1930-1940 (Gregory), rev. by RE, C133

"Poems of a Japanese Sojourn," rev. by RE, C582

Poems of Doubt and Belief, ed. Driver and Pack (1964), C192, C238, C254, C277

"The Poems of Gene Derwood," J1

"Poems of Richard Eberhart, Read by the Poet, Himself," G1

Poems of Today (1938), C76

Poems of Tomorrow . . ., ed. Smith (1935), B7, C76-78

Poems (Roy Fuller), rev. by RE, C120

Poems Since 1900 . . ., ed. Falck and Hamilton (1975), C161

Poems to Poets (RE), A38

"Poem ['The tears of the ancients']," C397, F153

"Poem ['There is an evil in the air']," C135

"Poem ['The truth hurt worse . . .']," C203

Poems to Remember, ed. Petitt (1967), C64

"Poem ['The vision of the world']," C103, F154

Poems: Wadsworth Handbook and Anthology, ed. Main and Seng, B25, C254, C295, C325

Poesia Americana del '900 (Izzo), I7

Poesis, C700

Poet, A33, B102, C335, C600, C712-13, C780

"The Poet," A39, A62, F158

"The Poet and His Work," C587

"The Poet as Teacher," A45, C368

"The Poet as Tightrope Walker," C211

"Poet at Full Ahead," E63

"Poet Eberhart Discusses Tragedy…," E11

"Poet Eberhart Feels Tug of Senses," E66

"Poet Eberhart's Reality Harbors Man in Nature," E34

"Poet Eberhart Captivates Wachusett," E44

"Poetess Discusses Poetry," E31

Poetic Horizons, C730

Poet in America: Winfield Townley Scott (Donaldson), D14

Poeti Inglesi e Americani (Rosati), I6

"The Poet Laureate Wore Bermuda Shorts," E52

Poet on a Scooter (Roskolenko), C420

"Poet-Prof Rhymes Delightful Paradox," E25

"Poet Relates Experiences," E47

Poetry (Chicago), B3, C31, C41, C48-51, C65-69, C85, C88-90, C101, C110, C120, C129, C132, C142-48, C150, C158, C169, C174-76, C197, C200-1, C229, C232, C235-40, C247, C259, C264, C279, C285-90, C301-3, C320-22, C328-29, C341, C359-61, C404, C434- 39, C478-82,

C614, C622-24, C628-29, C665-66, C773-74, C857-58
"Poetry," C681, F159
Poetry (London), A3b
"Poetry," B98
Poetry: A Closer Look, ed. Reid et al. (1963), C76
Poetry and Experience (MacLeish), C464
"Poetry and Games," A58, A62, F160
"Poetry and Politics," A45; as "No News Is Good Muse," C680
"Poetry and Religion," C379
Poetry: An Introduction, ed. Miller and Greenburg (1981), C76, C161
Poetry: An Introduction and Anthology, ed. Proffitt (1981), C628
The Poetry Anthology, ed. Hine and Parisi (1978), B136, C48, C436
Poetry as a Creative Principle, A12, A45
"Poetry as Individualism," C493
"Poetry as World Value," C846
"Poetry at Dartmouth," C488
Poetry Awards 1951, B29, C245
Poetry Brief, ed. Cole (1971), C64
Poetry Chapbook, C199
"Poetry Commentary," C824
Poetry Dial, C460
Poetry for Pleasure . . . (1960), C85, C254
"Poetry in Contemporary America," C473
Poetry in English, ed. Taylor and Hall (1963), B8, C76
Poetry in Our Time (Deutsch), rev. by RE, C303
Poetry-Ireland, C209
Poetry Is For People, ed. McDonough and Doster (1965), C143

Poetry Is For People, ed. Westermark and Gooch, A16a, C615
Poetry London / Apple Magazine, C676, C776, C800
Poetry London-New York, C345-46, C348-49
Poetry New York, C250-51, C589-91
Poetry Northwest, C430-31
Poetry Now, B144, C646, C709-11, C731-32, C754, C801, C807
The Poetry of Dylan Thomas (Olson), rev. by RE, C318
"The Poetry of Robinson Jeffers Read by Judith Anderson," J3
The Poetry of the Thirties, ed. Tolley (1975), C64
The Poetry of War 1939-1945, ed. Hamilton (1965), C161, C182
Poetry of War Resistance . . ., ed. Bates (1969), C161
Poetry Pilot, C703, E48
Poetry: Points of Departure, ed. Taylor (1974), C161
Poetry: Premeditated Art (Jerome), A13a, C76
Poetry Q, C157, C186
"Poetry Readings," E41
Poetry Review, C511, C520, C812
A Poetry Sampler, ed. Hall (1962), C76
Poetry: Sight and Insight, ed. Kirkland and Snders (1982), C76, C254
Poetry Society of America, E3, E29
Poetry II, ed. Peterson (1962), C76
"Poets and the European Sickness," C96
"Poet Says Verse Reveals an Age," E36
Poet's Choice, ed. Engle and Langland (1962), B64, C325

The Poet's Choice, ed. Murphy (1980), B142
Poet's Gold: Poems for Reading Aloud, ed. Ross (1956), C76
"Poet's Gold: Verses of Today," G6
Poets of the Year (series), A6
Poets in Progress, ed. Hungerford (1962), C257, C361
Poets of England and America, ed. Sanders et al. (1962), C64
Poets of the Pacific: Second Series (ed. Winters), rev. by RE, C216
Poets of Today, ed. Witt-Diamant and Fukuda, C325
Poets on Poetry, ed. Nemerov, B81
Poets On: Roots, C747
Poetspeak, ed. Janeczko (1983), B146, C325, C504
"Poets, Society, and Religion," E35
"A Poet Talks About His Craft," E53
Poets Theatre, A19a, B31, E51, E57
A Poet to His Beloved (Yeats), B153
"The Poet-Weathervane," A13, C252
"Politics," C236, G18
Pollard, Anne Carter, A47*n*
Pomegranate Press, A34
"Portrait of Rilke," A38-39, A62, C678
Posner, David, B129, D27
Postscript to *Twenty Five Dartmouth Poems* (1966), B84
Postscript to *Twenty One Dartmouth Poems* (1964), B77
Pound, Ezra, C204, C343, E68-69
"Pound's New Cantos," A45, B112, C204
"The Power of Art," C251
The Practical Imagination . . ., ed. Frye et al. (1980), C161
Practices of the Wind, C781
Prager, Kari, B95
Prairie Schooner, C371-72, C462, C684

Praise to the End (Roethke), rev. by RE, C268
"Prayer Is Intensely Individual," B49
"Prayer to the God of Harm, The Song of the Poet," A58, B140
"The Preacher Sought to Find Out Acceptable Words," A6-7, C167, G3- 4, G17
"Preamble I," A18, B40
"Preamble II," A18, C308
Preface by RE to *Childhood's Journeys* (Eaton), B118
Preface by RE to *Meditations on a Great Man Gone* (Slobodkin), B78
Preface by RE to *Seventy Dartmouth Poems* (1970), B104
Preface by RE to *Zineb*, B89
Premier Poets . . ., ed. Srinivas (1986), C629
Prentice-Hall (publ.), B93
"The Presentation," A33
"Presentation to Robert Lowell of the National Medal for Literature," C759
Price, Reynolds, A47*n*
Princeton University Library Chronicle, E30
"Prize-Winning Poet Still Searching for Truth at 72," E52
Proceedings of the American Academy and Institute . . . 1978, C759-60; 1984, C821
The Process (Triem), D29
Prompter, C246, C262
"Professor Richard Eberhart Honored; Poet Wins Bollingen Prize from Yale," E9
"Prof. Sees Spiritualism A True Poetic Concern," E27
Progressions (Cook), B66
"The Project," A20, A39, A62, B90, C322, G7

Prokosch, Frederick, B12, C94
"Prometheus," A20, A39, A62
Prophetic Voices, C813
"Prose, Poetry and the Love of Life,"
    rev. by RE, C324
Prosery, C784
Prose statement by RE on "This
    Fevers Me," B116
"Prospectus," F161
"The Protagonist," C164
"Protagonists," A18, A39, A62, B90,
    C392, G7
"Protection," A58
The Province of Poetry, ed.
    Benjamin (1966), C161, C254
PSA Bulletin (Poetry Society of
    America), C621, C687, E28
"Psalm 103," B13
"Psalm 124," B13
Pternodon, C782
Puddingstone, C161-62
"Pulitzer Poem Born Here," E23
"A Pulitzer Prize Poet Faces Life,
    Rain," E26
"Pulitzer Prize for Poetry Goes to
    Richard Eberhart," E22
"Pulitzer Prize Poem Born Here,"
    E23
"Pulling Out the Vines," A58
Pulse, C664, C674-77, E46
Pumphrey, Jean, D56
"Pure Poetry," A45, B98
"Purpose," C45
Pushcart Press, B151
The Pushcart Prize, IX, ed.
    Henderson (1984), B151, C819
Putah Creek Press, A44
Putnam (publ.), B51, B56, B59
Pym-Randall Press, A28

"Q's Revisions," C123
Quadrant, C667

Quality: Its Image in the Arts, ed.
    Kronenberger (1969), B98
"Quanta," A62
"Quarrel With a Cloud," A33, A39,
    A62, F162
The Quarry (RE), A20
"Quarry-Stone," A48, B133
*Quarterly Journal of the Library of
    Congress*, C777
Quarterly Review of Literature,
    C167-68, C197, C229, C340,
    C468, C604-6, C706
Quartet from the Golden Year
    (1961), C432
A Quarto of Modern Literature, ed.
    Bacon (1964), A13a, C85, C143
"Quern," C74
Quest, B97, C585-86
"Question Mark," A62, C812
A Question of Survival (Moore), D12
"A Quiet Tone from a Rich Interior,"
    rev. by RE, C530
Quinn, Kerker, B24
Quill, C821

Rain (RE), A56
"Rain," A56, A58
Rainscapes, Hydrangeas, Roses and
    Singing Birds," A20, A24, B63,
    C457, G29
Randall, Joanne, A52
Randlett, Mary, A27b
Ransom, John Crowe, A3b, C134
"The Rape of the Cataract," A2,
    A18, A39, A62, B90*n*, G27
"Rationalists and Naturalists," C460
Ray, David, B52
Raymond, Harold, A3a*n*
"Razzle-Dazzle," C723, F163
Razi, Michael ("Machi"), A40
"Reading an Old Poem," A58

A Reading Apprenticeship: Literature, ed. Brittin (1971), B14, C254

Reading Modern Poetry, ed. Engle and Carrier (1955), B38, C76, C194

"The Reading Room in the New York Public Library," A33, A39, A62, B141, C637, F164

Reading the Spirit (RE), A2

"The Real and the Unreal," C816

The Realities of Literature, ed. Dietrich (1971), B25, C161, C254, C325, C377

"Reality! Reality! What Is It?" A13, B42, C217, G18

"Realm (to W.H. Auden)," A3

Reaper, C793

Reason in Madness (Tate), rev. by RE, C134

"The Recapitulation," A7, A18, A39, A62, B16, B90

Recapitulation of a Poem Taken By the New Yorker (RE), A60

"Recapitulation of a Poem Taken by the New Yorker," A60

"Recipe for Abstinence," C165

"Recognition," A27, A39, A62, C29

"Recollection of Childhood," A3, A3an, A11, A18, A24, A39, A62, B14, G3, G17, G29

The Record, C325

"The Record," A20, C372

The Record of a Green Planet (Juergensen), D59

Rectangle, E46

"Redemption," A39, A62, C643

Reflections, E44

"Reflections on Wallace Stevens in 1976," A45, C752

"Refrains," A27, A39, A62

Reid, James M., C512

"Religious Consciousness and Poetry," C382

"Remarks on Auden," A45, C693

"Remenber the Source," A16

Renner, Lisanne, E56

"Renunciation," C26

"Request," A18, A38-39, A62, C398, F165

"Request for Offering," A2, A11, A18, A39, A62, B6, B90, C52, C74, G3

Residence on Earth and Other Poems (Neruda), rev. by RE, C183

"Resources of the World," C299, G19

Response, C493

The Responsible Man, ed. Howard and Tracz (1970), C85

The Resurrection of the Snails and Other Poems (Rinaldi), D36

"Retrospective Forelook," A6-7, A11, A18, A24, A39, A62, G3-4, G17

"The Return," A16, A18, A24, A39, A62, C389

Returning to Vienna 1947 (Spender), rev. by RE, C196

"The Return of Odysseus," A2, A11, A18, A62, C75, G2

"A Review," C40

The Review, E47

"Review of *Lord Weary's Castle*, B93

"Revolt on Seeing the Ciitro Monumentale di Milano," C33

Rexroth, Kenneth, A18a, A18b, A24, A33a, B140, C214, C283-84, C582

Reynolda House (Winston-Salem, N.C.), A56

"R.G.E.," A27, A39, A62, C177

Ricciardi, Jim, B157
Rice, Stanley R., B91
"Richard Eberhart," E32
"Richard Eberhart," G4
"Richard Eberhart Acceptance Speech for the National Book in Poetry, . . .," A45, F166
"Richard Eberhart at Eighty: The Long Reach of Talent," E71
"Richard Eberhart Awarded Pulitzer Prize . . .," E21
"Richard Eberhart: Poetry Topics to Think About . . .," F167
"Richard Eberhart Hits Zenith of U.S. Poetry," E45
"Richard Eberhart Is Singing Because He's a Poet," E64
"Richard Eberhart on the Character of Pound's Work," B112
Richard Eberhart: The Progress of an American Poet (Roache), A3a, B106, C1n, C54n
"Richard Eberhart Reading His Own Poems" (1941), G2
"Richard Eberhart Reading His Poems" (1958), G7
"Richard Eberhart Reading His Poems at a Recording Studio in Storrs, Connecticut, in 1953," G19
"Richard Eberhart Reading His Poems at His Home in Cambridge, Massachusetts, 13 May 1951," G18
"Richard Eberhart Reading His Poems in the Coolidge Auditorium, 12 March 1956," G20
"Richard Eberhart Reading His Poems in the Recording Laboratory, 2 December 1944," G17
"Richard Eberhart Reading His Poems with Comments in the Coolidge Auditorium, 28 September 1959," G21
"Richard Eberhart Reading His Poems with Comments in the Coolidge Auditorium, 24 Oct. 1960," G27
"Richard Eberhart Reading His Poems With Comment in the Coolidge Auditorium, 15 May 1961," G29
"Richard Eberhart Reading His Poetry," G15
"Richard Eberhart Reads From His Own Works," G14
"Richard Eberhart Reads, Talks at Goucher," E24
"Richard Eberhart: Some Thoughts on Verse Drama," E51
"Richard Eberhart: Two Plays," E10
Richards, Dorothy, A45
Richard, I.A., A45, E57, E72
"Riches," C439, F211
"The Rich Interior Life," A16
"A Rich Kiss," A58, C767
Richmond Times-Dispatch, E66
The Rider Book of Mystical Verse, ed. Cohen (1983), C524
"Rifkin Movement," A48, C764
Rinaldi, Nicholas, D36, D63, D83, D84
Rinehart & Co. (publ.), B42
Riverside Poetry 2 (1956), B43
"River Water Music," A62, B154, C818
Roache, Joel, A3an, A39a, A48, B106, C1n
The Road from Hiroshima (Kaminski), D73
Roadkills (1981), C325
Robert Burlen & Son, B125

Robert College (Istanbul), B88
"Robert Frost: His Personality,"
  A45, C542
"Robert Frost in the Clearing," C45,
  C115
*Robert Lowell: A Collection of
  Critical Essays,* ed. Parkinson
  (1968), B93
*Robert Lowell: A Portrait of the
  Artist in His Time,* ed. London et
  al. (1971), B105
Roberts, Michael, A2, B6
Robertson, Nancy, E68
Robert's Rules of Order (RE), A22
"Robert's Rules of Order," A23,
  A48, C528
Robert Worth Bingham Poetry Room
  (1966), B82
"The Roc," A16, C231, G18
"The Rock," C212
Rodman, Selden, B23
Roe, Dee, E47
Roethke, Theodore, C268, C424,
  C527, C531, E26
Roger Burt Press, B89
"The Rolling Eye," A27, F168
Rolling Stone Press, B142
Roman Epistles (Brooks), D70
"Room," C53
Rosati, Salvatore, I6
"The Rose," A46, A48
"A Rose and Milton" (after Borges),
  C624, F169
Roseliep, Raymond, B133, D47
Roseman, Mark A., E9
Rosenthal, Bob, B156
Roskolenko, Harry, C420
Routledge & Kegan Paul (publ.),
  B112
"Ruby Daggett," A20, A24, A39,
  A52, A62, C497
Ruffin, Paul, B161

Rukeyser, Muriel, A3b, C201, C391,
  C478, D13, D18
Rumination (RE), A8
"Rumination ['What I can hold…],"
  A7-8, A11, A18, A24, A36, A39,
  A62, B25, B42, G4, G15
"Rumination ['Already it has hap-
  pened']," A3, C105
"The Rush," A24
Rushlight, C328, C336
Russell-Rutter, Co., A26
Ruthrauff, Bourne, E11

"Sainte Anne de Beaupré," A16,
  A18, A39, A62
St. Louis Post-Dispatch, C254
St. Mark's School, A3*an*, E72
St. Martin's Press (publ.), B141,
  B143, B153
The Sacred Round (Palmer), D82
"The Sacrifice," A18, A39, A62,
  B356, E24, G7, G21
Safir, Natalie, D91
"Sagacity," A48, C730
"Sailing Away," F170
"Sailing to Buck's Harbor," A62
"Salem," A16, A18, A39, A62, B54,
  C339, G21
Saltmarshe, Christopher, B5
Salute (RE), A35
"Salute," A35, A58, B75
Sam Houston State Univ., B161
Sample, Paul, B65
"Sanders Theater," A27, A39, A62
The Sandpipers (Posner), B129, D27
"Santa Claus in Oaxaca," A27, A39,
  A62, B87, F171
Santos, Bienvenido, B79
"Sapphic," C742
Saturday Night at San Marcos
  (Packard), D81

Saturday Review of Literature, C210-11, C214, C243, C324, C347, C416, C453, C487, C498, C538, C579, C618, C646

"Saucy Love of Life," rev. by RE, C311

Saul, Milton, A9

Sayegh, Tawfig, I1

"The Scale," A58

"The Scarf of June," A3, A11, A18, A39, A62, C112, G2

Schlesinger, Arthur, Jr., B74

Scholastic Teacher, C254, C325

"Schopenhauer," C41, C48

Schott, Webster, B87

Schulte Publishing Co., B50

Schulze, Charles R., A20a

Schuyler, James, A60*n*

Schwaber, Paul, B74

Schwartz, Delmore, C156

Scott, Foresman (publ.), B38, B90, B116

Scott, Laurence, A22

Scott, Winfield Townley, C614, D2

"The Scouring," A39, A62, C669

Scribner's (publ.), B25, B75

Scrutiny, C76

"Sculptor," C27

"Sea Bells," A58

"Sea Burial from the Cruiser *Reve,*" A20, A24, A39, A62, B90, C477, G15, G29

"Sea-Hawk," A16, A18, A24, A39, A62, B54, B90, G7, G10, G14-15, G21, G29

"The Seal," A20, C491

"Seals, Terns, Time," A13, A18, A24, A39, A62, B42, B54, B63, B81, B90, F156-7, G7, G10, G14-16, G19-21, G29

"Searcher," B3, C5

"Search for Perfection," C169

"Searching Honesties of the Heart," B79

"Sea-Ruck," A20, A39, A62, C348

"Sea Scape with Parable," A13, C192, G18-19, I6

"The Seasons," A18, A39, A62, C275

"Sea Storm," A58, A62, C785

Seattle Post-Intelligencer, E23, E26

Seattle Times, E28

Secker & Warburg (publ.), B61

The Second Annual Wallace Stevens Program (1965), A13a

A Second Book of Poetry, ed. Peterson (1964), C76

Second Grace (Nixon), D33

Second Language (Mueller), D88

The Secret Heart (RE), A31

"The Secret Heart," A31, A33, A39, A62, C600, F172

The Seed of Darkness (Rukeyser), D13

"Seeing Is Deceiving," A16, A18, A39, A62, C302

Seeman Printery, A19a

Selected Essays of William Carlos Williams, rev. by RE, C234

Selected Poems (H.D.), C404

Selected Poems 1930-1965 (RE), A24

Selected Poems of Hölderlin, rev. by RE, C404

Selected Poems of Horace Gregory, rev. by RE, C269

The Selected Poems of John Holmes, rev. by RE, C537

Selected Poems (J.P. Bishop), rev. by RE, C133

Selected Poems (O. Williams), rev. by RE, C208

Selected Poems (Patchen), C416

Selected Poems (Ransom) rev. by RE, C169

Selected Poems (RE), A11

A Selection of Contemporary Religious Poetry, ed. Hazo (1963), C161, C254

"Select Seventy," rev. by RE, C214

The Self-Made Man (Whittemore), C453

Self-Portrait: Book People Picture Themselves, ed. Britton, J4

Self-portrait, drawing by RE, J4

"Self-Spinner Speaking," B111

Seltz, Rosalie, E42-43

"Seminar at the Library of Congress with Students and Faculty Members from American Univ., . . . 1959," G23

"Seminar at the Library of Congress with Students and Faculty Members from Catholic Univ., ...1959," G25

"Seminar at the Library of Congress with Students and Faculty Members from George Washington Univ., . . .1959," G22

"Seminar at the Library of Congress with Students and Faculty Members from Howard Univ., . . . 1960," G26

"Seminar at the Library of Congress with Students and Faculty Members from the University of Maryland, . . . 1959," G24

"Seminar at the Library of Congress with Students and Faculty Members from Coolidge and Roosevelt High Schools, . . . 1960," G28

Sense and Sensibility in Modern Poetry (O'Connor), rev. by RE, C234

Sentry Editions, B136

"Serenely Down Wide Water . . .," G1

"Sermon on the Amount of Love," C357

"Sestina," A16, A18, A39, A62, B26, B42, F173

Settling In in Hanover (Greenwood), B149

Seven, C105

Seven Centuries of Verse, English and American, ed. Smith (1957), C76

The Seven-League Crutches (Jarrell), rev. by RE, C269

Seventy Dartmouth Poems (1970), sel. by RE, B104

"73-Year Old Poet Driven by 'Psychic Energy'," E55

Sewanee Review, C170-72, C183, C241, C308, C365, C483, C518, C852

Sexton, Anne, E67

Shaman, C677

Shatterhouse (Connellan), D65

Shattuck, Charles, B24

"The Shell Vase," B1

Sheltered at the Edge (Pumphrey), D56

Shenandoah, C463, C489-90, C515-16, C619

"Shiftings," A58, C807

Shifts of Being (RE), A27

Shine, Carolyn, A44

"A Ship Burning and a Comet All in One Day," A18, A24, A39, A62, B50 B76, B81, C417, F147, G7, G10, G14, G16, G21, G27

Shipley, Vivian, D64

The Shivurrus Plant of Mopant, comp. Hausman, D11

"Shock or Shut Up," C543

Schonbrun, Margaret Thompson, E64

"Should Teach Poetry Early, Eberhart Advises Teachers," E7

Shows, Hal Stevens, B122

Siegel, Robert, A30, B114, D48. D57

Siegmeister, Elie, H3-4

Silbert, Layle, A39b

Silkin, Jon, B55

"Silver," C10

"Silver and Gold," C341

Simon and Schuster (publ.), B86

Simsen, John, E55

Sincerity (Erskine), rev. by RE, C71

"Singular, Desolate, Out of It," C857

Sitwell, Dame Edith, A11a, A18a, A18b, A39c, C296, C341, C398, E5

Sitwell, Osbert, C226

"VI ['How shall I quell . . .']," A26, C548

Six Mile Corner (Dawson), D9

"XVI ['Now, time, the armed master . . .']," A26, C550

Sixty Dartmouth Poems (1969), sel. by RE, B99

Skellings, Edmund, D37, D85

"The Skier and the Mountain," A13, A18, A39, A62, B90, C279, G19

"Slant Angle," A58, C794

The Sleeping Beauty (Harper), D78

Sliding Down the Wind (Axinn), D30

Slobodkin, Salem, B78

"The Slope Sun—1927," sec. title, C65

"Slow Boat Ride," A39, A62, C702

"Slow Fading," C837

Smith College Friends of the Library, E41

Smith, Dave, D86

Snow Day (Warren), D76n

"A Snowfall," A48, B135, C734

"Snowy Owl," A62

"Society of Friends," A16, B30

"Sociogramaphonology," F175

"Solace," A27, A39, A62

"A Soldier Rejects His Times Addressing His Contemporaries," A18, A39, A62, C423, G7

"Some from the Top of the Head, Others from the Heart," rev. by RE, C414

"Some Memories of Dylan Thomas," A45, B58, C323, F176

"Some Men Have It Early," B52, C316, G7

"Sometimes the Longing for Death," A13, A18, A39, A62, C119, C166, G3, G19

"Somewhere Else," A58, A62, C809

Song, C707

"Song ['And at Lake Geneva . . .']," A7, A11

Song and Idea (RE), A3

"Song ['Better have your say']," F177

"Song ['Cover me over, clover,']," C48

"Song for the Death of My Uncle in Illinois," A3, C90

"Song ['I see her in her feeble age']," A58, B9

"Song of Freedom," A3an

"Song of Remembrance," C370

The Song of the Cold (Sitwell), C206

"Song of the Nerves," C200

"Song of the Soul," A2

Songs for Eve (MacLeish), rev. by RE, C319

"Song ['There is a place in stoical autumn']," A3, A6, B17, C137, G3, G17

"Sonnet ['When all my victories . . .']," C56

"Sonnets," F178

Sontesifer, Richard J., C395

Sophian, E41

"The Soul," A33, C604
"Soul," A16, A18, A39, A62, C326, F179
"The Soul Longs to Return Whence It Came," A3, A3*n*, A11, A18, A24, A39, A62, B33, B76, B90, E72, G10, G14
"Soul's Reach," A13
"Soul's Struggle," F180
Sounds and Silences, ed. Boynton and Mack (1975), C143
South Coast Poetry Journal, C337-38
Southern Review, A3a, B8, B82, B116, C124, C138, C523-24, C531, C542, C554-58, C599, C609-13, C722-24, C752, C823
South Florida Poetry Journal, C600-03
Sou' Wester, C676
Southwestern Review, E51
Spaeth, Sigrid, A33b
Sparling, Reed, E54
"Speaker Explains Role of Poet," E20
"Speaking of Books," C304
Speakin of . . . Interpretation, ed. Lee (1975), C627
"Speaking Plain and Fancy," C537
"Specifications," A58
Spectrum, C377
"Speech of Acceptance," C858
"Speech from a Play," C243
"Speech from a Play: Enter the Poet Alone," B17, C162*n*
"Speech Given in Honor of Donald Hall . . .," C848
"Speech of a Protagonist," A7
"Speculative Nature Note," A48, C774
The Speed of Darkness (Rukeyser), rev. by RE, C584

"The Spell of Time," C380, F181
Spender, Stephen, C94, C196, E17
"Sphinx," A39, A62, F182
"The Spider," A20, A39, A62, B76, B90, C436
"Spirit," C462, G27
"Spirit Descends in the Man," A58, C781
"The Spirit of Poetry Speaks," B74
"Spirits Appearing," A58
Spite Fence (RE), A61
"Spite Fence," A58, A62
Splinters of Bone (Darweesh), D19
Spoken Arts, G16
"The Spoken Arts Anthology of 100 Modern American Poets," G16
"Sportive Accolade," C364
Spottiswoode, Ballantyne & Co., A11a
Squires, Radcliffe, C269
"Spring Man," C275
"Spring Mountain Climb," A18, A39, A52, A62, C432, G16, G29
Stafford, William, A57n
Stand, C780
"The Standards," A27, A39, A62
Stanford, Frank, C797
Stanford University Press, B46
"Statement," C744
Statement by RE about *Fire-Tested* (Juergensen), B147
Statement by RE about Robinson Jeffers's poetry, J3
Statement by RE on Vietnam War, B86
"The State of Poetry in America," E61
"Statue of Liberty," A62
"Stealth and Subtleties of Growth," A33, A39, A62, C599
Steele, Timothy, D41

Steinbrinker, Günther, I5
Steinman, Larry, E21
Stevens, Henry Bailey, B120
"The Stevens Prose," rev. by RE, C272
Stevens, Wallace, C185, C272, C313-4, C502, C625, C752, E14, E17, E19, E40, E46
"Still," A58
"The Still Spirit," C440, F183
Stinehour Press, A26, B48, B53, B62, B67, B77, B80, B84, B91, B95, B104, B110, B149
Stokesbury, Leon, D28
"A Stone," B45, G7
Stone Drum, C660
"Stone Fence," C856
Stone House Press, A57, B157
Stone, Lincoln, B122
"Stone Words for Robert Lowell," A48
Stopping a Kaleidoscope (RE), A54
"Stopping a Kaleidoscope," A37, A48, A54
"Storm and Quiet," A52, A58, C786
Strand, Mark, A60*n*
Straw for the Fire, ed. Wagoner, D15
Strohbach, Hermann, A58
"Strong, Sensitive and Balanced," rev. by RE, C355
Structure and Meaning, ed. Dubé et al. (1976), C85
"The Struggle," A20, A24, C479
The Student, B27, C31, C64, E69
Studies for an Actress (Garrigue), D17
Studying Poetry . . ., ed. Kroeber and Lyons (1965), C76
A Study of Literature . . . (Daiches), rev. by RE, C234
"Studying with Richard Eberhart," E4

"Stylistic Wizardry," C18
"Subdued Poetic Fire," C226
"The Suicide Gassed in the Brooklyn Garret," C141
"Suicide Note," A33, A39, A62, C617, F184
"Suite in Prison," A2, A11, A18, A39, A62
"Sumatra Shore Leave," C69
"Summer Incident," C844
"Summer Landscape," A16, A18, A39, A62, C344
Summit Books, B142
"Sunday in October," A16, A18, A39, B90, C328
Sundheim, Suzanne, B40
"The Sun-lit Ants Their Shadows Feign, Obsess," C140
"Sunset Over Florida," A55, A58
"The Supreme Authority of the Imagination," A18, A39, A62, B90, C371, F156, F185
Survivors (RE), A46
"Survivors," A46, A48, A58
Sussman, Robert, E4
Swallow, Alan, B20, B22
"The Swallows Return," A33, A39, A62, C585
"The Swans of Inverane," A27
Sweeney, John L. ("Jack"), A45, C685
Sweeney, Moira, A45
Swenson, May, A57*n*, A60*n*
Swimming the Channel (Meade), D54
"The Swinging Bridge," A48, A55, A58, A62, C757
"Swiss New Year," A27, B92, C579, F186
"The Symbol," A27
Syracuse Herald Journal, E20

Take Hold! . . ., ed. Hopkins, C238, C325, C359
"Talk at Dawn," C236, G18
"Talking Back to Nature," A58
Talking Bronco (Campbell), rev. by RE, C367
Tamarack, C811
Tamarisk, C762
Tambimuttu, B75
Tambimuttu & Mass, B75
Tampa Tribune, E36
"Target," A58, C790
Tate, Allen, C134
Taylor, Barnard, A57
Taylor, Henry, B124, C358b
Taylor, Joy, A48
Teague, Harry, B84
Tedlock, E.W., B58, C323
"A Telling," A58, C696
Tennyson, Alfred, E17, E53, E56, E72
Ten Poems (RE), A59
"A Testament," A18, A39, A62, C437, F187
"Testimony," A58, A62, B148, C792
Texas Review Press, B161
Text of RE's lecture at Mills College (1946), C184
"Thanks, John, For Being," B158
"That Final Meeting," A13, B29, C245, G18-19
Thee: A Poem (Aiken), C581
Thegze, Church, E31
"Theme from Haydn," A16, C242, G18
Themes from American Literature, ed. Genthe and Keithley (1972), C161, C339
"Themes of Recurrence and Unity in the Vision of an American Poet," E69
"Then and Now," A48

"The Theory of Poetry," A45, C184
"There Is an Evil in the Air," A6, A58, C62, C135, F188, G3
"There Is a Place in Stoical Autumn, a Glass," C137, F155
"There Is Something to be Said for Everything," B17
"Things As They Are," rev. by RE, C281
"Things Known," sec. title, C48
Things of This World (Wilbur), rev. by RE, C355
"Thinking: Being," A58
Third World Congress of Poets, B126
"13 Bards, and Prose in Praise of Poetry," E62
Thirteen Dartmouth Poems (1958), sel. by RE, B48
Thirty Dartmouth Poems (1959), sel. by RE, B53
38 Poems (Treece), rev. by RE, C120
Thirty Five Dartmouth Poems (1963), sel. by RE, B67, E15
Thirty One Sonnets (RE), A3an, A26
Thirty Two Dartmouth Poems (1965), sel. by RE, B80
"This Fevers Me," A1, A11, A18, A24, A39, A59, A62, B42, B116, G10, G14
"This Hunger for Death Is the Strangest Thing," F56, F189
"This Is," C58
This Is My Best . . ., ed. Burnett (1970), A25, A27a, B100, C555, C618
This Powerful Rhyme, ed. Plotz, A3a
Thistle, B133
Thistle Publications, B133
Thomas, Caitlin, D92
Thomas, Dylan, B58, C323, D92, E26

Thomas, Richard, B117
Thompson, Edmund B., A6
"Thoor Ballylee," A27, F190
"Those Who Love Struggle," A3,
    C125, G2
"A 3 x 5 Poem," A58
Three Dimensions of Poetry, ed.
    Stewart, A2a, C64, C254
Three Dozen Poems (Everson), C414
"Three Kids," A39, A62, C682,
    F191
"Three Poems," F192
Three Poems (RE), A28
"Three Poets," rev. by RE, C133
Three Rivers Press, A42
"Through the Sallow Wind of Cold
    Ocean," C60
"Throwing the Apple," A18, A39,
    A62, C449-50, G21
Throwing Yourself Away (RE), A57
"Throwing Yourself Away," A57-
    58, A62, C780
"Thrush Song at Dawn," A16, A18,
    A39, A62, B46, C361, G20
"Thumbsucking," rev. by RE, C581
Tiger's Eye, C202, C222
Tiller, Terence, B55
"Time," A58, B117, F193
"Time and Dylan Thomas," rev. by
    RE, C318
"Time Passes," A33, A39, A62,
    C629, F194
"Time's Clickings," A46, A48, C783
Times Literary Supplement, A43,
    A61a, C384, C442-43, C510,
    C593, C657, C682, C695, C715,
    C735, C740, C743, C758, C764,
    C796, C798, C802, C810
"Time's Offerings," B123
Times-Picayune, E52
A Time to Love, ed. Victor (1971),
    A27a

"Tin Gods," C13
"To a Dead Man," A37, A58
"To a Girl Suffering from a Leg
    Injury for Three Years," C116
"To Alpha Dryden Eberhart: On
    Being Seventy-Five," A58, B142
"To a Poet" (later titled "Go to the
    Shine That's on a Tree"), C108
"To a Poet Who Has Had a Heart
    Attack," A20, C489
"To a Proud Lady," C9
"To Arthur Dewing," A28
"To Auden on His Fiftieth," A20,
    A38-39, A62, C384, G7
"To a Young Greek Killed in the
    Wars," G7; later titled "A Young
    Greek Killed in the Wars"
"The Tobacconist of Eighth Street,"
    A13, A18, A24, A39, A59, A62,
    B27, B76, B90, C209, G7, G10,
    G14, G18-19, I3, I5
"To Bill Williams" (also as "To
    William Carlos Williams"), A20,
    A38- 39, A62, B50, C253, G7
"To Catch the Meaning," H4
"To Come Closer to Thee," C88
"To Critics," C109
Today's Poets, ed. Walsh (1964),
    A3a, A18a, B27, B75, C76, C85-
    86, C161, C209, C254, C333,
    C359, C417, C436, C481, C487
Todd, Ruthven, C342
To Eberhart from Ginsberg, B125
"To Evade the Whirlwind," C146,
    F197
"To Evan," A16, A18, A24, A39,
    A62, C294, F195-96, G7, G19,
    G27
To Face the Inscription (Safir), D91
"To Harriet Monroe," A27, A38,
    A39, A62, B75, F198
"To H.E.B.," C142

"To Helen With a Playbill," A16, C351, G20

"A Token," A58, C769

"To Kenya Tribesman, The Turkana," A33, A39, A62, C621, F199

"To Laughing, To Leering," B76

"To Maia," C55

"To Marianne Moore on Her 80th Birthday," E29

"The Tomb By the Sea With Cars Going By," A27, C545

"To: Members of the Department," F200

Tomlinson, Charles, F201

"To My Son, Aged Four," A13, C255

"To My Student, Killed in a Car Crash," A27

"To the Mad Poets," A27, A62

"Tonal Depth," C402

"The Tone Is Delicate," rev. by RE, C283

"Tones of Evening," C521, C525

"Tones of Spring," A24

"To My Son, Aged Four," A13, G19

"To One, Who, Dead, Sees His Poems in Print One Hundred Years Later," A13, C258, G19

"To One Returning," C82

To Play Man Number One, ed. Hannum and Chase, C458

To Read Literature, ed. Hall (1981), C76

The Total Experience of Poetry, ed. Thompson (1970), C76, C161

"To: The Department," F201

"To the Field Mice," A27, A39, A62, B88, F202

"To the Harps," C830

"To the Heart's Depths," rev. by RE, C342

"To the Mad Poets," A58, A62, F203

"To the Moon," A58

"Touch and Go," A58, C763

Touchstone, A58, C745, C814, C824

The Touch of a Poet, ed. Holmes and Souza (1976), C254

Toward Composition: Readings for Freshman English (1970), C76

Tower (Dartmouth College), C1-2, C5-8, C10, C12-19, C22-45, C528, C739

"To Whom It May Concern (2/14/55)," F204

"To Whom It May Concern (March 1, 1959)," F205

"To William Empson," F206; see "A Whack at Empson"

"Tones of Evening," F207

"Track," A33, A39, A62, C596, F208

"Tragedy as Limitation: Comedy as Control and Resolution," C474

Transatlantic Review, C451-52, C541

"The Transfer," A2, A11, A18, A39, A62, G1

"Transformation," A51, A55, A58, A62

Transition, C52, C83

Translations by American Poets, ed. Garrigue (1970), B101

Transports of Summer (Stevens), rev. by RE, C185

The Treasury of American Poetry, ed. Sullivan (1978), C76, C161

The Treehouse: An Introduction to Literature, ed. Stanley and Gillespie (1974), C85

"Tree Swallows," A18, A39, A62, B51, C411, F209

Tremblett, George, D92

Trial of a Judge (Spender), rev. by RE, C94

"A Tribute to W.H. Auden," A45, C693

Trident Press, B83

Triem, Eve, D29

Trinity Review, C310, C313-14, C386-88

Trinity Tripod, E14

"Trip," A48

"Triptych," A6-7, A18-19, A39, A62, C159

Triptych (Worth), D43

TriQuarterly, C433, C446

The Triumph of Life, ed. Gregory, A3a

Trolling (Lawder), D32

"True North," C385

Trumpet in the Twilight of Time (McCarty), D53

"The Truncated Bird," A33, A39, A62, B107

"Truth," C11

"The Truth," A58, A62

"Trying to be a Truth-Sayer," E52

"Trying to Hold It All Together," A38-39, A62, C687, F210

"Trying to Read Through My Writing," A27, C583

Tuckerman, Frederick Goddard, C530

Tuftonian, A4

Tufts College, A4

Tufts College Press, A4

Tufts, Jeanne, B31

Tulane Drama Review, C474-76

The Turning Path (Bottrall), rev. by RE, C110

Twayne (publ.), B27, B43

"12, Canterbury Street," C114

"The Twentieth Annual Poetry Awards (Long Island Univ.)," D87

Twentieth Century American Poetry, ed. Aiken, A3a, C76, C78, C124

Twentieth Century American Writing, ed. Stafford (1965), C76

Twentieth Century Authors: First Supplement, ed. Kunitz and Colby (1955), B41

Twentieth Century Literature, C815

Twentieth Century Poetry, ed. Brinnin and Read (1963), C161

Twentieth Century Poetry, ed. Marshall (1971), C161

"Twentieth Century Poetry in English: An Album of Modern Poetry," G8

The Twentieth Century Revised and Expanded, ed. Stern and Gross (1968), C76, C161

"21st Century Man," A62, C829

Twenty Five Dartmouth Poems (1966), sel. by RE, B84

"XXIV ['This is your marriage night, . . .']," A26, C552

Twenty One Dartmouth Poems (1964), sel. by RE, B77

"XXVI ['O fair vibrations . . .']," A26, C553

"Twenty-Two," C51

"XXII ['And law displaced . . .']," A26, C551

"II ['What shall I call . . .']," A26, C547

"Two for Rexroth," B140

"Two Loves," A3, A3an, A11, A18, A24, A39, A62, B15, B42, C121, G2-3

Two Poems (RE), A37

"Two Poems," F211

"Two Poets: Donald Hall, Ruth Pitter," rev. by RE, C598

'Two Translations from *Justice Without Revenge* . . .," A58

Tygers of Wrath, ed. Kennedy, B25

"Ultimate," C21

"Ultimate Song," A20, A39, A62, C484

Uncertainties and Rest (Steele), D41

Undercliff (RE), A13

"Undercliff Evening," A39, A62, C718

Under Milk Wood (Thomas), rev. by RE, C311

Under Open Sky, ed. Krapf, B157

"Undestanding of the Impossible," A58, C795

Understanding Poetry, ed. Brooks and Warren (1960, 1976), C76, C161

"Under the Hill," A48, B136, C48

Unicorn Press, B145

"Unique," C838

"United 555," A39, A62, C628, F212

The Unity of Literature, ed. Alssid and Kenney (1968), B27

University of Alabama Press, B138

University of Arizona Press, B66

University of Arkansas Press, B158

University of California, Davis, A44

University of Chicago Press, B52

University of Illinois Press, A45, B119

University of Iowa Press, B121

University of Kansas City Review, C263

University of North Carolina Press, A19a, A19b

University of Pennsylvania Press, B29

University of Texas Press, B94

University of Utah Press, B124, C358b

University of Washington Daily, E27

University Presses of Florida, B129

University Press of New England, B114, B154

University Press of Virginia, B127, B134

"Unknown Poet," C708

Untermeyer, Louis, B63

Untitled acceptance speech for the 1977 National Book Award in Poetry, C760

Untitled article about meeting Russian poet Sholokov, C441

Untitled autobiographical and artistic statement, B41

Untitled comment for "Twentieth Annual Poetry Awards" (Long Island Univ.), J5

Untitled comments by RE, E8

Untitled comments on living in Princeton, N.J., E30

Untitled comments on Marianne Moore, E29

Untitled comments on creativity, C496

Untitled comments on Richard Wilbur's "Love Calls Us to the Things of This World," B73

Untitled comments to a symposium on Ezra Pound's poetry, C343

Untitled contribution to "Jean Garrigue: A Symposium," C815

Untitled letter to John L. Sweeney, C685

Untitled letter to William Packard, B152

Untitled remarks from Jean Garrigue's memorial service, C703

Untitled remarks on Jean Garrigue, E48

Untitled review of *A Miscellany of American Poetry 1925*, C34

Untitled review of B.C. Heezen and C.D. Hollister, *The Face of the Deep*, C659

Untitled review of Conrad Aiken, *The Kid*, C180

Untitled review of David Daiches, *A Study of Literature*, and William Van O'Conner, *Sense and Sensibility in Modern Poetry*, C234

Untitled review of James M. Reid et al., *Poetry* . . ., C512

Untitled review of *New American and Canadian Poetry*, C653

Untitled review of John Erskine, *Sincerity*, C71

Untitled review of John Masefield, *Grace Before Plowing*, C603

Untitled review of Mary Owings Miller, *Wheel of Paper*, C215

Untitled review of Oscar Williams, *Selected Poems*, C208

Untitled review of Paul Engle, *The Word of Love* and *Poems from the Iowa Workshop*, C267

Untitled review of Reginald L. Cook, *The Dimensions of Robert Frost*, C422

Untitled review of Samuel French Morse, *Wallace Stevens*, C625

Untitled review of Witter Bynner, *Indian Earth*, C73

Untitled review of Yvor Winters, *Maule's Curse*, C99

Untitled statement about poetry, B126

Untitled statement about poetry, C712

Untitled statement about T.S. Eliot, C95

Untitled statement about Brewster Ghiselin, B124

Untitled tribute by RE to his high school English teacher, B155

Untitled statement for special anniversary issue of the *New York Quarterly*, C827

Untitled statement on contemporary poetry, C592

Untitled statement on the poetry of Philip Booth, C469

Untitled tribute to W.H. Auden, C688

Untune the Sky, ed. Plotz (1957), A13a, C108

"Ur Burial," A16, A18, A39, A58, A62, C409

"Ur-Review," C152

The Uses of Poetry (Stein), C76, C615

"Using the Meditative Means," C337

"Usurper," A39, A62, C692, F213

Valhalla and Other Poems (Francis), rev. by RE, C96

Valley News, E22, E45, E68

"Van Black, An Old Farmer in His Dell," A28, A33, A39, A62

Vanderbilt Poetry Review, C746

Van Doren, Mark, B43

Van Duyn, Mona, A60*n*

"Vast Light," A16, C362

The Vastness and Indifference of the World (RE), A21

"The Vastness and Indifference of the World," A21, A27, A39, A62, B90, C538, F214

Vechten, Carl Van, B12

Vegetaran World Publishers, B120

"Veil," C14

"Velvet Rocks," A62, C835

Vendler, Helen, A35

The Ventriloquist (Huff), B134, D31

"The Verbalist of Summer," A13, A18, A39, A62, C227, G10, G14, G18

Vermont Academy of Arts and Sciences, B115

Vermont History, C422

"Vermont Idyll," A39, A62, C665, F215

Verse, C830
Verse introduction by RE, B67
"Verse More or Less Topical," sec. title, C161-62
"Version Temporary," F216
Vertical, cd. Jolas, B16
"Vicente Huidobro (1893-1948)," C536
Vice Versa, A3b, C125, C130, C137
Vietnam War, RE on, E32, E43, E47
Views and Spectacles (Weiss), D42
"Vignettes," A58, C749, C755
"The Village Daily," B3, C48
"Villanelle," A18, A39, A62, B90, C377, G7, G21
Vindex (St. Marks School), B10
Viray, Manuel, B79
"The Virgin," A3, A18, A39, A62, B8
Virginia Quarterly Review, C96, C182, C206, C212-13, C277-78, C318, C421, C445, C620-21, C636-37, C651, C721, C783
"Vision ['I came into the street...']," C620
"Vision ['Two hummingbirds as evanescent as']," A20, A39, A62, B90, C503, F217-18
"The Visionary," A58, C705
"The Visionary Eye," C219, G18
"The Visionary Farms," A19, E51
"The Visionary Farms (Scene I-XIV)," B31, F219
"The Visionary Farms (Scene XV)," C340, F220
"Vision Through Timothy," A39, A65, C691
"A Vision of Life and Man That Drives the Poet On," rev. by RE, C419
"A Vision Welded to the World," rev, by RE, C265

"Visiting Poet Performs 'Aerial Wizardry'," E28
"The Visitor," C400, G7
"Visit with Eberhart," E59
"Vivid Poet, Rare Teacher," E50
Voces in Deserto (1960), B97
Voices, C280, C312, C336, C380, C410, C465
Voices of Poetry, ed. Kirschner (1970), C76, C161, C325
The Voice That Is Great Within Us, ed. Carruth, B8, C161, C504
Vox, C408, C433, E70
"The Voyage," A18, A39, A62, C288, G27, G29
"A Voyage of the Spirit," rev. by RE, C284
Vrobovska, Anca, B69, B92

Wachusett Regional High School, E44
"Wading Through the Thick Mud of Society," A3
Wagner Literary Magazine, C507
"The Wagner Poets: Comments on the Wagner Poets," C507
Wagoner, David, A60*n*, D15
Wain, John, A39c
"Waiting," A58, C747
Wake, C217-20, C230-31, C252-59
"Waiting for Something to Happen," A58, C745
"Waiting To Lean to the Master's Command," A62
Walker, David, B125
Walker, Sue, E67, E72
Wallace Press, A52
Wallace Stevens Journal, C749, C778
Wallace Stevens (Morse), rev. by RE, C625
Walls and Distances (Galler), C453

Walpole Printing Office, A6

Walsh, Chad, B75

Walton, John Boy, B117

Walt Whitman: A Centennial Celebration (1954), B37

"War and Poetry," A13, C244, C249, G10, G14, G18

War and the Poet, ed. RE and Rodman (1945), B23

"Warmth and Ease and Charm and Aptitude," C101

Warnings, B148

"War Poetry," B104

The War Poets (ed. Williams), A6, C76, C157, C161-62

"Warr," C589

Warren, Robert Penn, A11a, A24, A47, A60n, E33

Warren, Rosanna, A47n, D76

Washington and the Poet, ed. Rosenberger (1977), C452

Washington Post, E7, E52, E62

Washington Square Press, B83

Washington Star, E61

The Wasteland (Eliot), E67

Waterlily Fire (Rukeyser), C478

The Water of Light, ed. Taylor (1976), B124, C358b

"The Water-Pipe," A20, A24, B69

A Water Walk by the Villa (Garrigue), D3

"The Way It Is," F221

"A Way Out," A39, A62, B130, C715, F222

"Ways and Means," A20, A39, A62, B90, H4

Ways of Light (RE), A48

Wayzgoose Press, A8

W.B. Yeats: Interview and Recollections, ed. Mikhail (1977), B132, C393

W.B. Yeats (Parkinson), rev. by RE, C278

W.B. Yeats: The Tragic Phase (Koch), rev. by RE, C278

We Believe in Prayer, ed. Brings (1958), B49

"The Wedding," A33, A39, A62, C588, F223

"A Wedding on Cape Rosier," A27, A39, A62, B90, C557, F224, G1

We Have Lost Our Fathers (Rinaldi), D63

Weiss, Theodore, D42

We Moderns, B12

"Wentworth Place," C65

"West Coast Rhythms," A45, B125, C363

"West Coast Verse," rev. by RE, C216

Western Humanities Review, C358b

Western Review, C207, C221

West Hills Review, B37, C220, C779

"Wet June," A48, A55

"A Whack at Empson," A58, C776, F206

Whales: A Celebration, ed. Gatenby (1983), A18a

Whalesong (Siegel), D57

"What Gives," A18, A39, A62, G7, G20-21

"What Holds Us Here?" rev. by RE, C505

"What If Remembrance," A13, A24, B42, C225, G19

"What Is Art?" C387

"What Is the Question?" C312

"What the Senses Tell," A16

"What the World Is," C250, G18

"What You Keep on Your Mantlepiece," A48, C729

"W.H. Auden: A Memoir by Richard Eberhart," C686

Wheaton Alumnae Quarterly, E1

Wheaton College, A12, E1, E11

Wheel of Paper (M.O. Miller), rev. by RE, C215

"When Doris Danced," A3, A11, A18, A24, A39, A62, H4

"Whenever I See Beauty I See Death," A27, A39, A62

"When Golden Flies Upon My Carcase Come," A3, A3a*n*, A11, A18, A24, A39, A62, B42, B90

"When I Think of Her the Power of Poetry Arises," A3, C98, F16, F225

"When Love Has Given the Waylay to Our Powers," C139

"When Nature Falls Asleep," A27

"Where Are Those High and Haunting Skies," A2, A11, A18, A24, A39, A62, G2, G29

"Where Is My Ego Flown?" C93

Where Is Vietnam: American Poets Respond, ed. Lowenfels, A6

"Where I Want to Go," A33

Where the Compass Spins (Squires), rev. by RE, C269

Whetstone, C500, C508-9

"White Lily and Hail," C160

"White Night of the Soul," A27, C580

"White Pines, Felled 1984," A62, A154, C834

Whitman, Walt, C779

Whittemore, Reed, C183, C453

"The Whole View," A16, A58, C346

"Why?" A27, A39, A62

"Why I Say It in Verse," B34, B57 C304

"Why I Write Poetry," A45, C304

Widening Circle, C670

Wilbur, Richard, A11a, A33a, A47*n*, A60n, C193, C355

Wilderness Stair (Belitt), rev. by RE, C342

"Wild Life and Tamed Life," A39, A62, C672, F226

"The Wild Swans of Inverane," A62, F227

"Will," B100, C618, F228

"Will and Psyche in Poetry," A45, B60

William and Mary Review, E17

Williams, Cedric, D67

Williams, Jonathan, B131

Williams, Oscar, B17, B19, B21, B25, B33, B39, B82-83, G8, G11, G13

Williams, William Carlos, A18a, A18b, A39c, C198, C206, C233, C248, C265, C281, C324, C347, C819, C594, E17, E19, E33, E40, E46

William Carlos Williams (Koch), rev. by RE, C233

Willkie's Life and His World, rev. by RE, C391

Wilson Library Bulletin, C469

Wimsatt, W.K., Jr. B68

Wind and the Rain, C203, C256

The Wind and the Rain, ed. Braybooke (1962), B61

"The Wind As an Abstract God," C174

"The Wind Hugs the Blood" (Bouchet), trans. by RE, B101

"The Winds," A27, A92, C559

"Windy," C49

"Winter," A58

"Winter Man," C275

Winterfest, B85

Winterfest 1967(Boston), B85

"Winter Kill," A20, A24, A39, A52, A62, C482

Winter, Romney, B15

"Winter Squirrels in Pine Trees," A48, C690, F230

Winters, Yvor, C99, C216
"Wisdom," A13, G19
"The Wisdom of Insecurity," A16, A18, A24, A39, A62, B90, C331, G10, G14, G27
"With a Touch of the Poet," E52
"With Images of Actuality," rcv. by RE, C338
Wolk, Sheila, A36
"Wonder and Shadow," C20
Wonders: Writings and Drawings for the Child in All of Us, ed. Cott and Gimbell (1980), B142
Woodworth, Vicki, B122
Woolf, Cecil, B86
Worcester Review, C859
Word, Meaning, Poem, ed. Peckham and Chatham (1961), C85
The Word of Love (Engle), rev. by RE, C267
"A Word on Modern Poetry," C190
"Word Plays," C719
"Word-Prowess," A48, B131
"Words," A16, A18, A27, A39, A58, A62, B90, C330, F231, G7, G10
"The Words," A58, G14
Words Among America, ed. Gersmehl (1971), A18a
Words for the Wind (Roethke), C424
Words Into Flight . . ., ed. Abcarian (1972), C161
"Wordsworth Tintern Abbey," B83
Wordsworth, William, B83, E19, E53, E65
World Anthology (1980), B139
"The World Applauds," F232
"Worldly Failure," A38-39, C667
"World's Havoc," C321
"The World Situation," A20, C492
"World's Mere Environment," A2
A World-View (RE), A4
"World-View," A4, B17, C131

"World War," A6, A18, A24, A39, A62, G3, G17, I4
World War II, RE on, E19, E47, E56
World Wide Broadcasting Foundation, G1
Worley, John C., H2
"Worshipper," C19
Worth, Douglas, D43
"Wounds, Wounds, Wounds, Wounds," F233
Wright, Basil, B5
Wright, James, A27a
Wright, Stuart (publ.), A49-51, A59
The Writer (publ.), B57
Writing Poetry, ed. Holmes (1960), B57
W.W. Norton (publ.), B8

Yale Literary Magazine, C323
"Yale Series of Recorded Poets: Richard Eberhart," G10
Yankee, C339
"The Year," A58, B140
"Yeats," F234
Yeats, W.B., A45, B132, B153, C393, E57
Yevtushenko. Yevgeny, E45
"Yonder," A18, A39, A62, B52, C317, G7
Yorkshire Post, B76, C484, C500
"You Are Cold and Lovely, White-Armed One," C38
"The Young and the Old," A33, A38-39, A62, C654
"A Young Greek, Killed in the Wars," A18, A39, A62, C329, G21
"The Young Hunter," A3, A3an, A11, A18, A39, A62, C195, G3, G17
Young Pegasus (1926), B4, C31
Your AASA in 1958-59, B54

"Youth and Age," A58, B122
"You Think They Are Permanent But They Pass," A33, A39, A62, C656
"You, Too, Are Coming Up," A2
"You Would Think the Fury of Aerial Bombardment," C161

Zaturenska, Marya, C133
The Zephyr Book of American Verse, ed. Dabin, A3a, C76, C144, C147
Zineb (1968), B89
Zukovsky, Louis, C537
Zydek, Frederick, C768